AUSTIN

Celebrating the Lone Star Millennium

AUSTIN

Celebrating the Lone Star Millennium

Introduction by

◆ © DONOVAN REESE

Sponsored by the Greater Austin Chamber of Commerce ★

Dan Rather

Art Direction by
Geoffrey Ellis

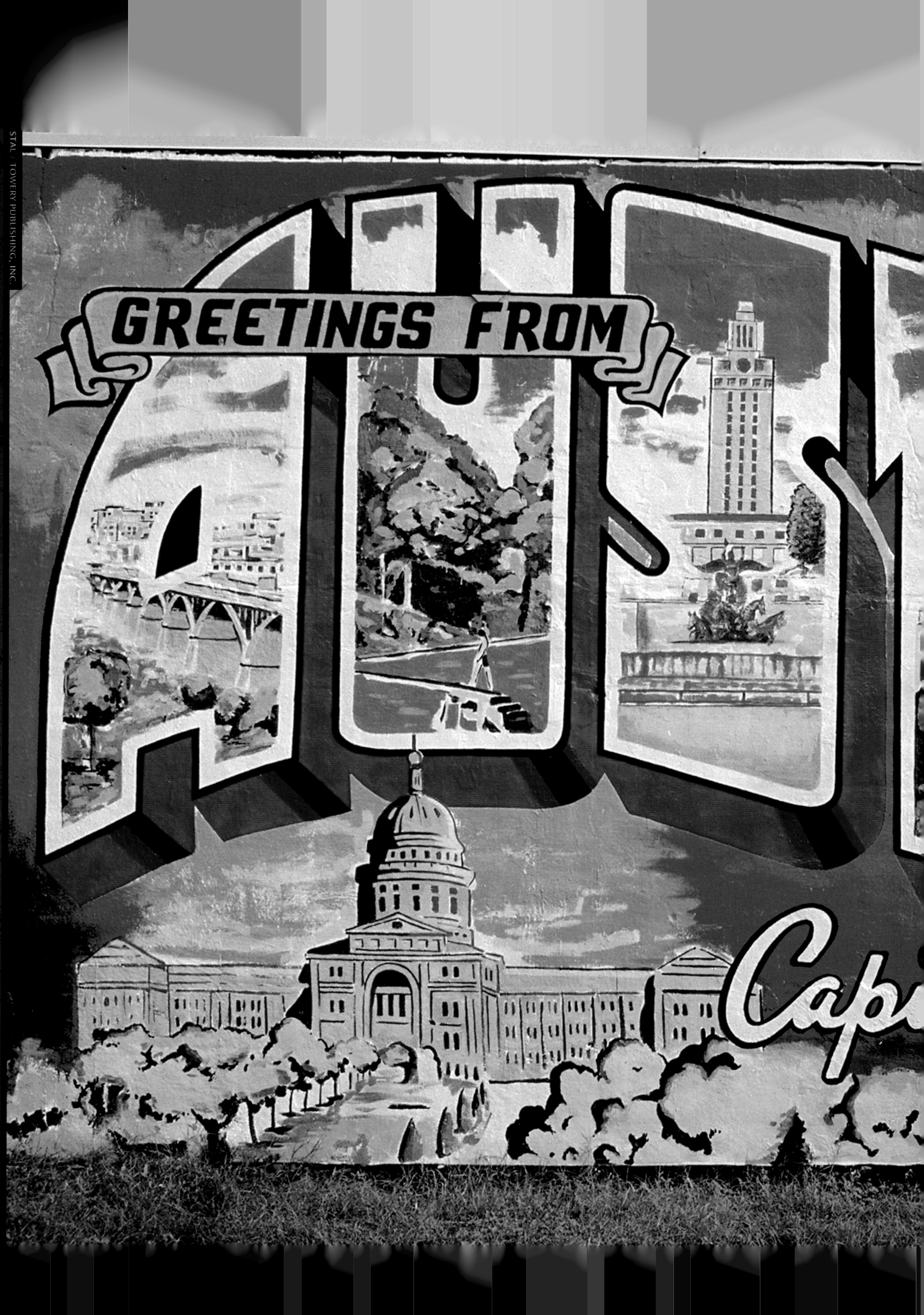

STAL / TOWERY PUBLISHING, INC.

Contents

Cataloging-in-Publication
data may be found on page 496.

ustin is home to me, although I wasn't born here. ★ Austin keeps welcoming me back, no matter how far I roam. ★ Austin welcomed me the first time I saw it. I was brought here by my parents, back in the late 1930s. We were driving in from Houston, where we lived, and my

parents, who believed (correctly) that Texas was the center of the universe and that Austin was the center of Texas, wanted to make sure we saw the state capital. I remember riding all day with my brother and sister in the back of the 1936 Ford my father had borrowed from a friend. The car had no air-conditioning, but we didn't notice. If any place or thing in Texas had air-conditioning at that time, we hadn't heard about it. Heat was just something you lived in, like air; you didn't think about it. The car had a

primitive radio, but despite my father's tinkering, it wasn't working that trip, so we sang to compensate for the silence. We believed that other cars on the road might not have radios, either, and so we sang extra loud for their benefit. And then, just as the sun was going down, we cleared a hilltop.

© JAMES A. DUMAS / SPECTRUM PHOTOGRAPHY

And there was Austin. Purple and gray in the setting sun. Lights sparkling. The capitol in the foreground, the Tower of the University of Texas just beyond it: These were the only two buildings of size in those days, and they stood out not only because of their hugeness, but also because of their colors. Then, as now, the capitol was a dusky pink; the Tower, illuminated a pale gold (which we later understood was not gold at all, but burnt orange).

It was like seeing all of Texas at once.

It still is. ☞

FILMMAKER RICHARD LINKLATER, CREATOR OF HITS INCLUDING *Dazed and Confused, Slacker,* AND *The Newton Boys*

My father pulled over to the side of the road so that we could admire the view. It is one I have never forgotten. I have tried to go back and find the hill or promontory where we stood that evening, but the city has grown up so much that I can't find the exact spot. I would like to show my own children, friends, and visitors that same perspective: I can only hope this book will do the trick.

People come to Austin and exclaim over the Hill Country, the beauty of the white, white limestone and the green, green trees. "It looks just like Provence!" they say.

"No," my wife, Jean, says, gently but firmly. "Provence looks like Austin."

Austin is supremely aware of the natural splendor of its setting. Other places may be more take-your-breath-away beautiful, but no other place is more *interesting* to look at and explore. Maybe that's why Austinites are so in touch with nature—more so even than most other Texans. Recreation to an Austinite means getting out of doors.

★ In springtime, that buttoned-down executive will go wandering through the wildflowers after work. Texas is rightly celebrated for its wildflowers, and many of the most beautiful are in the Austin area. The former first lady, Lady Bird Johnson, herself a precious natural resource, established the Lady Bird Johnson Wildflower Center just outside of town.

★ In summer, that college student is going to Barton Springs Pool after class—maybe not even waiting that long, but stealing away at lunchtime. (Slackers are an Austin invention, courtesy of filmmaker Richard Linklater.)

★ In fall, that pilot is going bird-watching to admire the ease with which other creatures take to the air.

★ In winter—well, there isn't really a winter to speak of. This is Texas, after all.

Austin loves its nature far beyond the limits other people set for themselves. Only in Austin could an infestation of bats turn into a beloved local institution and tourist attraction. ☞

But, let's be honest, the place is much, much bigger and much, much busier than it ever used to be. Old-timers (that is, anybody who arrived before 1980) delight in telling

newcomers how easy life used to be—especially the traffic. They will tell you that when they first came to the city, it was possible for an old hound dog to lie undisturbed all day in the middle of Congress Avenue, moving only with the sun. Now, of course, the only animal that can lie on Congress Avenue is a state legislator.

The Texas State Legislature is popularly known as the Lege. There are people, such as my friends at the CBS television affiliate K-EYE and at the *Austin American-Statesman*, as well as the renowned columnist Molly Ivins, who make their living doing nothing but explaining the Lege to others. You have no idea how much I envy them. I was actually assigned to cover the Lege many years ago. But it's an uphill job: The Lege defies description. Nobody ever believes the things these people do.

SYNDICATED COLUMNIST MOLLY IVINS

The name-calling, roughhousing, fistfights, and unclassifiable incidents involving marching bands and small animals are legion and legendary.

Their saving grace is how funny the legislators can be, mostly when they don't mean to be.

From its earliest days, the Lege has been home to some of the most colorful characters in a state that nobody ever called colorless. These men and women make Texas' governors look positively dull. As a body, they have passed legislation that confounds the powers of logic and credulity. Then, realizing that the original legislation may be . . . *imperfect* . . . they start improving it. And usually forget to stop.

They are a musical bunch, our legislators, and you are always hearing stories about somebody breaking into song in the middle of a session. Hymns are especially popular. Unfortunately, few legislators seem to be quite so gifted linguistically: Some Austinites fill notebooks collecting the malapropisms and other bizarre turns of phrase that our legislators regularly turn out. Many would qualify for the *Reader's Digest* column "Toward More Picturesque Speech," if anybody could figure out what they meant.

There are some decent lawmakers in Austin. It's just hard to hear them over the din. ☛

They meet only a few days a year. This is all they require. And it is all most of the rest of us can endure.

The other great institution in Austin is the University of Texas (UT): Just as the capitol and the Tower used to dominate the Austin skyline, and still do, they loom large in the city's personality.

Yes, there are other universities and colleges in the area, each one making special contributions to the community as a whole, but UT is the center of attention. It's so darned big. "You cannot get away," as the school's song insists, with the not-too-subtle suggestion that you'd better not *try* getting away either. UT boasts more students than most Texas towns, more buildings and acreage than some small countries, and more money than some solar systems, thanks to a state charter that endowed UT (and all the state universities) with land grants and oil money.

The character of the school infuses the rest of the city. UT is known as the only place in the entire state where the sixties were actually permitted to happen, and as a result, they've never entirely released Austin from their grasp. There are days when you can get a "contact high" just walking along Guadalupe, the main drag of the old campus, an unofficial landing strip for honest-to-Timothy-Leary hippies (better known as "drag worms").

The university is like an ant colony for intellectuals, world renowned for the excellence of its research and teaching staffs; the students did not come to Austin just to eat lunch. Some days, walking across campus, you can practically feel the heat from all the brainpower these people generate. They all live right on top of each other, but they don't seem to mind. (When I was in school, you had to transfer if you could see the smoke from another student's chimney.) ☞

University of Texas running back and Heisman Trophy winner Ricky Williams

You can't categorize UT students. You can't describe them. You can barely *count* them. They are diversity personified en masse, as varied as the state itself (and hundreds of them, so help me, aren't even Texans).

They still find time for football, which is practiced like a pagan religion, with equal measures of artistry and brutality (complete with human sacrifices), all over the state. UT has been conducting an especially fierce jihad with its ancient rival, nearby Texas A&M, for generations.

Of course, you can't tell an Aggie or a Longhorn just by looking at one, and that's the origin of one of the greatest social perils in the entire state. Many are the business relationships exploded, the friendships abruptly terminated because a Longhorn made the mistake of telling an Aggie joke, or an Aggie bragged about a football score in the wrong company.

Usually, Austin is about the most amiable place you could ever hope to be, and yet we have had our share of feuds and fights.

The trouble may have originated simply because Austin has always been such a great place: Nobody wanted to surrender an inch of it. Those first Austinites, the Tickanwatic people (whose name, I am assured, means "most like humans"—I don't know who they were comparing themselves to, and I'm not sure I want to know) were mostly friendly, but they managed to discourage the first Spanish settlers, who stuck around only for a year before hightailing it back to San Antonio in 1731. White settlers didn't repeat the attempt until 1838, when Jake Harrell pitched his tent where present-day First Street and Congress Avenue intersect.

The Tickanwatic people had given way to the Comanche tribes. The Comanche in

particular resented Harrell and the Yankees who followed, and for a couple of decades, they'd slip into town under cover of darkness, relieve a few skulls of their scalps, and slip back into the hills. (A&M's Aggies have been officially requested by their school administrators not to replicate such behavior in their feuds with modern-day Austinites.) For years, even the state capitol had a stockade around it.

Perhaps the most important feud in Austin's history is that between the first and second presidents of the Republic of Texas: the great Sam Houston and his successor, Mirabeau Bonaparte Lamar. Lamar visited Harrell in 1838. In those days, Harrell called his settlement Waterloo, and although it seems unlikely anybody called Bonaparte would cotton to any Waterloo, Lamar had at least inherited his namesake's dreams of empire, and Waterloo (renamed Austin) would be his capital.

But Sam Houston was already building his own sort of empire down to the south, centered around the New Orleans of the West, a little town called—you guessed right—Houston. Although the Republic's capital city was still Washington-on-the-Brazos,

Lamar rightly suspected that Sam was about to move the operation to Houston.

Unfortunately for Sam, old-time Houston was even more humid and swampy than it is now, and medical science hadn't come close to conquering the myriad plagues and fevers that swept through town periodically. Lamar hinted to state surveyors that they'd find fairer—and healthier—fields to the north, and the next year, 1839, they recommended that Austin be named the new capital. Houston's partisans complained that life in untamed Austin could never compare to civilized Houston, but theirs was a losing cause.

Now president of the Republic, Lamar arrived at the end of the year with his entire cabinet—and 50 wagon loads of paperwork. (Even in those days the bureaucracy—only three years old—was Texas-sized.) The next year, the town could boast two newspapers, one for every 428 residents.

But the Houstonians hadn't given up hope. Three years later, in 1842, Santa Anna set up camp in San Antonio: He appeared to be poised to retake Texas, ready to pounce on

STEPHEN F. AUSTIN

Austin. So Sam, president again, ordered the capital relocated to the city of Houston. That meant relocating all the paperwork, too. His troops got only as far as Round Rock before a band of Austinites tracked them down, reclaimed the papers, and brought them home again—where they've stayed ever since.

(So you see, the Lege can't really be blamed for getting so excited about their bureaucracy.)

One other early Austin feud deserves mention: the great Pig War of 1841, which nearly led to the declaration of armed hostilities between the Republic of Texas and the Empire of France.

A young adventurer called Jean Pierre Isidore Alphonse Dubois, Count de Saligny (possibly he had more names, but passports were only one page in those days) came to Austin and set himself up as the French chargé d'affaires, a lordly sounding title that (like his other title) he probably bestowed on himself. The French king, pleased enough to have representation in a promising re-gion, went along with the scheme.

© JAMES A. DUMAS / SPECTRUM PHOTOGRAPHY

De Saligny was better at putting on airs than paying his bills: To add insult to injury, rather than pay rent to his landlord, Richard Bullock, he bought the place next door, the fanciest house in town (you can still visit it). Bullock kept pressing for payment, and de Saligny replied only with richly accented epithets.

So Bullock did what any respectable Texan would do: He set his hogs loose in de Saligny's garden. De Saligny's garden wasn't merely decorative—it was his *dinner*, and in no time, the hogs had eaten every morsel.

He complained to the city authorities, who claimed there was nothing they could do. De Saligny ordered his servant to kill the hogs; Bullock whipped the servant instead.

THE DRISKILL

The city fathers, who seem to have been fed to the teeth with de Saligny's arrogance, smiled to themselves and continued to do nothing.

De Saligny stormed out of town, threatening to bring the King's Army back with him. The poor king! If he'd only taken de Saligny's advice, he might have been able to conquer Texas and sell it back to the United States, averting the Mexican War (1846-1848) and earning back some of the money France lost in the Louisiana Purchase. Instead, France's government brokered a diplomatic settlement, and de Saligny returned to serve another three years as chargé d'affaires—until the United States annexed Texas in 1845 and his services were no longer wanted.

There have been other feuds—people are still talking about the shoot-out in the lobby of the Driskill Hotel on Sixth Street in 1908—but the most serious dispute probably occurred in 1861. That was the year Texas decided to secede from the Union and join the Confederacy.

Austin and Travis County wanted to remain in the Union. So did the state's governor, Sam Houston. He risked his

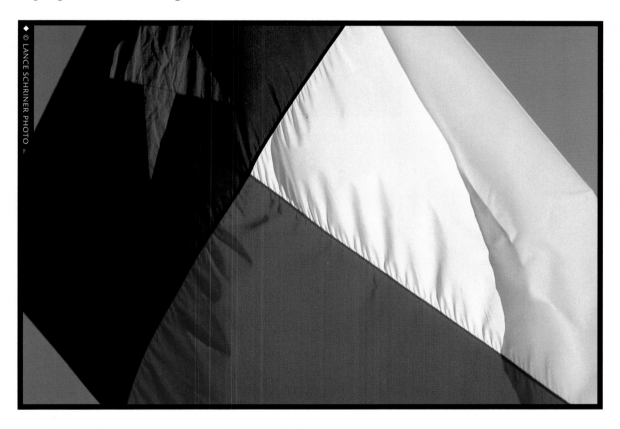

© LANCE SCHRINER PHOTO

whole reputation, and lost much of it, by fervently opposing the Confederacy. He was committed to the United States of America, which he'd fought so hard to get Texas into. But the Union was increasingly committed to the abolition of slavery, and too many other Texans and southerners did not feel as Sam (and Austin) did.

Which isn't to say that Sam was pro-abolition. He *was* pro-United States. But as long as his fellow Texans were talking of leaving the Union, he couldn't see why they'd want to sign on as part of some new country. Better they should start a new Republic of Texas—with Sam resuming his presidency.

In those days, the Lege was cotton-controlled, its purse strings held by Big Cotton

money from East Texas, the most populous (and most slaveholding) part of the state. Sam Houston must've known that he had no chance of winning this debate. But he faced a pivotal moment and made the best speech of all his life. He argued for the United States and against secession.

They rebuked him in the Lege, and kicked the Father of Texas Independence out of town. He got on his horse and rode away, beaten but unbowed, never to return to Austin. The first night, he slept within a few yards of where my wife, Jean, was born. Not much later, he died in his home in Huntsville.

Sam Houston had, as few others before or since, an innate sense of honor and principle. This is not to say that Sam Houston always lived up to that sense.

Do I need to tell you that I feel Sam's sense of honor and principle still hovering over Austin to this very day? Houston and his at-first-opposed, sometimes-resented capital city wound up as kindred spirits—and have stayed that way.

Sure, our governors have caroused a bit—Houston was not the last to spend time in Huntsville, although he had the privilege of sleeping *outside* the state penitentiary. The legendary Ma Ferguson became our state's first woman governor mostly because her husband, Pa, had been found guilty of transgressing a couple of statutes against bribery and corruption. Underscore for emphasis: Not everybody in Austin can uphold

Sam Houston's sense of honor and principle. But even when Austinites do wrong, even when they violate every principle in the book, they know it. And they feel really *bad* about it.

Some of our governors have managed to do some remarkably good things, of course: "Pappy/Pass the Biscuits" Lee O'Daniel not only led a successful career as a radio musician, he also hosted the biggest picnic (60,000 people) in state history to celebrate his inauguration in 1939, and two years later celebrated again with the biggest dinner party (a mere 20,000 spilling out of the Governor's Mansion and onto surrounding yards and streets).

The redoubtable Jim Hogg (who really did have a daughter named Ima, but would never dream of naming a daughter Yura) gave Texas the pecan as surely as Athena blessed Greece with the olive: He passed laws to protect pecan groves that were menaced by cotton fields, and in his honor, the pecan was named our state tree.

And Dolph Briscoe tried really, *really* hard to exterminate all the fire ants in the state. This was an impossible task, and he might have been forgiven for failing if he'd had any other policies during his two terms in office.

Ultimately, Austin is a storyteller's town. Not just the colorful characters in our state government, but every single person in town has got a story. Some of them have had

several stories to tell: O. Henry, Fred Gipson, J. Frank Dobie, Liz Carpenter, Bud Shrake, Kinky Friedman, Cactus Pryor. James Michener came to Austin and loved it so much he endowed a whole school for writers. Time was you couldn't consider yourself a real writer unless you'd come to Austin, bent your elbow at Scholz Garden, and dipped your toes in Hippie Hollow. My wife claims I came here just to build up my writerly credentials.

Wherever I've gone in the world, I've found that anybody who knows Austin, loves Austin. Tell people that you've just come from Austin, or you're on your way there, and they get a goofy little grin. "I love Austin," they say.

Here are some of the reasons people love Austin:

1. Austin tastes good. The state of Texas is blessed with a variety of the world's most delicious cuisines, and some of the best practitioners of each can be found within a few miles of the capitol dome. Mexican, Vietnamese, Middle Eastern—even the French have come back to town (evidently they have

decided not to press the hog issue any further). Austin was, for a long time, the capital city of *mechanized* Tex-Mex cuisine: The first machines to make tamales and tortillas were built and operated here.

2. Austin smells good. Did I mention those wildflowers?

3. Austin sounds good. I don't refer merely to our beloved state song, "Texas, Our Texas," which is often heard here and sometimes known to make strong men weep with joy and pride.

Austin's music is a guide, perhaps even better than its cooking, to the cultures that make Texas special. Sounds have come together, crossing distances of thousands of

miles, to blend in ways nobody could have imagined: The distinctive Texas *conjunto* sound, combining German polkas and Mexican mariachi, is only one such musical marvel. Tejano music de-emphasizes the German oompah sound and plays up traditional Mexican melodies. Scottish, Anglo, and Irish folk music came to the state with settlers (mainly from Tennessee), and all three continue to influence Austin's music. Scholars from the University of Texas were responsible for collecting and preserving many thousands of more-recent folk melodies from cowboys and railway workers (to name my personal favorites). African-American music—from spirituals, gospel, blues, and jazz to up-to-the-minute dance and international sounds—is perhaps more prevalent here than anywhere else in the state. Fresh waves of immigration keep adding new ingredients to the simmering musical stew.

And, perhaps most important, Austinites don't just leave this music lying around. They play, they listen, they dance. They go to clubs and concerts, they trade record

albums, they grab a guitar or harmonica and sit under a tree: Austinites seldom miss a chance to make a joyful noise. These are some of the most passionate consumers and practitioners of music in the world: Willie Nelson, Jimmie Dale Gilmore, Tish Hinojosa, Jerry Jeff Walker, Guy Forsyth, David Murray, Ray Wylie Hubbard, Joe "King" Carrasco, and Joe Ely aren't exceptions, they're the *rule*. If you spend more than a day in Austin without hearing something that makes you want to jump up and dance (maybe the Texas Two-Step or the Cotton-Eyed Joe)—then you're doing something wrong, pardner.

Oh, and by the way, there's a lively symphony orchestra (first in the state) and opera troupe, too. Austin's musical scene truly knows no limits.

4. Austin looks good. I am a little hesitant to mention this for fear of being thought a dirty old anchorman, but the fellow who rhapsodized about "the girls in their summer dresses" must have been thinking of Austin. The folks from UT like to remind us that actress Farrah Fawcett was once voted one of the 10 most beautiful girls on cam-

Musician and troubadour Joe Ely

AUSTIN SYMPHONY ORCHESTRA CONDUCTOR PETER BAY

pus (according to my source, unverified, she wasn't even number one, but number *three*).

But, yes, Austin abounds in *all* kinds of scenic beauty (I did mention those wildflowers, didn't I?)

5. Austin feels good. Even the heat is more tolerable here than it is in Houston (which is wetter than a Turkish bath with leaky plumbing) or Dallas (which is statistically windier than Chicago and thus resembles a metropolitan blast furnace). Some people credit Austin's slower pace: If you don't feel like hurrying, they say, you don't have to. Unfortunately, in many parts of the city, that's no longer true. Austin can be just as fast-paced as Houston or Dallas or (gulp) New York, but Austinites tend to hurry only when they have reason to.

I'm not sure why Austin feels better. It just does.

I'm comforted by the knowledge that the pictures in this book will help you understand Austin better than anything I could possibly say.

You will see the honky-tonks and the wildflowers, and you will understand that Austin can never really be tamed.

You will see the churches and schools, and you will know why so many people want to raise their children here. ☞

To tell the truth, our children *wish* we'd raised them here. Our grandson doesn't live here full-time—yet. But we've already begun bringing him down, letting him chase after clouds on the green grass of Austin under a Texas sky.

I've held him up to look at the capitol eye to eye. I've taken him wading in Barton Springs Pool. I've fed him a *tamal* at Rosie's, out by Lake Travis. I've shown him the ghost-faced bats of Bee Caves. I've told him of the world's first barbed wire, unspooled at Waller Creek in 1857, and of the buried Spanish treasure he just might find some day (providing there really is any). I've shown him the dappled deer and the shiny-scaled fish, none brighter than a little boy's eye.

I have tried to show him the things you will see in this book.

Like my grandson, you will see the friendly faces and the magical places, and you will know why we call Austin our home.

© RON DORSEY

In this book, Austin will spread out like a panorama before you, like the vista my parents showed me on that night many years ago.

You may feel the chill of excitement and possibility that I felt that night.

You may feel that Austin is a song you can never get out of your head, the music of the air and the water and the trees and the animals, in harmony with the tuning of your own soul.

Listen to Austin, the heartbeat of Texas.

Let Austin's magic work on you.

You can feel the spirit of Austin moving now, can't you?

Hear me as I whisper in my grandson's ear: "Welcome home!" ★

AUSTIN

DISTINCTIVE HOMES ABOUND throughout Austin and its surrounding hills, where various forms of "lawn art" reflect the city's penchant for individualism (OPPOSITE AND ABOVE). A recent high-tech boom in the area has drawn thousands of new residents seeking high-paying jobs and an accompanying quality of life (PAGES 40-45).

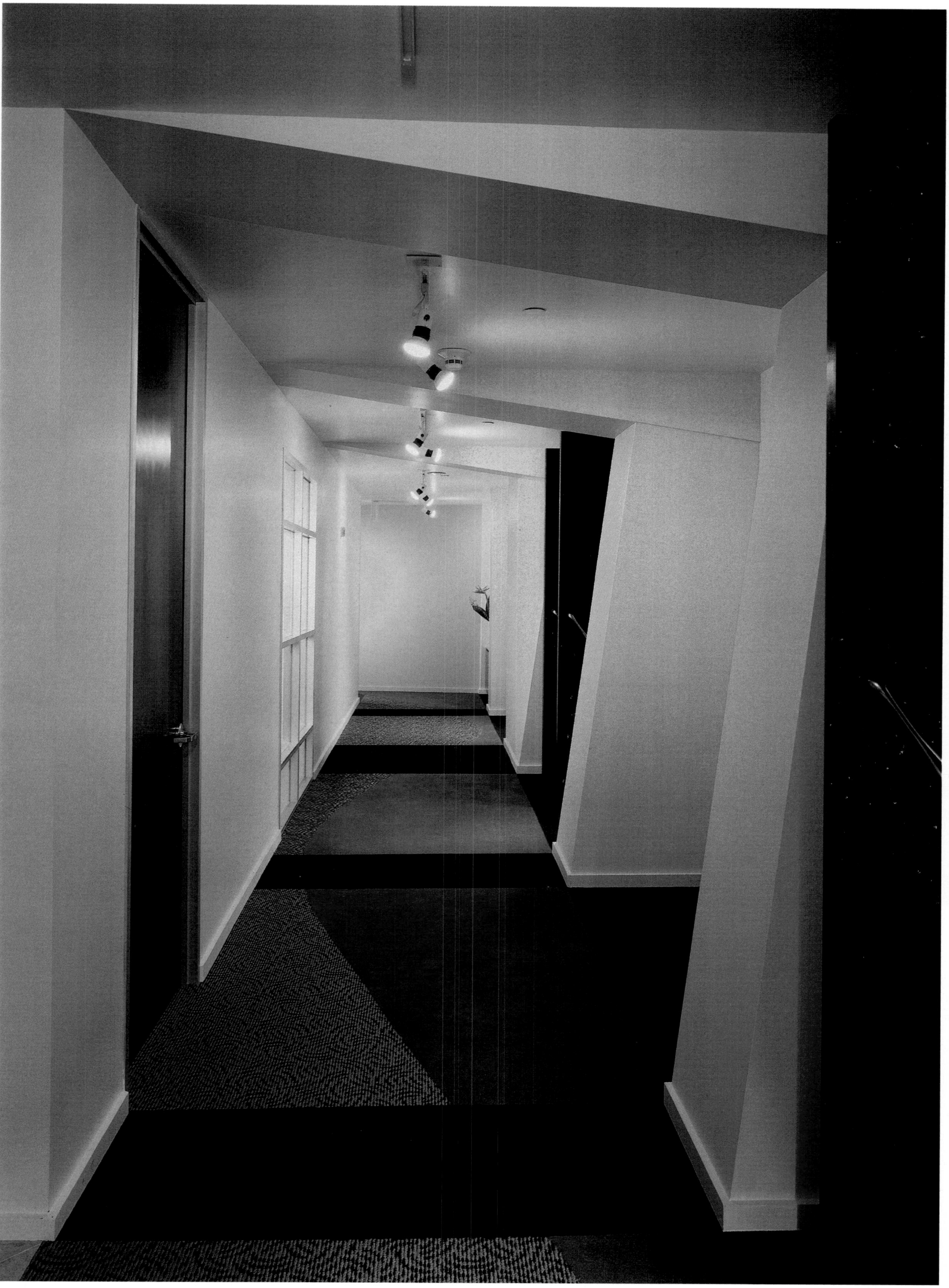

▲ © PETER TATA PHOTOGRAPHY

AUSTIN

AUSTIN

WITHIN A SHORT DRIVE of Austin are countless historic buildings with fascinating stories to tell. Claiborne House bed-and-breakfast (OPPO-SITE) off Highway 29 calls nearby Georgetown home. And join Waylon and Willie and the boys in Luckenbach, Texas, where the old post office harks back to the laid-back town immortalized in song.

THE JOHN BREMOND JR. house is one architectural component of what is known as historic Bremond Block, a series of elaborate 19th-century homes built for Austin banker Eugene Bremond and his family. The final piece of the puzzle, this Second Empire structure was completed in 1887 and contained the city's first indoor toilet.

BUILT IN 1899, THE MAJES- tic Caswell House is on the National Register of Historic Places. Originally home to the Daniel H. Caswell family, the restored site today is owned by the Austin Junior Forum and is open to the public.

DOWNTOWN'S ELEGANT Driskill Hotel was praised as the finest hotel in the South when it opened in 1886. A recent top-to-bottom renovation combined the best of the old and the new in the stately building, which has hosted presidents, legislators, celebrities, tourists, and a goodly number of honeymooners.

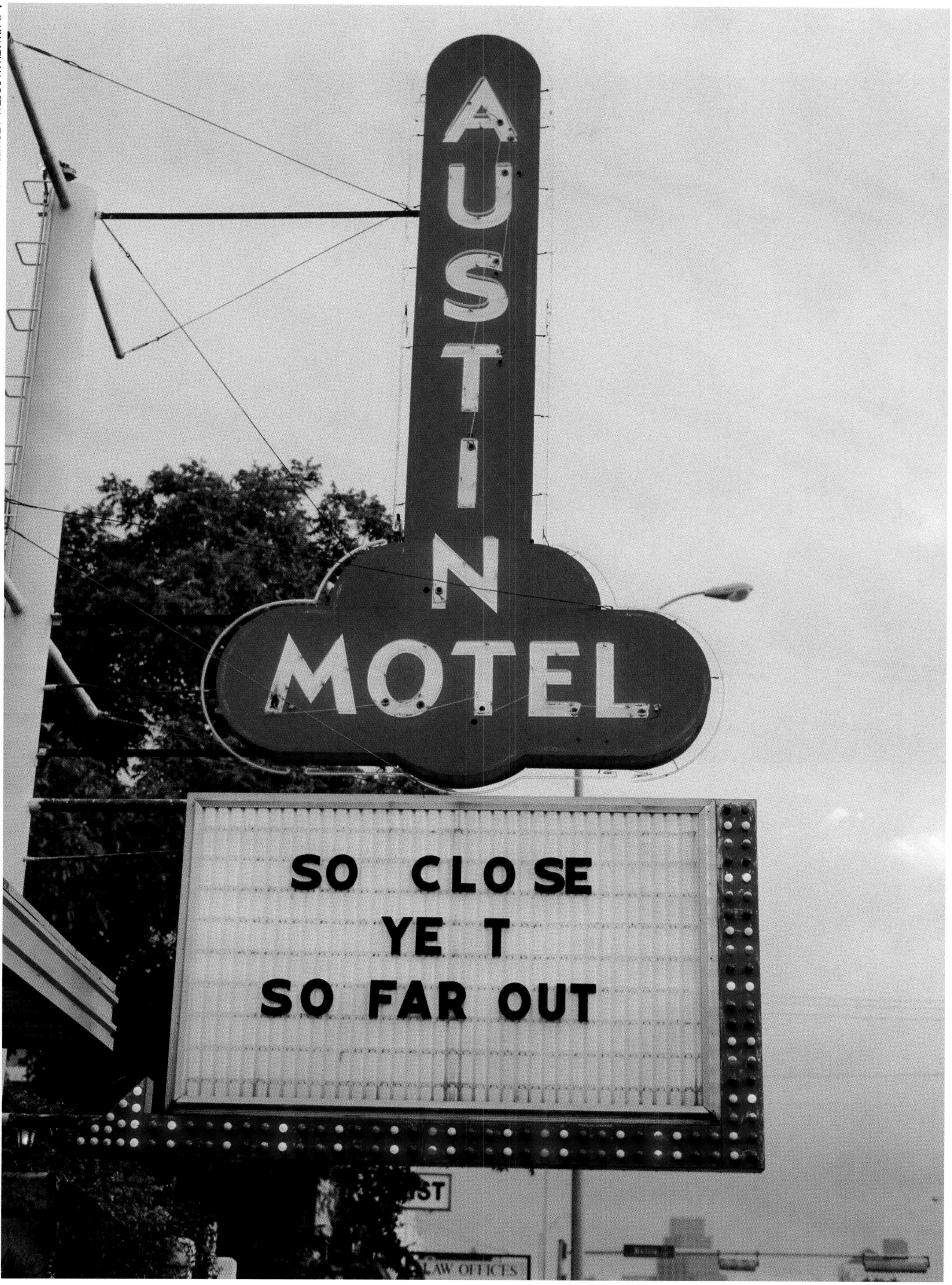
AUSTIN
MOTEL
SO CLOSE
YE T
SO FAR OUT
LAW OFFICES

54

NO NEED TO LOOK FAR TO find signs of Austin, not to mention the Lone Star State's famous mark (PAGES 56 AND 57). The emblem even makes a prominent appearance on the rotunda floor of the renovated capitol complex (PAGES 58 AND 59).

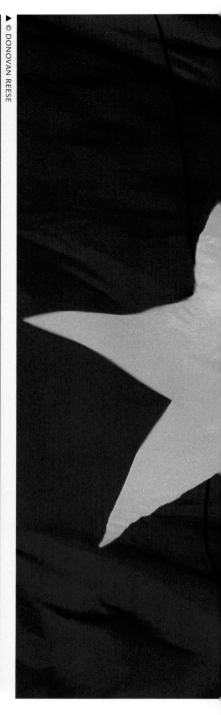

AUSTIN

THE STATE'S RED, WHITE, AND blue flag with the distinctive five-pointed star was officially adopted in 1839 by the Republic of Texas. The motif has been put to use in many forms over the ensuing years.

AUSTIN

TEXAS IS ONE OF THE MOST recognizably shaped states in the nation, and natives love to show it off in forms ranging from front yard shrubbery to rocks in the park.

THE SHADOW KNOWS: ATOP every true Texan is the familiar shape of a Stetson cowboy hat.

HUMORIST AND FAMOUS Austin resident William Sydney Porter (better known as O. Henry) is credited with coining the nickname City of the Violet Crown. Many believe that the phrase refers to the purple haze often seen hanging on the hills outside of Austin at dusk.

A POPULAR LOCAL ADAGE commands, "If you don't like the weather in Texas, wait a minute." Area forecasters frequently look to the skies for signs of change, and these curious clouds in the Hill Country make for some fascinating viewing.

AUSTIN

AUSTIN'S CROWN JEWEL sparkles during special-event light shows. Because the state capitol is one of the tallest in the country—taller than even the U.S. Capitol—Texans take any opportunity they can to show it off.

74

A LOOK UP AND AROUND IN the capitol complex is as impressive as the view from outside (PAGES 74-77). Its ornate rotunda and dome are at the intersection of the facility's main corridors.

76

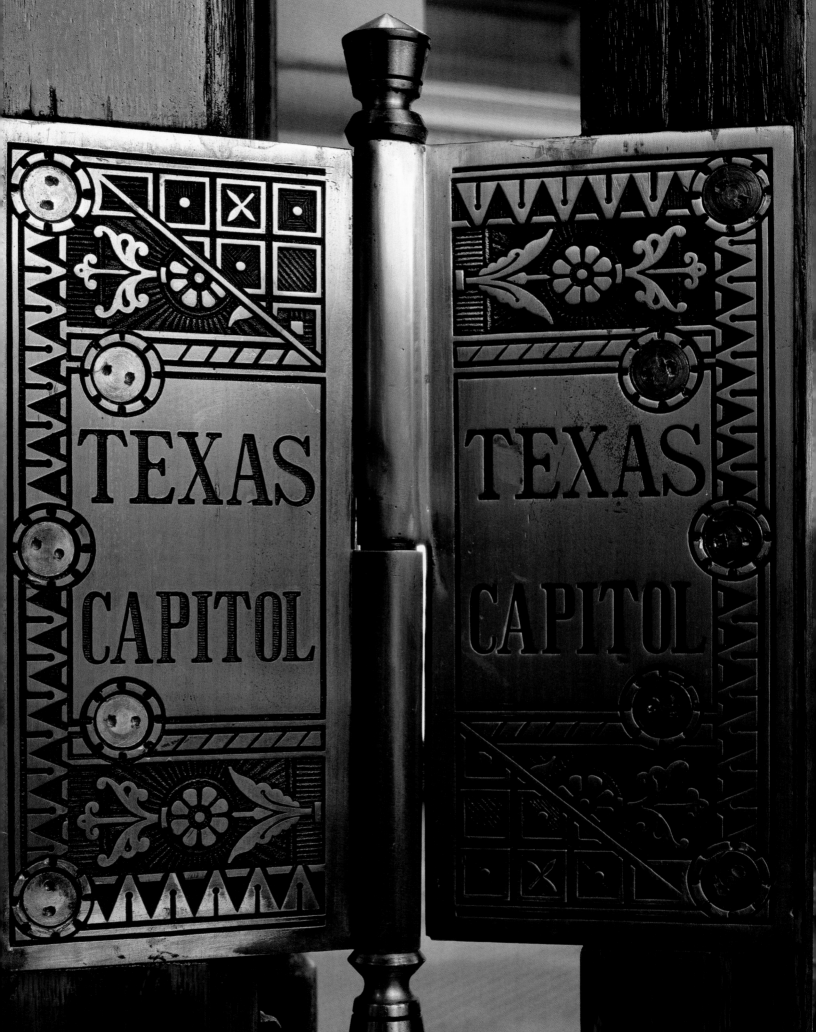

N 1881 FIRE DESTROYED THE original Texas capitol, but vestiges of the past still remain throughout its replacement, completed in 1888. Thanks to a massive, $187.6 million renovation completed in 1995, the building has been restored to its original glory.

AUSTIN

I n Austin, what's under the rainbow is just as important as what's over it. The city's tribute to native son and singer-ute to native son and singer- songwriter Stevie Ray Vaughan stands overlooking Town Lake (opposite).

THE GRACEFUL, ARCHING lines of a Town Lake bridge mimic nature's after-storm contribution to the city. Nearly 100 miles to the west, a more permanent natural fixture exists—legendary Enchanted Rock (PAGES 84 AND 85). The second-largest batholith (an underground rock formation uncovered by erosion) in the United States, the pink-granite boulder is 425 feet tall and covers 640 acres.

THE DOMED EDIFICE OF Palmer Auditorium has been an Austin presence since 1958. Adjacent to downtown along the shores of Town Lake, the facility has hosted countless civic, cultural, and performance events. In 1998, voters approved a plan to renovate the venue into a performing arts center.

ARCHITECTURE BUFFS AND late-night revelers alike find what they're looking for on a famed stretch of Sixth Street (PAGES 88 AND 89). Lined with popular bars, restaurants, and shops, the historic blocks between Congress Avenue and Interstate 35 always provide a rich sampling of live music and people watching.

IN 1843, A PRIME DOWNTOWN lot sold for just $10. Today's Austin is a complementary mix of high-rise office buildings and well-preserved historic structures.

AUSTIN

THE MOUNT BONNELL over-
look (OPPOSITE)—at 785
feet, the highest point in the
area—provides a stunning view
of the city and surrounding Hill
Country. Reflected in its many
sites and buildings, the changing face of Austin reveals a new
focus on a revitalized downtown
with an ever increasing mixture
of business, residential, and entertainment spots (PAGES 93-97).

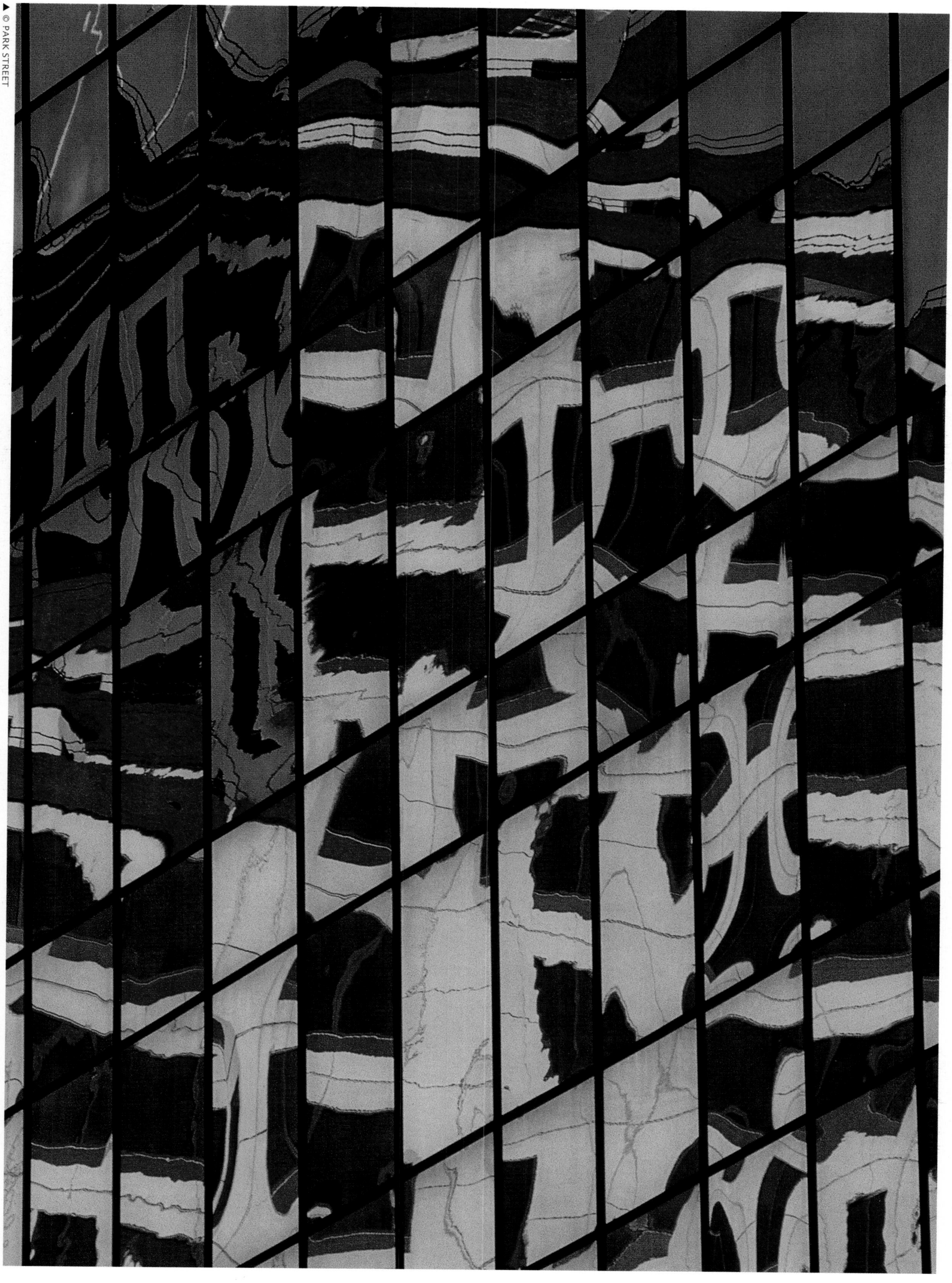

▲ © PARK STREET

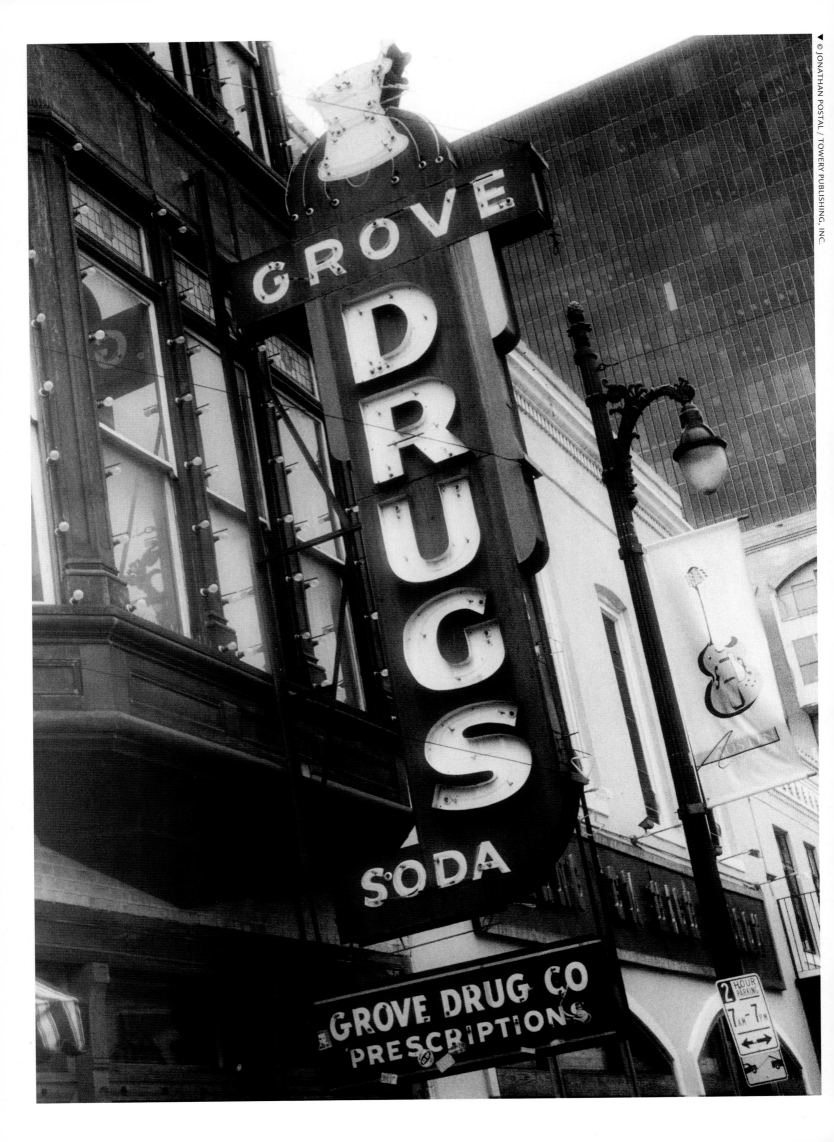

WHAT'S OLD IS NEW AGAIN in downtown Austin, where restored landmarks sit side by side with high-rise office buildings.

FROM URBAN MEADOW TO country store, there are few places like Austin for man's best friend to call home.

WARNING
WHEN SIREN BLOWS
FLOOD GATES WILL BE OPENED
LOOK OUT FOR SWIFT WATER

THE SWEEPING CURVE OF Mansfield Dam mirrors the rolling hills near the Uni- versity of Texas at Austin—yet another local site where the scenery reigns supreme.

ANY TIME IS THE RIGHT TIME to take a quick spin on Lake Austin or Lake Travis. The cool waters of the Highland Lakes, a 150-mile-long chain created by a series of dams, offer year-round recreation for skiers, sailors, and swimmers alike (PAGES 106-109).

AUSTIN

THE SMOOTH WATERS OF LAKE Austin make an ideal playground for jet skiers. The truly brave choose to dip in near Mansfield Dam, where the constant-level lake flows from the bottom of Lake Travis.

ONLY NONMOTORIZED CRAFT such as canoes, kayaks, and paddleboats are allowed on this long, straight stretch of Town Lake, making it the perfect spot for serious scullers or casual canoeists.

WHAT BETTER WAY TO SEE Town Lake than from a double-decker, paddle wheel riverboat? Chartered cruises and sunset rides offer visitors a scenic tour of Austin's hills and houses, as well as a close-up view of the city's famed bats as they make their evening exodus from underneath the Congress Avenue Bridge.

AUSTIN

WILD CREATURES AND COLorful characters abound, from Eeyore's Birthday Party at Pease Park (OPPOSITE TOP) to the Littlefield Memorial Fountain on the University of Texas at Austin campus (TOP). Many Austinites can recall the most bold—if not the most buoyant—entries in the annual Great River Raft Race, where a monster squid can come head-to-head with waterproof cowboys (BOTTOM AND OPPOSITE BOTTOM).

BARTON SPRINGS POOL IS A place where people have always come to clear their heads or share their thoughts while enjoying the serene natural set- ting. The lifelike *Philosophers' Rock* sculpture (OPPOSITE) by art- ist Glenna Goodacre captures an animated conversation between Austin's own historian Walter Prescott Webb, naturalist Roy Bedichek, and humorist and folklorist J. Frank Dobie. Mean- while, five bathing beauties strike a more refined pose.

KIDS OF ALL AGES LOVE THE cool, spring-fed waters of Austin's treasured Barton Springs Pool, which stays a chilly 68 degrees Fahrenheit throughout the year. Home to the endangered Barton Springs salamander, the site has long been a focal point of environmental preservation in Austin.

NOTHING BEATS A GOOD swimming hole in the hot Texas summer, and Hamilton Pool (OPPOSITE TOP), Barton Creek (OPPOSITE BOTTOM), and Barton Springs (THIS PAGE) are favorite spots in which to cool off.

THE ENCHANTING WATERFALL at Hamilton Pool is well worth the short drive from Austin. The pool was formed when the dome of an underground river collapsed thousands of years ago, and now swimmers and hikers enjoy the scenic result.

RECENT RAIN BRINGS THE sweet sound of rushing water to Pedernales Falls State Park. The Pedernales River and its spectacular falls are the centerpiece of the 5,211-acre park near Johnson City.

AUSTIN

STRETCHES OF BARTON CREEK and the Guadalupe River might be a little fast-paced, but tubing is a favorite pastime of Central Texans. Grab an inflated inner tube, a few friends, and a cooler, and enjoy a leisurely float downstream.

AMED FOR ITS FOUNDER, THE Lady Bird Johnson Wildflower Center opened its new, 42-acre facility in 1995 and has since become one of Austin's most popular spots. German mission and ranch-style stone buildings feature North America's largest rooftop rainwater collection system, which provides water for the center's 23 perennial and seasonal gardens.

IN APPRECIATION OF OUR FOUNDER, LADY BIRD JOHNSON, WHOSE LOVE OF NATURAL BEAUTY HAS LEFT A TIMELESS IMPRINT UPON THE AMERICAN LANDSCAPE FOR THE BENEFIT AND ENJOYMENT OF THIS AND FUTURE GENERATIONS, THE BOARD OF DIRECTORS HEREBY PROUDLY AND AFFECTIONATELY DEDICATES THE NATIONAL WILDFLOWER RESEARCH CENTER'S NEW FACILITY AS THE

Lady Bird Johnson Wildflower Center

MARCH 31, 1995

AUSTIN

DURING THE SPRING AND summer months, fields of bluebonnets—the Texas state flower—and prickly pear cacti paint the local landscape with colors so vivid that it's common to see people stop on the side of the road just to take pictures.

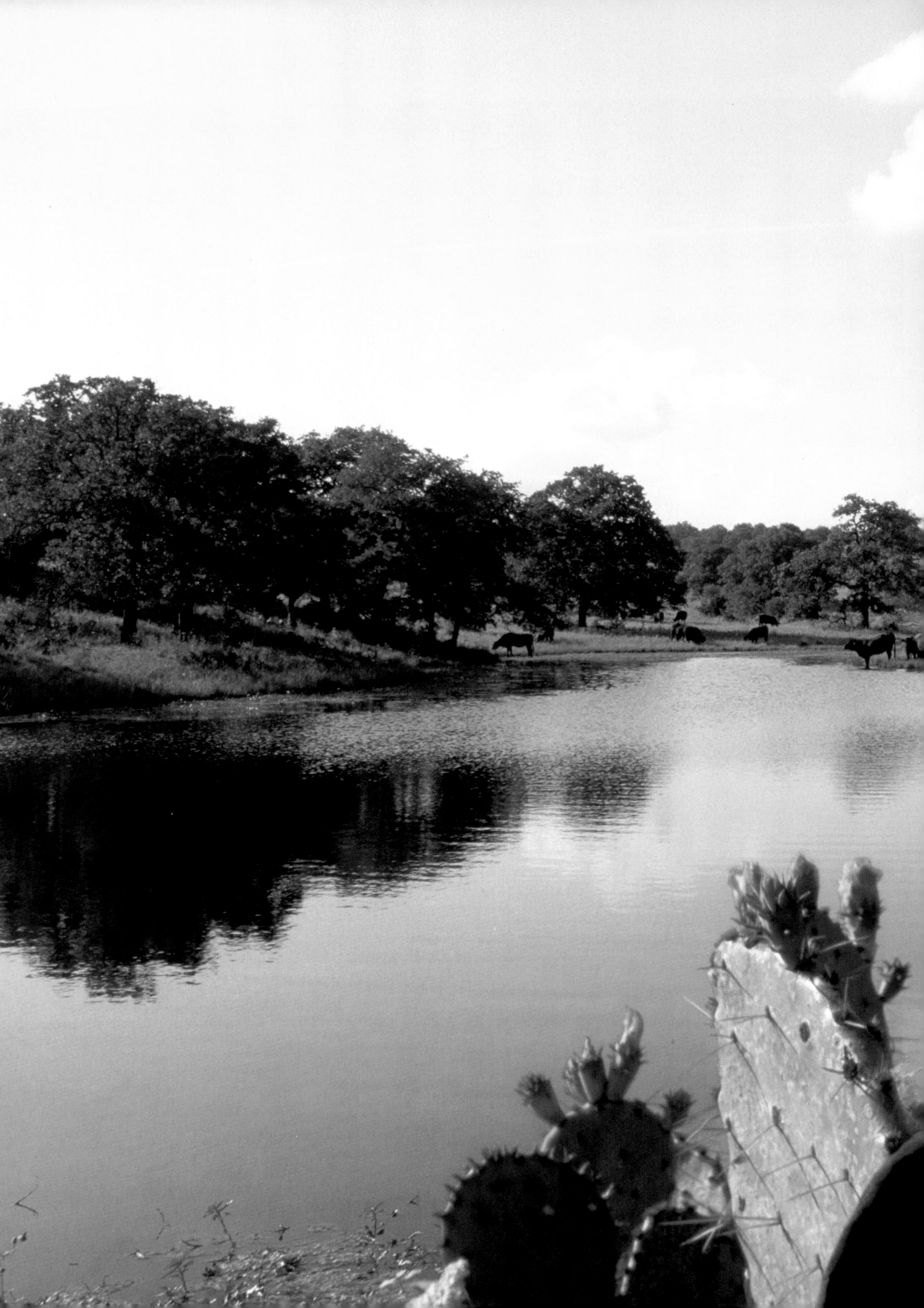

◆ © COLES HAIRSTON

HATS OFF TO WILLIE NELSON, Austin's adopted native son. Born in Abbott, Texas, the Red Headed Stranger made his way to Austin by way of Nashville in the early 1970s, and now lives and works on a ranch just outside of the city. Willie's Austin concerts are always a welcome-home party at which delighted fans sing along to their favorite songs.

AUSTIN OFFICIALLY ADOPTED the nickname Live Music Capital of the World in the early 1990s, but it has long been a ha- ven for tunesmiths and music lovers alike. Local legends Jimmie Vaughan (OPPOSITE) and Alejandro Escovedo (ABOVE) both came from musical Texas families, and have made significant contributions to the music scene with their unmistakable styles.

STEVE WERTHEIMER, OWNER of South Austin's famed Continental Club, and Amy Farris, fiddler for singer Kelly Willis, are just two of the influential faces that help shape the Austin music scene.

BRIAN HOFELDT (OPPOSITE LEFT) and Tony Villanueva (OPPOSITE RIGHT) of the Derailers, the immortal Stevie Ray Vaughan (LEFT), street musicians on Sixth Street (RIGHT), and every musician who's ever passed through Austin leave behind lingering notes that comprise an incredible collective of music, describable only as "the Austin sound."

TODAY'S AUSTIN SYMPHONY Orchestra, conducted by Peter Bay, is a sophisticated cousin of yesterday's musical ensembles such as the Ballerstedt family orchestra or the 1920s All American Dance Orchestra.

STEPPING UP TO THE MIKE means different things for singer Toni Price and radio talk show host Jim Hightower. Price, once referred to as "the best singer you never heard of," sings her country-rock-blues tunes all around the city. Hightower, the state's former agriculture commissioner, now broadcasts *Live from the Chat & Chew Café* out of Threadgill's World Headquarters restaurant.

SINGER-SONGWRITER Jon Dee Graham (OPPOSITE) has entertained loyal fans with his distinctive, rocking melodies ever since his early days in the Skunks and True Believers. Tango composer Glover Gill brings more than 20 years' experience on the Austin music scene to his latest band, Tosca.

THE PULSE OF THE CITY BEATS a little louder and a little later each March during the annual South by Southwest (SXSW) music festival, at which close to 1,000 bands perform at more than 50 venues over four days.

AUSTIN FASHION HAS ALWAYS been, well, a little heady. But horned helmets and big hair aside, the city's a great place to find a new look.

AT TEXAS HATTERS, THEY'VE been topping the best for more than 60 years. Owner Joella Gammage-Torres and her mother, Norma, run the hat-making business, which has crowned the renowned from presidents to celebrities.

REIGNING QUEENS OF THE Kendall County fair, these young ladies have got the Texas look down to a fine art.

AUSTINITES HAVE ALWAYS loved a celebration, be it the championship victory of a 1906 city baseball team or a local Dia de los Muertos parade.

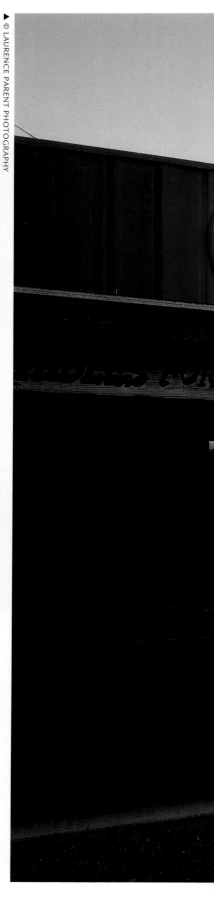

ARGUABLY THE CITY'S PRE-eminent country music dance hall, the Broken Spoke is known for—among other things— giving rise to the early career of singer Willie Nelson, and some boot-scootin'-delicious chicken-fried steak.

AUSTIN

WHETHER THEY'RE JUST learning the two-step or they've perfected their waltz to- gether over the years, dancers of all ages glide on the well-worn floor of the Broken Spoke.

AUSTIN

ALTHOUGH HE DEPARTED IN the spring of 1999, Ballet Austin's former artistic director Lambros Lambrou left his mark on the troupe. The company presents a season of five ballets each year at Bass Concert Hall on the University of Texas at Austin campus, as well as performances throughout the state.

OVER THE YEARS, AS AUSTIN has become a mecca for cultural events, ballet has pirouetted into the mix. But some things never change. Take the cowboy boot. From CEOs to musicians to politicians to students, the well-heeled footwear is as familiar in a boardroom as it is in a barn (PAGES 163-165).

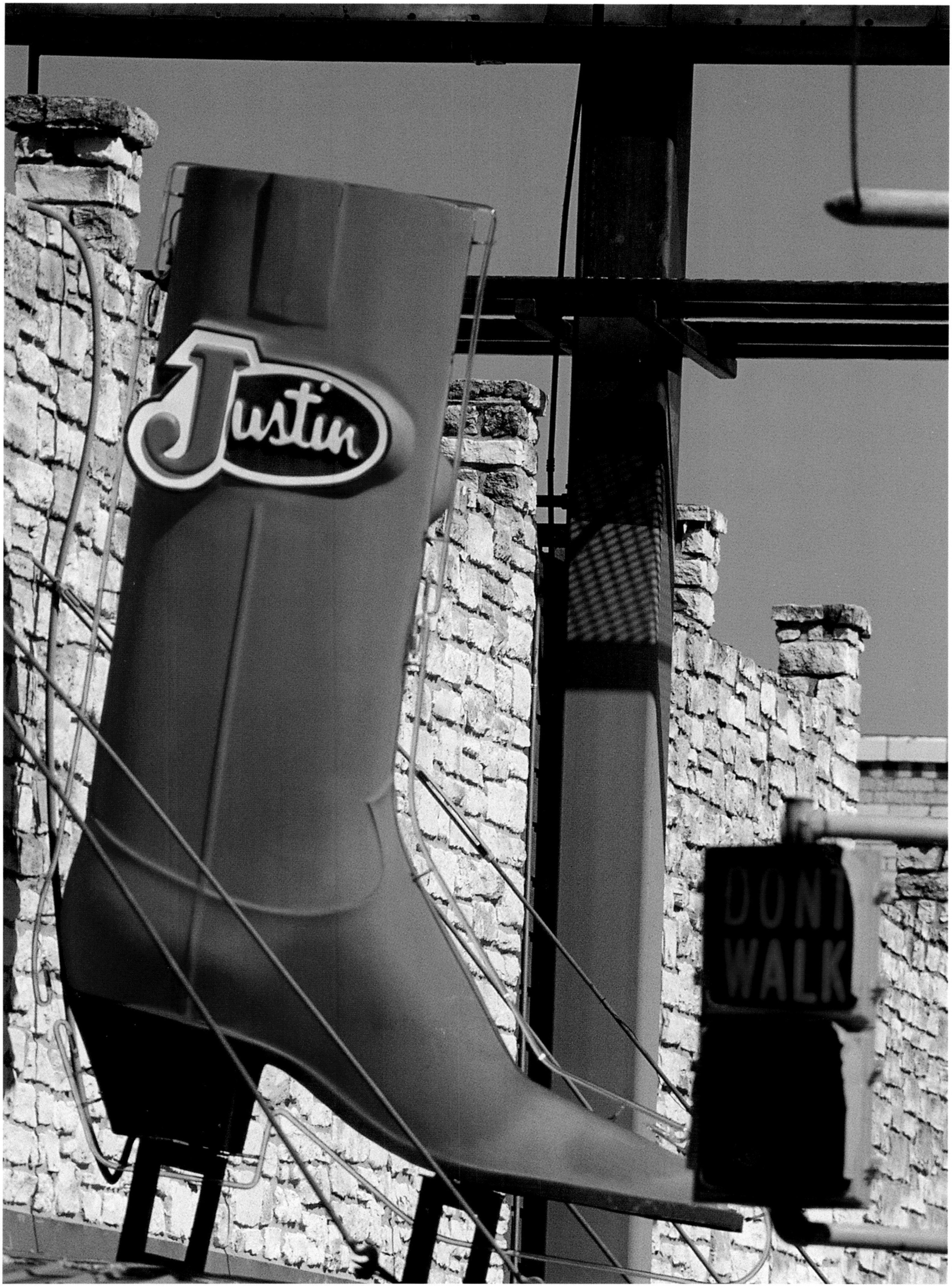

▲ © JONATHAN POSTAL / TOWERY PUBLISHING, INC.

FANCY BOOTS AND SHOES aren't the only hot commodities in Austin. True to their Texas roots, the city's residents consume their share of red chili peppers.

NOTHING'S MORE COMFORTable than a handmade pair of leather boots or a custom-made saddle refined by local craftsmen. The folks at Capitol Saddlery are legend in Austin, where they have been making high-quality leather goods since 1930.

IT'S HEAVY METAL ALL AROUND. The now defunct Electric Lounge (OPPOSITE) was once home to some of Austin's most eclectic acts from poetry slams and performance art to music. Sculptor Andy Colquitt, meanwhile, relies on heat, hammer, and anvil to come up with his whimsical pieces (PAGES 172 AND 173).

AUSTIN

ALTHOUGH AREA WELDERS and Austin sculptor Barry George (OPPOSITE) might use similar tools, their end products are quite different. George works primarily with found objects to create his pieces.

AUSTIN IS A HUB FOR ART-
ists and artisans such as
Faith Gay (OPPOSITE) and shop
owners Steve and Lisa Dean
from Under the Sun. The city's
eclectic mix of galleries, creative
studios, and retail shops offers
everything from one-of-a-kind
sculpture to vintage western
wear and music memorabilia.

LOCAL ARTIST AMADO PEÑA'S distinctive works (OPPO-SITE) are representative of the Latin American influence found throughout the Austin area. The contemporary Latin American art collection at the Jack S. Blanton Museum of Art on the University of Texas at Austin campus (ABOVE) contains some of the finest such pieces in the state.

CREATIVITY IS ONE OF AUSTIN'S most abundant natural resources. From spots such as the Ellos Gallery (OPPOSITE) to BMC Software's collection featuring a painting of Congress Avenue by Pamela Johnson (ABOVE), every corner of the city is a showcase of artistic talent.

LOOKING AT AUSTIN THROUGH the lens is keeping both surveyors and filmmakers busy. The varied scenery, good weath- er, and creative talent mean new residents, new businesses, and Hollywood have all come calling.

SXSW PRESENTS AUSTIN PREMIERE 'EDTV'
FROM UNIVERSAL PICTURES & IMAGINE ENTERTAINMENT

AUSTIN'S PARAMOUNT THE-atre rolled out the red carpet for the premiere of *EdTV* during the 1999 SXSW Film Conference and Festival. SXSW cofounder Louis Black (OPPO-SITE), editor of the *Austin Chronicle* weekly newspaper, joined direc-tor Ron Howard (ABOVE) for the big event.

WHEN HE'S NOT HANGING out at Julio's Restaurant, cyberpunk denizen and Austin resident Bruce Sterling is cook-ing up the future. In novels including *Heavy Weather*, *Holy Fire*, and *Distraction*, Sterling has explored the far-reaching reper-cussions of technology and its effect on the human race.

RELAXING OVER COFFEE WITH Hotel San Jose co-owner and lawyer Liz Lambert, writer Marion Winik (ON RIGHT), whose books include *First Comes Love* and *The Lunch-Box Chronicles: Notes from the Parenting Underground*, has been called Austin's Dorothy Parker. Sadly for the city, she moved away in the spring of 1999.

CRAFTSMANSHIP COMES IN all forms. Pulitzer Prize-winning cartoonist Ben Sargent (OPPOSITE) keeps local politicos on their toes with his illustrations in the *Austin American-Statesman*. Applying the same diligence and skill to their trade are the artisans at Heirloom Gold Leaf Frames.

G RAFFITI IS A PART OF EVERY big city, but in Austin it appears inside and out, as the vivid images that adorn the walls of the Smokin' Grill demonstrate (TOP AND OPPOSITE BOTTOM).

BIKERS OF ALL AGES ARE sportin' tattoos in Austin, where even the outside of a shop gets in on the art.

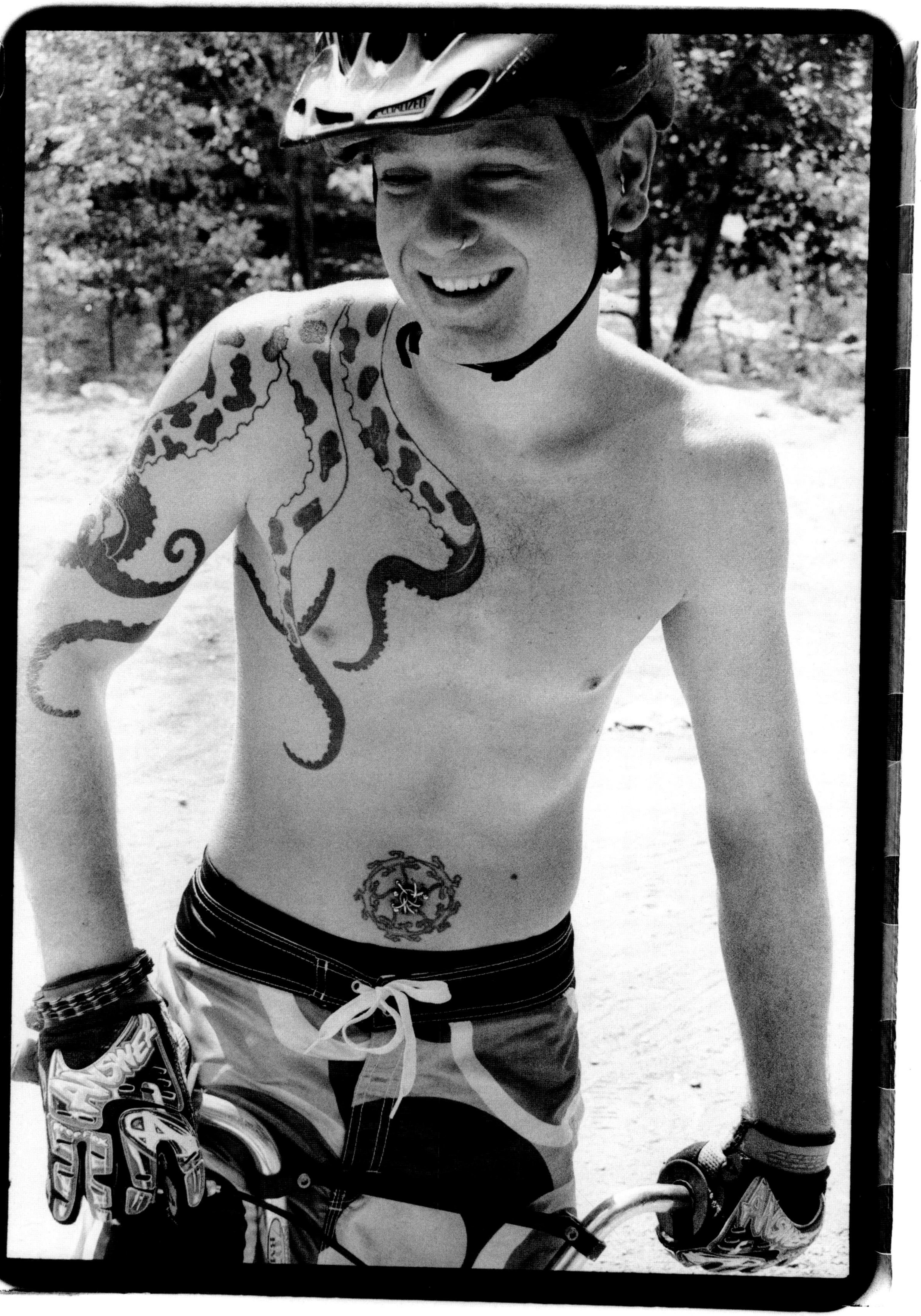

▲ © JONATHAN POSTAL / TOWERY PUBLISHING, INC.

FROM THE CITY'S EARLIEST days, Austin firefighters and police officers patrolled and protected. Still as dedicated to-day, members of both departments benefit from a bit fancier equipment than that used in the early 1900s (PAGES 194-197).

IT'S UP TO TRAVIS COUNTY Sheriff Margo Frasier (OPPOSITE) to help keep the peace around town. Local celebrity Leslie Cochran, meanwhile, stops just short of disturbing it with his unpredictable ensembles and political statements on display along Congress Avenue.

IF IMITATION IS INDEED THE highest form of flattery, country crooner Willie Nelson should be really flattered by his look-alike, Nellie Wilson, a con- testant in the annual chili cook-off in Luckenbach. In the 1940s, when Lyndon Baines Johnson (ABOVE, SECOND FROM RIGHT) served Texas as U.S. senator, it was the Harmony barbecue that drew him—and a less flamboyant crowd.

LIKE FATHER LIKE SON? Politically speaking, it's been a pretty easy ride for two-term Governor George W. Bush (OPPOSITE). Namesake and son of former President George Bush, he has aspirations bigger than, well, Texas.

204

FIRST LADY OF TEXAS LAURA Bush devotes much of her time promoting literacy initiatives throughout the state. For University of Texas Longhorns running back Ricky Williams, the 1998 Heisman Trophy winner, it's been reading the opponent's defense—not to mention barreling through it—that has gotten his name in print.

AN ATTORNEY BY TRADE, Austin Mayor Kirk Watson has served the city since June 1997. Another well-known local politician, Lyndon Baines Johnson left his legacy on both Texas and the United States. His presidential library and museum in Austin house some 40 million historical documents, as well as highlights of his political career and a replica of the Oval Office.

THE SUCCESS OF MAJOR HIGH-tech companies such as IBM and Dell Computer Corporation led *Fortune* magazine in 1998 to name Austin the Best City for Business in North America in its 10th annual ranking.

THE HIGH-TECH LURE OF multicolored computer chips is the look of the future for Austin. But who can resist a bit of nostalgia at the sight of a spinning Ferris wheel on a moonlit night?

THE UBIQUITOUS "BUNNY suit" is common work attire for employees of many of Austin's high-tech companies, where clean rooms rival hospitals for antiseptic honors.

A140

SE
TR:450
TE:11/Fr
EC:1/1 16kHz

CTLBOT
FOV:28x21
3.0thk/0.0sp/I

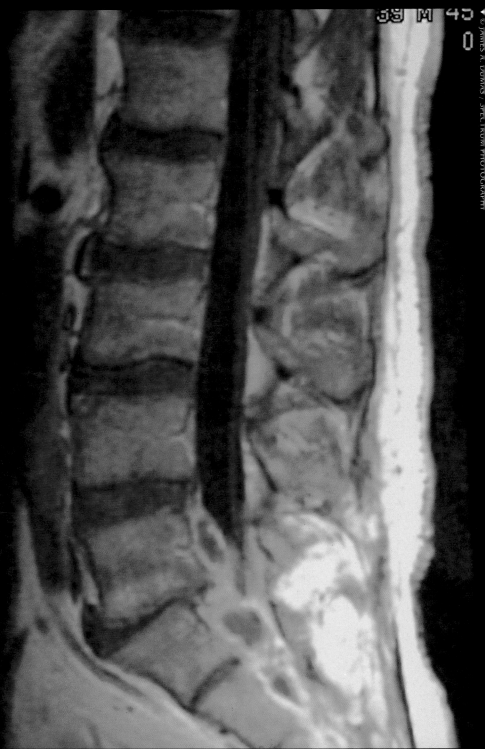

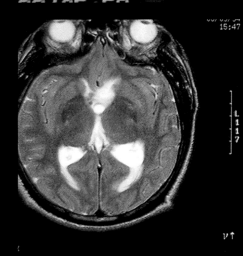

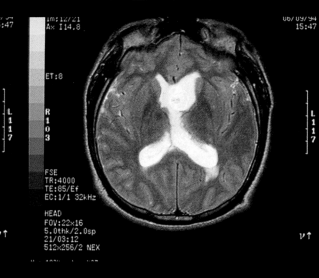

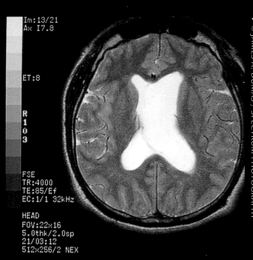

A USTINITES PLACE A STRONG emphasis on health, and the region is home to some of the top medical facilities in the country.

KICKING BACK MEANS DIF-ferent things to different folks around Austin. For residents of the Island on Lake Travis retirement community (OPPOSITE), a stunning view of the water lends itself to peaceful repose. On the University of Texas campus, students needing a break from the hectic pace of classes can visit the Student Union.

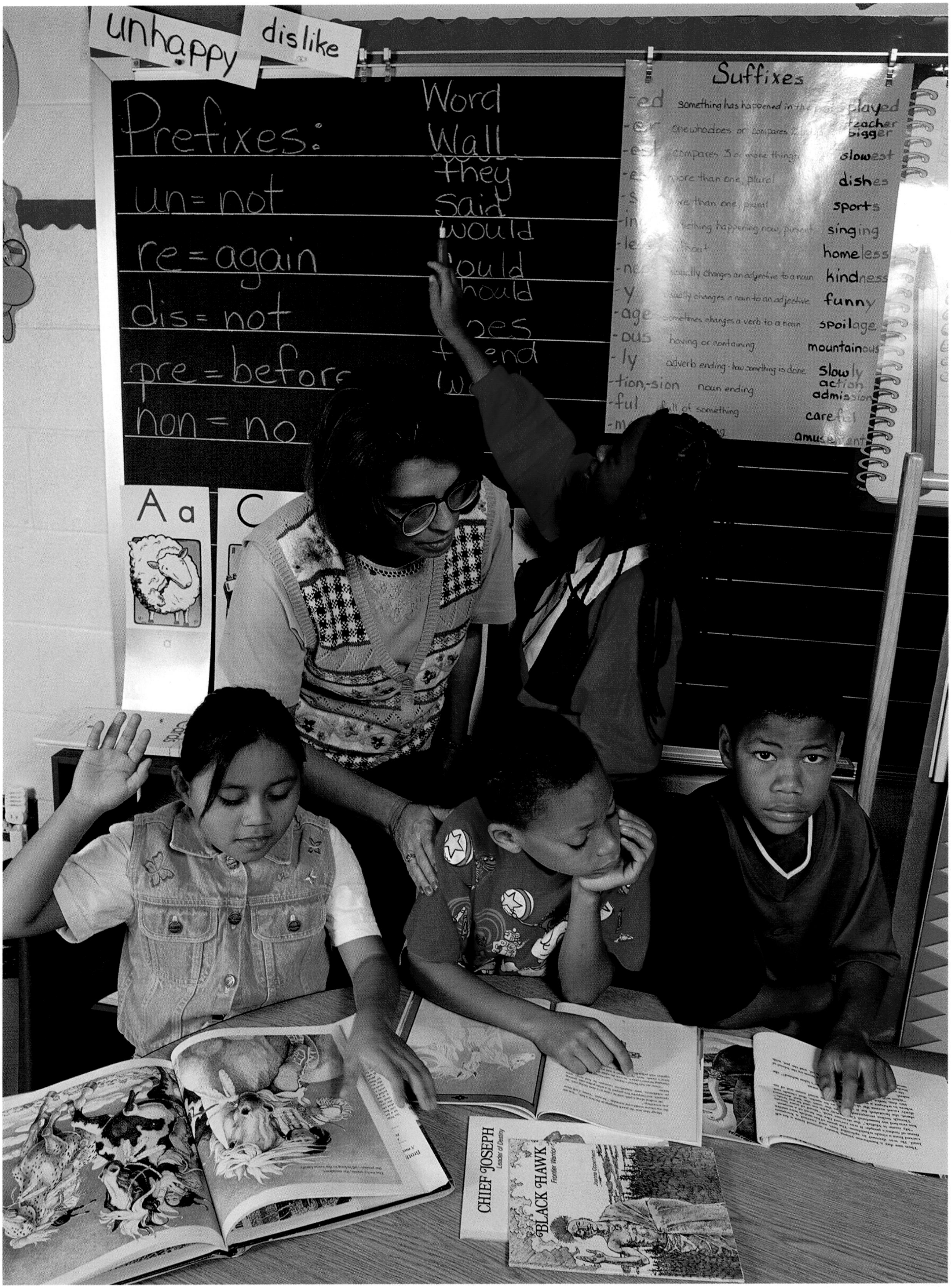

© JONATHAN POSTAL / TOWERY PUBLISHING, INC.

STUDENTS AT CAMPBELL Elementary School get a head start in readin', 'ritin', and 'rithmetic with teacher Mary Silver (OPPOSITE). One of the nation's most highly educated communities, Austin boasts an estimated one in nine adults currently enrolled in an area college or university, such as historic St. Edward's University.

THE NINE-BANDED ARMADILLO is such a common sight around Central Texas that it's not surprising to see anyone, including former Governor Ann Richards, holding the odd-looking critter. After all, it is the official state mammal.

BIRTHDAYS ARE ONE OF THE best parts of being a kid, especially when your dad's Texas Governor Daniel Moody Jr. and your party's on the lawn of the governor's mansion. Festivities aside, nothing beats the down-home feel of a pair of overalls.

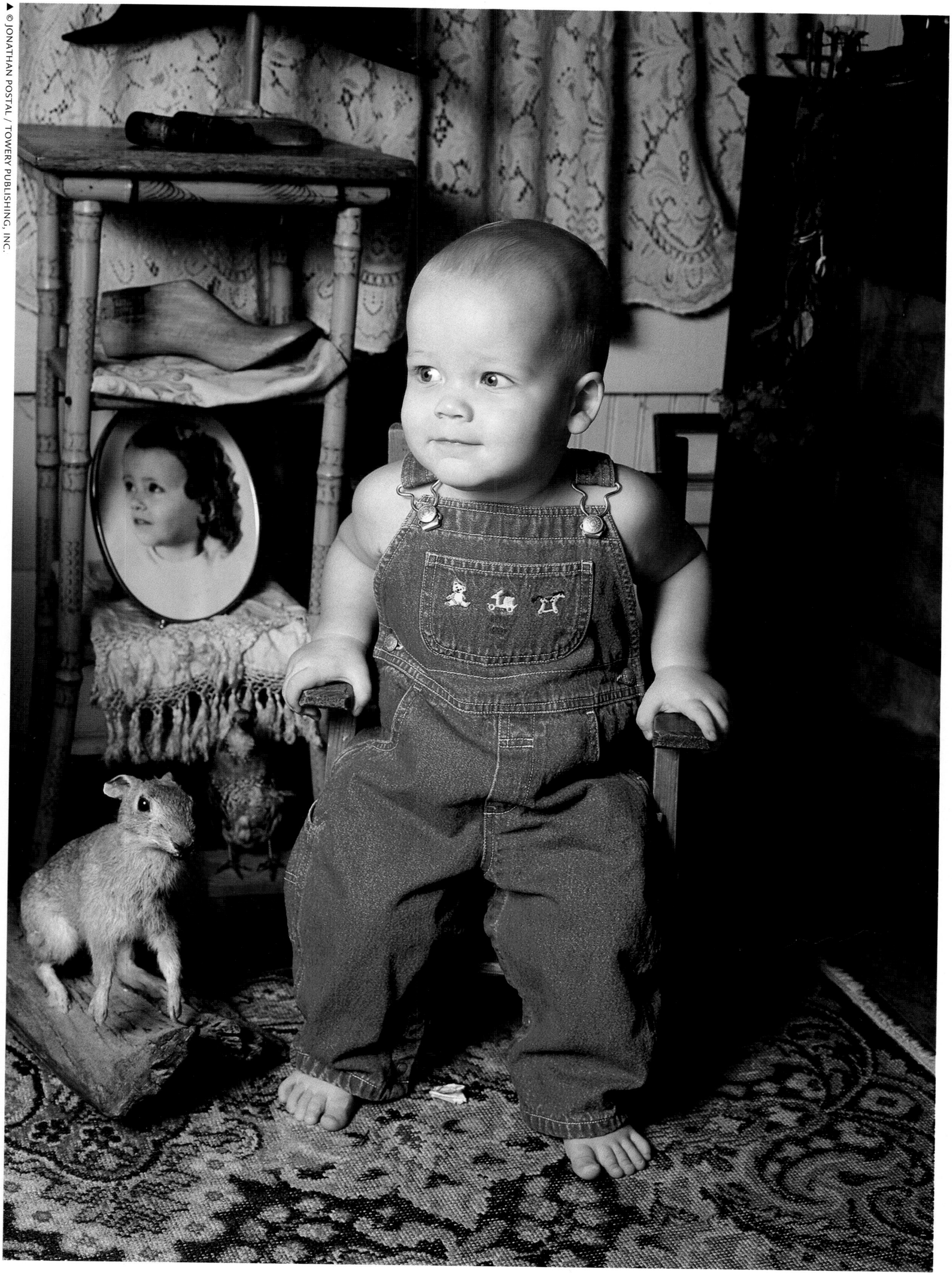

▲ © JONATHAN POSTAL / TOWERY PUBLISHING, INC.

AUSTIN IS A WONDERFUL place to raise children, and the city's cultural and geographic diversity provides ample opportunities for celebrations and fun activities for everyone.

AUSTIN

I T'S ALL A MATTER OF ACCES-
sorizing, pardner. For these
two, the attraction of the Wild
West was just too good to pass up.

AUSTIN

THE ROMANCE OF RODEO life leaves many sitting tall in the saddle. But one bull rider's about to learn a whole new meaning for the term "cowpoke."

232

A WIDE VARIETY OF TALENTS— some comical, some practical—are needed for a full complement of rodeo magic.

AUSTIN

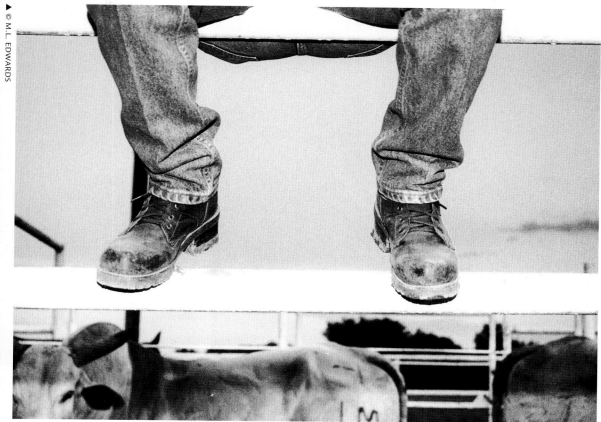

THE RIGHT STUFF: QUALITY equipment and the patience to watch and wait can make for a long ride in rodeo life.

TEXAS COWGIRLS NEVER GET
the blues—as long as they
can show off their Texas pride.

ELEBRATING VETERANS DAY, Cinco de Mayo, and Fourth of July, participants and onlookers alike share the excitement and fanfare of a parade.

CELEBRATING THE LONE STAR MILLENNIUM

240

STANDING STATUE-STILL IS ALL in a day's work for these Austinites. About 40 miles northeast of the city, Taylor, Texas, is the site for the annual rattlesnake roundup (OPPOSITE RIGHT) that draws hundreds to the city park, where the first contestant to bag 10 diamond-backs is the lucky winner.

TRIBUTES TO THE DECEASED are expressed in a variety of ways, from the military precision of headstones in a New Braunfels veterans' cemetery to the decorative ornamentation of other grave sites (PAGES 242-245).

ALL KINDS OF CREATURES ARE taking flight in Austin, where travelers to and from the city can experience the amenities of the new Austin-Bergstrom International Airport (OPPOSITE).

TRANSPORTING FOLKS VIA A "clean machine" helps Austin preserve the city's air quality while decreasing traffic hassles. In addition to operating the UT shuttle bus service and the free downtown Dillo Dash trolley-style bus, the Capital Metropolitan Transportation Authority bus system serves a 500-square-mile area surrounding Austin.

AUSTIN

FROM THE REAL THING TO THE wheel thing, the Texas longhorn is the mascot of the people.

OLDSMOBILE
19 TEXAS 65
NWV427

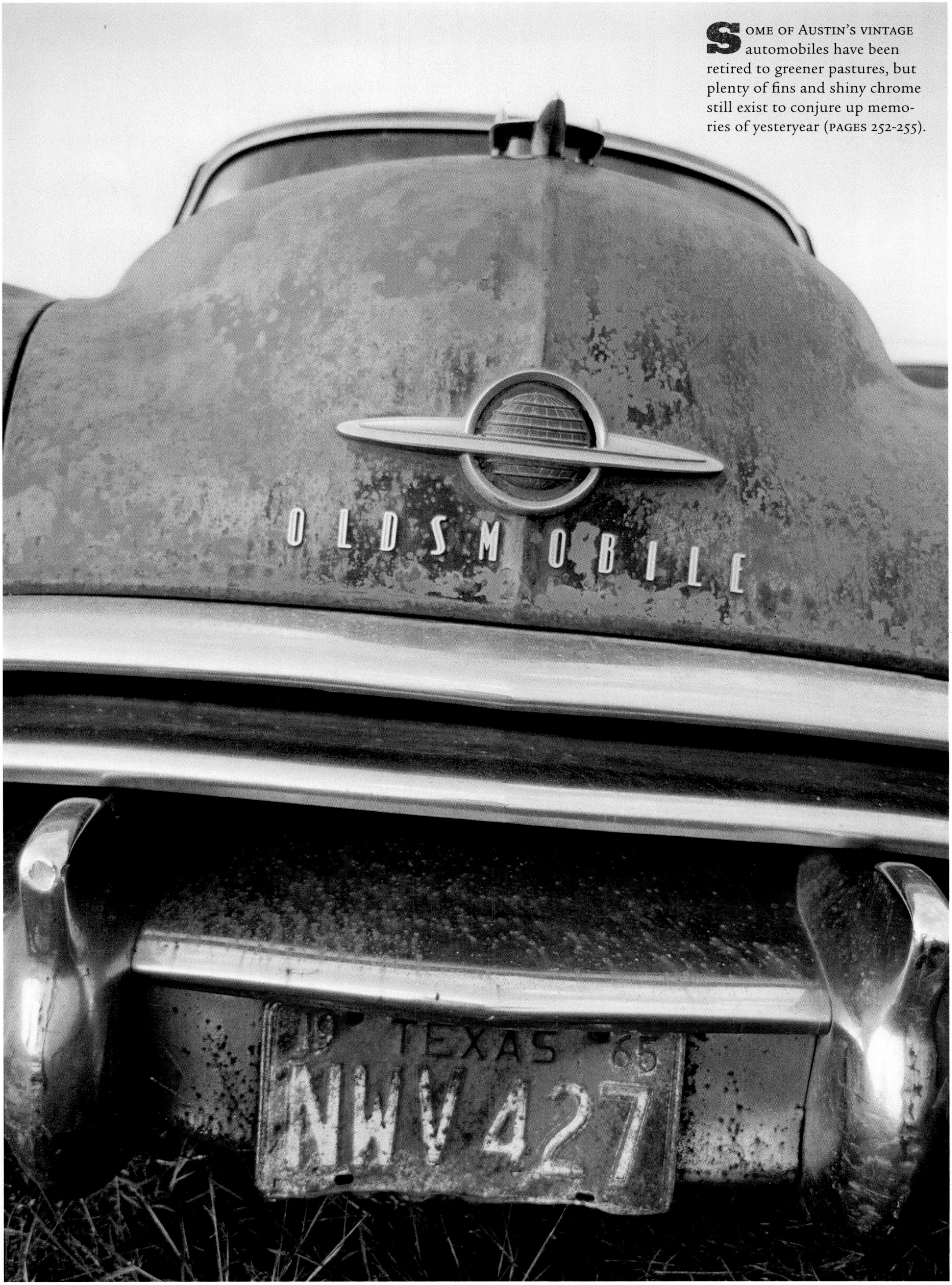

Some of Austin's vintage automobiles have been retired to greener pastures, but plenty of fins and shiny chrome still exist to conjure up memories of yesteryear (pages 252-255).

▲ © Jonathan Postal / Towery Publishing, Inc.

ALTHOUGH IT'S GENERALLY the exception to the rule these days, a few Austinites still enjoy relaxing with a cigarette in hand.

IN A CITY WHERE WISHES CAN come true, it's little wonder the genie population is high. Carrying the weight of artist Rory Skagen on its shoulders, one such lucky charm undergoes a touch of restoration work.

260   A U S T I N

A SPECTACULAR VARIETY OF dining and drinking experiences awaits the taste buds of Austinites. Chef James Fisher offers exquisite Asian and Middle Eastern dishes at Mars (OPPOSITE). For some of Austin's more down-home flavors, try the burgers at Fran's Hamburgers. But if it's majestic dining you're looking for, you're too late. The Majestic (PAGES 262 AND 263) closed a few years ago, leaving only good memories behind.

CELEBRATING THE LONE STAR MILLENNIUM

AUSTIN'S WONDERFUL weather makes dining alfresco a year-round treat, as patrons of Shady Grove on Barton Springs Road and the Oasis on Lake Travis will attest.

FIXTURE ON THE CITY'S culinary scene for generations, Sam's Bar-B-Que on East 12th Street serves a mean plate of ribs. With Willie Mays Sr. behind the counter and Willie Jr. along to help, a visit to Sam's is sure to put a smile on your face.

TAKE ADVANTAGE OF THE local bounty at a roadside stand, where you can spice things up or cool things down in just a matter of miles.

OSTRICHES BONNIE AND
Clyde—unlike their
namesake counterparts—have no
reason to be on the lam, thanks
to their good home, courtesy of
Sid McQuary. But while ostrich
eggs are sought after largely for
their monetary value, it's the
healing power of the ordinary
chicken egg that has others
enraptured.

272

Coach Jody Conradt has led the University of Texas women's basketball team since 1976 and has won more games than any other coach in the history of women's basketball. In 1999, she was inducted into the prestigious national Women's Basketball Hall of Fame. With a slam dunk of his own, a salesman at a local farmer's market shows off his prize-sized pumpkin.

he Darrell K. Royal–Texas Memorial Stadium fills with more than 74,000 avid Longhorn fans for every football home game. Renamed for the legendary head coach in 1995, the arena's major renovation in 1998 added several thousand more seats, a new upper deck, and 52 stadium suites.

WO OF THE MOST RECOGNIZ-
able landmarks in Austin
are the Darrell K. Royal-Texas
Memorial Stadium (OPPOSITE)
and the University of Texas
Tower. The tower's observation
deck, closed since 1975, reopened
to visitors after a major renovation in 1999.

WHILE ALL THE LONGHORNS are a proud lot, some choose to wear their support on their chests.

VICTORY WAS SWEET FOR THE Longhorns after the 1999 Cotton Bowl. Fans in Austin knew their team had won as soon as they saw the UT Tower lit orange.

DIE-HARD DALLAS COWBOYS fans once waited in the hot sun for hours to see their favorite players—like quarter-back Troy Aikman—practice at St. Edward's University. Rampant disappointment set in when the team moved its summer training camp from Austin to Wichita Falls in 1998.

A LOVE FOR SPORTS, ESPECIALLY football, starts at a very young age in Texas, where high school and Little League games are a favorite pastime for members of the community.

AUSTIN

WHATEVER THE SPORT, Austin youngsters and teenagers alike put their best foot forward.

COME RAIN OR SHINE, HUN-dreds of sports teams play every week in city leagues. Base-ball, basketball, soccer, and soft-ball all are popular sports around town.

AUSTIN SPORTS AFICIONADOS can go from the batting cage to the Bat Cave, the new nickname of the Travis County Exposition Center and home of Austin's very own minor-league hockey team, the Ice Bats.

I F IT'S BOXING THAT'S YOUR sport of choice, lessons are available from Richard "Ironman" Lord (OPPOSITE) or Anissa "The Assassin" Zamarron (THIS PAGE).

AUSTIN PROUDLY CLAIMS some of the world's best golfers as its own. Tinsley Penick, son of legend Harvey Penick, shows off some of his dad's coaching form in front of the Loop 360 bridge. Perhaps a potential student, a youngster tastes victory after a hotly contested round of miniature golf.

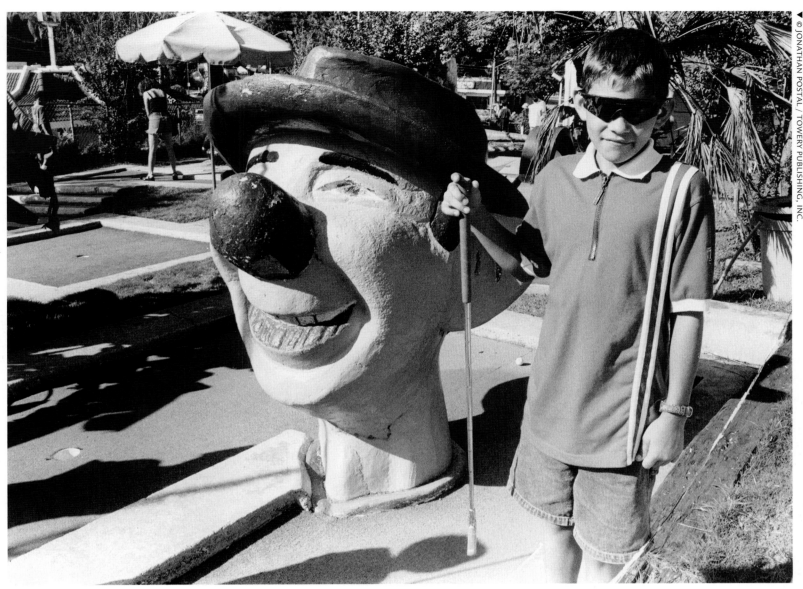

AUSTIN

CLOWNING AROUND AT PETER Pan Mini-Golf, these two characters have it made in the shades.

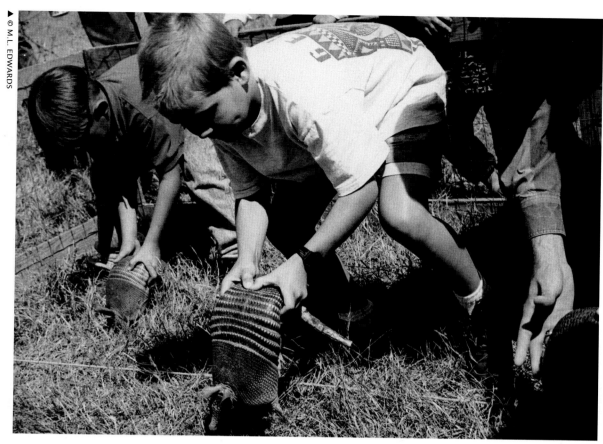

THE LITTLE DOG CERTAINLY laughed when he saw this cow jump over the moon on Congress Avenue. Some friendly competition brings out the creativity among contestants in an armadillo race, a mini tractor race, and the Capitol 10,000 10K.

I WASN'T BORN IN AUSTIN, BUT I got here as fast as I could," says a popular bumper sticker.

The same could likely be said of these avian Austinites, who seem to fit right in.

WHOA THERE, PARDNER. THE COWBOY image is larger than life in Austin, where Clark Lee Walker (BOTTOM) shows that his roping skills are on par with his screen-writing talents. Walker is noted for his work on the scripts for *Slacker* and *The Newton Boys*.

COWBOYS AREN'T THE ONLY reminders of the days of old. Antiques, collectibles, hard- to-find goodies, and just plain ol' cool stuff abound in Austin's many eclectic shops and stores.

306

COLLECTORS ARE A FOCUSED lot, and one axiom holds true for them all: Whatever your memorabilia of choice, you've got to have a place to display it.

Time keeps on ticking, but things just seem to improve with age in Austin, the city where the Lone Star millennium promises to usher in a new season of growth and celebration.

◆ © DONOVAN REESE

PROFILES IN EXCELLENCE

A look at the corporations, businesses, professional groups, and community service organizations that have made this book possible. Their stories—offering an informal chronicle of the local business community—are arranged according to the date they were established in Austin.

AMD ★ Americus Diamond ★ Analysts International Corporation ★ Apple Americas Customer Support Center ★ Armstrong Moving & Storage, Inc. ★ Ascension Orthopedics, Inc. ★ AT&T ★ Austin American-Statesman ★ Austin-Bergstrom International Airport ★ Austin Community College ★ Austin Energy ★ Austin Radiological Association ★ AXA Advisors L.L.C. ★ Bank of America ★ BMC Software ★ BookPeople ★ Brigham Exploration Company ★ Brock Consulting Group, Inc. ★ Brown Distributing Co. ★ Brown McCarroll & Oaks Hartline, L.L.P. ★ Calcasieu Lumber Company ★ Capital City Container ★ CarrAmerica Realty Corporation ★ Chase Bank of Texas, N.A. ★ City of Austin ★ City of Austin Water and Wastewater Utility ★ Clear Channel Radio, Inc. ★ Clinical Pathology Laboratories, Inc. ★ Commemorative Brands, Inc. ★ Computer Sciences Corporation, Financial Services Group ★ Cook-Walden Funeral Homes and Cemeteries ★ The County Line, Inc. ★ Cypress Semiconductor (Texas), Inc. ★ Delgado Design Group, Inc. ★ Dell Computer Corporation ★ DuPont Photomasks Inc. ★ EDS/NHIC ★ EEA (Energy Engineering Associates, Inc.) ★ Encore Orthopedics, Inc. ★ Faulkner Construction Company ★ Fisher-Rosemount Systems ★ The Gottesman Company ★ Greater Austin Chamber of Commerce ★ GSD&M ★ Herman & Howry, L.L.P. ★ Higdon & Higdon, Inc. ★ Homestead Village ★ Huston-Tillotson College ★ ICG Communications, Inc. ★ IntelliQuest Information Group Inc. ★ IXC Communications, Inc. ★ Jackson Walker L.L.P. ★ Jeffrey's ★ Keane, Inc. ★ Korn/Ferry International ★ Merrill Lynch ★ Micro-Media Solutions, Inc. ★ National Instruments ★ O'Connell Robertson & Associates, Inc. ★ Omnifax ★ ORIGIN Systems Inc. ★ Personique ★ Pervasive Software Inc. ★ Pinnacle Construction of Austin, Inc. ★ The Porter Company, Mechanical Contractors ★ The Progressive Corporation ★ PromiseLand ★ PSI Technologies Corporation ★ Randalls Food Markets, Inc. ★ Renaissance Women's Center ★ Riverbend Church ★ r.j. kolar ★ Roger Beasley Automotive Group ★ St. Edward's University ★ St. Stephen's Episcopal School ★ SAS Institute Inc. ★ SETON Healthcare Network ★ Shoreline Christian Center ★ SI Diamond Technology, Inc. ★ SicolaMartin ★ The SMT Centre Inc. ★ Solectron ★ State Farm Insurance Companies ★ Stewart Title ★ Sulzer Orthopedics Inc. ★ Surrey, Inc. ★ TechWorks, Inc. ★ TECO-Westinghouse Motor Company ★ 3M ★ Tokyo Electron America, Inc. ★ Trammell Crow Company ★ Trilogy Software, Inc. ★ The University of Texas at Austin ★ VTEL Corporation ★ Wallingford Electronics, Inc. ★ Watson Bishop London Galow, P.C. ★ The Wattinger Group ★ Wayne ★ Wells Fargo ★

1839-1970 ★

1839 City of Austin
1871 City of Austin Water and Wastewater Utility
1895 Austin Energy
1999 Austin-Bergstrom International Airport
1871 Austin American-Statesman
1875 Huston-Tillotson College
1877 Greater Austin Chamber of Commerce
1883 Calcasieu Lumber Company
1883 The University of Texas at Austin
1885 St. Edward's University
1886 The Wattinger Group
1888 Cook-Walden Funeral Homes and Cemeteries
1890 Bank of America
1892 AXA Advisors L.L.C.
1898 AT&T
1902 SETON Healthcare Network
1934 Chase Bank of Texas, N.A.
1938 Brown McCarroll & Oaks Hartline, L.L.P.
1938 Jackson Walker L.L.P.
1940 Merrill Lynch
1946 Stewart Title
1947 The Porter Company, Mechanical Contractors
1948 Clinical Pathology Laboratories, Inc.
1949 St. Stephen's Episcopal School
1950 O'Connell Robertson & Associates, Inc.
1954 Austin Radiological Association
1962 Brown Distributing Co.
1962 Faulkner Construction Company
1968 Commemorative Brands, Inc.
1968 Computer Sciences Corporation, Financial Services Group
1968 PromiseLand
1968 Trammell Crow Company
1969 Capital City Container
1970 BookPeople

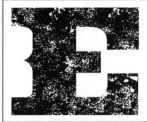

EVERYONE WHO HAS STUMBLED INTO AUSTIN—FROM nomadic Indian tribes to Spanish missionaries to the first American settlers—has discovered the city's many charms. The beauty of the area's natural resources greatly impressed those who visited in the

past, as it still does today.

In 1839, the congress of the Republic of Texas approved a permanent site for its capital and named the city in honor of Stephen F. Austin, leader of the early settlement effort in the Territory of Texas. Little did the founders know that their new capital would become the booming metropolis it is today.

Austin continues to be one of the fastest-growing large cities in the nation, with a ranking of 18th largest, according to the 1999 population estimates by the City of Austin. Austin is home to more than 615,000 people, with an estimated 1 million within the metropolitan area. To meet the growing

needs of that diverse population, the City of Austin is pursuing its goal of making the Texas capital the most livable community in the country.

"Everyone has a different definition of what 'livable' means," says City Manager Jesus Garza. "Whether that's affordable housing, a good sense of community, or overall quality of life, we try to achieve it."

PLENTY TO SHOUT ABOUT

Ask any number of Austinites what they like best about their city, and each one will probably have a different answer. Thanks to an average annual temperature of

70 degrees, climate and outdoor activities often top the list. With 150 miles of Highland Lakes, more than 23,200 acres of dedicated parkland, plenty of hiking and biking trails, the Hill Country, and Barton Springs, there are boundless opportunities to enjoy the area's beautiful weather.

As the Live Music Capital of the World, Austin has more than 100 clubs providing live entertainment for practically every taste. The city's diverse population also supports countless cultural activities throughout the year. An emphasis on environmentalism is prevalent, and Austin has established itself as a Clean Air City, which means smoking is prohibited in public buildings unless authorized.

Austin is considered one of the country's most highly educated communities, with 31 percent of adults completing 16 or more years of schooling. This level of education is due in part to the fact that Austin is home to the nation's largest university, with about 50,000 students. The University of Texas has 14 colleges and schools, with 53 departments and 308 degree programs. The area also boasts six other colleges and universities, and the Austin

CLOCKWISE FROM TOP:
THE COLORADO RIVER WINDS ITS WAY THROUGH TEXAS' CAPITAL CITY, PROVIDING A PEACEFUL RESPITE FROM THE HUBBUB OF DOWNTOWN AUSTIN.

A CROWD RELAXES AT ONE OF THE MANY BARS AND RESTAURANTS IN THE SIXTH STREET ENTERTAINMENT DISTRICT IN DOWNTOWN AUSTIN.

AUDITORIUM SHORES, ALONG THE SOUTH BANK OF THE COLORADO RIVER PORTION KNOWN AS TOWN LAKE, HOSTS MANY CONCERTS IN THE LIVE MUSIC CAPITAL OF THE WORLD. THE CONCERT VENUE IN DOWNTOWN AUSTIN DRAWS THE "BOOTS, SUITS, AND OLD HIPPIES" THAT TYPIFY THE CITY'S DIVERSITY.

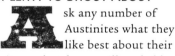
J. GRIFFIS SMITH

J. GRIFFIS SMITH

Independent School District operates 94 elementary, junior high, and high schools.

Austinites are not alone in recognizing their city's qualities. In 1998, *Fortune* magazine ranked Austin number one on its list of the best cities for business in North America; *Money* magazine listed it as one of the best large cities in the South; and *Financial World* magazine ranked Austin among the top five best financially managed cities in the country. Austin has been noted by *Parenting* magazine as one of the 10 best cities for raising children; by *Walking City* magazine as number one in the Fit City, USA category; and by *Time* magazine as number three among its top 15 cities for job growth. In 1998, *Town & Country* magazine ranked two West Austin neighborhoods as Platinum Addresses in a nationwide survey.

SERVING THE COMMUNITY

The City of Austin is one of the largest public employers in the area, with a staff of approximately 10,000 in 23 departments. The day-to-day operations of the city are overseen by seven council members (headed by the mayor) and the council-appointed city manager. Elected at large, council members serve a maximum of two three-year terms. "Our council is truly representative of the community as a whole," says Garza.

From the municipally owned utilities to the new Austin-Bergstrom International Airport to the fire, police, and emergency medical services departments, the City of Austin constantly strives to improve service to its citizens. The Planning, Environmental and Conservation Services Department promotes a number of unique offerings and incentives designed to help maintain Austin's natural beauty and resources. Innovative programs seek to meet the specific needs and concerns of citizens, including one that works with individual neighborhood associations to create long-term neighborhood plans.

To help achieve its vision well into the next century, Austin's city council recently developed the comprehensive Smart Growth initiative to manage overall development. "In assuring the creation of a healthy economy while maintaining the city's quality of life, the answer is smart growth," says Garza. "By managing and directing where and how the city grows, we can improve our economic development while protecting the best aspects of the city and the reasons we're all here."

In 1998, voters approved almost $1 billion for city improvements in bond elections. Among other things, the money will help replace the City Coliseum with the Community Events Center; renovate Palmer Auditorium; purchase and build new parks and greenbelts; build new police, fire, and ambulance facilities; reconstruct damaged streets; expand water and wastewater facilities; build the Mexican American Cultural Center near the Austin Convention Center; and expand the George Washington Carver Museum.

As its history tells, this community has always been a site of incomparable natural beauty, of active growth and business, of education and knowledge, and of shared cultures and ideas. Building on more than a century and a half of progress, the City of Austin plans to do its part to take the Texas capital into the new millennium.

BURIED DEEP BELOW AUSTIN'S STREETS AND ROADWAYS IS a vast and complex maze of more than 3,500 miles of pipes and tunnels that range in diameter from four inches to 96 feet. They are a part of everyday life in Austin, though most locals don't even realize they're there, nor do many of them know the history behind the company that oversees this feat of modern engineering—the City of Austin Water and Wastewater Utility.

The Water and Wastewater Utility has roots dating back to 1871, when a private company began pumping water from the Colorado River to local citizens under a franchise granted by the City of Austin. By May 1893, Austin Dam spanned the Colorado River, and new pumps, generators, and metering equipment provided the city with its first reliable water and power source. After a devastating flood destroyed the dam, Austin turned to a pump and infiltration well system to supply water service. In 1923, Dr. E.P. Schoch, a chemical engineering professor at the University of Texas at Austin, recommended a simple chemical treatment that used lime to disinfect river water.

Austin included this treatment method in the design of a new facility that was introduced in 1925. The facility, then named Thomas C. Green Water Treatment Plant, consisted of a chemical building, mixing baffles, a sedimentation basin, filters, and a clearwell for water storage. Modern water treatment had become a reality in Austin.

Austin's wastewater service began in 1917. The city's first wastewater facility used a tank system, which was later replaced by the Govalle Wastewater Plant, a revolutionary facility utilizing a relatively new treatment process using activated sludge. Since then, new facilities using a wide range of treatment methods, combined with periodic expansion and modernization projects, have enabled the Water and Wastewater Utility to meet the city's needs. The Walnut Creek Plant was built in 1977, and, most recently, the South Austin Regional Plant was completed in 1988.

The utility draws water from the Colorado River into three water treatment plants—Green, Davis, and Ullrich—that have a rated capacity of 227 million gallons per day and a combined storage capacity of 39 million gallons. The utility also has plans to build a fourth treatment plant to serve the northwest part of the city, which has recently seen considerable growth.

Over the years, many additions and improvements have kept the system in step with both evolving technology and Austin's increasing population. Today, the city supplies water to customers within the corporate city limits of Austin, as well as to the cities of nearby Rollingwood and Sunset Valley; a water control and improvement district; five water supply corporations; seven municipal utility districts; three private utilities; and customers outside the city limits. The utility also has contracts with Pflugerville and Round Rock.

PROTECTING THE ENVIRONMENT

We put much more research and effort into developing innovative water and wastewater

THE CITY OF AUSTIN WATER AND WASTEWATER UTILITY TREATS WATER FROM THE COLORADO RIVER TO PROVIDE AUSTIN'S DRINKING WATER.

THE THOMAS C. GREEN WATER TREATMENT PLANT, LOCATED IN DOWNTOWN AUSTIN, WAS BUILT IN 1925.

treatments than most other communities, to ensure that the water we put back in the system is cleaner than what we take out," says Randy Goss, director of Austin's water and wastewater services. "Our environmental and conservation efforts are in direct response to a long-standing community interest." One such program recycles high-quality wastewater for customer use in landscaping irrigation and evaporating/air-conditioning systems. The utility is also looking at aquifer storage and recovery as a means of slowing demand and delaying plant expansion.

The Water and Wastewater Utility's environmental efforts have won numerous quality awards at the local, state, and national level from a host of agencies and groups—from the Environmental Protection Agency (EPA) and the Texas Department of Health, to the Greater Austin Chamber of Commerce and the Association of Metropolitan Sewerage Agencies. The Texas Natural Resource Conservation Commission rated Austin's drinking water system as superior. In 1993 and 1996, the Water and Wastewater Utility won a Significant Merit Award from the Austin Quality Forum, and in 1995 it was awarded the American Planning

Association of Texas award for its water and wastewater long-range planning guide. In 1998, Austin's water supply was selected as the best-tasting water in Central Texas by the Texas Water Utilities Association.

The Hornsby Bend Bio-Solids Management Facility is the site of the utility's nationally and state-recognized Beneficial Re-Use Program. The EPA recognized Hornsby Bend in 1996 as the Best Operating Facility in the United States for the second time. Using a multifaceted process, sludge is pumped from the utility's three other wastewater treatment plants and composted into an EPA-approved product known as Dillo Dirt. This organic compost product is sold to the public by local garden retailers and used throughout the city by the Parks and Recreation Department as a nutrient rich soil conditioner.

Hornsby Bend is also the site of the Center for Environmental Research, a joint project of the Water and Wastewater Utility, the University of Texas, and Texas A&M University. The center conducts research to develop solutions to long-term environmental concerns.

The Water and Wastewater Utility works directly with the

community to offer education and awareness of conservation efforts and environmental issues. Communication programs range from outreach to schoolchildren to conducting neighborhood discussions on its projects. Each May, the utility celebrates Drinking Water Week and opens its water treatment facilities for school and public tours. "We like to show people exactly what's behind those mysterious brick walls and what kind of staffing it takes to provide water services to a city this size," says Goss.

Every one of the utility's 1,000 employees plays a part in providing seamless water service, whether they wear rubber boots and climb into the tunnels or wear white coats and develop new ways to treat water. Says Goss, "Each member of our diverse team contributes to our effort to provide superior service to the community, so that we can continue to provide the best and most competitive water and wastewater services in the region."

CLOCKWISE FROM TOP LEFT: WALNUT CREEK WASTEWATER TREATMENT PLANT HAS WON GOLD AND SILVER AWARDS FROM THE AMERICAN METROPOLITAN SEWERAGE ASSOCIATION.

THE HORNSBY BEND BIO-SOLIDS MANAGEMENT FACILITY AND THE CENTER FOR ENVIRONMENTAL RESEARCH ARE TWO OF THE UTILITY'S AWARD-WINNING ENVIRONMENTAL PROGRAMS.

MANY CHILDREN PARTICIPATE IN BLUE THUMB DAY, THE UTILITY'S CELEBRATION OF NATIONAL SAFE DRINKING WATER WEEK. EXHIBITORS USE HANDS-ON EXPERIMENTS TO RAISE CHILDREN'S AWARENESS OF WATER ISSUES.

AUSTIN ENERGY

USTIN ENERGY IS AUSTIN'S ENERGY. TWENTY-FOUR hours a day, seven days a week, Austin's community-owned electric utility provides the reliable, affordable electricity that makes the dynamic city go. ★ Austin voters established the city-owned

CLOCKWISE FROM TOP LEFT: AUSTIN IS THE ONLY CITY IN THE WORLD WHERE THE HISTORIC MOONLIGHT TOWER LIGHTING SYSTEM IS FOUND.

THE SEAHOLM POWER PLANT, BUILT IN 1949, REFLECTS THE DELICATE BALANCE BETWEEN INDUSTRY AND NATURE. AUSTINITES CONTINUE TO ENJOY THE CLEAN HIKE-AND-BIKE TRAILS NEARBY.

COMMUNITY SUPPORT IS A KEY FOCUS FOR AUSTIN ENERGY, AND MANY EMPLOYEES VOLUNTEER TO ASSIST OTHERS THROUGH THE MEALS ON WHEELS PROGRAM.

electric utility in 1895 by approving funding for the construction of Austin Dam across the Colorado River. The first electricity from the dam provided the soft light of Austin's famous Moonlight Towers, 17 of which remain standing today.

Austin Energy reflects the values of its citizens by providing low-cost, clean power and the most comprehensive array of energy conservation programs in Texas. In fact, total energy conservation improvements implemented in homes and businesses in Austin are equal to the output of a 379-megawatt power plant—enough electricity to power 214,000 homes year-round.

Like any good business, Austin Energy works hard to deliver a reliable service at the lowest possible price while ensuring profitability. Each year, $55 million in Austin Energy profits flow back into the community to help fund

police, fire protection, schools, and community parks and libraries. These profits have served over the years to offset the need for an increase in taxes. Austin Energy also takes care of a variety of other community needs, such as erecting lighting for city-owned athletic fields or performing electrical work for other city departments,

saving millions over the years. At the same time, Austin Energy residential electric rates are some of the lowest of any major city in Texas.

At Austin Energy, customer service is an established priority. A new, state-of-the-art Customer Service Center processes and directs 80,000 calls each month to a cadre of ser-

CLOCKWISE FROM TOP:
A BEAUTIFUL SKYLINE ALONG TOWN
LAKE IS ONE REASON AUSTIN CON-
TINUES TO BE ONE OF THE MORE
POPULAR SPOTS IN THE NATION.
IN 1998, AUSTIN WAS CHOSEN THE
BEST CITY FOR BUSINESS IN NORTH
AMERICA BY *Fortune* MAGAZINE.

THIS SOLAR PLANT AT THE AUSTIN-
BERGSTROM INTERNATIONAL AIR-
PORT PROVIDES ENERGY TO
AUSTIN'S ELECTRIC GRID.

AUSTIN ENERGY INSTALLED LIGHTS
AT 31 COMMUNITY SPORTS FIELDS AS
A PUBLIC SERVICE, ADDING TO THE
QUALITY OF LIFE FOR MORE THAN
9,000 YOUTH AND THEIR FAMILIES.

THE AUSTIN ENERGY CUSTOMER
SERVICE CENTER PROVIDES ONE-
STOP SERVICE FOR ALL AUSTIN UTILI-
TIES, INCLUDING ELECTRIC, WATER,
WASTEWATER, AND SOLID WASTE
SERVICES.

vice representatives, who challenge themselves to satisfy each customer on the first contact—whether concerning a bill or a request for service.

The customer-friendly approach adopted by Austin Energy for its tree-trimming program is unique in the state of Texas. Because tree limbs contacting power lines are the number one cause of outages during storms, tree trimming is a priority. Austin Energy representatives meet with each property owner prior to the trimming of trees and even provide a sketch of how the trimming will look.

Striving to perform well beyond its charge to provide reliable, low-cost electric service, Austin Energy is a valued community asset. Like most utilities, Austin Energy is responding to the changing utility environment by updating itself and using the opportunity to determine how it can better serve the Austin community. The result has been to solidify performance that is second to none, and to assure an asset that will continue to grow and care for the Austin community through the next millennium.

USTIN'S NATURAL BEAUTY, DIVERSE CULTURES, BOUND-less entertainment, and unique opportunities appeal to both locals and visitors alike. Few places reflect this enchanting and unique character as well as the Austin-Bergstrom International Airport (ABIA).

Opened for passengers in 1999, ABIA's four-level, three-story Barbara Jordan Passenger Terminal stretches approximately three city blocks with 25 gates and the capacity to add 30 more. Natural light pours in through the high windows of the modern, crescent-shaped building, allowing travelers to take in the big Texas sky.

From the concessionaires to the artwork, ABIA reflects the best of Austin. A central courtyard area, called the Market Place, showcases Texas-flavored shops; a cybercafé to help travelers stay connected; restaurants offering tastes of barbecue, Tex-Mex, ice cream, sandwiches, and more; and a stage area where local musicians routinely play.

A multiuse facility, ABIA serves general aviation needs, the State Aircraft Pooling Board, and the Texas Army National Guard. Through the airport's air cargo operations, opened in 1997, Austin's high-tech shippers can send and receive more cargo than ever before. With 1.3 million square feet of parking and up to 400,000 square feet of warehouse space, the air cargo facility can also accommodate the largest aircraft in the world.

ABIA is just minutes from downtown Austin, with direct access from Texas Highway 71/Ben White Boulevard and major road access via U.S. 183. An attractive, landscaped parkway greets visitors, and separate arrival and departure levels ensure a smooth traffic flow. Both surface parking and garage parking are available, doubling the amount of parking available at Austin's former airport.

AUSTIN'S ROBERT MUELLER MUNICIPAL AIRPORT'S SECOND ADMINISTRATION AND TERMINAL BUILDING OPENED IN 1942. THIS WOOD-FRAME STRUCTURE REPLACED THE ORIGINAL SMALL COTTAGE, BUILT IN 1930, WHICH SERVED AS THE AIRPORT'S FIRST OFFICE AND TERMINAL.

TURNING LEMONS INTO LEMONADE

In the late 1980s, the city recognized that its existing airport, Robert Mueller Municipal Airport, was quickly losing its ability to handle the dynamic growth of cargo and passengers. Without a new airport, Austin's leap into the 21st century would soon be hobbled. Since there was no room to expand, Austinites selected the nearby farming community of Manor as the site of a new airport.

But in 1990, when Congress closed Bergstrom Air Force Base after 50 years of distinguished

THIS 50-FOOT CONTROL TOWER BEGAN OPERATION AT AUSTIN'S AIRPORT IN 1943. IT REMAINED IN USE UNTIL 1961, WHEN THE PRESENT 86-FOOT TOWER OPENED. WHEN THIS TOWER WAS CONSTRUCTED IN 1943, AUSTIN'S AIRFIELD WAS ONE OF THE BUSIEST IN THE NATION DUE TO THE WAR EFFORTS. THERE WERE APPROXIMATELY 12,000 NON-MILITARY AIRCRAFT LANDINGS AND 120,000 ARRIVING PASSENGERS AT THE AIRPORT THAT YEAR.

service, locals saw a different solution to their problem. The loss of a long-standing military base could have been a difficult blow, but Austin created a plan to turn the Bergstrom base into a world-class airport. As Mayor Kirk Watson says, "Austin turned lemons into lemonade."

The conversion of the former base offered planners the unique opportunity to preserve local history while reusing and recycling much of the existing infrastructure and facilities. Military housing was moved off the property and made available to low-income families, fuel tanks were reused, and more than 40 trees were relocated on the site. The cylindrical former 12th Air Force Headquarters building, fondly referred to as the doughnut, became a hotel.

One of the biggest cost savings came from recycling Bergstrom's existing 12,250-foot runway, avoiding 75 percent of the cost of building a new one. One of the longest in the state, it allows Austin to accommodate nonstop overseas flights. ABIA's twin runway layout adds a 9,000-foot runway parallel to Bergstrom's existing runway. Aircraft can land and take off simultaneously, greatly enhancing efficiency and reducing passenger travel time.

The Federal Aviation Administration bestowed on the city an Environmental Achievement Award for ABIA's efficient airfield layout, which minimizes aircraft taxi distances, resulting in lower fuel use and reduced air emissions. Importantly, ABIA's location dramatically reduced the number of residents affected by noise from more than 30,000 at Robert Mueller Municipal Airport to approximately 1,500.

FLYING TOWARD THE FUTURE

THE AIR TRAFFIC CONTROL TOWER AT AUSTIN-BERGSTROM INTERNATIONAL AIRPORT (ABIA) IS 227 FEET TALL, MAKING IT THE SECOND TALLEST IN TEXAS. ENGINEERED TO SWAY ONLY ONE INCH IN AN 80-MILE-PER-HOUR WIND, THE TOWER WALLS ARE CONSTRUCTED OF CONCRETE PANELS 20 INCHES THICK AND REINFORCED WITH 1.75-INCH-DIAMETER REBAR.

THE ABIA PASSENGER TERMINAL, WHICH HAS 25 GATES, INCLUDES CUSTOMS AND IMMIGRATION FACILITIES AND THE CAPABILITY TO HANDLE INTERNATIONAL FLIGHTS.

 BIA's forward-thinking planning, design, and construction mirror Austin's commitment to the environment. In fact, many Austinites contributed ideas and comments through public meetings hosted by the Airport Advisory Board, which communicates regularly with local residents through meetings. The board itself represents diverse community populations across the city and will continue to solicit feedback from citizens on the airport's operation.

Owned by the City of Austin and designed to meet the needs and wishes of the local community, the airport uses no federal income taxes, city sales taxes, or local property taxes. The entire budget is paid by the airport users and the national aviation system.

Any revenue generated from the airport goes back into its operations, helping defray costs.

Just as Austin is welcoming the 21st century, ABIA is welcoming the world. And thanks to its state-of-the-art terminal, environmentally friendly facilities, and countless amenities for the traveler, the airport is flying into the Lone Star millennium in style.

REPORTING THE NEWS SINCE 1871, THE *Austin American-Statesman* is an old tradition with a fresh approach. It's Not Your Same Old Statesman is the apropos slogan for the newspaper, and Central Texans are taking a second look. ★ Originally published by the Texas

Democratic Executive Committee as part of its effort to restore the state's pre-Civil War political order, the newspaper is owned by Cox Newspapers, a wholly owned subsidiary of Cox Enterprises, Inc.

Today, the *Austin American-Statesman* is Central Texas' main source for news, sports, entertainment, business, features, classifieds, and countless other topics. More than 383,000 readers pick up the paper each day, while 476,300 peruse the Sunday edition. Several special sections offer readers in-depth information about a plethora of interests, such as an enhanced Sunday Travel section, Tech Monday section focusing on high technology, Friday's Health and Fitness page, and Thursday's XLent, a complete, colorful entertainment guide.

Readers have long relied on the *American-Statesman* for in-depth coverage of important local, national, and international news. The newspaper's editorial staff is well respected in the community for its dedication to thorough, comprehensive, and investigative reporting.

CLOCKWISE FROM TOP:
THE *Austin American-Statesman* HAS BEEN REPORTING THE NEWS FOR AUSTINITES SINCE 1871.

FOR MORE THAN 20 YEARS, THE *American-Statesman* HAS HOSTED THE CAPITOL 10,000 RACE, WHICH RAISES THOUSANDS OF DOLLARS FOR AREA ORGANIZATIONS AND PROJECTS.

Austin American-Statesman
PUBLISHER MICHAEL LAOSA

IT'S NOT YOUR SAME OLD STATESMAN

As technology increasingly affects where, when, and how the public receives information, the *American-Statesman*'s innovative new services reach beyond the printed word to link Central Texas to the world.

"The extraordinarily high use of the Internet is one example of the changes taking place in our region," says Publisher Michael Laosa. The *American-Statesman*'s Web site, www.austin360.com, has become a frequent focal point for many of those users. "Integrating our newspaper and our Web site allows us to provide news, information, and advertising 24 hours a day," Laosa says. Response has been tremendous; the *American-Statesman*'s Web products receive more than 12 million page views per month.

A subsidiary of Cox Enterprises, Austin360.com was launched in late 1994, and links users to everything they need to know about Austin, from news and sports to bats and music. And for those die-hard high school football fans so prevalent in Texas, www.hometeam360.com provides continuous updates on area high school sports teams.

The *American-Statesman* is the largest classified advertising marketplace for the Austin area, and ran nearly 2.3 million classifieds in 1998. With a Web-site approach to classifieds via austinclassifieds.com, the *American-Statesman* hopes to facilitate the process of buying a car, finding a job, locating a home, and much more. On-line classified users will find a more in-depth content in an easily navigable format. For example, users moving to the area can search related information such as housing, schools, property tax information, or nearby shopping.

The paper's Inside Line is a telephone information system and fax service offering Central Texans free access to hundreds of topics 24 hours a day. Smartline, an Internet and fax service, gives subscribers quick access to civil, criminal, and public record filings from surrounding counties.

As the market evolves at breakneck speed, the *American-Statesman* has changed its technological capabilities not only in the way it disseminates news and informa-

tion, but also in the way it does business. "Our advertising and marketing professionals are continually undertaking initiatives that provide our advertisers with effective and efficient connections to their markets," says Laosa.

NEWSWORTHY COMMITMENT

Each year the *American-Statesman* and its staff serve the community by supporting more than 400 charities and nonprofit organizations. "We believe in the adage 'as our community goes, so goes our company,'" remarks Laosa. "As a result, we are extremely involved in community development. Beyond reporting, analyzing, and voicing opinion on issues of importance to the community and donating hundreds of thousands of dollars annually to worthy causes, our employees contribute countless hours to make our region a better place to live."

For more than 20 years, the *American-Statesman* has hosted the Capitol 10,000, the state's largest footrace. The 10-kilometer run is held each spring and brings almost 20,000 participants along a downtown/Town Lake racecourse. The event raises thousands of dollars for area organizations and projects.

The American-Statesman is located on Town Lake, near the home of Austin's Mexican free-tailed bats. In fact, the newspaper hosts thousands of curious bat watchers each summer at its public viewing area.

As part of its ongoing outreach in the community, the *American-Statesman* has developed several education-related activities, including an annual scholarship contest

(cosponsored by 3M Austin) and workshops in schools with curriculum designed to interest students in news. The paper's Awesome Texas, a youth-friendly Wednesday page with stories, cartoons, and other fun features, won a national award from the Southern Newspaper Publishers Association.

This award is just one of a myriad that the paper and its individual reporters, editors, photographers, designers, columnists, and cartoonists garner each year from a diverse group that includes the American Association of Sunday and Feature Editors, Texas Sports Writers Association, Texas Daily Newspaper Association, Texas Press Association, and many

others. The *American-Statesman*'s more than 1,000 employees also receive internal kudos through several programs recognizing and rewarding exceptional employee performance.

The newspaper's slogan reflects the many changes that have occurred in the last several years and those that will carry the paper into the next millennium. "As Austin and Central Texas continue to grow and advance, we are committed to continue developing a world-class newspaper and information company," says Laosa. "Professional, credible, objective, and thorough journalism, regardless of the medium, will continue to be the core of our franchise."

THE *American-Statesman*'S EDITORIAL STAFF IS WELL RESPECTED IN THE COMMUNITY FOR ITS DEDICATION TO THOROUGH, COMPREHENSIVE, AND INVESTIGATIVE REPORTING.

THE *American-Statesman* IS LOCATED ON TOWN LAKE, NEAR THE HOME OF AUSTIN'S MEXICAN FREE-TAILED BATS. THE NEWSPAPER HOSTS THOUSANDS OF CURIOUS BAT WATCHERS EACH SUMMER AT ITS PUBLIC VIEWING AREA.

As Huston-Tillotson College approaches the 125th anniversary of its inception, it is celebrating a rich history and looking to a bright future. At Huston-Tillotson, the mission is to educate a diverse, multicultural community of students for leadership and service in the 21st century.

"We seek to be a center of excellence for preparing young men and women to be leaders in the community and the workforce," says Dr. Joseph T. McMillan Jr., the college's president.

"WE SEEK TO BE A CENTER OF EXCELLENCE FOR PREPARING YOUNG MEN AND WOMEN TO BE LEADERS IN THE COMMUNITY AND THE WORKFORCE," SAYS DR. JOSEPH T. MCMILLAN JR., PRESIDENT OF HUSTON-TILLOTSON COLLEGE (RIGHT).

HUSTON-TILLOTSON WAS CREATED BY THE MERGER OF TILLOTSON COLLEGE, FOUNDED IN 1875, AND SAMUEL HUSTON COLLEGE, FOUNDED IN 1876. AS HUSTON-TILLOTSON APPROACHES ITS 125TH ANNIVERSARY, THE COLLEGE REMAINS TRUE TO ITS MISSION: TO EDUCATE A DIVERSE, MULTICULTURAL COMMUNITY OF STUDENTS FOR LEADERSHIP AND SERVICE IN THE 21ST CENTURY (BELOW).

Huston-Tillotson was created by the merger of two historically black, church-related colleges. Tillotson College, Austin's first institution of higher education, was founded by Congregationalists in 1875. In 1876, Samuel Huston College was established nearby by Methodists. Combining the best of both schools' traditions and history, Samuel Huston and Tillotson merged in 1952 under the motto "In Union, Strength." Today, Huston-Tillotson is affiliated with both the United Church of Christ and the United Methodist Church, but has always welcomed students of all ages, races, nationalities, and faiths.

ACADEMICS AND MORE

Huston-Tillotson offers bachelor of arts and bachelor of science degrees in five academic areas: education, business, social sciences, natural sciences, and humanities. Through the Cooperative Education Program, students can alternate periods of study with employment. The college's challenging curriculum includes a dynamic general studies program, a vigorous program of major and minor concentrations, and a community service requirement.

Campus life is much more than academics at Huston-Tillotson. Students can choose from many groups and activities, including national sororities and fraternities, performance groups, professional and academic associations, honor societies, and religious, sports, and service organizations. The Huston-Tillotson Rams compete in the Red River Conference, under the guidelines of the National Association of Intercollegiate Athletes. Students participate in intercollegiate-level competition in men's and women's basketball, men's baseball, men's soccer, women's volleyball, and men's and women's track and cross-country.

Community service programs include adopting local elementary schools, teaching computer literacy skills to children in neighboring housing projects, and providing AIDS education outreach to the community. The college's highly successful AusPREP program assists junior high students in math, science, and engineering during an eight-week summer session.

Through Upward Bound, funded by the U.S. Department of Education, Huston-Tillotson hosts a six-week program for high school students to help them succeed while preparing for college. And through the Delta program, developed in conjunction with the Austin Independent School District, Huston-Tillotson helps high school dropouts with a self-paced, evening curriculum taught by certified teachers.

"Our students are very passionate and energetic in their commitment to our volunteer programs," says McMillan. "They truly enjoy making a difference in the community."

TOP-NOTCH FACULTY

Equally committed to making a difference, Huston-Tillotson's faculty of more than 50 men and women is dedicated to teaching and to the college's mission. Sixty percent of Huston-Tillotson's faculty members possess a doctoral or equivalent degree. PhDs and department chairs teach even introductory courses.

As it enters the 21st century, Huston-Tillotson College will continue to fulfill its mission of preparing students for the future. "We've come so far and accomplished so much with so little," says McMillan. "We will enter the new era by helping another new generation succeed."

USTIN'S SKYLINE MAY HAVE CHANGED OVER THE PAST century, but the stunning view of the city from St. Edward's University has remained the same since its founding in 1885. Built on donated land, the university was established by Father Edward Sorin, Superior

General of the Congregation of Holy Cross and the founder of Notre Dame University.

A small, Catholic, liberal arts university, St. Edward's today serves a culturally diverse student body of more than 3,000. Its mission is to provide a values-focused education, reinforcing ethics, integrity, and community responsibility throughout its rigorous curriculum. The university prides itself on academic excellence and nontraditional course structures as it continually explores new ways of teaching and learning.

St. Edward's serves two distinct student populations: traditional undergraduate students and working adults. The university offers undergraduate degrees in 33 areas of business, humanities, science, social service, arts, and education. Graduate programs include human services and business administration. Through its innovative New College undergraduate program, St. Edward's tailors a curriculum to meet the needs of adults whose access to higher education is often limited by career, family, or other demands. Started in 1974, New College allows students to develop a self-paced degree program that offers flexible hours and college credit for real-life experience.

A WELL-ROUNDED EDUCATIONAL EXPERIENCE

St. Edward's focuses on excellence in teaching and learning in an environment that encompasses the campus classroom, student life programs, and the broader community. The university takes pride in its small class size and student-faculty ratio of 15-to-1—both of which promote personal attention to students and a sense of community.

The historic, 180-acre campus offers many traditional student

RICK PATRICK

services, including a swimming pool, a career resources center, a health center, a bookstore, recreational sports facilities, a theater, and computer labs. Approximately 600 students live in four dormitories and student apartments—all wired with Internet access. The campus' newest star is a 61,000-square-foot campus center, the centerpiece of a recently completed $27 million capital campaign. The new center contains state-of-the-art dining facilities, meeting rooms, a ballroom, and a 250-seat auditorium.

St. Edward's places a strong focus on experiential learning by building relationships in the community. Programs encourage students to participate in internships with area businesses, forging strong partnerships with individuals and institutions. Through St. Edward's Community Mentor Program, students serve as mentors to nearly 500 at-risk elementary school students.

Its innovative programs and commitment to the community are not the only reasons St. Edward's is set apart from other schools. Its endowed Center for Teaching Excellence aims to continuously raise the level of academic quality. In 1993, St. Edward's was one of 20 colleges designated by the American Association of Colleges as a Re-

source Institution for Core Curriculum Development. And in 1997, the school was named to the Honor Role for Character-Building Colleges by the John Templeton Foundation. *Hispanic Magazine* lists St. Edward's in its *Guide to the Top 25 Colleges for Hispanics*. The university is the only private school in the country with a College Assistance Migrant Program, a nationally acclaimed program for children of migrant farmworkers.

Such accolades—combined with the school's recent growth in enrollment and endowment, its strong sense of purpose, and its focus on learning—will ensure St. Edward's University's reputation for values-based, dynamic education well into the 21st century.

RICK PATRICK

RICK PATRICK

INCE 1877, THE GREATER AUSTIN CHAMBER OF COMMERCE has served as the voice of business in the Austin area, playing a key role in economic and community development. Over the years, the Chamber has become the area's largest business organization, representing a diverse

coalition of companies and individuals.

First known as the Austin Board of Trade and later as the Austin Chamber of Commerce, the organization adopted its current name in 1989 as it became more convinced that economic development was not just for Austin, but for the entire region. With a membership of 3,000 firms, the Chamber represents virtually every industry segment and interest.

BUSINESS AND COMMUNITY LEADERS FROM THE REGION GATHER EACH YEAR TO HEAR THE GREATER AUSTIN CHAMBER OF COMMERCE'S ECONOMIC REVIEW AND FORECAST.

▲ JAMES A. DUMAS, SPECTRUM PHOTOGRAPHY

A STRATEGY FOR GROWTH

ver the last decade, the economic development efforts of the Greater Austin Chamber of Commerce have resulted in some of the most impressive successes in the nation, producing a robust local economy anchored by state government, higher education, and technology.

In late 1997, the Chamber commissioned ICF Kaiser International Economic Strategy Group to conduct a landmark study to create a visionary, long-range action plan for economic development for the five-county region of Bastrop, Caldwell, Hays, Travis, and Williamson counties. The study—The Next Century Economy—builds on the area's economic strengths and recommends strategic initia-

tives to ensure success in the 21st century.

The report highlighted Austin's recent transition to a cluster-based economy, one composed of and driven by interrelated expanding core clusters—semiconductors and electronics, computers and peripherals, and software—and emerging industries that have the potential to become core clusters. The seven emerging clusters identified by the ICF Kaiser report and the Chamber are logistics and distribution, biosciences products, film, music, multimedia, telecommunications, and transaction services.

To reflect the changing dynamics and needs of these industry clusters, as well as the region's established industry sectors, the Chamber created individual cluster

groups to facilitate communications between industries and the community. "Our commitment is to become even more relevant to our traditional industries as we reach out and become relevant to the emerging clusters," says 1999 Board Chair Earl Maxwell.

Today, the Chamber is structured in two spheres of programming: economic development and community development. "These two spheres are important, interrelated, inseparable, and institutionalized," says past Chamber president Glenn E. West. "Virtually everything we do in the Chamber can be related to one, or both, of these spheres."

The new structure supports the efforts of cross-functional teams, focusing on strategic initiatives and driven by the work of task forces that address major issues. The economic development sphere encompasses prospects and inquiries, new industry recruitment, mature industry clusters, emerging industry clusters, international business development, entrepreneurship, and research. The community development sphere focuses on workforce development, education, transportation, governmental relations, regional and strategic partnerships, social equity, leadership development, and environment.

THE CHAMBER'S WORKFORCE DEVELOPMENT EFFORTS ARE ENHANCED BY KEYSTONE INTERNATIONAL, REPRESENTED HERE BY STUDENTS IN A COMPUTER ASSEMBLY CLASS.

◀ SUSAN HOERMANN, EVERGREEN STUDIOS

VOLUNTEERING TO LEAD

As a true grassroots organization, the Chamber is fueled by volunteer leadership and participation. Volunteers commit financial resources by providing membership dues, and, in addition, by working on a variety of committees and programs. They help the Chamber shape issues and accomplish goals that are essential to the economic vitality of the community. Fifty-five board members serve three-year terms, and a 26-member executive board adopts policies. The Chamber's programs and initiatives are implemented by a staff of 40 professionals in close conjunction with the organization's volunteer leadership.

This volunteer-led organization plays a key role in identifying and developing new and emerging leaders in the community. "We recruit people from all walks of life to become volunteer leaders and to get involved at all levels of the community," says 2000 Board Chair Mary Scott Nabers.

The Chamber's many individual programs create hundreds of opportunities for volunteer participation. Formerly called Austin Adopt-A-School, the Partners in Education program has grown into one of the top business education partnerships in the nation. Annually, through more than 2,100 partnerships, volunteers have given more than 340,000 hours to local schools, in addition to cash and in-kind contributions. In the 15 years since the program's inception, contributions have totaled almost $47 million. The Chamber and the City of Austin created the Capital Area Training Foundation to pro-

vide Austin-area employers with a better skilled and prepared workforce, and to provide opportunities for youth and adults to enter high-skill/high-wage careers.

Leadership Austin provides a unique forum for networking and leadership training, Austin Quality Council provides quality management education to businesses and other organizations, and the Sports Foundation promotes Austin as a venue for major sports events. The Next Century Economy Initiative, formerly known as Advantage Austin, provides critical funding for these flagship programs and fuels some of the region's most important economic development activities.

The Chamber often plays the role of collaborator, serving as a liaison between the business community and diverse governmental and educational agencies to build dynamic coalitions that work for the welfare of all Austinites. One of the most significant collaborations came when the Chamber brokered an agreement between the Save Our Springs Alliance and the Real Estate Council of Austin,

which includes setting aside tens of thousands of acres in southwest Austin as dedicated open space. The Area Council Program serves to facilitate communication with members in all areas of town. The Austin Technology Incubator— a collaborative project of the Chamber, the University of Texas, and the City of Austin—is a national model for helping technology firms get started. Even the Chamber's new Web site— www.austinchamber.org—serves as an informational resource and forum, fostering increased communication with and between members and prospects.

The Austin area is on the verge of two historic events: the dawn of the 21st century and the region's transformation into one of the world's top technology centers. Focusing on diverse economic and community development efforts, the Greater Austin Chamber of Commerce continues a long history of innovation and leadership to make Austin an even better place to work, to start businesses, to raise families, to visit, and to live.

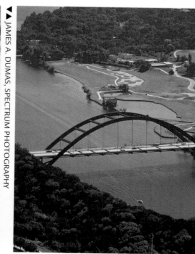

CLOCKWISE FROM TOP LEFT: HAMILTON POOL OFFERS A REFRESHING RESPITE TO SWIMMERS DURING SUMMER MONTHS.

THE CHAMBER'S PARTNERS IN EDUCATION PROGRAM FOCUSES COMMUNITY RESOURCES ON ELEMENTARY STUDENTS.

THE GRACEFUL ARCHES OF THE LOOP 360 BRIDGE SPAN LAKE AUSTIN AND HIGHLIGHT THE NATURAL BEAUTY OF THE AREA.

AUSTIN'S DOWNTOWN SKYLINE IS FRAMED BY BEAUTIFUL TREES AND THE COLORADO RIVER.

CALCASIEU LUMBER COMPANY

THE CITY OF AUSTIN WAS BUILT WITH VISION, TALENT, AND Calcasieu lumber. Family-owned and -operated since 1883, Calcasieu Lumber Company has grown with Austin and continues to make its mark on the entire area. ★ Founded by brothers William and Carl Drake, the company took its

name from Calcasieu Parish, Louisiana, an area known for its fine longleaf yellow pine. The brothers began selling Calcasieu lumber on the banks of the Colorado River, where they converted a one-room brewery into a bustling business. In fact, the Drakes are credited with creating one of the first delivery services in Austin: They would ride out on horses to meet settlers arriving in wagon trains, take orders for building supplies, and ride back to assemble the materials before the wagons had even crossed the river.

BUILDING A HISTORY

When the company was first established, the population of Austin was approaching 10,000, a new university was being built, and more than 50 homes were under construction. With a well-placed foot in the door, Calcasieu Lumber Company quickly grew with the city. By 1905, the company occupied four city lots, providing customers with everything from wallpaper to custom millwork. Many Austin landmarks, such as the Butler Mansion, the Caswell House, and the old Mansfield

Dam, were built with materials from Calcasieu.

By the 1920s, William Drake had become the sole owner of the company. He introduced a monthly installment plan for financing home building, and was later credited by many historians as the catalyst of Austin's residential building boom in the 1920s. Calcasieu financed and built Austin's first suburb, Enfield, and at one point the company supplied lumber for half of Austin's homes.

The Great Depression posed a new challenge, as the building boom abruptly ended. The Calcasieu family of employees pulled together, and Drake dipped into his personal savings to help his staff buy groceries. When Drake died in 1934, a close family friend, R.G. Mueller (for whom Austin's Mueller Airport was named), was chosen to run Calcasieu.

World War II proved another turning point for the company, when Calcasieu received military contracts to supply sections of Camp Swift and Fort Hood. Calcasieu's 300-plus employees worked around the clock to operate 17 line yards to meet the demand.

Upon his return from the war in 1947, Bill Drake Jr., William's son, became president of Calcasieu. His direction of the company led to many innovative marketing ideas, including the development of the Complete Home Center, a three-story building showcasing different building materials in actual use.

A NEW ERA BEGINS

Calcasieu continued to grow, and today is headed by a member of the family's third generation, T.N. "Nick" Morris, who began working for the company at the age of 12. Company president since 1983, Morris bought Calcasieu outright in August 1997. After discussions with several large, out-of-state holding companies, Morris, with the support and encouragement of the board of directors and shareholders of the company, decided that Calcasieu should continue as a family-owned and -operated business. A local bank created a financial package that enabled him to purchase the company, and Calcasieu entered a new phase with the slogan An Austin Tradition Continues . . . A New Era Begins. Other members of the family work alongside Morris in the business, including nephews, cousins, two sons, and a son-in-law.

Today's Calcasieu employs approximately 400 people at its Burleson Road manufacturing and sales site and its Round Rock lumberyard, which opened in 1996. The 32-acre Burleson Road site houses a massive lumberyard with stacks of all types of lumber stretching as far as the eye can see. The administrative and sales departments are on-site, as are the window, wood window, millwork, and truss departments. The consolidated wholesale division sells

CALCASIEU LUMBER COMPANY BEGAN IN AUSTIN IN 1883, SELLING THE BEST MATERIALS AND FINEST LONGLEAF YELLOW PINE LUMBER FROM CALCASIEU PARISH, LOUISIANA.

directly to other lumberyards throughout South and Central Texas. A recent addition, the turnkey framing department, provides customers with professional crews to do on-site framing.

One of Calcasieu's corporate goals is to earn its customers' loyalty by providing good service, quality products, and competitive prices, while showing a sincere appreciation for each customer's business. This focus, and the company's resulting reputation, retains Calcasieu's loyal customers. "We treat every customer as our only customer. This allows us to keep more in touch with the changing needs of the marketplace, and to meet and exceed their expectations," says Morris. These principles helped the company reach a 1997 revenue of $81 million in sales and $100 million in 1998. The company was named Retailer of the Year by *Building Supply Home Centers* magazine in June 1993, and Pro Dealer of the Year by *Pro Dealer Magazine* in December 1998.

In maintaining its Austin roots, Calcasieu contributes directly to both the Austin economy and the community. The company prides itself on civic involvement and supports a number of programs in the community, such as

Advantage Austin, a Chamber of Commerce organization focusing on economic development and recruitment of business to the area. Morris and many of Calcasieu's employees are members of the Texas Capital Area Builders Association. The company also supports local nonprofit organizations and athletic teams, and supports Austin Partners in Education, a program sponsored by the Austin

Independent School District and the Greater Austin Chamber of Commerce.

Morris credits the company's success to its focus on the community. "For my family, Austin is, and will continue to be, home. We are committed to this community, our customers, and our employees, and we are proud to be part of a new era in a continuing Austin tradition."

THE FAMILY OF COMPANY OWNER NICK MORRIS AND HIS WIFE, MOLLY: (FROM LEFT) SON BOBBY MORRIS AND WIFE JACQUE; MOLLY MORRIS; SON-IN-LAW RON ROSS; GRANDSON HUDSON ROSS; NICK MORRIS; DAUGHTER KIM ROSS; AND SON TREY MORRIS AND WIFE ANNA-MARGARET

▲ PARISH PHOTOGRAPHY, INC.

THE UNIVERSITY OF TEXAS AT AUSTIN

FOUNDED IN 1883 ON 40 ACRES NEAR THE state capitol, The University of Texas at Austin (UT Austin) is a major comprehensive research university with a broad mission in undergraduate and graduate education, research, and service to society.

THE UNIVERSITY OF TEXAS AT AUSTIN TOWER—THE STATE'S MOST FAMOUS COLLEGIATE SYMBOL—OFTEN GLOWS ORANGE TO CELEBRATE OCCASIONS OF GREAT DISTINCTION AND ACHIEVEMENT IN THE LIFE OF THE UNIVERSITY (LEFT).

"THE GREAT PUBLIC UNIVERSITIES OF AMERICA ARE AMONG THE MOST EXQUISITE CREATURES OF THE HUMAN SPIRIT," SAYS PRESIDENT LARRY R. FAULKNER. "THEY SEE AND FOSTER THE BEST IN HUMAN NATURE. THEY ARE WORTHY PLACES IN WHICH TO INVEST OUR LIVES, AND THEY ARE INDEED DOORS TO THE FUTURE" (RIGHT).

Today, the university enrolls almost 49,000 students annually, with about 25 percent in graduate and professional programs. Although UT Austin is a large university, it is made up of many smaller learning communities centered on the common goal of expanding knowledge and human understanding.

Says President Larry R. Faulkner, "For Texas to lead in the future, we must have in this state a core of critical talent; a productive volume of research, development, and enterprise in critical technical domain; strong mutual support between individuals and organizations; a venturesome spirit; and the willingness to form productive partnerships with the private sector. The university has an important place in all of these aspects."

A RESOURCE FOR THE REGION

The university makes an incredible impact on the community, providing public service and cutting-edge research; connecting Austin to history and culture through world-class museums and outstanding libraries; and entertaining thousands at special events and athletic competitions. UT Austin's reach extends well beyond its 357-acre main campus. With 2,700 faculty members and 17,000 staff members, UT Austin is one of the city's largest employers.

UT Austin strives to achieve its core purpose: To transform lives for the benefit of society through learning, discovery, freedom, leadership, individual opportunity, and responsibility. Such basic human values are reflected in the slogan "We're Texas," which is the theme of a seven-year fund-raising campaign launched in 1997.

The university's public service efforts include a criminal defense clinic that provides legal advice for people unable to afford a lawyer; an advisory service to owners of small businesses; the Neighborhood Longhorns Program, which encourages youths to stay in school; and outreach programs that help diverse groups of K-12 students prepare for college.

UT Austin has been a significant force in the city's development as a technology center. Its 87 organized research units—which received

nearly $291 million in funding in 1997-1998—are a breeding ground for talented students and faculty. In addition to generating numerous spin-off technologies and companies, the university has attracted many new businesses to the area.

HOME TO THE ARTS AND ATHLETICS

With its outstanding library system, the university boasts one of the top five academic libraries in North America. Its Nettie Lee Benson Latin American Collection is one of the world's most important collections of its kind, and the Tarlton Law Library is the fifth-largest academic law library in the nation. The Lyndon Baines Johnson Library and Museum includes the papers of the 36th president of the United States and rare historical objects illustrating 20th-century American political life. The Harry Ransom Humanities Research Center (HRC) is an internationally recognized rare book and manuscript library, home to a Gutenberg Bible and the world's first photograph.

UT gives Austinites access to outstanding permanent and visiting art collections. The Jack S. Blanton Museum of Art, formerly the Archer M. Huntington Art Gallery, will open a new facility in 2002 and will be one of the foremost university art museums in

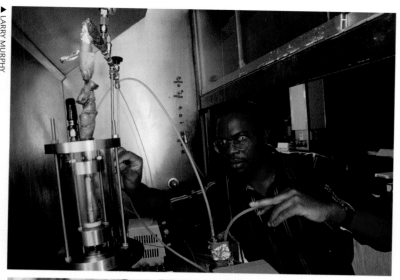

the nation. The 100,000-square-foot building will enable the Blanton to exhibit a significant portion of its permanent collection, including an extensive collection of European art from the Renaissance and baroque periods, such as the world-renowned Suida-Manning Collection of Old Masters paintings.

Austin also enjoys the many cultural performances hosted each year at the Performing Arts Center, which includes several venues ranked among the best on any American campus. The 18,000-seat Frank C. Erwin Jr. Special Events Center hosts more than 250 shows a year, including circuses, college basketball, and concerts by major artists ranging from master tenor Luciano Pavarotti to singer Reba McIntire.

The UT Tower—the state's most famous collegiate symbol—often glows orange to celebrate occasions of great distinction and achievement in the life of the university, including the many victories of UT's athletics program. University athletic facilities range from Texas Memorial Stadium, which seats more than 81,000, to the state-of-the-art Texas Swimming Center. Competing in the Big 12 Conference, UT Austin ended 1998 on a high note with one of its own—tailback Ricky Williams—winning the coveted Heisman trophy, collegiate football's highest honor.

AMONG THE BEST IN THE NATION

T Austin is home to students from all 254 counties in Texas, all 50 states, and some 115 foreign countries. The university has the largest Hispanic enrollment of any flagship teaching and research university in the nation. African-Americans and Hispanics comprise approximately 16 percent of the student population.

UT Austin is a magnet for talented students and is ranked among the top three universities in the nation in number of National Merit and National Achievement Scholars. The university offers more than 50 honors programs, and its Plan II liberal arts honors program is a national model. UT Austin's graduate offerings in law, education, business, engineering, and public affairs are consistently ranked among the nation's best. Through the UT Graduate School of Business, more than 450 companies recruit new employees each year. UT Austin, with programs such as the Institute for Latin Ameri-can Studies, is fast becoming the nation's most important source of expertise about Latin America.

More than 100 undergraduate degree programs and 170 graduate degree programs are offered by the university's 15 colleges and schools, as well as the Graduate School and the Division of Continuing Education. UT's ability to attract and retain outstanding faculty, including Nobel laureates, Pulitzer prize winners, and members of prestigious scholarly academies, is bolstered by its 1,000 privately endowed chairs, professorships, fellowships, and lectureships.

"The great public universities of America are among the most exquisite creatures of the human spirit," says Faulkner. "They see and foster the best in human nature. They are worthy places in which to invest our lives, and they are indeed doors to the future."

CLOCKWISE FROM TOP LEFT: FOUNDED IN 1883, UT AUSTIN TODAY IS HOME TO STUDENTS FROM ALL 254 COUNTIES IN TEXAS, ALL 50 STATES, AND SOME 115 FOREIGN COUNTRIES.

UT AUSTIN IS A MAJOR COMPREHENSIVE RESEARCH UNIVERSITY WITH A BROAD MISSION IN UNDERGRADUATE AND GRADUATE EDUCATION, RESEARCH, AND SERVICE TO SOCIETY.

UT AUSTIN OFFERS CULTURAL EVENTS RANGING FROM FOLKLORIC BALLET TO THE MASTERPIECES DISPLAYED IN THE JACK S. BLANTON MUSEUM OF ART. SHOWN HERE IS *The Annunciation* BY VERONESE, FROM THE MASTERPIECES OF EUROPEAN PAINTING FROM THE SUIDA-MANNING COLLECTION, HOUSED AT THE BLANTON.

COMPETING IN THE BIG 12 CONFERENCE, UT AUSTIN ENDED 1998 ON A HIGH NOTE WITH ONE OF ITS OWN—TAILBACK RICKY WILLIAMS—WINNING THE COVETED HEISMAN TROPHY, COLLEGIATE FOOTBALL'S HIGHEST HONOR.

MANY MAJOR AUSTIN LANDMARKS—BOTH OLD AND new—owe their existence to the Wattinger Group, a family of companies that, over the years, has completed more than 400 projects, ranging from the original Travis County Courthouse to multimillion-

dollar, high-tech facilities.

The Wattinger family began building in Central Texas in 1886, when Jacob Wattinger, a stonemason by trade from Switzerland, started a general construction business. "Jacob was the founder of the companies," says Vernon Wattinger, Jacob's great-grandson and chairman of the Wattinger Group of Companies.

Included among Wattinger's projects are schools, universities, hospitals, health care facilities, high-tech office/manufacturing facilities, state institutional work, commercial buildings, and retail centers. The group focuses primarily on the Austin and Central Texas area, usually staying within a 100-mile radius of Austin.

ALL IN THE FAMILY

The family tradition has carried on, and the Wattinger Group is now being run by fourth- and fifth-generation family members. The

various Wattinger companies include VRW Construction; Wattinger Company, Inc.; Wattinger Management Company; and Wattinger Service Company, Inc. VRW Construction, which began its general construction business as Austin Rio Construction Co. in 1975, today offers construction management, general contracting, and

design/build services for selected projects. Started in 1929, Wattinger Company, Inc. is a mechanical contractor handling major projects for such clients as *Austin American-Statesman*, Advanced Micro Devices, Motorola, Samsung Electronics, Texas Instruments, and 3M, as well as underground utility work. Tom Wattinger, Vernon's brother and president of Wattinger Company, stresses the firm's expansion into new piping and duct work technology in the past 10 years, as well as its capabilities in HVAC and plumbing, including sheet metal and pipe fabrication shops. Wattinger Service Company was started in 1980, and is today one of the leading commercial air-conditioning and heating service companies in Austin.

Working together as a group of companies provides a system of checks and balances in cost control and efficiency in the construction of every project. "We not only have the oldest construction company in Austin, but we have one of the most complete," says Vernon. "We have done—and can do—every aspect of the business."

THE WATTINGER GROUP HAS A LONG HISTORY IN CENTRAL TEXAS, AND OVER THE YEARS HAS COMPLETED MORE THAN 400 PROJECTS, RANGING FROM THE ORIGINAL TRAVIS COUNTY COURTHOUSE (PICTURED AT RIGHT) TO MULTIMILLION-DOLLAR, HIGH-TECH FACILITIES.

SINCE 1980, VRW CONSTRUCTION HAS HANDLED MOST OF THE CONSTRUCTION AT ST. EDWARD'S UNIVERSITY, INCLUDING RESTORATION OF THE OLD MAIN BUILDING IN 1986 (BOTTOM).

AMONG WATTINGER'S HEALTH CARE PROJECTS ARE THE EXPANSIONS AT ST. DAVID'S COMMUNITY HOSPITAL, WHICH INCLUDE THE EAST CAMPUS PROJECT.

CENTRAL TEXAS LANDMARKS

The Wattinger Group has enjoyed long relationships with many of its clients—so long, in fact, that it has received the contracts to remodel buildings originally constructed by prior generations of Wattingers. The group has collectively built 21 buildings at the University of Texas, including the Drama Building, Roberts Hall, Andrews Hall, Biological Laboratories, Education Annex, and University Teaching Center. The 1978 acquisition of B.L. McGee Construction Company, which had also constructed many campus buildings, cemented the Wattingers' alliance with the university.

Other education landmarks constructed by the group are the administration building at Sul Ross State University in Alpine, Texas; numerous projects for Austin, Georgetown, Rockdale, Bastrop, and San Marcos school districts; and Austin's original city library (now the Austin History Center). Since 1980, VRW has handled most of the construction at St. Edward's University, including restoration of the Old Main Building in 1986 and construction of the Ragsdale Campus Center and the Recreation and Convocation Center. At Southwestern University in Georgetown, VRW is responsible for the Fine Arts Theatre Building, McCombs Campus Center, Brown Cody Residence Hall, F.W. Olin Building, Recreational Activities Center, and Fondren Jones Science Building Addition.

Among Wattinger's health care projects are the Kerrville VA Hospital, Seton Northwest Ambulatory Healthcare Center, and the expansions at St. David's Community Hospital, which consist of a three-building complex: Rehabilitation, Surgical, and Psychiatric hospitals. High-tech companies have also found the Wattinger Group: VRW/Austin Rio has constructed several major high-tech complexes, including the new Intermedics Orthopedics, Inc. headquarters.

BUILT ON RELATIONSHIPS

The Wattinger Group is extremely proud of the diverse nature of its projects, which range in size from $1 million to $30 million. The firm has a substantial impact on the local economy, thanks to the 50 to 60 direct subcontractors and suppliers that must be hired for each project, and its approximately 200 full-time employees. Quality and safety are key concerns on every job, and the company has won numerous outstanding building construction awards and local/national safety awards.

The Wattingers are big believers in repeat business, as evidenced by their long-term relationships with many clients, subcontractors, architects, and engineers. According to Vernon's son, Trey Wattinger, president of VRW Construction Company, "We work as a team and perform 110 percent on every project we have. By working with our own forces, we can offer hands-on management from top to bottom."

Building relationships with customers and business associates comes easy to the Wattinger Group. It is an active member of Associated General Contractors (Trey is a past president), Greater Austin Chamber of Commerce, and Mechanical Contractors Association of Texas (Tom is a past president), and is involved with the Construction Specifications Institute, Associated Building Contractors, and American Institute of Architects. The firm also contributes to numerous charitable and civic causes. The Wattinger Group will continue to leave its mark on Austin and Central Texas for many more years to come. Future generations of company leadership are sure to build on the Wattinger tradition of quality and service, adhering to one of the fundamental principles of the company: not to be the biggest in town, but rather the best.

AT SOUTHWESTERN UNIVERSITY IN GEORGETOWN, VRW CONSTRUCTION IS RESPONSIBLE FOR THE FINE ARTS THEATRE BUILDING, MCCOMBS CAMPUS CENTER, BROWN CODY RESIDENCE HALL, F.W. OLIN BUILDING (PICTURED), RECREATIONAL ACTIVITIES CENTER, AND FONDREN JONES SCIENCE BUILDING ADDITION.

COOK-WALDEN FUNERAL HOMES AND CEMETERIES

COOK-WALDEN FUNERAL HOMES AND CEMETERIES, ONE of the oldest businesses in Austin, operates six full-service funeral homes, two additional chapels, and three perpetual care cemeteries, and employs approximately 140 funeral staff, prearrangement counselors, and cemetery personnel.

When Samuel E. Rosengren started his funeral establishment in the 400 block of Congress Avenue in the late 1800s, he could not have imagined his downtown storefront facility growing into the premier funeral service provider in Central Texas. At the time, Austin was a small community known primarily as the home of the capitol and the state university in an era when undertaking was often combined with a livery stable or furniture store.

Circa 1920, Charles B. Cook purchased Rosengren's business, and in 1924, moved it into a grand,

three-story building located prestigiously between the Governor's Mansion and the Capitol building. He named it Cook Funeral Home, and it quickly became the number one ambulance and funeral provider in Austin.

Competition flourished as Austin grew, and in 1971, Charles Walden (who had been in the funeral business since 1942) purchased Cook Funeral Home, and the Cook-Walden era began. After 50 years of operating from a facility at 11th and Colorado streets, the dynamic, new leadership of Cook-Walden spearheaded the completion of a new site on North Lamar. It is a beautiful, unique

facility with two complete chapels and closed-circuit television for the convenience of overflow funeral services. Beautifully landscaped and easily recognized by the fountain on the front grounds, the funeral home remains Cook-Walden's landmark.

A VISIONARY APPROACH

Walden, a visionary in the funeral industry, was innovative in bringing new ideas of service into the age-old need of society to bury its dead with dignity. Both pragmatic and philosophical, Walden believed that to make a difference and be a positive influence in the community, one must be willing to lead. This philosophy helped change Austin's funeral industry.

The vision of providing complete service to a fast-growing community culminated in the purchase of two adjacent cemeteries on North IH-35. Capital Memorial Gardens and Memorial Hill Cemeteries became Cook-Walden Capital Parks, and operated under the Perpetual Care Laws of the state of Texas. Immediate plans were made to upgrade both burial parks. An award-winning mausoleum with an inside chapel was constructed, new sections were opened in the cemeteries to accommodate different groups, and the

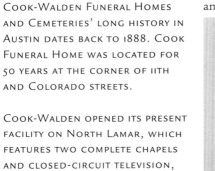

CLOCKWISE FROM TOP RIGHT: COOK-WALDEN FUNERAL HOMES AND CEMETERIES' LONG HISTORY IN AUSTIN DATES BACK TO 1888. COOK FUNERAL HOME WAS LOCATED FOR 50 YEARS AT THE CORNER OF 11TH AND COLORADO STREETS.

COOK-WALDEN OPENED ITS PRESENT FACILITY ON NORTH LAMAR, WHICH FEATURES TWO COMPLETE CHAPELS AND CLOSED-CIRCUIT TELEVISION, IN 1974.

CHARLES WALDEN BECAME THE OWNER OF COOK FUNERAL HOMES IN 1971.

BETTE MAYFIELD PHOTOGRAPHY

entire burial gardens were made even more beautiful.

During this period, there was a movement to include funerals in estate planning. As a leader in the industry, Cook-Walden implemented a complete program of prearrangement whereby a funeral could be not only planned but prepaid. This was, and continues to be, strongly regulated by the State of Texas Banking Department. Because it met a need, the endeavor was very successful and appreciated.

In 1985, Cook-Walden enlarged its service area with the acquisition of the Davis Funeral Home in Georgetown and the Young Funeral Home in Florence, both operated by the highly respected Davis family. The dream continued, and soon a beautiful, serene section of wooded ground was purchased on Anderson Mill Road just off Highway 183 North, and in 1985, Cook-Walden/Chapel of the Hills was dedicated to serve the Hill Country.

In 1992, Cook-Walden took the opportunity to become affiliated with Service Corporation International (SCI), a publicly held company. SCI is the largest death care corporation in the world, providing people in need with a local, national, and worldwide network of facilities and services not available to an independent company.

Subsequently, the Forest Oaks Funeral Home and Cemetery in Oak Hill and the Condra Funeral Home in Round Rock also became a part of the Cook-Walden family of funeral service providers. Following the philosophy of meeting the demands and needs of the public, a new, full-service funeral home was opened in 1997 within the grounds of Capital Memorial Park Cemetery.

The master growth plan had come to fruition. As Walden says, "To see a lifetime dream come true is an unparalleled and rewarding experience."

A New Era

Memorializing the dead is an important part of human history. However, the state of flux in funeral customs is so gradual as to go almost unnoticed. For

CAPITAL PARKS IS ONE OF COOK-WALDEN'S THREE PERPETUAL CARE CEMETERIES.

BETTE MAYFIELD PHOTOGRAPHY

example, the death mask used in ancient Egypt and the Roman Empire extended to early American times, but it is no longer considered appropriate. Neither do modern Americans now have the body embalmed in the home, where it used to remain for the wake and mourning period prior to the funeral service.

"The defining difference of Cook-Walden is that we refuse to be relegated to the past," says Allan Akens, Cook-Walden area vice president. "Although we hold in high esteem our own rich heritage, we know that we must continue to be progressive in service."

The high-tech and multicultural society that defines Central Texas today makes Cook-Walden's motto—Yesterday, Today, and Tomorrow—even more relevant. Custom and pragmatism may change, but old-fashioned care remains the pivotal component in a business that began in the 19th century and now moves into the 21st. Cook-Walden will continue to give the same dedicated service that has made it the respected firm it is today.

The company's goal is well stated in a quote by Walden in a 1975 edition of the *Austin Citizen*: "Cook-Walden will, of course, maintain the traditions which have distinguished it for more than 100 years."

ALLAN AKENS, AREA VICE PRESIDENT FOR COOK-WALDEN

THIS AWARD-WINNING MAUSOLEUM IN CAPITAL PARKS CEMETERY WAS CONSTRUCTED IN 1980.

PILLAR OF THE AUSTIN COMMUNITY, BANK OF AMERICA traces its local roots back more than a century to predecessor bank Austin National Bank, which was founded in 1890. Today, as a result of a merger between NationsBank and BankAmerica Corpora-

tion, the new Bank of America is the first nationwide, coast-to-coast bank.

In business to help people realize their dreams, Bank of America provides financial solutions to a broad, diverse range of customers—individuals, families, small businesses, corporations, and community institutions. Whether an individual is expanding a business, improving a home, or buying a car, Bank of America strives to make banking work for its customers in ways it never has before.

HIGH-TECH SERVICE

s consumers continue to seek more convenient options to do their banking, Bank of America continues to respond with products and services to fit their needs. With more than 1,400 ATMs and 400 banking centers, Bank of America has the largest banking center franchise and bank-owned ATM network in Texas.

Bank of America gives customers access to their money at any time, from anywhere—24 hours a day, seven days a week, 365 days a year. With the personal computer

product Managing Your Money, customers can set up budgets, organize finances, and pay bills. Also, customers can choose to go on-line to access their accounts by visiting the bank's Web site (www.bankofamerica.com), and, with a toll-free telephone system, account information is just a phone call away.

Even with an extensive service menu, Bank of America is always looking for new ways to meet consumer needs. "We spend a great deal of time developing ways to improve the quality of life of the people and the communities we serve," says Lew Little Jr., president, Bank of America in Austin. "We want to help consumers meet life's opportunities and challenges, whether it's helping a small business succeed or providing a family with their first mortgage."

Whether its customers want to finance a home, a new car, a child's education, or a vacation, Bank of America has an array of products and services available for every level of financial need. In addition to consumer products, Bank of America covers commercial products for small and large

businesses, including loans for real estate and agriculture.

SERVING THE COMMUNITY'S NEED

ith the resources of a large organization, Bank of America is investing in Texas. The bank's 500-plus Austin employees contribute many volunteer and leadership hours to a wide variety of civic, cultural, and educational initiatives. Whether volunteering at local schools through Austin Partners in Education, or coordinating participation in activities such as the March of Dimes Walk America, Texas Book Festival, or United Way's Day of Caring, Bank of America associates bring both a personal and a professional commitment to their work in the community.

"We believe we are only as successful as the communities we serve," says Little. "To us, that means more than just financial transactions. From volunteering our time, to making charitable contributions, it means investing in people by helping the families, businesses, and communities we serve."

AUSTIN-AREA ASSOCIATES GATHER TO CELEBRATE DAY ONE OF OPERATIONS AS THE NEW BANK OF AMERICA IN AUSTIN (RIGHT).

BANK OF AMERICA AUSTIN REGIONAL EXECUTIVE ANDY ELLIOT AND BANKING CENTER MANAGER CHUCK FUQUAY UNVEIL THE NEW BANK OF AMERICA SIGN DURING DAY ONE ACTIVITIES AT THE NEW BANK (LEFT).

I N 1914, CHARLIE MERRILL AND EDDIE LYNCH MET IN A pickup basketball game in New York—and soon afterwards, they formed a new company with a new vision. Almost nine decades later, Merrill Lynch's business philosophy of bringing Wall Street to Main Street prevails, and its dedication

to its clients is greater than ever.

Merrill Lynch serves more than 4 million households, small- to mid-sized businesses, and regional financial institutions using a planning-based financial service approach. Among the many features available to its clients are brokerage, personal credit, insurance, home financing, and trust services, as well as retirement and group employee benefit services and business financing. Merrill Lynch clients are served by more than 18,200 financial consultants in more than 900 branch offices worldwide. As of December 31, 1998, investors had entrusted Merrill Lynch with more than $1.4 trillion in client assets.

"We work face-to-face with real people," says Austin Resident Vice President Thomas J. Mosley Jr. "Whether our clients want to educate their children, plan for a secure retirement, or manage the succession of a small business, we help them meet real goals."

Within the Austin area, Merrill Lynch's 85 trained financial consultants work closely with each client to identify the steps to help them meet their personal financial goals. The company's qualitative approach to financial planning begins with a detailed training program for each financial consultant, and provides them with numerous opportunities for continuing education.

TRUSTED ADVISERS SINCE 1940

errill Lynch's Capitol of Texas Complex consists of nine offices in the Greater Austin area, including Georgetown, Fredericksburg, Kerrville, Lakeway, Marble Falls, and Temple. Each offers a full range of brokerage services, including securities brokerage, business lending, investment banking, asset management, mortgages, 401(k) services and other retirement plans, and personal financial planning. The company provides these services to a wide array of clients, including individual investors and small- to mid-sized businesses.

Merrill Lynch was the only brokerage house in Austin when it opened its office in 1940, and Financial Consultant Theodore Quadlander, who has been with the company since 1951, remembers when its average daily volume was less than 1 million shares. "Now we handle that much in the first minute we're open each day," he says. But one thing that has not changed over the years is Merrill Lynch's dedication to the community. The company's 150 Austin employees are active participants in Austin's many civic and charitable organizations. The Merrill Lynch Capitol of Texas Complex even funded and built its own house for Habitat for Humanity in just 20 weeks, the first company in Austin to do so. The company and its employees are also active in organizations such as the United Way, Boy Scouts of America, Red Cross, Greater Austin Chamber of Commerce, and Austin Lyric Opera.

Merrill Lynch continues to expand rapidly in Central Texas, and expects to grow at double-digit rates both in number of employees and in assets under management. "Austin is one of the most dynamic markets in the country," says Mosley. "Having been a vital part of the community for so long, we enjoy helping our clients find success—whatever that may be."

MERRILL LYNCH AND ITS EMPLOYEES ARE ACTIVE PARTICIPANTS IN AUSTIN'S MANY CIVIC AND CHARITABLE ORGANIZATIONS, INCLUDING HABITAT FOR HUMANITY. THE MERRILL LYNCH CAPITOL OF TEXAS COMPLEX FUNDED AND BUILT THIS HOUSE FOR THE ORGANIZATION IN JUST 20 WEEKS (RIGHT).

"AS PEOPLE THINK TOWARD THE FUTURE AND THE VALUE OF FINANCIAL PLANNING, THEY TURN TO MERRILL LYNCH AS A TRUSTED ADVISER. WE BELIEVE IN PERSONAL ATTENTION BECAUSE EACH DOLLAR WE INVEST COMES FROM AN INDIVIDUAL, FAMILY, OR BUSINESS IN THIS COMMUNITY— AND EACH ONE HAS INDIVIDUAL GOALS," SAYS AUSTIN RESIDENT VICE PRESIDENT THOMAS J. MOSLEY JR. (SEATED), WHO IS PICTURED WITH KAREN BEBEE, ADMINISTRATIVE MANAGER, AND KERRY GUNNARSON, SERVICE MANAGER (LEFT).

AXA Advisors, L.L.C.

I N THESE CHALLENGING TIMES, MANY PEOPLE ARE SEEKING TO determine how the realities of today's rapidly changing world will affect their financial decisions of tomorrow. Dedicated to helping citizens meet the demands of today's intense financial climate, The Equitable Companies Inc.—parent

company of The Equitable Life Assurance Society of the U.S.—has undergone a revolution of its own and has recently changed its name to AXA Financial Inc. This name change reflects The Equitable Companies' continuing evolution into a premier, full-service financial planning company. Texas, a state whose history is steeped in important revolutionary beginnings, is at the forefront of the company's historic mission.

"WE WANT TO BE THE WORLD'S PREMIER PROVIDER OF FINANCIAL PLANNING, INSURANCE AND ASSET MANAGEMENT PRODUCTS, AND SERVICES FOR FINANCIAL SECURITY AND RETIREMENT SAVINGS," SAYS KENT ABNEY, EXECUTIVE VICE PRESIDENT OF AXA ADVISORS' AUSTIN OFFICE (TOP).

FOR MORE THAN A CENTURY, EQUITABLE HAS SERVED AS A TRUSTED ADVISER TO AUSTIN-AREA CLIENTS, PROVIDING THEM WITH THE PRODUCTS, SERVICES, AND SOLUTIONS TO HELP MEET A WIDE RANGE OF NEEDS DURING THEIR FINANCIAL LIFE CYCLES (BOTTOM).

To understand the significance of this evolution, as it relates to Texas, one must understand the history of the company. For more than a century, Equitable has served as a trusted adviser to Austin-area clients, providing them with the products, services, and solutions to help meet a wide range of needs during their financial life cycles. One of the largest insurance companies in the United States, Equitable traces its roots in Austin back to its first on-site agent in 1867. Its first office opened in 1892.

◄ EVERGREEN STUDIOS

Building on a rich history of innovation in the insurance industry, Equitable, since its inception in 1859, has been quick to embrace change to keep up with a shifting marketplace and evolving needs. In 1976, for instance, to stay ahead in an increasingly competitive industry, Equitable was the first U.S. insurer to sell variable life insurance. And when facing a harsh economy in 1990, Equitable made a bold move to demutualize and became publicly held as part of The Equitable Companies, Inc.; it was the largest mutual insurance company to do so. And shortly after, in 1991, The Equitable Companies Inc. became a member of the global AXA Group when AXA made a strategic $1 billion investment in the company, and subsequently became its majority shareholder.

Despite having experienced tremendous growth—the company currently employs 4,200 people nationwide, in addition to a field force of approximately 7,300—

Equitable is redefining its mission by becoming a fully integrated financial services entity. Capitalizing on its alliance with AXA, which has created new dimensions of global reach and strength, is key. Under the leadership of its chairman and CEO, Ed Miller, Equitable's efforts toward this goal include restructuring its sales force to enhance growth opportunities, strengthening its penetration in advanced markets and creating a new advertising campaign that positions associates as comprehensive planning professionals.

The name Equitable, long associated with the best in insurance and annuity products, didn't reflect the broad-based financial services provider the company had become, nor its access to the global array of products and services provided through AXA. So on May 19, 1999, shareholders voted to change The Equitable Companies Inc. name to AXA Financial, Inc. Housed under the AXA Financial Inc.

umbrella is AXA Advisors L.L.C., formerly known as EQ Financial Consultants, which represents the financial planning and broker/dealer arm of the company; Equitable Life, which will continue to manufacture insurance and annuity products; Donaldson, Lufkin & Jenrette Inc.; and Alliance Capital Management LP.

Austin, in addition to other Texas cities, has a unique role in AXA Financial Inc.'s journey. It is one of the company's chosen sites for its Texas financial planning pilot program: the seed that blossomed into AXA Advisors. "We want to be the world's premier provider of financial planning, insurance, and asset management products and services for financial security and retirement savings," says Kent Abney, executive vice president of AXA Advisors' Austin office. "While the Equitable name definitely has a unique place in America's history books, it didn't necessarily signify our new ability and what we had become to our customers. We feel this new brand represents a much broader value proposition to our consumers, focusing on advice, access, and service."

Associates of AXA Advisors and its in-house professionals work hand-in-hand with clients to develop a sound financial strategy that helps them meet their goals and objectives through fee-based financial planning services. Once objectives are established, clients have the option to continue to work with associates of AXA Advisors to implement the plan with a full portfolio of products and services. "This approach helps our associates objectively focus on the client's overall needs and to provide products to fit the client's planning needs," explains Abney.

State-of-the-art electronic communication systems are also key in helping associates service clients more effectively. At the touch of a button, associates can keep abreast of their clients' needs, as well as see how these needs are affected by the overall market.

AXA Advisors' qualified sales associates cover a range of professional and financial disciplines, including CFP, accounting, legal, and banking backgrounds. In fact, the company is ranked number one

in terms of sales associates who hold both the Chartered Financial Consultant (ChFC) and Chartered Life Underwriter (CLU) certifications from The American College, an independent, accredited, nonprofit institution that provides graduate and professional education in the financial services and insurance fields.

The majority of AXA Advisors' financial planning clients are individuals, ranging from small-business owners to top executives at some of Austin's largest companies. "The city has experienced prolific economic growth, and as a result, our clients are looking for full-service financial service partners," says Abney. "In addition to financial planning, as registered representatives of AXA Advisors and associates of Equitable, we offer a broad array of financial products, including insurance products, securities, mutual funds, annuities, and other related financial products and services."

Just as AXA Financial Inc. is dedicated to providing financial assurance to Austin residents, it is also dedicated to enriching the city on a community level. Associ-

ates are involved in many different organizations, including the Greater Austin Chamber of Commerce, Advantage Austin, United Way, the Austin Children's Museum, and the Ronald McDonald House. "We support charities that are close to our hearts on both a corporate level and a personal level," says Abney. "We truly enjoy giving back to this city that has supported us in so many ways for so many years."

SALES ASSOCIATES OF AXA ADVISORS AND ITS IN-HOUSE PROFESSIONALS WORK HAND IN HAND WITH CLIENTS TO DEVELOP A SOUND FINANCIAL STRATEGY TO HELP THEM MEET THEIR GOALS AND OBJECTIVES.

EVERGREEN STUDIOS

EVERGREEN STUDIOS

OR MORE THAN A CENTURY, AT&T HAS BEEN AN INTEGRAL part of Austin's development. Its roots in the city reach as far back as 1898, when the AT&T long-distance network first connected to Austin. More than 50 years later, network television programming found its way to the capital city

when AT&T built and operated the facilities that television networks used to send their programs to affiliates throughout the nation. On November 21, 1952, AT&T opened a microwave relay link for television connecting Austin to Dallas, and from there to the networks of Los Angeles and New York.

Today, AT&T is still right at home in Austin, with more than 900 employees throughout the city. "Just as Austin has played an important role in our corporate history, AT&T is committed to playing an important role in the city's development," says Jim Davis, AT&T vice president and chief advocate for the company's law and government affairs operations in Texas and the Southwest.

Going Mobile

T&T is the nation's largest long-distance service provider, but the company also is a leader in

digital wireless communications and Internet service. AT&T's WorldNet Internet service went on-line in 1996 and was the first Internet service provider to introduce flat rate pricing for surfing the Net. Also, AT&T was the first wireless communications provider with a plan that charges a monthly flat rate for all calls made from a wireless phone with no roaming and no long-distance charges. Digital technology allows cellular phone users access to services like call waiting, caller identification, voice mail, and text messaging.

"The future is here," says Kevin McKeand, vice president and general manager of AT&T's wireless operations. "AT&T is making it much easier for our customers to connect to the people, programming, and information they want, anytime, anywhere." Mergers with companies like TCI, the nation's largest cable television service, mean AT&T soon will provide the advanced technology that will en-

able customers to receive phone service, data transmission, cable television, and Internet access through a single cable.

Caring for Austin

T&T employees are active in Austin and throughout Texas, serving on boards of civic and cultural organizations and volunteering their personal time for causes that benefit the community. AT&T Cares, a company program that encourages AT&T employees to dedicate a full workday to community service, has resulted in countless human resources all focused on making Austin a better place. From hammering nails during a Habitat for Humanity Blitz Build in East Austin to ushering crowds and helping children read at the Texas Book Festival, AT&T employees actively care about Austin.

As part of the AT&T Cares program, AT&T's Austin employees recently took a day off from their regular work schedules to survey historic Oakwood Cemetery in East Austin. Employees surveyed the monuments and tombstones to develop a written record in the first step of a master plan to renovate the 64-acre cemetery. "Oakwood Cemetery plays a significant role in Texas history, and we're helping to preserve that legacy for the future," Davis says.

Additionally, the AT&T Foundation has contributed to Austin's success in cultivating educational, artistic, and community service programs. Since its grand opening as a formal Austin institution, the Austin Children's Museum has been supported by the AT&T Foundation. AT&T's focus on innovation and technology makes it a perfect match in supporting the museum's vision. Through AT&T support, children of Austin

AT&T EMPLOYEES LARRY PRICE AND MARY BROOKS MAKE A RUBBING OF A 19TH-CENTURY HEADSTONE DURING A VOLUNTEER PROJECT AT OAKWOOD CEMETERY. AT&T WORKERS SURVEYED THE MONUMENTS AND TOMBSTONES TO HELP DEVELOP A PLAN TO RENOVATE THE HISTORIC CEMETERY ON MARTIN LUTHER KING BOULEVARD.

REBECCA McENTEE/AUSTIN AMERICAN-STATESMAN

and Central Texas are exposed to the world of culture, the arts, and technology.

In a thriving city of artists and different art forms, the AT&T Foundation has long been a supporter of new works presented by the Austin Symphony Orchestra, Austin Lyric Opera, and Ballet Austin. Beyond just bringing innovation to the stage, AT&T also has brought innovation and art to Main Street, sponsoring free concerts and performances for schoolchildren and the Greater Austin area population over the years.

Innovation sparked AT&T's recent support for production of *The Texas State Capitol: A Virtual Tour*, an interactive CD-ROM focusing on the historic Texas capitol, an Austin icon. Some 3,500 copies of the CD-ROM were donated to schools across the state so that students who have never seen the capitol are able to get a glimpse of the historic building, the largest capitol in the United States.

"The capitol is one of the state's most popular tourist attractions, but it also is a place where students can learn about Texas heritage, our local form of government, and our leaders," Davis says. "We wanted teachers to be able to use the CD-ROM to create lessons in Texas history." The CD-ROM showcases 15 areas of the capitol, highlighting the history of each area and its present-day use. The CD-ROM includes segments on the capitol's construction, an explanation of

▲ STATE PRESERVATION BOARD/AT&T FOUNDATION

ABOUT 3,500 COPIES OF THE INTERACTIVE CD-ROM *The Texas State Capitol: A Virtual Tour* WERE DONATED TO SCHOOLS ACROSS THE STATE SO STUDENTS CAN VIEW THE HISTORIC TEXAS CAPITOL, AN AUSTIN ICON. THE PROJECT WAS UNDERWRITTEN BY THE AT&T FOUNDATION.

how a bill becomes a law, and a suggested reading list on state history.

LOOKING FORWARD

Telecommunications is one of the world's fastest-changing industries. As a result, people can do, see, hear, and learn things today that no one would have thought possible just 10 years ago. Wireless communication and global services mean people can stay in touch with others halfway around the world, 24 hours a day. The fantastic growth of the Internet means unlimited learning opportunities for anyone with access to a computer. And it is now possible to receive literally hundreds of cable television channels, where once there were only three.

AT&T enters the 21st century as a leader in the communications industry. During this new millennium, AT&T will continue blazing the trail for new ways to connect to people, places, and information, with the same reputation of excellence in technology and customer care for which it's been known for more than 100 years.

ROBO-CITY, AT THE AUSTIN CHILDREN'S MUSEUM, WAS SELECTED BY THE AT&T NEW EXPERIMENTS IN ART AND TECHNOLOGY PROGRAM TO SHOWCASE THE EDUCATIONAL AND ARTISTIC INSTALLATION OF INTERACTIVE TECHNOLOGY USING ROBOTICS, CYBERHUMANS, ROBOTIC LIGHTING, AND A MUSICAL DANCE SURFACE.

▲ AUSTIN CHILDREN'S MUSEUM

HE CENTRAL TEXAS COMMUNITY HAS EXPERIENCED TREMENdous growth in recent years, with no signs of slowing down. As the new millennium approaches, this means more people, jobs, and houses. A growing community also has growing needs for infrastructure—police and fire services, schools, roads, and health care for all.

As the region's leading health care provider, its largest nonprofit community service organization, and its safety net health care provider for the poor, the SETON Healthcare Network is reaching out in new, creative ways to serve one of America's most dynamic communities, while fulfilling its century-long commitment to Central Texas and to the nearly 400-year-old mission of the Daughters of Charity.

CLINICAL EXCELLENCE

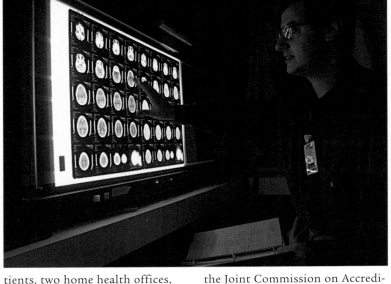

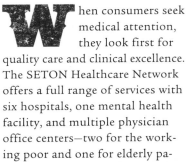

MORE THAN 1,600 PHYSICIANS ARE MEMBERS OF THE SETON HEALTHCARE NETWORK'S MEDICAL STAFF. PHYSICIANS, NURSES, DIETITIANS, TECHNICIANS AND STAFF WORK TOGETHER TO ENSURE PATIENTS GET THE BEST POSSIBLE CARE.

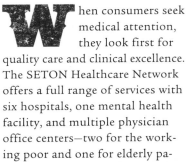hen consumers seek medical attention, they look first for quality care and clinical excellence. The SETON Healthcare Network offers a full range of services with six hospitals, one mental health facility, and multiple physician office centers—two for the working poor and one for elderly patients, two home health offices, and two cancer centers. This comprehensive network allows SETON to provide distributed community care close to where people live or work.

SETON is accredited as an integrated health care network by the Joint Commission on Accreditation of Healthcare Organizations (JCAHO), the nation's oldest and largest accrediting body of its kind. In fact, SETON has earned accreditation with commendation, the highest level awarded by the organization. "This outstanding level

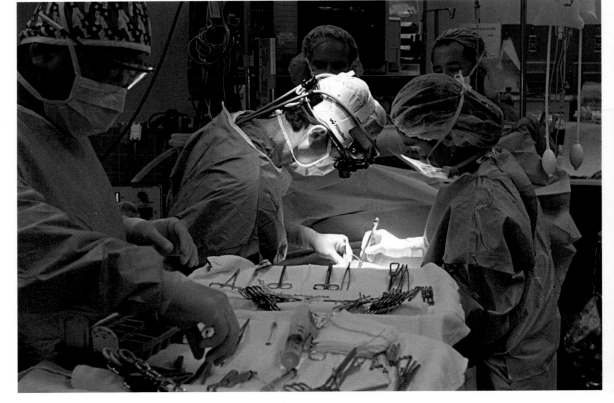

THE SETON HEART CENTER HAS A HISTORY OF CARDIAC EXCELLENCE, AND PROVIDES THE REGION'S FIRST AND ONLY HEART TRANSPLANT AND PEDIATRIC HEART PROGRAMS.

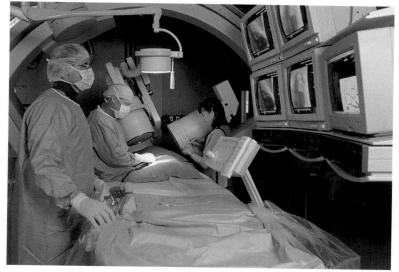

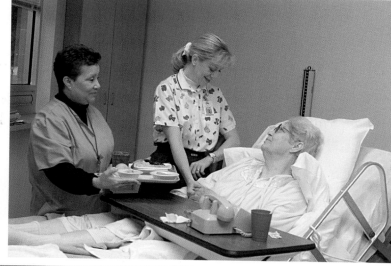

of achievement reflects the successful efforts of your health care network to provide high-quality care for those you serve," says the JCAHO report.

SETON's facilities have received numerous Quality Leader awards from the National Research Corporation—attesting to the community's high preference for the care provided within the SETON Healthcare Network. Additionally, all four Austin facilities have been part of the Top 100 Hospitals: Benchmarks for Success study conducted by HCIA Inc. and William M. Mercer.

Children's Hospital of Austin, the region's only children's hospital, serves the 46-county area with access to specialized pediatric services and doctors. Physicians and staff at Children's diagnose and treat children not as miniature adults, but as individuals with their own illnesses, emotional realities, and forms of and responses to treatment. In addition, 'Specially for Children, a group of pediatric subspecialists, provides Central Texas families with specialized pediatric care previously unavailable without traveling to Dallas or Houston.

The regional Trauma Center at Brackenridge, the third-busiest center in Texas, serves the area with 24-hour trauma and emergency medical care, medical helicopter services, and emergency medical services.

The Seton Heart Center has a history of cardiac excellence, offering the region's first and only heart transplant program (Medicare-certified) and pediatric heart program. Many cardiac firsts took

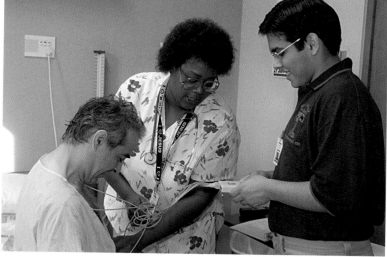

place in SETON facilities, including the launch of the region's first heart program in 1958, the first adult and pediatric heart catheterizations in 1959, the first open-heart surgery in 1961, and the first heart transplant in 1986. State-of-the-art cardiac catheterization labs offer quicker diagnosis and treatment for adult and pediatric patients, including the only cath lab in Central Texas with specialized pediatric capabilities.

SETON offers the region sophisticated neonatal care with the Marialice Shivers Regional Neonatal Center at Seton Medical Center and the Children's Hospital of Austin Neonatal Intensive Care Unit at Brackenridge, both Level III neonatal units. SETON's specially equipped transport units respond to hospitals in surrounding areas to transport infants and pediatric patients, ensuring they receive appropriate care during the trip.

In an effort to strengthen the community's medical safety net,

SETON acquired and supports the Central Texas Medical Foundation (CTMF), the area's only graduate medical education residency training program.

The SETON network has expanded its continuum of care with regional hospitals in Burnet and Caldwell counties, and a full-service mental health facility in Austin. SETON also is reaching out to meet the needs of geographically underserved areas by opening new facilities.

To provide primary medical care and meet other health and social service needs of people 65 years of age and older, the Seton Senior Health Center in Northwest Austin offers primary medical care, laboratory services, nutrition and pharmaceutical counseling, and case management. In addition, the Seton Health Plan offers Seton SeniorCare, a supplemental plan for Medicare patients, which reduces paperwork and provides cost savings for seniors and the disabled.

CLOCKWISE FROM TOP LEFT: STATE-OF-THE-ART CARDIAC CATHETERIZATION LABS OFFER QUICKER DIAGNOSIS AND TREATMENT FOR ADULTS AND PEDIATRIC PATIENTS.

SETON'S NURSING STAFF ASSIST LOCAL HEALTH VOCATION PROGRAMS BY EXPOSING HIGH SCHOOL AND COLLEGE STUDENTS TO PATIENT CARE.

PATIENTS COUNT ON QUALITY CARE AND CLINICAL EXCELLENCE AT SETON FACILITIES. SETON'S SIX HOSPITALS HAVE APPROXIMATELY 50,000 INPATIENT VISITS EACH YEAR.

COMMUNITY CARE

Providing medical care, support, and services to people who are unable to pay for them is a fundamental expression of SETON's Catholic heritage and its mission to build a healthier Central Texas community. SETON contributes about $50 million each year to care for the poor and benefit the community, touching the lives of almost 200,000 Central Texans in the process.

The Children's Hospital of Austin/Austin Independent School District (AISD) Student Health Services Program is an innovative, nationally recognized collaborative effort in which SETON's clinical staff provide health services for more than 75,000 Austin schoolchildren. Children's Hospital and AISD work together to ensure appropriate medical services in the schools and to help find primary

care homes for children in need.

SETON has two community health centers for the working poor, Seton East and Seton South. A third center, Seton Topfer Community Health Center, opens in early 2000. These neighborhood clinics offer holistic primary medical care, pharmacy and laboratory services, social and psychological services, and educational programs.

The Seton Good Health School and the Seton Good Health Club (for seniors over 65) offer a variety of wellness classes, immunizations, and screenings. In addition, SETON's Web sites (www.goodhealth.com and www.childrenshospital.com) offer consumers easily accessible health information on-line.

The SETON network approaches healing from a holistic approach, treating the entire person—mind, body, and spirit. In

addition, The Seton Cove interfaith center offers spirituality-focused programs that work toward integrating spirituality and wholeness into healing.

Two organizations provide a philanthropic structure for compassionate Central Texans who want to contribute to SETON programs—The Seton Fund and Children's Hospital Foundation of Austin. The efforts of these two organizations help make it possible for SETON to carry out its mission with services and programs such as the community health centers and school health program.

PARTNERSHIPS WITH THE COMMUNITY

Truly meeting the medical and health needs of Central Texas' indigent and working poor requires the efforts, resources, and expertise of more than one health care provider. As a result, SETON partners with public and private organizations to fill service gaps and address unmet needs. As the region's safety net provider, for example, SETON leases and manages two hospitals owned by the City of Austin.

Through efforts like the Indigent Care Collaboration (ICC), a corporate alliance of private and public primary care providers, local organizations, including SETON, are working together to help the poor find medical homes

SETON IS COMMITTED TO MEETING THE NEEDS OF THE WORKING POOR. THE COMMUNITY HEALTH CENTERS PROVIDE A MEDICAL HOME WITH HOLISTIC PRIMARY MEDICAL CARE, SOCIAL AND PSYCHOLOGICAL SERVICES, AND EDUCATIONAL PROGRAMS.

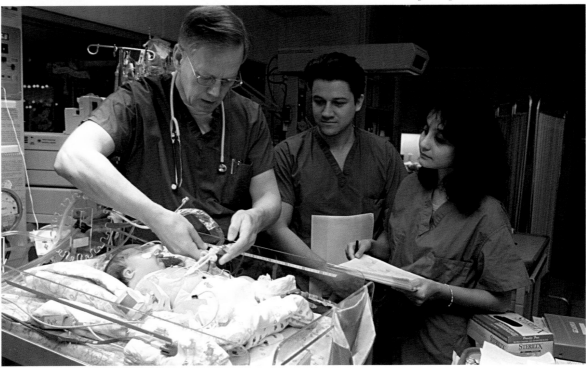

SETON PROVIDES SOPHISTICATED REGIONAL NEONATAL CARE WITH STATE-OF-THE-ART UNITS AT BRACKENRIDGE AND SETON MEDICAL CENTER.

and reduce unnecessary emergency room visits. For example, the ICC identified a need for after-hours assistance for clinic patients. Co-operatively funded, the Seton Call Center is available 24 hours a day and answers calls after normal business hours. Registered nurses assess patients' medical needs, help determine whether they need emergency or less-urgent attention, and schedule clinic appointments in some cases.

THE NEW MILLENNIUM

Throughout the 20th century, SETON's mission has been to care for and improve the health of the people it serves to build a healthier Central Texas. In that role, the organization has accepted new responsibilities, entered new collaborations, and brought new thinking to its position as the leading health care provider in a growing region of more than a million people.

The continued growth of Central Texas brings the hope of new opportunities and better lives for people throughout the region. As the community grows in size and wealth, the SETON Healthcare Network is committed to making sure it also grows by providing quality care for all who need it, by developing innovative partnerships, by exploring the reaches of holistic care, and reinvesting in the healthy growth of Central Texas into the new millennium.

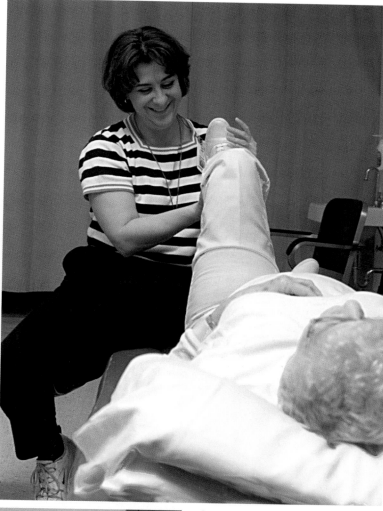

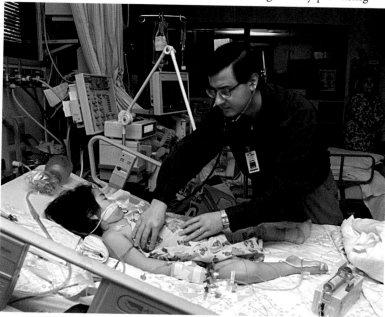

CLOCKWISE FROM TOP LEFT: CHILDREN'S HOSPITAL HAS SPECIALLY TRAINED PHYSICIANS AND STAFF PROVIDING PEDIATRIC CRITICAL CARE.

THE DEMAND FOR OUTPATIENT SERVICES—DIAGNOSTICS, REHABILITATION, AND DAY SURGERY—HAS INCREASED DRAMATICALLY IN RECENT YEARS. SETON PROVIDES MORE THAN 735,000 OUTPATIENT VISITS EACH YEAR.

CENTRAL TEXAS FAMILIES RECEIVE SPECIALIZED PEDIATRIC CARE AT CHILDREN'S HOSPITAL.

Chase Bank of Texas, N.A.

HASE BANK OF TEXAS IN AUSTIN REFERS TO EVERY ONE OF ITS 325 employees as a "banker," a reflection of its deep commitment to service throughout every level of the organization. Austin's second-oldest bank, Chase Bank of Texas, N.A., began in 1934 as Capital National Bank, which later

became the 33rd member of Texas Commerce Bancshares in 1977 and changed its name to Texas Commerce Bank-Austin in 1981. In 1987, Texas Commerce Bancshares merged with Chemical New York Corporation. Then, in 1996, Chemical and Chase Manhattan Bank merged to create the largest bank holding company in the United States, with more than $350 billion in assets. Texas Commerce Bancshares officially adopted the name of Chase Bank of Texas, N.A. in 1998.

Chase-Austin is one of the city's most respected financial institutions, both for its exemplary service and its involvement in the community. Maintaining consistency in its staff and leadership throughout the organization is a result of teamwork and communication, according to Joe Holt, chairman and CEO of Chase-Austin.

With the power of a global company behind it, Chase Bank of Texas capitalizes on its longtime local presence and its local advisory board of directors. "Our entire team—people our clients have known and trusted for years—can make local decisions with the ability to deliver global products and services," says Holt. From its downtown location and its eight branches across the city, Chase-Austin provides a full range of financial services to clients representing a true cross section of Austin's community and industry.

ALL ASPECTS OF BUSINESS

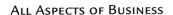

hase Bank of Texas focuses on all aspects of business, with particular emphasis on corporate, commercial, private, and retail banking. "We are really a one-stop shop for our customers," says Holt. As a result, the majority of Texas companies with sales between $1 million and $250 million use Chase Bank of Texas. In addition, Chase is the leading middle-market commercial lender in Austin; more than 30 percent of area businesses with sales exceeding $3 million are clients.

Through its commercial banking services, Chase offers substantial financial experience to entrepreneurial businesses. Virtually every major technology company in Austin has a significant relationship with Chase-Austin's high-technology lending group, which began more than 10 years ago. The bank's real estate lending group is the leading commercial real estate financier in the Austin area.

Chase also provides a broad range of retail banking services, including PC/home banking products and small business banking.

Chase is the leader in providing large Austin and Central Texas companies with investment banking services, including loan syndications, merger and acquisition advisory services, private equity, investment grade corporate debt, and high yield/leveraged corporate finance debt products. Chase also provides a complete and thorough treasury management product menu and maintains a large treasury staff in Austin. The bank's risk management services help customers design and execute strategies to mitigate financial risk through interest rate hedging and other financial management products.

Chase offers full international trade services, including letters of credit, foreign payment and collections, bankers' acceptance financing, and export financing. Through the Chase Manhattan Corporation's Global Trade Finance and Advisory Network, Chase-Texas has access to offices in more than 50 countries and a worldwide correspondent banking network. Local foreign exchange representatives help execute foreign currency drafts and other international services.

As the largest trust institution in the nation, Chase helps customers with corporate debentures, tax-exempt financing, asset-backed securities, and indemnification and general escrows. Through its retirement and investment management services, Chase offers a wide array of products and services for commercial and corporate clients. The Chase Private Bank provides specialized services to individuals, including business owners and professionals, designed to build personal wealth.

FROM ITS DOWNTOWN LOCATION AND ITS EIGHT BRANCHES ACROSS THE CITY, CHASE BANK OF TEXAS PROVIDES A FULL RANGE OF FINANCIAL SERVICES TO CLIENTS REPRESENTING A TRUE CROSS SECTION OF AUSTIN'S COMMUNITY AND INDUSTRY.

TOMMY HOLT

▲ TOMMY HOLT

THE SENIOR MANAGEMENT TEAM OF CHASE-AUSTIN IS COMPRISED OF (BACKROW, FROM LEFT) EILEEN SALING; KEN SAMPLE; RICK NELSON; WILL GARNER; TERESA KETNER; JEFF TARR; (FRONTROW, FROM LEFT) CAROL KERN; JOE E. HOLT, CHAIRMAN AND CEO; MILAM JOHNSON; AND CINDY MATULA.

Chase's affiliate, Chase Securities of Texas, Inc., manages more than $1.2 billion in investment assets in Austin, helping customers with public financing, U.S. government and federal agency securities, corporate and municipal bonds, mortgage-backed securities, and money market mutual funds.

LONG-TERM INTEREST

Chase's slogan, The Right Relationship Is Everything, is reflected in the bank's acute focus on customer service and high level of commitment to the community. "Our bankers are committed to providing the highest level of service possible, a goal that is facilitated by building relationships within the community," says Holt. Indeed, Chase's broad support of charitable, community, and social endeavors makes it one of the most visible organizations in town.

Chase-Austin employees participate in numerous corporate volunteer projects involving such organizations as United Way, Austin Partners in Education, Children's Hospital, Boy Scouts, and the Austin Children's Museum. Chase is a major supporter of the arts, and annually contributes thousands of dollars to more than 100 nonprofit agencies. In 1997

and 1998, the bank won the Highest Corporate Gift Per Capita award from the United Way Capital Area.

Every year, the bank participates in the Chase Global Day of Caring by sponsoring a local event, such as 1997's fall festival to benefit the Center for Battered Women. In 1994 and 1997, Chase received an outstanding rating on its Community Reinvestment Act examinations—

an honor received by only 7 percent of the nation's financial institutions.

"We are extremely proud of our commitment to the Austin community and the level of involvement throughout our organization," says Holt. "It's one more way for us to enjoy our strong partnership with Austin and its people."

CHASE-AUSTIN EMPLOYEES PARTICIPATE IN NUMEROUS CORPORATE VOLUNTEER PROJECTS INVOLVING SUCH ORGANIZATIONS AS UNITED WAY, AUSTIN PARTNERS IN EDUCATION, CHILDREN'S HOSPITAL, BOY SCOUTS, AND AUSTIN CHILDREN'S MUSEUM.

NE OF AUSTIN'S OLDEST LAW FIRMS IS TODAY ONE OF ITS largest, and Brown McCarroll & Oaks Hartline, L.L.P. credits its success to a wealth of resources, an exemplary track record, and an unwavering dedication to cost-effective and client-focused legal representation.

Brown McCarroll & Oaks Hartline was founded in Austin in 1938. The firm quickly emerged as a leader in the Texas legal community by delivering effective solutions tailored to the state's unique legal, political, and business needs. Today, Brown McCarroll is a regional firm with full-service capabilities and offices in Austin, Dallas, Houston, Longview, and Round Rock. The firm serves not only Texas-based companies, but also national and international corporations that have significant legal needs throughout the region.

With more than 120 lawyers skilled in such areas as corporate law, finance, real estate, health care, civil litigation and appeals, product and professional liability, environmental law and toxic torts, and comprehensive estate planning, Brown McCarroll has the background to skillfully handle clients' wide-ranging needs.

FULL-SERVICE CAPABILITIES

Whether managing and closing massive real estate acquisitions or industrial developments, or handling high-profile, large-scale litigation for companies such as the Ford Motor Company and General Electric, Brown McCarroll supports companies and transactions of any size.

"We have the capability to tailor a staff and program specific to the needs of each client. Whether we're helping major international corporations expand in Austin or helping small local companies negotiate licensing agreements, we have the depth of experience to handle every facet of our clients' business," says Managing Partner Bob Werner.

Whether organizing a new business or developing an industrial plant, Brown McCarroll attorneys take a proactive stance, helping clients with all aspects of planning, structuring, negotiating, and documenting both domestic and international business transactions. Brown McCarroll's business attorneys also work extensively with the firm's labor and employment lawyers to ensure compliance with the complicated array of employment laws and regulations. Brown McCarroll's

BROWN McCARROLL & OAKS HARTLINE WAS FOUNDED IN AUSTIN IN 1938, AND QUICKLY EMERGED AS A LEADER IN THE TEXAS LEGAL COMMUNITY BY DELIVERING EFFECTIVE SOLUTIONS TAILORED TO THE STATE'S UNIQUE LEGAL, POLITICAL, AND BUSINESS NEEDS.

BROWN McCARROLL'S REAL ESTATE ATTORNEYS PROVIDE THE SERVICES NECESSARY TO CLOSE ANY TYPE OF TRANSACTION, WORKING WITH CORPORATIONS, BROKERS, LENDERS, AND INVESTMENT TRUSTS OF ALL SIZES IN THE ACQUISITION, DEVELOPMENT, AND DISPOSITION OF PROPERTY (LEFT).

BROWN McCARROLL HAS ONE OF THE LARGEST AND MOST EFFECTIVE LITIGATION PRACTICES IN TEXAS. SERVING CLIENTS ON A REGIONAL AND NATIONAL BASIS, THE FIRM'S MULTIDISCIPLINARY TEAM OF ATTORNEYS HAS SUCCESSFULLY DEFENDED CASES RANGING FROM INDIVIDUAL AND SMALL GROUP CLAIMS TO CLASS ACTION LAWSUITS AND PATTERN LITIGATION THROUGHOUT TEXAS STATE COURTS AND FEDERAL DISTRICT COURTS (RIGHT).

real estate attorneys provide the services necessary to close any type of transaction, working with corporations, brokers, lenders, and investment trusts of all sizes in the acquisition, development, and disposition of property.

In addition to the firm's extensive business and real estate practice, Brown McCarroll's heath care attorneys assist local, regional, and national clients in the creation and operation of managed care organizations; compliance with federal and state statutes governing the various billing and compensation arrangements of medical practices; fraud and abuse analysis and compliance programs; structuring new organizations or expanding existing ones; and contracting with insurance companies or government entities.

In environmental, public utility, and telecommunications law, Brown McCarroll's attorneys are recognized throughout the state and nation, and serve as key legal resources for many national and international business entities. The firm advises clients regarding federal, state, and local laws and regulations; licensing certification; resource planning; rate design and carrier relations; arbitration; rulemaking; and franchising. Attorneys also assist companies of all sizes in obtaining permits and authorizations required for the construction, operation, or modification of facilities.

The firm has an extensive governmental affairs practice and takes an active role in the legislative process. Attorneys can develop short-term opposition to a specific policy or can prepare a detailed, long-term legislative program to track pertinent legislation, draft proposed legislation, assist in the preparation and presentation of testimony, provide advice to legislators, and participate actively throughout the legislative process.

Brown McCarroll has one of the largest and most effective litigation practices in Texas. Serving clients on a regional and national basis, Brown McCarroll's multidisciplinary team of attorneys has successfully defended cases ranging from individual and small group claims to class action lawsuits and pattern litigation throughout Texas

state courts and federal district courts. "Our litigators have the skills and experience to win cases while helping clients manage litigation risk," says Werner. "We help meet their goals while controlling costs though careful communication, planning, and budgeting."

A Long-Term Partner

Brown McCarroll's success comes from working closely with clients to adapt to their individual situations and business objectives. Says Werner, "We get to know our clients and their businesses, we determine what is most important to them, and we take the most effective course of action for each one. Our objective is to create a long-term relationship with each client to provide legal solutions that make sound business sense. Our goal is to function as an extension of our clients' legal or executive staff in an environment of trust, efficiency, and cooperation."

With approximately 60 lawyers and close to 190 additional staff in Austin, Brown McCarroll & Oaks Hartline has a significant presence

in the community as well as in the legal arena. The firm is strongly committed to community involvement, and encourages employee participation in community affairs, mentorship programs, and service organizations. Through the donation of time and/or money, many of the firm's attorneys and staff are personally involved in community service organizations, including the United Way, Goodwill Industries, Special Olympics, Muscular Dystrophy Association, Boy Scouts of America, American Cancer Society, Court Appointed Special Advocates, Austin Partners in Education, St. David's Foundation, and Boys & Girls Clubs of Austin.

Brown McCarroll also contributes to the community through its pro bono work, much of which is delivered through volunteer legal service programs. "We are deeply committed to each community in which we have a presence," says Werner, "and our history in Austin makes it especially meaningful to us when we are able to give something back and help make a difference."

JACKSON WALKER L.L.P.

BUILDING ON A STRONG HERITAGE OF BUSINESS AND COMMUnity involvement, the Austin office of Jackson Walker L.L.P. combines the strengths of two of the state's oldest and most prestigious law firms. Small, Craig & Werkenthin's attorneys officially joined Jackson Walker on January 1, 1999. The consolidation was described by T. Michael Wilson, managing partner of Jackson Walker, as "an alliance between two firms whose philosophies of operation and histories of success closely mirror one another."

The new entity retains the name of Jackson Walker L.L.P. and carries on a long tradition of delivering quality, client-centered legal services with priorities on responsiveness, accessibility, and communication. The firm's commitment to excellence emphasizes a focus on practical, cost-effective solutions for clients based on the highest professional standards.

A HISTORY OF SERVICE

Jackson Walker is one of Texas' oldest and largest law firms, having been founded in Dallas more than 110 years ago. The origin of Small, Craig & Werkenthin can be traced back more than 60 years, when C.C. Small Sr. and the other founders began practicing law in Austin.

The two firms were clearly bound by historical threads. The late A.W. Walker, a name partner in Jackson Walker, and the late C.C. Small Jr., a name partner in Small, Craig & Werkenthin, first crossed paths at the University of Texas Law School, where they began developing their respective expertise in oil and gas law and land title law. Their association continued throughout the middle of the 20th century, when they argued cases together, helping to define and develop the laws that govern the Texas energy industry today.

Each firm also played an important part in the economic growth of Texas—Small, Craig & Werkenthin through its role in the development of some of the most important legislation and regulations affecting industries throughout the state, and Jackson Walker through its involvement in the creation of thriving corporate entities such as Dallas County Gas Company, known today as Lone Star Gas. By bringing these legacies together, Jackson Walker has fused both firms' long-standing reputations for delivering high-quality legal counsel focused on the needs and goals of clients, creating a firm of history and distinction.

Jackson Walker's ability to provide superior service has been enhanced by the addition of the Small, Craig & Werkenthin attorneys, many of whom have practiced in the Austin area for decades. "Our long-standing presence in the Austin area and familiarity with the legislature and state regulatory agencies is of great value," says Austin office Partner-in-Charge Jim Alsup. "This experience helps us to better understand our clients' needs, provide more effective legal services, and truly assist our clients in achieving their goals."

GRANT • GUERRERO PHOTOGRAPHY

GRANT • GUERRERO PHOTOGRAPHY

EDWARD C. SMALL, GOVERNMENT AFFAIRS PARTNER, IS THE SON OF THE LATE C.C. SMALL JR., FORMER NAME PARTNER IN SMALL, CRAIG & WERKENTHIN (TOP).

JACKSON WALKER L.L.P.'S AUSTIN OFFICE HAS ROOTS REACHING BACK MORE THAN 60 YEARS (BOTTOM).

THE FIRM'S OFFICE IS LOCATED ON CONGRESS AVENUE.

With the addition of the Small, Craig & Werkenthin attorneys, the firm has a greater number of practice areas and stronger core services in virtually every area of law. These areas include administrative, agricultural, banking, bankruptcy, corporate and securities, employment, energy, environmental, governmental, health care, insurance, intellectual property, international, litigation, media, probate and estate, real estate, tax, technology, and transportation.

Jackson Walker has a geographic presence that encompasses offices in Austin, Dallas, Fort Worth, Houston, San Angelo, and San Antonio. On an international scale, the firm extends its capabilities further as a founding member of Globalaw™, a worldwide network of affiliate law firms in the United States and more than 60 foreign countries.

"Just as business is no longer localized, we are expanding to better serve our clients locally, nationally, and internationally," says Partner Fred B. Werkenthin. "The size and strength of our combined legal talent will increase the depth of expertise available to all our clients."

NATIONAL PRESENCE, LOCAL INVOLVEMENT

Remaining active in both the business and civic communities is an important part of the Jackson Walker culture. "Almost every individual here is involved in the community, not only as members of local organizations, but as leaders," says Alsup.

Current members of the firm carry on its well-established tradition of serving as board members of major civic organizations in Austin. These organizations include the United Way, Greater Austin Chamber of Commerce, Austin Museum of Art, Young Men's Business League, Austin Parks Foundation, Caritas, Seton Fund, Austin Community Nursery Schools, Big Brothers/Big Sisters of Austin, LifeWorks, Ronald McDonald House, American Heart Association, Capitol Area Food Bank, and SafePlace. Significant involvement in providing pro bono legal services to the poor has led to Jackson Walker attorneys' earning numerous honors from Volunteer Legal Services of Austin. Attorneys at the firm have also served the legal community in positions such as president of the Travis County Bar and the Texas Young Lawyers Association. Additionally, the firm's employees work hand in hand with Campbell Elementary through Austin Partners in Education.

"We have a true desire to be involved in the community," says Alsup. "We have always had lawyers who contribute their energy to civic activities, public service, and politics—all with the goal of making Austin a world-class community."

(SEATED, LEFT TO RIGHT) T. MICHAEL WILSON, MANAGING PARTNER; FRED B. WERKENTHIN, FORMER NAME PARTNER IN SMALL, CRAIG & WERKENTHIN; AND JAMES M. ALSUP, PARTNER-IN-CHARGE OF THE AUSTIN OFFICE; (STANDING, LEFT TO RIGHT) PARTNERS LAWRENCE A. WAKS, EDWARD C. SMALL, CARLA J. COX, AND C. WADE COOPER

STEWART TITLE IS A FAMILY-RUN COMPANY WHOSE ROOTS GO back more than 105 years. The company can trace its beginnings to 1893, when Maco Lee Stewart purchased his first abstract company in Galveston. Those abstracts became the foundation records for Stewart Title Guaranty

Company. Incorporators and original directors included brothers Maco and Minor Stewart and their brother-in-law W.C. Morris. Today, the company is headed by the family's third generation and has more than 5,000 issuing locations worldwide.

With its Austin office, opened in 1946, Stewart Title maintains the tradition of a family atmosphere at the company. "The most important part of our business is our people," says Austin President Nicki Tyler. "We have 70 employees in Austin, and we're all part of the family here."

EMPHASIS ON EMPLOYEE SATISFACTION

Stewart Title's emphasis on family is evident in the company's structure and its attention to employee satisfaction. Whether creating phased job schedules to accommodate employees with children, hosting annual parties and picnics, or sending lunch to an entire branch if closings prevent them from going to lunch, Stewart Title helps ensure a happy and loyal staff.

Open communication plays a key factor in the company's internal and external successes. A Junior Board solicits employee feedback and suggestions for improvements, benefits, and fun activities. Through the Stewart Bond Program, employees award recognition bonds for coworkers' outstanding service. At the end of the year, employees can cash in their bonds for rewards ranging from movie tickets to a set of golf clubs. An internal newsletter, the *Plaid Review*, features articles by employees and about employees, as well as other issues of interest.

The company empowers employees to assess customer satisfaction, and an internal measurements team surveys the accuracy of information provided to customers. Process controls also help Stewart Title track every step of the closing process to review procedures and increase efficiency.

There is also frequent communication among the local branches of Stewart and the corporate office downtown. A traveling team of company trainers visits local offices to conduct ongoing training and program coordination. In addition, each local president provides a regular report on meeting the company's core elements of success, including leadership, process management, business results, and customer satisfaction. By placing a regular focus on each of these issues, Stewart Title ensures quality and service at every level of the company.

MAKING A DIFFERENCE

Stewart Title employees carry their team effort outside the office into the local community, volunteer-

STEWART TITLE EMPHASIZES EMPLOYEE SATISFACTION, TEAM WORK, AND OPEN COMMUNICATION. THE EMPLOYEES CARRY THEIR TEAM EFFORTS INTO THE COMMUNITY, VOLUNTEERING FOR NUMEROUS CHARITABLE AND SERVICE ORGANIZATIONS, SUCH AS THE ANNUAL UNITED WAY AUCTION (TOP).

STEWART MORRIS JR., PRESIDENT OF STEWART TITLE, ACCEPTS A DIVIDEND FROM NICKI TYLER, PRESIDENT OF STEWART TITLE AUSTIN, INC. (BOTTOM)

ing for numerous charitable and service organizations. The calendar is always full of activities, including adopting needy families during the holidays, participating in numerous walkathons such as the March of Dimes Walk America and the American Heart Walk, helping with Habitat for Humanity, or sponsoring youth at the Sunshine Camp or the Travis County livestock show and rodeo. Stewart Title also supports Seton Hospital, American Heart Association, YMCA, and SafePlace. The company even hosts its own internal auction to benefit the United Way, inviting clients, associates, and retired employees to bid on items ranging from home-baked goods to a day off. "We really like to get involved in activities that are important to both the community and to our employees," says Tyler. "We've found that the more involved we are in such worthy outside events, the closer we become as a company."

Company management plays an active role in the Austin business community, serving in leadership positions in the Real Estate Council of Austin, Texas Capital Area Homebuilders Association, Austin Board of Realtors, Downtown Alliance, and Greater Austin Chamber of Commerce.

The open and familial atmosphere helps Stewart Title maintain a very low attrition rate; in fact, one Austin employee boasts more than 50 years with the company. Opportunities abound for upward mobility in the company, both in Austin and around the world.

THE STAFF OF THE COMMERCIAL DIVISION FOR STEWART TITLE AUSTIN, INC. (TOP)

RECOGNIZED FOR THEIR TENURE WITH STEWART, THESE ASSOCIATES HAVE A MINIMUM OF 15 YEARS WITH THE AUSTIN OFFICE; PAUBLA GUTIERREZ (CENTER, STANDING) CELEBRATED HER 52ND YEAR WITH THE COMPANY IN 1999 (BOTTOM).

CLOSING THE DEAL

One of the nation's top four title insurers, Stewart Title has diversified within the real estate information industry to better serve customers by providing information technology, advanced electronic data interchange solutions, surveying, and geographic information services. In 1994, Stewart Information Services Corporation, the holding company for Stewart Title Guaranty Company, was listed on the New York Stock Exchange.

With four offices in Austin, Stewart Title combines the latest technology with the highest level of service to expedite the closing process. Researching, sorting, and analyzing vast quantities of information on each closing, Stewart relies on fine-tuned internal processes and cutting-edge real estate information services to complete each transaction with industry-leading speed and efficiency.

In coordinating each real estate closing, Stewart Title works with a number of different parties, including real estate agents, buyers, sellers, brokers, lenders, builders, land developers, attorneys, governments, and businesses of all sizes. "Since we're in the middle of the process, we try to make the closing as quick and pleasant an experience as possible," says Tyler. "Imagine coordinating 400 to 600 closings a month and making every one special. That's just what we do."

THE PORTER COMPANY, MECHANICAL CONTRACTORS

ROM TRADITIONAL HVAC AND PLUMBING TO COMPLEX PIPING and clean room filtering systems, The Porter Company's broad range of mechanical contracting projects demonstrates how the company has evolved since it began in 1947. ★ Founded by T.B. Porter as Porter Plumbing and

Heating Company, the firm started out primarily as a plumbing and heating contractor. Since the 1950s, the company has specialized in HVAC, medical gas, and plumbing systems in hospitals. The Porter Company also provides mechanical and plumbing systems for numerous commercial customers, including high-tech companies, educational institutions, and several of the landmark high-rise office buildings that dot the Austin skyline.

Just as the skyline and key Austin industries undergo continued transformation, the innovative Porter Company has evolved to meet the changing needs of its customers. Today, the company provides a full complement of mechanical and specialty piping systems, not only for typical commercial systems, but also for semiconductor manufacturers, high-tech fabrication facilities, pharmaceutical companies, medical facilities, and other highly specialized institutions. The company designs, manufactures, and installs sophisticated chemical piping and filtering systems, including chemical distribution units and piping for the delivery and recovery of high-purity and ultrahigh-purity

chemicals. "We enjoy challenges—the more technically demanding or specialized the project, the greater we excel," says President and CEO David Richards, who bought the company in 1992. The Porter Company also operates its own sheet metal and pipe fabrication facilities.

To better serve its customers with ultrahigh-purity environments, the company built its own clean room—which is certified by the National Environmental Balancing Board—in 1996. One of the few contractors capable of providing this service, The Porter Company fabricates high-purity materials for fast installation on the job site.

The company also specializes in commercial and industrial mechanical services, through The Porter Service Company. With strong capabilities in mechanical retrofitting and equipment upgrade and maintenance, The Porter Service Company specializes in commercial and industrial mechanical services for all brands of chillers, air handlers, pumps, boilers, packaged equipment, and ancillary products.

Exceptional expertise, service, and quality typify The Porter Company's dedication to its customers. "We've built this company with a focus on our customer," says

Richards. "We have proven that listening to our clients and responding to their needs has set us apart from our competition. We partner with our clients and help them get the most value for their construction dollar." Ensuring customer satisfaction on every project has helped the company grow more than 500 percent since 1992.

While its range of services has expanded through the years, its small company atmosphere has not changed. Located just south of Austin in Manchaca, The Porter Company employs approximately 250 people who work together as

CLOCKWISE FROM TOP:
THE PORTER COMPANY, MECHANICAL CONTRACTORS IS HEADQUARTERED IN AUSTIN.

THE COMPANY DESIGNS, MANUFACTURES, AND INSTALLS SOPHISTICATED CHEMICAL PIPING AND FILTERING SYSTEMS, INCLUDING CHEMICAL DISTRIBUTION UNITS AND PIPING FOR THE DELIVERY AND RECOVERY OF HIGH-PURITY AND ULTRAHIGH-PURITY CHEMICALS.

THE PORTER COMPANY PROVIDED THE HVAC AND PLUMBING FOR THE LYNDON B. JOHNSON PRESIDENTIAL LIBRARY.

RICK PATRICK PHOTOGRAPHY

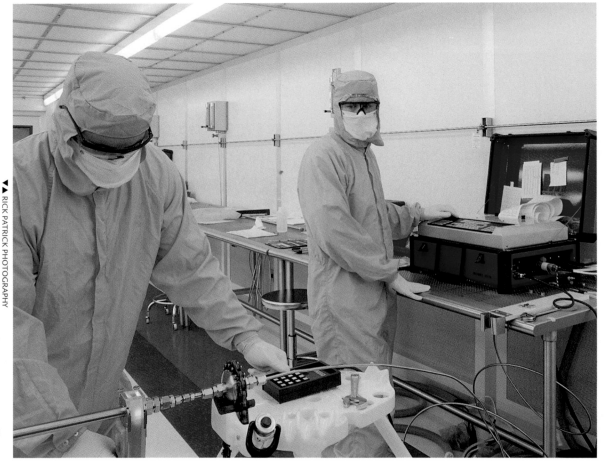

a team. The company has long been active in the Mechanical Contractors Association, Semiconductor Equipment and Materials International (SEMI), Building Owners and Managers Association (BOMA), and the Greater Austin Chamber of Commerce.

The company's managers and supervisors average more than 25 years of experience and have been involved in overseeing mechanical contracting on dozens of multi-million-dollar projects. Staff members handle everything from procurement to fabrication to postinstallation service. In addition, the skilled craftspeople employed by The Porter Company each complete a rigorous four- to five-year apprenticeship program.

The company provides additional training, including manufacturer certification courses and cross-training in a variety of specialized areas.

While half of the company's mission focuses on providing exceptional value and service to customers, the focus of the other half, says Richards, is "to offer our

employees unique opportunities for professional growth and satisfaction." This dedication to both groups is the impetus behind The Porter Company's many long-term relationships with satisfied customers and loyal employees, and it is the reason Porter will continue to thrive in the future.

CLOCKWISE FROM TOP:
TODAY, THE COMPANY PROVIDES A FULL COMPLEMENT OF MECHANICAL AND SPECIALTY PIPING SYSTEMS, NOT ONLY FOR TYPICAL COMMERCIAL SYSTEMS, BUT ALSO FOR SEMICONDUCTOR MANUFACTURERS, HIGH-TECH FABRICATION FACILITIES, PHARMACEUTICAL COMPANIES, MEDICAL FACILITIES, AND OTHER HIGHLY SPECIALIZED INSTITUTIONS.

PORTER COMPANY EMPLOYEES IN A CLEAN ROOM SETTING PERFORM ORBITAL WELDING FOR HIGH-PURITY STAINLESS STEEL FABRICATION.

A SAFETYCASE® SAMPLING STATION ILLUSTRATES THE PORTER COMPANY'S ABILITY TO CUSTOM DESIGN AND MANUFACTURE CHEMICAL CONTAINMENT EQUIPMENT TO ANY SPECIFICATIONS REQUIRED BY THE CUSTOMER, WITH JUST-IN-TIME DELIVERY AND EXPERT INSTALLATION COMPLETING THE GOAL OF EXCEEDING CUSTOMER EXPECTATIONS.

CLINICAL PATHOLOGY LABORATORIES, INC.

S RELIABLE AS CLOCKWORK—AND WORKING AROUND THE clock—Clinical Pathology Laboratories, Inc. (CPL) is a full-service medical laboratory that performs comprehensive clinical and anatomical pathology testing for hospitals, physicians, managed care organizations,

and industries throughout Texas.

Dr. Charles Pelphrey, Austin's first formally trained pathologist, founded CPL in 1948. Pelphrey, a native Austinite, envisioned a full-service pathology lab, the type of which did not exist at the time, that would help raise the practice of medicine to a new level. As the laboratory's reputation grew, it attracted more business and more pathologists. Today, the company employs close to 400 people in Austin, including 20 on-staff doctors providing professional pathology services. After more than 50 years of service to the area, CPL remains one of the last physician-owned, independent reference laboratories in any major city in the country.

Following medicine's trend of becoming increasingly regional, CPL decided to expand its presence beyond Austin, and in 1992 opened a facility in San Antonio. The company has since extended its reach across the state and now owns labs in Kerrville, Bryan, Dallas, Houston, San Marcos, Waco, and Fort Worth.

NONSTOP SERVICE

A well-known name in the medical field, CPL exists to support physicians, health care organizations, and clinics. Using the most advanced medical laboratory instrumentation available, the lab handles all major types of testing, including blood testing, tissue processing and biopsies, and drug screens. Through a network of patient service centers, multiple testing locations, and a radio-dispatched courier fleet, CPL provides comprehensive clinical and anatomical pathology services 24 hours a day, 365 days a year. CPL's Austin headquarters receives thousands of samples every day for overnight testing, the results of which are sent electronically to clients' offices first thing the next morning.

Each of CPL's pathologists is board certified in anatomic and clinical pathology. But, says Robert Connor, M.D., chairman of the board and chief executive officer of CPL, "we look beyond formal education and training in selecting pathologists. We search for people who genuinely care about their contributions to the clinician and the patient." CPL instills a dedication to top-notch service at all levels of the company, from pathologist to technician and receptionist to courier.

The on-staff and affiliated statewide network of pathologists

AUSTIN IS HOME TO CLINICAL PATHOLOGY LABORATORIES' (CPL) CORPORATE HEADQUARTERS AND MAIN TESTING LABORATORY (TOP).

CPL OFFERS MEDICAL PROVIDERS UNIQUE LABORATORY SERVICES NOT OTHERWISE AVAILABLE IN THE CENTRAL TEXAS AREA (BOTTOM).

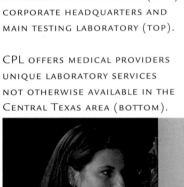

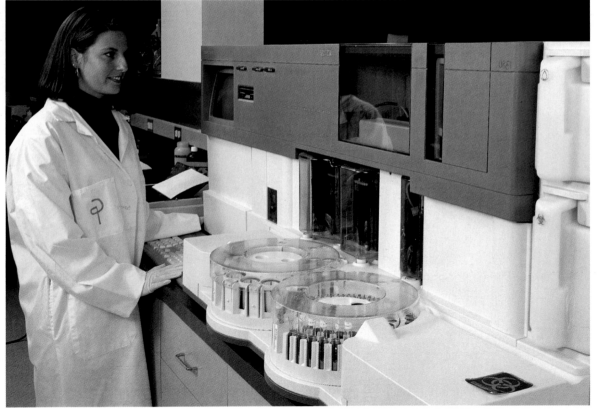

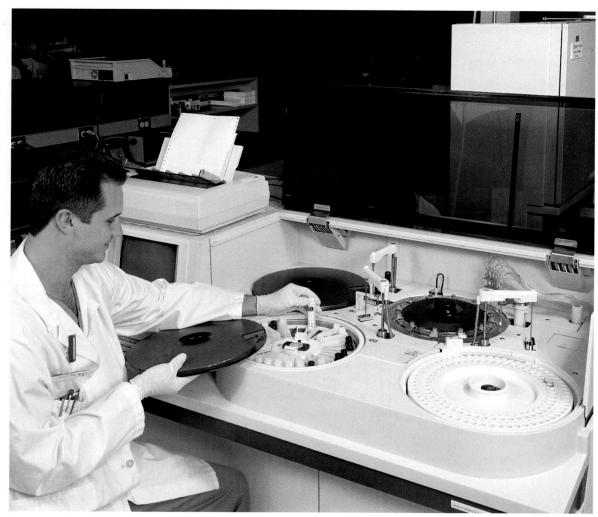

provides a vast pool of expertise, facilities, and resources upon which CPL can call to provide accurate and timely test analysis. "We have a broad-based group of pathologists in just about every specialty you can imagine," says Connor. "We are available around the clock to answer clients' questions, help them with difficult laboratory cases, or arrange additional services."

A Scientific Management Approach

Connor attributes CPL's growth to three things: providing the best laboratory services available, providing them at the lowest possible cost, and operating the laboratory like a business. "CPL combines the science of testing with business economics to deliver the highest-quality services possible at the lowest possible price," says Connor. CPL's ability to develop efficient services in each local market is founded on the principle of increasing volume while maintaining low overhead and channeling the savings to enhance services to clients.

CPL is unique in that it is managed as a traditional company rather than as part of a group practice. A physician-CEO leads the executive management team of business, financial, and technical personnel with industry-specific knowledge. CPL's board of directors is composed of six pathologists with more than 80 years of combined experience in the operation of inpatient, outpatient, and reference laboratory facilities.

CPL is approved by governmental agencies such as the Department of Health and Human Services, is CLIA (Clinical Laboratory Improvement Act) certified, and is accredited by the College of American Pathologists. The company is active in many local and national professional and charitable organizations, including the Rheumatology Foundation, American Cancer Society, American Heart Association, St. David's Foundation, Seton Fund, and the Travis County Medical Society's HealthFest. CPL also provides expertise and support to the People's Community Clinic, and many employees volunteer for a

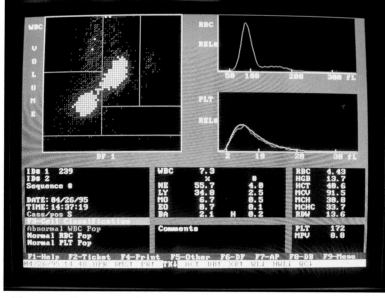

wide range of causes on their own time.

"Our connection to Austin extends well beyond our service in the medical community," says Connor. "Having been here for more than 50 years, we've really grown with the city. We are very proud of our Austin history and of our continued success as a locally owned business. We plan to be here for a long time to come."

SITUATED ON A BEAUTIFUL 428-ACRE CAMPUS OVER-looking Lake Austin, surrounded by trees, fields, and spectacular views of the Hill Country, St. Stephen's Episcopal School is much more than a college preparatory school—it's a home away from home.

St. Stephen's is a coeducational boarding and day school for students in grades six through 12. Founded by Bishop John E. Hines, the school has seen dynamic changes and growth in its 50-year history. Remaining faithful to the promise of its founding headmaster, Reverend William Brewster, St. Stephen's is dedicated to education that concerns the whole person—mind, body, and spirit. The school upholds this philosophy through rigorous academic preparation and stimulating physical activities, and by instilling moral virtues within a caring, diverse Christian community that values the potential and the dignity of every student.

Parents and students choose St. Stephen's not only for the school's outstanding faculty; small, discussion-based classes; rigorous curriculum; and high expectations, but also for the programs beyond the standard four-year academic course. Exciting options include a student ex-change program in Japan; summer courses in Spain, Greece, Turkey, and Italy; a dance/theater program in Ireland; or a climbing expedition in Ecuador.

A Full-Time Experience

Unlike any other school in Austin, St. Stephen's maintains a focus on boarding, with approximately 40 percent of students in full-time residence. Students come from all over the world to experience the ethnic, religious, and economic diversity that is the school's unique learning environment. "We spend a lot of time focusing on what we have in common, rather than on our differences," says Headmaster A. Frederick Weissbach. "We create a harmonious community while embracing an incredible amount of diversity in all its many forms." More than 50 teachers and their families also live on campus.

The school's close-knit community envelops both boarding and day students, and activity at St. Stephen's doesn't cease when the last class ends. "We are truly an around-the-clock community," says Weissbach. Faculty and students regularly dine together, and a full slate of activities—from student publications and drama to music and wilderness programs—keeps everyone busy during the week and on weekends.

Physical education and athletics are also considered an integral part of the educational process at St. Stephen's. The school provides a full range of traditional varsity sports, as well as alternative activities such as caving, dance, mountain biking, and rock climbing. St. Stephen's also offers intensive, year-round tennis and soccer programs for those athletes who hope to further their sports careers at the collegiate level. Additional information on programs at St. Stephen's can be found on the school's Web site, www.sss.austin.tx.us.

Importance of the Spirit

As a church school, St. Stephen's challenges its students—through daily chapel and required theology courses—to bring their own life experience to the task of thinking about the spiritual side of human existence. "Matters of the spirit are important to us," says Weissbach. "We engage each other on moral values; teach respect, dignity, and compassion; and differentiate right from wrong and how to act accordingly."

Educating the whole person is a philosophy that has worked extremely well for St. Stephen's and its students, 100 percent of whom pursue higher education. Alumni credit their years at the school for providing unforgettable experiences pivotal in shaping exciting futures and opportunities still to come.

St. Stephen's Episcopal School is a coeducational boarding and day school for students in grades six through 12 that provides rigorous academic preparation and challenging athletic activities, while seeking to instill moral virtues within a caring, diverse Christian community. (Photo by Christopher Caselli)

OR 50 YEARS, THE ARCHITECTS AND ENGINEERS AT O'Connell Robertson & Associates, Inc. have developed the blueprint for success. ★ Over the course of its history, the firm has completed nearly 1,000 projects ranging from small residential additions to multi-

GENO ESPONDA

GREG HURSLEY

million-dollar university and medical complexes. O'Connell Robertson's project experience represents diverse fields, including health care, education, finance, industrial, government, commercial, and residential work. With projects in Austin and across the state of Texas, its clients include the Austin Independent School District, Metroplex Healthcare System in Killeen, Veterans Administration in Temple, University of Texas at Austin, Georgetown Healthcare System, Georgetown Independent School District, Seguin Independent School District, and General Services Commission.

The firm was founded in 1950 by Bill O'Connell, the first architect employed by the Texas Department of Health, and his partner, Victor Probst. O'Connell's strong background in health care led to an emphasis on hospital design for 25 years. In 1989, the firm changed its name to O'Connell Robertson & Associates, Inc. Since then, the company has grown consistently, diversifying its client base while also strengthening its foundation in health care and education.

A FULL-SERVICE FIRM

O'Connell Robertson provides a full-service approach to the planning and development of its projects, offering extensive architectural planning experience in conjunction with engineering expertise. With the in-house capabilities to handle all aspects of a project, the firm's services include programming/master planning, architectural design, engineering (including mechanical, electrical, plumbing, fire protection, life safety, and communications design), construction management, and energy conservation and management. A new interior design department further enhances the

firm's ability to see a project through from conception to completion.

As an architecture and engineering firm, O'Connell Robertson takes a careful process approach to developing effective, efficient facilities. "We worry less about the latest design trends and more about developing creative solutions to meet specific needs," says President Noel Robertson. "We don't build for ourselves, we build for our clients."

With a staff of more than 45 professionals, O'Connell Robertson is large enough to complete the most challenging projects while giving clients the attention and dedication their projects demand. "We look at each job as a long-term relationship, not just as a project," says Robertson.

O'Connell Robertson takes its client commitment an extra step by contributing time and expertise to help clients further their own goals. A strong proponent of school-to-career initiatives, the firm works closely with education clients to develop innovative job shadowing programs, work site visits, and internships. The company is also actively involved in a variety of professional and community organizations, including the

ROBERT PANDYA

American Institute of Architects (AIA); American Society of Heating, Refrigerating and Air-Conditioning Engineers (ASHRAE); Texas Hospital Association; Texas Association of School Business Officials; Greater Austin Chamber of Commerce; Austin Partners in Education; Hispanic Chamber of Commerce; and United Way.

In addition, employees enjoy the unique experience of internal programs such as ORA University, a monthly meeting featuring a wide range of personal and professional development topics. Such ongoing communication and development helps the progressive, professional staff of O'Connell Robertson draw from 50 years of experience while building for the future.

PRINCIPALS OF O'CONNELL ROBERTSON & ASSOCIATES, INC. INCLUDE (STANDING, FROM LEFT) RICHARD J. BURNIGHT, AIA, VICE PRESIDENT; WILLIAM L. ADAIR, PE, VICE PRESIDENT; (SEATED, FROM LEFT) NOEL G. ROBERTSON, PRESIDENT; AND JERRY R. HAMMERLUN, CSI, VICE PRESIDENT.

O'CONNELL ROBERTSON PROVIDED ARCHITECTURE AND ENGINEERING SERVICES FOR THE STUDENT CENTER AT THE AUSTIN PRESBYTERIAN THEOLOGICAL SEMINARY (TOP RIGHT), AND THE UNIVERSITY OF TEXAS AT AUSTIN MONCRIEF-NEUHAUS COMPLEX (BOTTOM).

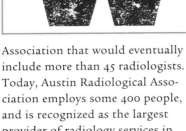

WHEN RADIOLOGIST DR. ROBERT SNIDER BEGAN practicing medicine in Austin in 1954, he had no idea that the overtures he would make into the medical field would result in a medical practice operating under the name of Austin Radiological

Association that would eventually include more than 45 radiologists. Today, Austin Radiological Association employs some 400 people, and is recognized as the largest provider of radiology services in Central Texas.

Radiologists are medical doctors who have completed an undergraduate degree, four years of medical school, and four years of a radiology residency program. Additionally, many radiologists also complete a one- to two-year fellowship, where they receive training and qualifications to conduct very specialized imaging tests and procedures. These medical imaging tests are crucial in assisting other physicians, such as primary care physicians, internists, pediatricians, and gastroenterologists, in the diagnosis of diseases and other medical conditions.

PAST AND PRESENT

In addition to the work he was doing in 1956 with the Austin hospitals, Snider was instrumental in opening an outpatient X-ray clinic on Rio Grande Avenue. These modest beginnings, coupled with a merger with Radi-

ology Consultants in 1996, set the stage for the arena in which Austin Radiological Association now operates, providing radiologist interpretation services at eight hospitals in Austin and surrounding areas, and operating 13 outpatient clinics in a geographical area that reaches from Round Rock, 15 miles north of Austin, to the community of San Marcos, 35 miles south of Austin. The comprehensive medical imaging services provided by Austin Radiological Association include routine X rays, such as chest and spine X rays;

fluoroscopy, such as upper GI series; small bowel studies; mammography and stereotactic breast biopsies; sonography; nuclear medicine; computerized axial tomography (CAT scans); magnetic resonance imaging (MRI); bone densitometry exams; and outpatient myelograms.

RELATIONSHIPS CRUCIAL IN GROWTH

Austin Radiological Association was built on service relationships, and today, these relationships extend to working with approximately 2,500 referring physicians serving more than 100,000 patients per year, and participating in more than 30 managed care plans. According to Snider, "Austin Radiological Association grew with Austin, and grew with the increasing number of physicians who came to the city." Regarding the many changes in health care today, Snider comments that an integral part of Austin Radiological Association in the early days was the provision of good service to doctors and patients. The company's commitment to good service is still evident, with special teams employed to ensure that exceptional customer service is in place and that continu-

PRESIDENT LARRY HILL, M.D. HAS GUIDED AUSTIN RADIOLOGICAL ASSOCIATION FOR 15 YEARS, EMPHASIZING ACCESS TO SERVICE AND BUILDING RELATIONSHIPS WITH PHYSICIANS.

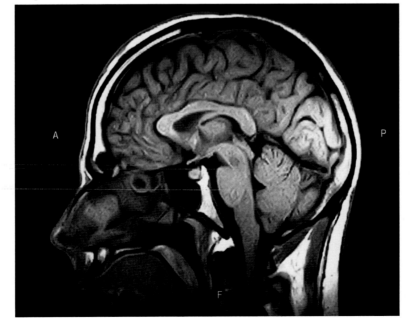

THE TYPE OF MEDICAL IMAGING TESTS PERFORMED AT AUSTIN RADIOLOGICAL ARE CRUCIAL IN ASSISTING OTHER PHYSICIANS, SUCH AS PRIMARY CARE PHYSICIANS, INTERNISTS, PEDIATRICIANS, AND GASTROENTEROLOGISTS, IN THE DIAGNOSIS OF DISEASES AND OTHER MEDICAL CONDITIONS.

ous quality improvement is a priority of the organization.

EXPANSION OF SERVICES

Over the last 15 years, radiologist Dr. Larry Hill has guided the organization in his role as president. Under his leadership, the radiologists of Austin Radiological Association have focused on expanding services through multiple locations and in participating in agreements with a large number of insurance and managed care providers.

Hill attributes the growth and success of Austin Radiological Association, in part, to convenient access for patients. The 13 outpatient facilities operated by Austin Radiological Association are situated within close distance to physicians' offices and hospitals. Of these 13 locations, there are two facilities, the Women's Imaging Center and the Austin Breast Screening House, that offer mammography and other related services specifically for women. Mammography is also provided at eight other outpatient locations in Austin, Round Rock, and San Marcos. Additionally, there are two facilities, located at the Medical Park Tower next to Seton Medical Center and at West Avenue Imaging, that cater specifically to those patients needing CT scans and MRI exams. CT and MRI scans are also offered at various other Austin Radiological Association outpatient locations.

NEW INITIATIVES

In June 1998, John Relic came on board as the CEO to guide the day-to-day operations of this growing organization. Some of the initiatives that he has implemented are the installation of an open MRI unit to address the needs of the claustrophobic or obese patient; renovating a general radiology outpatient clinic to a main pediatric facility; developing special focus teams to ensure customer service; and involving key management and physicians in a long-range planning process. Relic is an advocate of true quality improvement. Says Relic, "We may not win any awards for continuously improving our quality and maintaining it at a high level. I don't know that there are any. But we will know quality is there and, more important, our patients and physicians will know it is there."

Under Relic's administration, Austin Radiological Association is developing a strategic plan to ensure that this 45-year-old, stable, growth-oriented organization will further expand its relationships and services to serve the people of Austin and surrounding areas far into the 21st century.

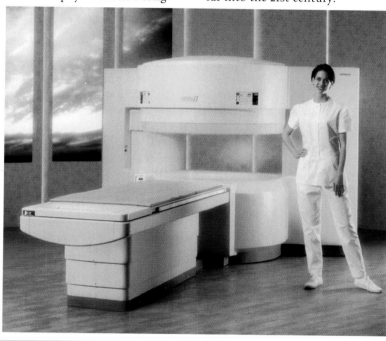

THE GROUP HAS ONE OF THE NEWEST AND MOST ADVANCED OPEN MAGNETIC RESONANCE IMAGING SYSTEMS IN AUSTIN.

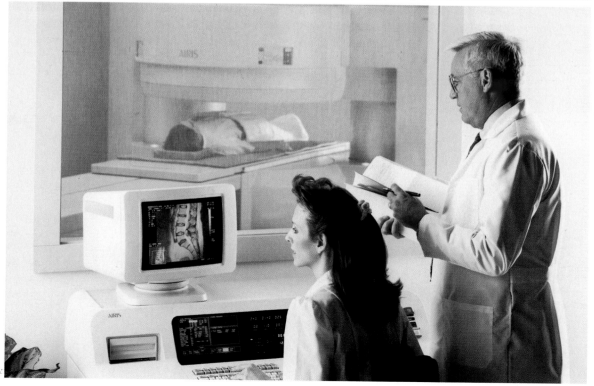

THE OPEN MAGNETIC RESONANCE IMAGING SYSTEM USED BY AUSTIN RADIOLOGICAL ASSOCIATION PROVIDES HIGH-QUALITY IMAGING AND IS OFTEN USED FOR CLAUSTROPHOBIC OR LARGE-BONED PATIENTS.

BROWN DISTRIBUTING CO.

IKE COLD BEER AND SPICY BARBECUE, LONGTIME partners Brown Distributing Co. and Anheuser-Busch make a great match. President J. Dan Brown founded the company that bears his name in 1962 at age 27, and ever since then, Brown Distributing has been the exclusive

CLOCKWISE FROM LEFT: IN 1998, BROWN DISTRIBUTING HAD A 50 PERCENT MARKET SHARE IN AUSTIN AND SOLD 7.2 MILLION CASES OF BEER.

PRESIDENT J. DAN BROWN FOUNDED BROWN DISTRIBUTING IN 1962, AND LAURIE BROWN WATSON SERVES AS VICE PRESIDENT OF THE COMPANY, WHICH IS THE EXCLUSIVE ANHEUSER-BUSCH DISTRIBUTOR IN AUSTIN.

THE COMPANY'S NEW HEADQUARTERS, WHICH WILL FEATURE CORPORATE OFFICES, A 75,000-SQUARE-FOOT, CLIMATE-CONTROLLED WAREHOUSE, AND AMPLE SPACE FOR THE BROWN FLEET OF MORE THAN 250 VEHICLES.

Anheuser-Busch distributing company in Austin.

Brown Distributing sold only three brands of beer in the beginning, but today sells 28 brands of beer and has a 50 percent market share. "A large part of the reason we've been so successful is because we've maintained our exclusive relationship with Anheuser-Busch," says Brown. "Both businesses are also family managed. There's a certain pride in a family business you can't compare to any other. We carry on the legacy and tradition of quality and service established by Anheuser-Busch."

SERVICE WITH A SMILE

When Brown opened his distributorship, he sold beer to licensed retailers, delivering the kegs and packages himself with

the help of four employees. Today, with more than 300 employees, Brown still stresses the personal touch that prevails at all levels of the business. "We treat the customer who buys two cases a week as well as we treat the one who buys 200," says Laurie Brown Watson, vice president.

In 1998, Brown Distributing sold 7.2 million cases of beer for approximately $94 million in gross sales. The company is scheduled to move into a new, 236,000-square-foot headquarters, located on 30 acres off Highway 290 East. In addition to expanded corporate offices, the new building will feature a 75,000-square-foot, climate-controlled warehouse and ample space for the Brown fleet of more than 250 vehicles, including delivery trucks, 18-wheelers, delivery vehicles, automobiles, and pickups.

GIVING BACK TO THE COMMUNITY

Brown Distributing has a high profile in local community programs, annually donating more than half a million dollars to charitable, civic, and educational organizations, including Children's Hospital of Austin, Greater East Austin Youth Leagues, and Huston-Tillotson

Scholarship Fund. Each year, the company helps to sponsor more than 450 special events in Austin, such as the Austin Travis Country Livestock Show and Rodeo, Bob Marley Festival, and Pecan Street Festival, as well as cultural events celebrating Cinco de Mayo, Diez y Seis, Juneteenth, and Black History Month. The company is a strong supporter of KLRU-TV, *Austin City Limits*, the University of Texas and Southwest Texas State University athletics programs, and is an active promoter of Anheuser-Busch's consumer awareness and educational program, Know When to Say When.

Brown Distributing instills in its employees a pride in both the company and the product. "Everyone here lives and breathes Budweiser and Bud Light," says Watson. Goal-setting programs create an environment that fosters both productivity and teamwork. One recent program set an unprecedented sales goal in one month. Not only did the energetic Brown team meet the goal, they exceeded it. "We stress working hard, but having fun at the same time," says Watson. "Even though we've grown so much, there is still a family atmosphere at Brown Distributing."

366

IN 1968, PASTOR KENNETH PHILLIPS AND HIS WIFE, WANDA, FOUNDED a small church on Avenue D with just 65 members. In 1971, they dedicated the sanctuary at 1504 East 51st Street, and the World of Pentecost was born. Today, the 26-acre site is home to the new PromiseLand auditorium, an educational building, the PromiseLand theater, a bookstore, a softball/soccer field, and the Central Austin Events Centre (known as Home Court).

Located just five minutes from the state capitol, the PromiseLand and its diverse membership represent the heart of Austin. "Our congregation is multicultural, multiracial, multitalented, and multistatus," says Phillips. "Everyone is welcome."

The congregation's jubilant and unconventional style of worship is just one reason so many people attend. "We provide an 'un-church,' with a fresh, joyful approach," says Phillips. "We want people to know that God is not an angry old man, but his arms are outstretched and waiting to receive everyone who will come."

Each Sunday and Wednesday, the PromiseLand holds celebration services featuring a full band and a 150-member choir in a 2,200-seat sanctuary with Jumbotron video screens and state-of-the-art sound and lighting. The church's Easter pageant, Jesus the Miracle, has become an internationally renowned event with more than 10,000 people in attendance each year. Pastor Randy Phillips—son of Kenneth Phillips and a member of gospel music's award-winning Phillips, Craig & Dean—describes the ministry as energetic, dramatic, and emotional. "No one sleeps in our church, that's for certain," he explains.

REACHING INTO THE COMMUNITY

The PromiseLand is a strong asset for the entire metro Austin community. Special outreach programs include youth camps, a ministry for the homeless, a prison ministry, and a television ministry. The auditorium, theater, and education building are fre-

quently used by community groups or other religious congregations. And the Home Court activity center, complete with a game room, basketball and handball courts, pool tables, an exercise room, classrooms, and conference rooms, is often used by groups such as the Travis County Sheriff's Office, the Austin Police Department, the DARE program, University of Texas basketball camps, and Austin's Banks Festival.

The PromiseLand also places a strong emphasis on supporting its own congregation through education and activities. The Sunday night Xit program, a refuge for Generation Xers, features live music, comedy, and creative communication, while an active singles group hosts regular Bible studies and a variety of social activities. Every Friday and Wednesday night, the church also hosts a special Youth World service followed by fun activities and socializing. "We offer a safe place for kids to come and enjoy themselves where they'll hear something spiritual

PASTOR KENNETH PHILLIPS (SEATED), FOUNDER OF THE WORLD OF PENTECOST, AND HIS SON, PASTOR RANDY PHILLIPS

and practical as well," says Randy Phillips.

The PromiseLand is Austin's only church with a father/son pastoring team. Kenneth Phillips, who has preached at conferences and crusades worldwide, says that the most rewarding aspect of his job is the challenge of it all: "We've baptized more than 17,000 people, and to see the great change and the improvement in lives is a wonderful thing. Over the years, we have tried to improve everything we've touched, and I believe we have."

THE WORLD OF PENTECOST IS HOME TO THE PROMISELAND AUDITORIUM, AN EDUCATIONAL BUILDING, THE PROMISELAND THEATER, A BOOKSTORE, A SOFTBALL/SOCCER FIELD, AND THE CENTRAL AUSTIN EVENTS CENTRE.

FAULKNER CONSTRUCTION COMPANY

OOKING AROUND AUSTIN, ONE WOULD HAVE DIFFICULTY finding an area where Faulkner Construction Company has not made its mark. Based in Austin, with branch locations in San Antonio, the Rio Grande Valley, and Mexico City, Faulkner Construction Company provides

general contracting, design/build, and construction management services to a broad spectrum of institutional, educational, commercial, and industrial clients. Founded in 1962, the company primarily serves the Southwest construction market, although it has managed many projects in major cities elsewhere.

During its 38 years in business, Faulkner has served as construction manager, design/builder, or general contractor on many high-profile and challenging projects. As Austin industry has evolved, Faulkner has been deeply involved in the advanced technology fields of semiconductor manufacturing, pharmaceuticals, and health care. While building its expertise in these areas, the company has also maintained its edge in the arena of conventional construction and continues to be a leading builder of office buildings, school and university projects, hospitals, airports, assisted-living centers, general manufacturing facilities, and retail developments.

Faulkner is the oldest of seven corporations comprising The Faulkner Group of Companies, which collectively provide jobs for more than 2,500 people in Central Texas. The 550-employee Faulkner Construction is one of the Southwest's most successful construction enterprises and is the only Austin company to be consistently listed in *Engineering News Record* magazine's Top 400 U.S. Contractors and Top 50 General Building Contractors.

MEETING THE CLIENTS' NEEDS

Understanding that the client's investment and Faulkner's own good name and reputation are at the forefront of every project, the company applies sound business and project control standards to each job, particularly with respect to quality and safety. The firm has won numerous awards from both the Austin and the Texas building branches of the Associated General

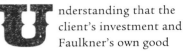

FOUNDED IN 1962, FAULKNER CONSTRUCTION COMPANY HAS SERVED AS CONSTRUCTION MANAGER, DESIGN/BUILDER, OR GENERAL CONTRACTOR ON MANY HIGH-PROFILE AND CHALLENGING PROJECTS. THE SCOPE OF FAULKNER'S WORK RANGES FROM MIDSIZE OFFICE BUILDINGS TO MAJOR BUILDINGS AND CAMPUSES FOR MANY OF THE COMMERCIAL, GOVERNMENTAL, AND WELL-ESTABLISHED MANUFACTURING ENTITIES IN AUSTIN. RECENT PROJECTS INCLUDE RIVERBEND CHURCH (TOP) AND CLEAN ROOM MANUFACTURING AND CORPORATE OFFICES FOR APPLIED MATERIALS (BOTTOM).

Contractors of America. Faulkner prides itself on the level of technology and diversity it has brought to the institution of construction. The company is clearly on the leading edge with respect to communications and project management systems.

Faulkner works with its clients every step of the way, from conceptualization to completion. The company carefully selects a qualified, skilled team to meet the specific needs of the client, drawing from its long-standing relationships with established design professionals, subcontractors, suppliers, and consultants across Texas and the Southwest.

"We really develop long-term relationships with everyone we work with," says Chief Executive Officer Steve Nelson. "Our customers become our friends." As validation, the company's client list contains more than 65 percent repeat customers.

The scope of Faulkner's work ranges from the midsize office buildings completed early in the company's history to major buildings and campuses for many of the commercial, governmental, and well-established manufacturing entities in Austin. Faulkner entered the high-tech arena in the 1970s and 1980s with work for Advanced Micro Devices, Motorola, and Sematech. Recent high-tech projects include clean room manufacturing and corporate offices for Applied Materials, Samsung, Motorola, Cypress Semiconductor, and Apple Computer.

As impressive as Faulkner's high-tech portfolio is its expertise in other commercial construction areas, schools, churches, and health care facilities. Among its recently completed local projects are the Plaza 7000 office building at MoPac and Far West boulevards; the Village at Westlake shopping center; Mills and Hart elementary schools; new high schools for Austin, Leander, and Del Valle Independent School Districts; and Riverbend Church.

The company's health care business has also grown steadily over the years, both in Austin and beyond. Seton Northwest Hospital and the Heart Hospital of Austin are Faulkner projects, as are the Arkansas Heart Hospital in Little Rock, McAllen Heart Hospital, Edinburg Regional Medical Center, the South Texas Cancer Center at Brownsville, and, more recently, SETON Southwest Healthcare Center.

THE FAULKNER TRADITION

Faulkner's longevity and success are due in large part to its leadership and loyal employee base. While Royce W. Faulkner, chairman of the board and founder, leads the way in number of years with the company, several employees have been with Faulkner Construction for 20 to 25 years. The Faulkner management team collectively boasts hundreds of years of experience in construction, business, law, estimating, value engineering, project management and scheduling, team building, and staffing.

The people of the Faulkner Group of Companies are individuals for whom participation in local and community affairs is the norm. Faulkner officers and employees are or have been members and officeholders on City of Austin boards and commissions, Austin Community College Board, State of Texas Workers Compensation Commission, civic organizations, Chamber of Commerce committees, special community task forces, and diverse church, civic, and property owners organizations. Staff members also contribute time and energy to local schools through the Junior Achievement program.

Creating deep ties in Austin, both in the construction industry and in the community, Faulkner Construction continues to build on its tradition of quality, with big plans for its next 38 years.

VAN REDIN

VAN REDIN

AMONG FAULKNER CONSTRUCTION COMPANY'S RECENTLY COMPLETED LOCAL PROJECTS ARE THE PLAZA 7000 OFFICE BUILDING AT MOPAC AND FAR WEST BOULEVARDS; THE VILLAGE AT WESTLAKE SHOPPING CENTER; MILLS ELEMENTARY SCHOOL (TOP); SETON NORTHWEST HOSPITAL AND THE HEART HOSPITAL OF AUSTIN; AND WESTECH 360 OFFICE PARK (BOTTOM).

RESERVING MEMORIES BY THE MILLIONS, COMMEMORATIVE Brands, Inc. creates jewelry and other products to help people celebrate and record such special events as graduations, the birth of a new baby, and even winning the World Series. ★ One of the largest manufacturers of

COMMEMORATIVE BRANDS, INC. CREATES JEWELRY AND OTHER PRODUCTS TO HELP PEOPLE CELEBRATE AND RECORD SUCH SPECIAL EVENTS AS GRADUATIONS, THE BIRTH OF A NEW BABY, OR EVEN PLAYING IN THE SUPER BOWL.

class rings in the United States, Commemorative Brands also creates special occasion jewelry and graduation-related fine paper products and accessories. The company markets and distributes its class rings at retail to independent and chain jewelers under the names ArtCarved® and R. Johns® and to mass merchants under the names Keystone®, Class Rings, Ltd.®, and Master Class Rings®. It markets in high schools under the Balfour® name, and on college campuses under the ArtCarved® and Balfour® names.

LASTING TRADITIONS

The majority of the company's class ring sales are to high school students, who can choose gold or white metal rings featuring a choice of more than 50 different stones, more than 400 different designs, and emblems of more than 100 activities or sports. Depending on student preferences, personalized rings can range in cost anywhere from $75 to more than $500. "Between our different product lines, we probably make more custom rings than almost any other com-

pany in the world," says Charlyn Cook, senior vice president, operations. "And because of the choices in customization, each ring is different from every other."

Commemorative Brands, under its various product lines, is the exclusive class ring supplier to many colleges and universities, including Notre Dame and Baylor University. Under the Keepsake® name, the company is the exclusive supplier of the official University of Texas ring. And across the globe, Aggies can recognize the official ring of their alma mater, supplied exclusively to Texas A&M University by Balfour®. In fact, traditions associated with the Aggie ring are so strong that the buy rate is more than 100 percent, according to Cook, since some customers lose them, but always replace them.

College class rings are often larger and have a more complex design than high school rings, but both are designed and produced in the same factory. For every ring manufactured, an individual wax casting from a mold is developed according to the features specified by the customer. "We use a lost-wax casting method that dates back to the Byzantine era," says Cook.

Under the Balfour® and Keepsake® names, the company manufactures and markets licensed consumer sports jewelry for fans and members of professional, amateur, and collegiate teams. It

has created championship rings for participants in the Olympic Games, as well as for winners of the World Series and the Super Bowl. From national championships in all major sporting events to minor-league championships, Commemorative Brands makes jewelry not only for football, basketball, baseball, and hockey teams, but also for such events as golf, horseback riding, figure skating, bowling, and auto racing.

To celebrate special life events like births and baptisms, and other family celebrations like Mother's Day and Valentine's Day, Commemorative Brands makes personalized family jewelry under its Celebrations of Life®, Generations of Love®, and Namesake® lines. Another product category is corporate recognition and reward jewelry, including rings, pins, and other items designed to commemorate employees' accomplishments or anniversaries.

The company prides itself on the quality of its products, caliber of its sales force, customer service, and comprehensive distribution network. "We set the industry standard for the fast delivery of a custom product," says Cook, noting that customized class rings are produced and shipped within several weeks.

A LOCAL GEM

While the company's presence in Austin began in 1968, Commemorative Brands, Inc. is a relatively young entity—the result of mergers and acquisitions of many key players in the class ring business. The ArtCarved brand name has been associated with numerous technical and marketing innovations during its more than 50 years in the jewelry industry, and has been used for class rings since 1976. Since the inception of the retail

sales channel in 1963, ArtCarved and its predecessor have been the leading supplier of high school rings in the in-store market, as well as a leading supplier of college class rings.

Balfour began as an insignia jewelry manufacturer in 1913 and entered the class ring industry in 1922, eventually becoming a significant producer of class rings, service awards, and recognition products. In 1996, Castle Harlan Partners II, L.P., a Delaware limited partnership and private equity investment fund based in New York, acquired ArtCarved from CJC Hold-

ings and Balfour from Town and Country to form Commemorative Brands, Inc.

With its corporate headquarters tucked away just off I-35 in South Austin, the company is not easily noticed by passersby. However, Commemorative Brands is one of the largest employers in the city, with 1,350 employees. "We recruit the majority of our employees from Austin and the surrounding area," says Cook. "Over 100 folks have worked here for more than 20 of our 30 years in Austin. Experience like that is hard to beat."

OR 40 YEARS, COMPUTER SCIENCES CORPORATION (CSC) has helped clients around the world use information technology to achieve their business objectives. Based in El Segundo, California, CSC provides management and information technology consulting, systems integra-

tion, application software, operations support, and information services outsourcing to government and commercial clients. Today, CSC is a $7.7 billion company with 50,000 employees and 700 locations in more than 60 countries. The company is ranked among the top information technology and services providers worldwide.

CSC's Financial Services Group, headquartered in Austin, is the focal point for delivery of the full range of CSC's capabilities to the worldwide financial services industry. This global organization was created in 1997, following CSC's acquisition of the Austin-based Continuum Company and its Hogan Systems unit, leading providers of software, consulting, and services to the insurance, banking, and financial services industries. In forming the Financial Services Group, CSC integrated Continuum and Hogan with its existing financial services skill sets and customer base.

PETE BOYKIN, PRESIDENT, COMPUTER SCIENCES CORPORATION (CSC), FINANCIAL SERVICES GROUP

"CSC's approach is unique in that we provide specialized financial services knowledge and offerings, coupled with a broad set of end-to-end service capabilities, through a single business unit," says Pete Boykin, president of CSC's Financial Services Group. "We draw on the total capabilities of CSC and tailor a solution to meet each customer's particular requirements."

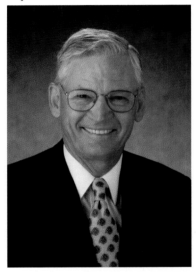

A GLOBAL FOCUS

hile it is headquartered in Austin, CSC's Financial Services Group has a global focus, with almost half of its business outside the Americas. Its customers include more than 1,000 banks, insurers, investment firms, consumer finance companies, and other major financial services organizations worldwide.

"To serve the increasingly global financial services market, we must have a strong global organization," says Boykin. "CSC is committed to delivering products that can be adapted to the needs of the various geographic markets. Our service approach combines the benefits of a large, worldwide infrastructure with local support and staff who understand regional requirements."

CSC's Financial Services Group has three major divisions covering the major financial services markets: the Americas Division, headquartered in Austin; the Europe, Middle

CSC'S FINANCIAL SERVICES GROUP HAS ITS HEADQUARTERS IN AUSTIN. THE GROUP ALSO HAS REGIONAL HEADQUARTERS IN CAMBERLEY, ENGLAND (EUROPE, MIDDLE EAST AND AFRICA DIVISION), AND SYDNEY, AUSTRALIA (ASIA-PACIFIC DIVISION).

East and Africa Division, head-quartered in Camberley, England; and the Asia-Pacific Division, headquartered in Sydney, Australia.

CREATING CUSTOM SOLUTIONS

CSC integrates strategy and technology to help customers succeed in the increasingly competitive financial services market. Rather than just providing a product to meet a single specific requirement, or performing a one-time systems integration project, CSC looks at the client's overall business objectives and works with the client to meet those goals.

"We emphasize total solutions," says Boykin. "That means providing the right combination of products, services, methodologies, and people to advance the client's strategies. Technology and business processes are so intertwined today that it is necessary to approach them in an integrated fashion if you are going to deliver significant business improvements.

"The financial services industry is undergoing a time of radical change," Boykin adds. "Industry sectors such as banking, insurance, and investments are converging; the industry is consolidating through mergers and acquisitions;

customers are becoming more sophisticated; and technology is changing the way business is conducted. Companies need a partner who can work with them to take advantage of the opportunities and surmount the challenges of this environment."

CSC helps its clients meet business goals such as managing customer relationships, improving profitability, bringing new products to market quickly, or expanding their distribution channels. "We focus on the things our customers want most, whether it's helping an insurance company reduce the cost of claims, or assisting banks in making better decisions on issuing credit," says Boykin. "We don't just create software—we develop entirely new business models based on our work with clients and industry best practices."

This strategy is a highly successful one, and the proof lies in the rapid growth of CSC's financial services business. The Austin office alone has grown to 1,500 employees, and worldwide CSC has approximately 10,000 people supporting its financial services clients. To meet the growing demand for services, the Financial Services Group has implemented several innovative training and recruitment programs, including

a program to help recent college graduates quickly learn CSC's business and products. This program also is designed to accommodate recruits from non-technical professions who want to pursue an information technology career.

CSC also partners with the communities in which it does business. In Austin, the Financial Services Group is the title sponsor of the CSC Spot Run 15K race and relay, which last year raised more than $20,000 for the Court Appointed Special Advocates (CASA) of Travis County. CSC also has participated in charitable events around the world, such as a charity run and a cycling event in Australia, and a rafting expedition along Scotland's River Tay.

Combining the strengths of a prosperous past with the opportunities of a bright future, CSC looks forward to continued successful partnerships with its customers and local communities. "We are extremely optimistic about our future," says Boykin. "The rapid change going on in the financial services industry provides a great opportunity for us. Austin provides an excellent environment for our headquarters and a tremendous pool of talent to help support our growth."

TRAMMELL CROW COMPANY

RAMMELL CROW COMPANY, THE NAME BEHIND MANY OF Austin's most noted real estate developments, has helped set new standards since coming to the capital city in 1968. With the area's largest portfolio of owned, leased, and managed property, the company today is a full-service real estate firm offering management, brokerage, development, construction, and retail services.

Founded in Dallas in 1948, Trammell Crow is one of the largest diversified commercial real estate service companies in the United States. Trammell Crow Central Texas, one of the corporation's eight regional divisions, handles operations in Austin, San Antonio, Corpus Christi, and South Texas.

An Austin Mainstay

rammell Crow's local work literally covers the map, from the downtown high-rise at 301 Congress Avenue, to the state-of-the-art office complexes of Research Park and Braker Center, to the multiuse developments of Expo Center and Southpark. The company is also known for its involvement in high-quality retail developments, such as Stassney Heights Shopping Center, the Village at Westlake, and Sunset Valley Village.

Trammell Crow developed the city's renowned Arboretum Complex, a multiuse property combining office and retail space with a luxury hotel. Each year, thousands of locals and visitors choose the Arboretum to shop or dine, stroll the tree-lined walkways, take in a movie, or enjoy free concerts under the stars.

Known in Austin and beyond for its high-quality development and attention to detail, Trammell Crow pursues environmental sensitivity in all of its development activities. Every project is designed with nature in mind, and aims to exceed city standards while maximizing water quality, maintaining existing trees, enhancing curb appeal, and minimizing impervious cover.

Locally Focused

he key component in Trammell Crow's business philosophy

and success, says Austin City Leader Stan Erwin, is helping enhance the communities it serves. Trammell Crow is as well known for community involvement as it is for real estate expertise. In fact, the company makes a substantial commitment to various local organizations, and its 135 Austin employees contribute time and energy to a number of causes important to them, as well as to their customers. Groups such as the American Cancer Society, Boy Scouts of America, Daughters of Charity, Jewish Federation of Austin, Big Brothers/Big Sisters of Austin, Seton, Junior Achievement, and Austin Jaycees benefit greatly from the generosity of Trammell Crow.

The company also works very closely with the Greater Austin Chamber of Commerce, reiterating its belief in making a positive impact at the local level.

"We work on projects we're proud of," explains Erwin. "We build the kind of shopping centers we would like to shop in and the kind of office buildings we want to work in. What we do helps to augment the quality of life that is the real reason we're all here."

TRAMMELL CROW COMPANY'S WORK IN AUSTIN LITERALLY COVERS THE MAP, FROM THE DOWNTOWN HIGH-RISE AT 301 CONGRESS AVENUE (TOP), TO THE STATE-OF-THE-ART OFFICE COMPLEXES OF RESEARCH PARK AND BRAKER CENTER, TO THE MULTIUSE DEVELOPMENTS OF EXPO CENTER (BOTTOM RIGHT) AND SOUTHPARK.

TRAMMELL CROW DEVELOPED THE CITY'S RENOWNED ARBORETUM COMPLEX, A MULTIUSE PROPERTY COMBINING OFFICE AND RETAIL SPACE WITH A LUXURY HOTEL (BOTTOM LEFT).

At Austin's BookPeople, the management and staff agree that there's nothing better than a good book. Unless, of course, you find it among the eclectic gifts, comfortable chairs, and cozy coffee shop that characterize the city's largest independent bookstore.

"Customers come in looking for one thing, and find so much more than they expected that they leave with something else," says CEO Stan Biderman, who, along with President Abe Zimmerman, is locally known as one of the Book Guys. Biderman goes on to say, "We're a number of stores within one."

Customers can find everything from best-sellers and cookbooks to hard-to-find texts on metaphysics and alternative health. BookPeople orders from 36,000 publishers, including all major publishing houses, as well as smaller independent and university presses. In addition to standard literary fare, the store offers titles in such sub-specialties as religious studies, psychology, Texana, children's literature, high technology, architecture, and local authors.

"We're the last large independent bookstore in Texas," says Zimmerman. "We're committed to the alternative, independent voice of the written word, and we want to serve as a resource for the entire region."

Beyond the thousands of books it stocks, BookPeople offers a selection of gifts from around the world. Buying Director and General Manager Tracey Tarlton and her staff scour the globe for unique nostalgia toys, one-of-a-kind art pieces, candles, cards, pens, handmade gift boxes, menorahs, wind chimes, jigsaw puzzles, meditation cushions, T-shirts, and jewelry crafted by countless artisans. Comfortable chairs and couches welcome browsing customers, and a coffee shop serves flavorful brews and pastries from local bakeries.

"People walk through the door and immediately see that they're in a different kind of bookstore," says Biderman. "We combine a comforting environment, an extremely knowledgeable and help-ful staff, and one of the deepest selections of subjects anywhere."

THREE DECADES OF SERVICE

BookPeople was founded as Grok Books by a group of University of Texas students in 1970. Originally located in an old house on West 17th Street, the store's goal was to provide the community an alternative selection of books with special emphasis on small press literature, Eastern/Western studies, and politics.

Grok had one full-time employee and stocked about 3,000 titles. By 1984, the store had outgrown its space, moved into the Brodie Oaks Shopping Center, and changed its name. The new name was taken from Ray Bradbury's *Fahrenheit 451*, in which the so-called book people preserved the written word by memorizing entire texts before the books were incinerated. In 1995, BookPeople made its move to become a world-class bookstore, moving to its location in the heart of Austin and expanding to more than 150,000 titles.

The store hosts book signings almost nightly, and hundreds of authors, ranging from Jimmy Carter and Walter Cronkite to Anne Rice and Deepak Chopra, draw crowds as diverse as their books. The store also welcomes dozens of local authors, and is an active participant in the Austin Writers' League and the Texas Book Festival.

"We are dedicated to our community, to local authors, and to the free word," says Biderman. "We're proud of being home-grown and we're proud of being eclectic. BookPeople genuinely reflects everything that makes Austin so dynamic."

◄ RAQUE KUNZ

◄► RAQUE KUNZ

CLOCKWISE FROM TOP: IN 1995, BOOKPEOPLE MADE ITS MOVE TO BECOME A WORLD-CLASS BOOKSTORE, MOVING TO ITS LOCATION IN THE HEART OF AUSTIN.

CUSTOMERS CAN FIND EVERYTHING FROM BEST-SELLERS AND COOKBOOKS TO HARD-TO-FIND TEXTS ON METAPHYSICS AND ALTERNATIVE HEALTH.

"CUSTOMERS COME IN LOOKING FOR ONE THING AND FIND SO MUCH MORE THAN THEY EXPECTED THAT THEY LEAVE WITH SOMETHING ELSE," SAYS CEO STAN BIDERMAN (RIGHT), WHO, ALONG WITH PRESIDENT ABE ZIMMERMAN, IS LOCALLY KNOWN AS ONE OF THE BOOK GUYS.

CAPITAL CITY CONTAINER LIKES A CHALLENGE. "THE SHAPE or size of a product makes no difference to us," says Managing Shareholder David Patten. "If you can make it and ship it, we can come up with a package for it." ★ Since 1969, more than 1,000 companies have made Capital City

Container their packaging supplier. Local Central Texas customers include Dell Computer Corporation, IBM, Motorola, Texwood Furniture Corporation, Serta Mattress, Kimberly-Clark, Lancer Corporation, Hart Graphics, Sony, and hundreds of others, ranging from small, family-owned businesses to major international corporations. "We pride ourselves on selling to the smallest company operating out of the family garage and to the largest Fortune 500 company," says Patten. "No customer is too small or too large for us."

FOUNDED IN 1969, CAPITAL CITY CONTAINER IS THE PACKAGING SUPPLIER FOR MORE THAN 1,000 COMPANIES.

QUALITY AND SERVICE

Capital City Container makes its high-quality industrial and retail packages from materials such as cushioned packaging, wood products, corrugated sheeting, and fiberboard. "We've made boxes to house everything from car engines to taxidermy mounts to computers to food products," says Managing

CAPITAL CITY CONTAINER USES THE BEST AND LATEST TECHNOLOGY AND EQUIPMENT AT ALL STAGES OF PRODUCTION.

Shareholder Duane Alford. The company primarily manufactures custom boxes, but also carries a wide variety of stock boxes in different shapes and sizes.

Capital City Container provides customers turnkey package design, development, certified testing, and manufacturing, as well as just-in-time delivery, a concept Patten pioneered in this market area. "When I entered the world of packaging sales, most container companies required that customers give them two weeks' notice to deliver an order," he says. "We were the first to warehouse boxes for our customers so that we had them on hand and ready to deliver whenever they needed them."

The company celebrates its 30th anniversary in 1999. "From the beginning, we've been very service oriented," says Patten. "When the company was founded, we were dealing in a world of

giants. We had to play the role of David with a slingshot and a stone, and we had to be very accurate."

Taking careful aim to provide the best product for its customers, Capital City Container uses the best and latest technology and equipment at all stages of production. An on-site development and engineering lab helps the company create the best package for each customer and each product, and state-of-the-art testing equipment employs the latest technology to ensure boxes are strong enough to meet not only Capital's own high standards, but also those of the ISO.

The company has kept pace with the ever changing Austin market by continually adding to its fleet of trucks, doubling the size of its design and test lab, and adding a four-color press that prints high-quality graphics directly on corrugated sheeting. Capital City Container helps customers build boxes that protect their product and also help sell it. "With direct printing techniques and the latest in four-color label laminating, we have the talent and technology

necessary to develop packages that cut through the clutter," says Patten. In fact, other box companies often call on Capital City Container to print their jobs for them.

Capital City Container has invested in serious research to develop cushioned packages that not only protect the customer's product, but are environmentally friendly as well. In addition to using recyclable materials in its production process, the company gathers, binds, and recycles all cardboard scraps left over after the printing and cutting process.

A Dedicated Employee Base

Approximately 125 people work at Capital City Containers, many of whom have been with the company for years. "We're like family around here," says Patten. "We always communicate about how we're doing as a company, and we share whatever we can, whether we're going through good times or tough times."

The Buda, Texas-based company also enjoys long-term relationships with many of its customers, the

majority of whom are within a 100-mile radius of Capital City. "In our industry, you really stay near the people you serve," Patten says. This philosophy of meeting the needs of local customers was one reason the company helped to found the original Buy Greater Austin Campaign. The company remains active at all levels of the community, and is a gold member of the Greater Austin Chamber of Commerce.

Patten attributes much of the company's growth to partnering with clients, many of whom have honored Capital City Container with quality and service awards. "We are blessed with wonderful customers and we appreciate our close relationships with them," he says.

Patten sees a future of steady growth for the company, based on both new business and repeat business from existing clients. "We provide good quality and old-fashioned service at a fair price," he says. "That's the philosophy that we started with, and it's still our top priority. And customers know that good things come in Capital City containers."

1971-1985 ★

1971 Armstrong Moving & Storage, Inc.

1971 GSD&M

1971 Roger Beasley Automotive Group

1971 State Farm Insurance Companies

1971 TECO-Westinghouse Motor Company

1972 Austin Community College

1972 Wayne

1975 Jeffrey's

1975 The County Line, Inc.

1976 National Instruments

1976 Surrey, Inc.

1976 The Progressive Corporation

1977 EDS/NHIC

1977 EEA (Energy Engineering Associates, Inc.)

1977 Personique

1979 AMD

1979 Riverbend Church

1981 Fisher-Rosemount Systems

1981 Sulzer Orthopedics Inc.

1982 Clear Channel Radio, Inc.

1982 PSI Technologies Corporation

1983 Americus Diamond

1983 ORIGIN Systems Inc.

1984 3M

1984 Dell Computer Corporation

1985 BMC Software

1985 IntelliQuest Information Group Inc.

1985 SAS Institute Inc.

1985 SicolaMartin

1985 VTEL Corporation

Armstrong Moving & Storage, Inc.

ARMSTRONG MOVING & STORAGE, INC. BRINGS MORE than a half century of care to every move it makes. As one of the leading business and residential moving organizations in the southwestern United States, Armstrong provides moving, storage, and relocation services for local, intrastate, interstate, and international moves. In addition to moving households, the company handles office and industrial relocations, special commodities transportation, air freight service, household goods storage, commercial warehousing and distribution, packing, and custom crating. Whether moving households, corporate offices, trade shows, or art exhibits, Armstrong provides the highest level of customer service.

ARMSTRONG MOVING & STORAGE, INC. MOVED ITS HEADQUARTERS TO AUSTIN IN 1991, AND NOW ALSO HAS OFFICES IN LUBBOCK, SAN ANTONIO, MIDLAND, AND EL PASO.

IN ADDITION TO MOVING HOUSEHOLDS, THE COMPANY HANDLES OFFICE AND INDUSTRIAL RELOCATIONS, SPECIAL COMMODITIES TRANSPORTATION, AIR FREIGHT SERVICE, HOUSEHOLD GOODS STORAGE, COMMERCIAL WAREHOUSING AND DISTRIBUTION, PACKING, AND CUSTOM CRATING.

Founded in Lubbock in 1946, Armstrong Moving & Storage is run by Richard Anderson, the son of founder Gene Anderson. The company moved its headquarters to Austin in 1991, and now also has offices in Lubbock, San Antonio, Midland, and El Paso. Armstrong is one of 120 shareholder agents that own United Van Lines, the largest moving organization in the world.

Full-Service Office and Home Relocations

While household moving comprises the majority of Armstrong's business, the company has built an excellent reputation for full-service office relocations. When moving the entire operation of an Austin business, Armstrong custom designs the relocation to keep interruptions of business operations to a minimum. Using a proven and tested planning process for relocations, including budget development, checklists, regular planning meetings, written guidelines for supervisors and employees, and on-site project coordination, Armstrong ensures that all of the details are understood and expectations are met.

Each of Armstrong's five facilities includes an expansive storage facility, and its just-in-time program takes the storage burden off manufacturing customers by holding components and delivering them as needed. Armstrong's extensive customer service department provides a single point of contact that monitors a move from beginning to end. A leader in information services, Armstrong uses computer tracking to provide status reports, and equips its trucks with satellite tracking and communication systems. The company can even provide comprehensive destination information on more than 7,000 cities, including reports on geography, climate, taxes, schools, transportation, and child care services.

Commitment to Quality

Armstrong's dedication to customer service is at the heart of every move, and satisfied customers consistently place the five Armstrong offices within United's highest ranks of quality service. In recognition of the Armstrong focus on quality, United established the Gene Anderson Excellence Award, presented annually to members of its worldwide team who demonstrate exceptional achievement.

The company's dedication to its customers begins with its own employees. A stringent pre-employment program helps find the most qualified employees, who then attend at least 200 hours of training and certification programs. As a result of investing in its own staff, Armstrong consistently wins awards of excellence in packing, cargo claims, safety, and agency superiority.

Armstrong finds that its most successful business development comes simply from word-of-mouth referrals. "We don't just move people—we build a relationship with them," says Richard Anderson. "Some customers have called us to move them five or six times. We want people to think of us wherever they are, and we'll be there for them."

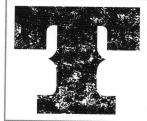

HE ORIGINAL SOURCE IN AUSTIN FOR FINGER-LICKING barbecue, The County Line is a local legend that has achieved international renown. Since opening its first restaurant in 1975, the company has continued to please people and palates from across the world. ★ The County

Line started out with a concept of sophisticated barbecue in a casual setting. The sophistication comes from buying the best pork and beef available, and then slow-smoking only the leanest cuts to the peak of tenderness.

Staying true to its Central Texas German heritage, The County Line serves beef and pork ribs, brisket, and sausage, as well as a full array of side dishes such as flavorful potato salad, coleslaw, and beans. Patrons can order country-style barbecue (all you can eat) for everyone at the table, or select individual entrées like barbecue plates, grilled fish, or steak. Homemade cobbler and ice cream always bring the feast to a sweet end.

AUSTIN AND BEYOND

 longtime favorite for locals and visitors alike, The County Line has found widespread acclaim with its restaurants in Austin, El Paso, Lubbock, Oklahoma City, Albuquerque, Denver, Houston, Corpus Christi, Colorado Springs, and San Antonio. Each location is filled with authentic roadhouse decor and the tantalizing aromas of the company's world-famous barbecue.

The original restaurant, known as County Line on the Hill, is housed in a historic rock building on Bee Caves Road. In addition to great food, the location offers a 20-mile view of the Texas Hill Country from a beautiful stone patio perched on one of the highest peaks in the area. The company's second Austin location, County Line on the Lake, opened in 1980 in an old lodge on FM 2222 and quickly established itself as the best place around to take out-of-town guests.

County Line is authentic local Austin cuisine—and barbecue is one of the few remaining regional

foods. Diners can find good Mexican cuisine all over the world, but to get real Texas barbecue, they have to stay pretty close to Texas.

To satiate the demand of its large number of fans who don't have easy access to a County Line restaurant, the company began its popular Air Ribs delivery service. True barbecue enthusiasts can cure their cravings by ordering next-day delivery of juicy ribs, sausage, sliced brisket, smoked turkey, the restaurant's famous private-label sauces, and much more.

A FOCUS ON SERVICE

he County Line aims to provide not only the best food around, but also the best service. For example, every employee goes through an in-depth training period that focuses heavily on customer service.

Fortunately for Austin, the company's commitment to service, combined with an atmosphere of camaraderie, extends throughout the organization. The County Line works with its 250 Austin employees to benefit local nonprofit orga-

nizations including SafePlace, KLRU, Paramount Theater, Boy Scouts of America, Big Brothers and Big Sisters, and Candlelighters. County Line employees enjoy getting to know people both in the restaurants and throughout the community.

Whether they come to savor a huge plate of mouthwatering ribs, enjoy a casual evening with friends and family, or take in the stunning local vistas, County Line patrons never go home unsatisfied.

THE COUNTY LINE SERVES SOPHISTICATED BARBECUE—THAT IS, BARBECUE PREPARED FROM THE BEST PORK AND BEEF AVAILABLE—IN A CASUAL SETTING.

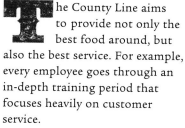

EACH COUNTY LINE LOCATION IS FILLED WITH AUTHENTIC ROADHOUSE DECOR AND THE TANTALIZING AROMAS OF THE COMPANY'S WORLD-FAMOUS BARBECUE.

GSD&M

**I**N 1971, SIX UNIVERSITY OF TEXAS GRADUATES STARTED AN ADVERTISing agency based on the premise that big ideas generate big results. Over the years, GSD&M has grown from a group of college kids with a big idea to a nationally acclaimed, full-service agency with 300 employees and billings that top $500 million a year.

"We learned a long time ago that we are not in the advertising business," says GSD&M Founder/President Roy M. Spence Jr. "We are in the idea business. We are in the business of building our clients' businesses and winning in the marketplace—that's the thrill of it all."

A SOLID FOUNDATION

SD&M has achieved a winning record by following a quest for visionary ideas and operating under a set of ideals the founders have always shared, but only recently defined. These core values—community, winning, restlessness,

freedom and responsibility, curiosity, and integrity—still drive the company today. "[These values] are grounded in our people and are even carved in stone at our offices," says Spence. "They affect the way we go to market for our clients and are crucial to understanding the kind of agency we are."

As GSD&M has endeavored to become a visionary company, it has learned the importance of forming strong partnerships with other companies whose leaders are committed to similar goals. "Visionary clients make it easier to develop visionary ideas," says Spence. "The right fit is important to us and to our clients. Mutual respect and

a passion for winning are what count most with us in building strong marketing relationships."

By building relationships with some of the most outstanding companies and industries in the United States, GSD&M has amassed a track record that speaks for itself. Longtime client Southwest Airlines is the country's most profitable major airline. GSD&M created a strategy based on core values that helped Wal-Mart become the world's largest retailer. The agency launched a campaign for Texas Tourism, which turned the Lone Star State into the number two vacation destination in the United States. Another client, the Texas Lottery, broke world records with first-day and first-week sales, and in 1995, became the number one lottery in the United States and number five in the world. GSD&M also helped the Texas Department of Transportation develop the Don't Mess with Texas campaign, the most successful litter-prevention effort in U.S. history.

Clients such as Pennzoil, Anheuser-Busch Theme Parks, Brinker International, the PGA Tour, Fannie Mae, Lennox Industries, and many others credit GSD&M's vision for similar success stories.

A VALUED TEAM

With almost 30 years of success under its belt, GSD&M knows that visionary, business-building ideas don't just happen. They develop out of a sound strategic process based on values marketing, which differs from other strategic planning processes that tend to be product-benefit-based.

"Values marketing goes beyond attributes to connect with the values people hold dear," says Spence. This theory is the base of

GSD&M IS LOCATED IN THE HEART OF AUSTIN. IDEA CITY, AS THE OFFICE SPACE IS CALLED, COMBINES THE COMMUNITY-BUILDING SENSE OF PUBLIC SPACE FOUND IN ANCIENT GREEK CITIES WITH THE CULTURAL IDENTITY CONCEPTS OF NEW YORK CITY'S GREENWICH VILLAGE AND LONDON'S SOHO.

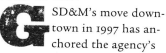

GSD&M's move downtown in 1997 has anchored the agency's longtime commitment to its vision and to its birthplace. In the heart of Austin on Sixth Street and Lamar Boulevard, Idea City, as the office space is called, embodies the concept of the city as a place for visionaries. The two-story fountainhead of creativity combines the community-building sense of public space found in ancient Greek cities with the cultural identity concepts of New York City's Greenwich Village and London's Soho.

"Idea City is a concrete demonstration of how intent we are on sustaining and nurturing our culture," say Spence. "When we began planning a new building, we realized it would need to reflect the natural flow not only of Austin, but also of our people and culture."

Building on its success, vision, and synergy with the city it calls home, GSD&M looks forward to a prosperous future. "We love Austin," says Spence. "It's often referred to as the 'idea capital,' with high-tech, music, and film industries that impact the nation. We love the energy of the city, the openness and excitement here. In all our years here, we've learned that where we live is as important as what we do."

GSD&M HAS ACHIEVED A WINNING RECORD BY FOLLOWING A QUEST FOR VISIONARY IDEAS, AND BY LEARNING THE IMPORTANCE OF FORMING STRONG PARTNERSHIPS WITH OTHER COMPANIES WHOSE LEADERS ARE COMMITTED TO SIMILAR GOALS.

GSD&M'S CORE VALUES—CARVED IN STONE AT IDEA CITY—DRIVE THE COMPANY.

Values Based Branding, GSD&M's proprietary process that helps the agency discover the strongest bond between an audience and a brand, then develop a strategic hinge to connect the two.

Not only does this process bring fast results for clients, but it also spreads ownership of winning ideas among people throughout the agency and its client organizations. The constant creative buzz fueling GSD&M's big ideas comes from its many talented and energetic employees, a self-described "curious and restless bunch." Working in such a fast-paced environment requires a common passion and vigor, and the result is something more akin to a family relationship than a typical business culture.

Giving back to each other as well as to the community is a privilege and a responsibility taken very seriously at GSD&M. "Investing in our community means more than just doing the right thing. It's a way of life," says Spence. "Our mission is to bring value to our community by touching people's lives in positive, meaningful ways." GSD&M focuses its contributions and support on programs, projects, and institutions dedicated to education, children, health, community development, and the environment.

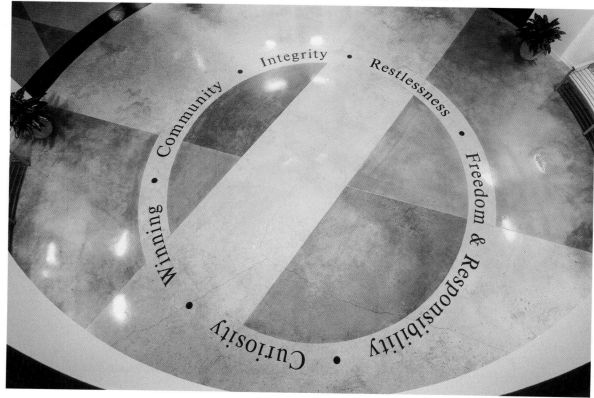

NE SIMPLE DOCTRINE—TAKE CARE OF THE CUSTOMER AND the business will take care of itself—is the driving force behind Austin's premier automobile dealerships. And it is a philosophy that Roger Beasley, president of the Roger Beasley Automotive Group, has instilled in his

employees through more than 30 years in the business. The customer-first approach has helped Beasley grow automobile dealerships from the ground up and turn faltering franchises into profit centers.

Today, the Roger Beasley Automotive Group operates nine franchised organizations in Greater Austin: three Mazda dealerships, two KIA dealerships, and individual Volvo, Porsche, Saab, and Suzuki franchises. Additionally, the homegrown company will soon open its newest stores, a Mazda/Volvo dealership in Georgetown and a Honda dealership in San Marcos.

A SIMPLE PHILOSOPHY

fter graduating from the University of Texas (UT), Beasley began his career in Austin as a mortgage banker. In the early 1970s, he decided to go into the automobile business. Unhappy with the treatment he had received from existing local dealerships, he knew what he wanted to do—and he knew how to do it.

Beasley's philosophy was simple and crystal clear: Sell cars at a fair price, back them up with the very best service, and do what you say

you are going to do. With this basic premise, Beasley founded what has become one of Austin's best-known and most successful businesses.

Starting out, Beasley established a Renault-Peugeot-Lotus-Jeep dealership on North Burnet Road. Soon thereafter, he was presented with the opportunity to open a franchise for Mazda, which was, at the time, the newest Japanese import in the U.S. market. Beasley had so much confidence in the new line of cars that he agreed to part with everything except his Jeep franchise to obtain the Mazda line. Looking back, he admits there were times when he

second-guessed his own decision. However, even when Mazda experienced problems with its early rotary engines, Beasley's customer service was never an issue. Local Mazda owners knew they could depend on the Austin dealership. Fortunately for everyone, the manufacturer began producing piston-driven engines, and Mazda quickly developed a reputation for engineering a product that the public wanted at a very reasonable price.

Beasley established that first successful dealership—still known as Roger Beasley Mazda—in North Austin in 1971. Since then, he has turned the business into one of the most successful Mazda franchises in the nation today. In March 1994, he bought Mazda South, an existing dealership in South Austin. With Beasley's good name and solid reputation behind it, the new acquisition became the fastest-growing Mazda dealership in the nation.

Jim Bagan, vice president and managing partner of Roger Beasley Imports, began working with Beasley in 1987 in the company's finance office. "When I started, we had one store and were selling about 150 cars a month," says Bagan. "By the

ROGER BEASLEY (SEATED), PRESIDENT, ROGER BEASLEY AUTOMOTIVE GROUP; JIM BAGAN (LEFT), MANAGING PARTNER, ROGER BEASLEY MAZDA SOUTH; DAVID STEIN, MANAGING PARTNER, ROGER BEASLEY PORSCHE/ SAAB AND ROGER BEASLEY VOLVO

ONE SIMPLE DOCTRINE—TAKE CARE OF THE CUSTOMER AND THE BUSINESS WILL TAKE CARE OF ITSELF—IS THE DRIVING FORCE BEHIND AUSTIN'S PREMIER AUTOMOBILE DEALERSHIPS.

time I left Roger Beasley Mazda to go to Mazda South, we had grown it into one of the top five stores in the country." In similar fashion, adds Bagan, Mazda South had average sales of 75 cars a month when Beasley took over; it now sells approximately 300 cars a month and is the seventh-largest Mazda dealer in the nation.

In 1997, through Beasley's tireless efforts and unwavering commitment to excel, both of his Mazda dealerships and their personnel earned the Japanese automaker's highest award, membership in the 1997 President's Club. Roger Beasley Mazda also won the President's Award of Honor, a prestigious award given to the top 15 Mazda dealers of comparable size. In addition to sales achievement, exemplary customer satisfaction is a requirement of membership in the President's Club. Today, Beasley's two Mazda dealerships in Austin are ranked number one and number seven in total sales in the nation, and Roger Beasley Mazda is ranked number one nationally in truck sales. In addition, Beasley recently opened a new Mazda operation in Bastrop, which is already enjoying steady sales growth.

Beasley's other operations report similar successes. In July 1993, Beasley purchased an existing Volvo dealership. In one year, he turned the franchise around and received the highest award for customer service awarded by the Swedish automaker. In fact, Roger Beasley Volvo has received the Dealer of Excellence award every

year since 1995. The franchise is currently ranked 14th in the nation in new car sales and second in sales of Volvo Select pre-owned, certified used cars. In 1998, Roger Beasley Volvo completed construction of the first ground-up Volvo Select facility in the United States.

Beasley's Volvo franchise leads the nation and the industry in

other ways as well, including the use of a new satellite repair system that links car repair specialists directly to the manufacturers and design engineers in Sweden and Germany. Known as the Vehicle & Administrative Diagnostic Information System (VADIS), the technology helps technicians diagnose and repair problems immediately.

ROGER BEASLEY VOLVO HAS AN INTENSELY LOYAL CUSTOMER BASE, SAYS DAVID STEIN, VICE PRESIDENT AND MANAGING PARTNER OF THE VOLVO DEALERSHIP AND OF THE PORSCHE/SAAB FRANCHISES THE COMPANY ACQUIRED IN APRIL 1997.

IN JULY 1993, BEASLEY PURCHASED AN EXISTING VOLVO DEALERSHIP. IN ONE YEAR, HE TURNED THE FRANCHISE AROUND AND RECEIVED THE HIGHEST AWARD FOR CUSTOMER SERVICE AWARDED BY THE SWEDISH AUTOMAKER. IN FACT, ROGER BEASLEY VOLVO HAS RECEIVED THE DEALER OF EXCELLENCE AWARD EVERY YEAR SINCE 1995.

Beasley has maintained a personal atmosphere that draws customers back year after year.

PUTTING PEOPLE FIRST

Roger Beasley Automotive Group has built its reputation on a promise unique to most automotive dealerships—putting people first and profits second. The philosophy under which all Roger Beasley dealerships operate is the same. First and foremost, the goal is to take care of the customer and follow up on every sale and visit. Second, the company strives to hire and retain the finest dealership personnel and to provide them with the best tools and equipment available. Management and staff undergo year-round training, and each dealership participates in and supports every manufacturer program offered.

Beasley credits his personnel for the success of each dealership. For example, Roger Beasley Mazda's sales manager was ranked first in the automaker's President's Guild for a customer satisfaction index in sales and delivery of 93.7 percent. Out of 1,165 salespeople in Mazda's Gulf sales region, all 11 of Roger Beasley Mazda's sales staff members were ranked in the top 15, and six were in the top 10.

Empowerment is a key element at Roger Beasley Automotive Group, and employees at all levels are encouraged to make decisions to better serve the customer. "As a group, we are committed to the best customer care and safety," says Beasley. "Everyone here is

Roger Beasley Volvo has an intensely loyal customer base, says David Stein, vice president and managing partner of the Volvo dealership and of the Porsche/Saab franchises the company acquired in April 1997. "At least 80 percent of our customers buy both new and used cars from us a second, third, or fourth time," he says. The company's attention to service is reflected in such customer benefits as a fleet of 70 Volvos, Porsches, and Saabs used solely as loaner cars. Customers who return to the Beasley dealerships for service can conveniently borrow the same kind of car they are accustomed to driving.

In June 1995, Beasley added two KIA franchises to his dealer group. The stores have flourished and consistently lead the region in sales and customer satisfaction. What's more, after Beasley acquired existing Austin franchises for Porsche and Saab, sales increased by 60 percent in the first year, and

the dealerships' current customer satisfaction index is close to 100 percent.

In addition to the more than 40 makes and models of new cars it sells, Roger Beasley Automotive Group does a brisk business in used car sales. Each car is carefully inspected and certified to ensure its safety and the high quality for which the dealerships are known.

"Quality and value are talked about a lot in this business," says Stein. "We strive diligently to extend the concepts. Formal customer satisfaction surveys are a part of our business plan, and we constantly look outside the car business to other industry leaders to compare customer satisfaction levels."

Beasley credits the success of his business to the combination of a popular, quality product, a fair price, and a strong commitment to service—all of which lead to loyal customers. Even with the incredible growth of his business,

BEASLEY CREDITS HIS PERSONNEL FOR THE SUCCESS OF EACH DEALER-SHIP. FOR EXAMPLE, ROGER BEASLEY MAZDA'S SALES MANAGER WAS RANKED FIRST IN THE AUTOMAKER'S PRESIDENT'S GUILD FOR A CUSTOMER SATISFACTION INDEX IN SALES AND DELIVERY OF 93.7 PERCENT.

able to make management-level decisions to provide timely answers and service to customers."

Active in the Community

Roger Beasley Automotive Group maintains a strong commitment to the community as well, giving profits back to the public through numerous charitable and service organizations. The company and its 350 Austin employees support Operation Blue Santa, the UT athletics program, and local anti-drug school education campaigns. Roger Beasley Automotive Group and its employees also provide daily mentoring and tutoring to students at Langford Elementary and support the Learning by

Earning program sponsored by the Austin Automobile Dealers Association.

The attitude and philosophy that Beasley himself brings to the automobile business permeates his entire organization and is directly responsible for the reputation his dealerships maintain in Austin and throughout Central Texas. Looking ahead to continued success, Beasley says, "As we enter the 21st century, we are excited about the changes that are in store, from new product lines to increased satisfaction levels."

By focusing on customers and the community—rather than concentrating solely on profits—Roger Beasley Automotive Group strives to redefine success and instill a strong sense of pride among

employees. "We all live here in the Austin area and work directly with the Austin community," says Bagan. "Whether we're at a UT football game or out to dinner with our families, we know that we can go anywhere and hold our heads high."

"This is a great organization to be involved with," adds Bagan. "We have an incredibly loyal staff and more long-term employees than just about any other dealer-ship in town. Everyone here admires Roger's commitment to Austin and the way we do business, which is to do what is best for the consumer and for Austin, as well as for the company. It's the reason why Roger Beasley Automotive Group has been so successful in this town."

IN JUNE 1995, BEASLEY ADDED TWO KIA FRANCHISES TO HIS DEALER GROUP. THE STORES HAVE FLOUR-ISHED AND CONSISTENTLY LEAD THE REGION IN SALES AND CUSTOMER SATISFACTION.

State Farm Insurance Companies

IN 1922, AFTER 20 YEARS OF FARMING, ILLINOIS RESIDENT GEORGE Mecherle left the land for a new calling in the insurance industry. As he began selling auto insurance, Mecherle suggested to his company the idea of creating a rate system that would suit the needs of farmers, who drove less than people living in cities.

When his idea was rejected, he founded the State Farm Mutual Automobile Insurance Company.

Today, the State Farm Insurance Companies still follow Mecherle's doctrines of fairness and customer service—practices that helped the company become the largest property and casualty insurance company in the world, with more than 65 million policyholders and 70,000 employees. After 75 years, the company's mission is still to provide excellent customer service, as well as to help people manage the risks of everyday life, recover from the unexpected, and realize their dreams. State Farm currently writes policies in State Farm Mutual, State Farm County Mutual, State Farm Fire & Casualty, State Farm Lloyds, and State Farm Life Insurance Companies. Headquartered in Bloomington, Illinois, the State Farm Insurance Companies have insured Texans since 1931.

The company's Texas Regional Office opened in Austin in 1971 and now serves Central Texas, Houston, San Antonio, Corpus Christi, and the Rio Grande Valley. Originally built in North Austin, the site expanded three times before opening, in 1994, its current facility on a gracefully landscaped, 70-acre site in Northwest Austin.

Through nearly 700 area agents, State Farm writes fire, auto, life, and health insurance for more than 2.5 million policyholders in the region. Because each agent is an independent business owner and works exclusively with State Farm, he or she is better able to know customers on a one-to-one basis and to provide personal, customized service. To ensure a quick response to policyholders' needs, State Farm's Claim Central operation in Austin is open until 9 p.m. and the State Farm customer response center takes calls 24 hours a day.

A Good Neighbor

The slogan "Like a good neighbor, State Farm is there" aptly describes both State Farm's customer service and its community involvement. The company's 1,600 Austin employees and agent volunteers have participated in events all over the South Texas region. Regular volunteer activities include participation in the March of Dimes Walk America, in SAT Pre-Game Clinics for student athletes, and in local high schools' Project Graduation programs.

Volunteers from all over the region also donate their time and talents by sponsoring and presenting safety programs to children in hundreds of classes from kindergarten through sixth grade. State Farm has developed several highly regarded educational programs and learning kits that teach safety to children. The curriculum teaches important issues including calling

STATE FARM INSURANCE COMPANIES' TEXAS REGIONAL OFFICE OPENED IN AUSTIN IN 1971, AND THE COMPANY EXPANDED THREE TIMES BEFORE OPENING ITS CURRENT FACILITY IN 1994 ON A GRACEFULLY LANDSCAPED, 70-ACRE SITE IN NORTHWEST AUSTIN.

STATE FARM EMPLOYEES ARE DEDICATED TO PROVIDING QUALITY CUSTOMER SERVICE—WITH A SMILE.

911 and the operator, traffic light safety, pedestrian safety, and flood safety. State Farm's popular Bicycle Safety Rodeo utilizes a hands-on course where children can bring their own bikes and bike helmets for an inspection, and run an obstacle course. Additional education and safety kits developed by State Farm teach children about fire prevention, heroism, responsibility, self-esteem, and even auto insurance basics.

Through an active speakers bureau, State Farm employees meet with various community groups to discuss important insurance issues and to help educate the public about both their choices and their responsibilities.

Ensuring Employee Satisfaction

State Farm is committed to its employees and provides a wide variety of special employee services. To help employees balance their jobs with their personal and family responsibilities, State Farm offers flexible work arrangements, as well as a unique employee services program with dry-cleaning pickup and delivery, film processing, shoeshine and shoe repair, and a company store.

Competitive benefits include a fully funded retirement plan, in addition to a 401(k) plan, annual salary reviews, performance bonuses, immediate paid vacation and sick leave, and a contemporary, busi-

ness casual dress environment. The regional office houses its own credit union for State Farm employees and agents. As a special touch, employees receive a card and a rose on their birthdays.

Teamwork is highly encouraged, as is employee participation and initiative. Through its Discovery Program, State Farm rewards employees for suggestions on improving efficiency. Lifelong learning is an ongoing priority,

and State Farm provides extensive skills-based training and life issues training. An on-site resource center provides employees with a wide selection of self-development books, periodicals, software, and walk-up computers with tutorials and Internet access, as well as a video setup for practice presentations and mock interviews. The resource center is open until 10 at night and on the weekends, and some classes are held in the evening so employees' spouses can attend.

State Farm provides excellent job training for employees, and internal career opportunities result in a high degree of upward mobility based on employee skills, ability, performance, and personal development.

Regional Vice President Bill King describes State Farm as an employee-oriented company, and that translates into better service for customers. "By providing the best environment and opportunities for our employees and our agents," says King, "we create a ripple effect that touches every aspect of our business, and ultimately results in outstanding service and value for our policyholders."

STATE FARM'S GOOD NEIGH BEAR HELPS CHILDREN AND THEIR PARENTS LEARN ABOUT BICYCLE SAFETY.

POLICYHOLDERS RECEIVE GOOD NEIGHBOR SERVICE FROM THEIR PERSONAL STATE FARM AGENTS.

TECO-WESTINGHOUSE MOTOR COMPANY

ROM THE FIRST GLIMPSE OF THE THREE TEXAS LONGHORN steers grazing in front of its rust-colored building just off Interstate 35, visitors know that the TECO-Westinghouse Motor Company is a unique place. The longhorns represent TECO-Westinghouse's singular culture—at once

strong, admirable, different, and distinctively Texas. For more than 25 years, the company has aimed to maintain the authenticity of this culture, while bringing new technology and innovation to the industry and the area.

A strong Central Texas presence since 1971, the company's focus on heavy manufacturing truly stands out in the vast array of local high-tech companies.

TECO-Westinghouse builds alternating current (AC) and direct current (DC) motors for major domestic industries and utilities, as well as for customers worldwide. The company is the leading supplier of power plant motors for utilities, and industrial applications for its motors include pumps and compressor drives for industries such as petrochemical, pipeline, paper, and cement.

Building motors ranging from 500 to 50,000 horsepower, the company helps customers run oil fields, steel mills, gas turbines, and assembly lines across the world.

THE NEW GAME IN TOWN

When Westinghouse Electric Corporation's Gas Turbine Division opened its Round Rock facility in 1971, the new satellite manufacturing plant was the only game in town. "When the company put down its roots in Central Texas, it was certainly big news in this part of the country to open a manufacturing plant of this size," says TECO-Westinghouse President David Pipes.

After successful manufacturing of initial production units, operations were shut down due to the poor market conditions caused by the energy crisis of the early 1970s. In 1975, the company formed the Heavy Industry Motor Division (HIMD) and began operations in the Round Rock plant. The HIMD product line consisted of "heavy" DC motors for the steel and surface mining industries, as well as AC motors (above 4,000 horsepower) for industrial and electric utility applications.

After more than 10 years of market shifts and industry consolidations, the Westinghouse Motor Company was founded in 1988 as a separate company from Westinghouse Electric Corporation. The company was purchased by TECO Electric Machinery Company, Ltd. in Taiwan, and officially became the TECO-Westinghouse Motor Company in July 1997.

As a subsidiary of TECO, the company provides the engineering, technology, testing, quality assurance, marketing, and manufacturing for a wide range of motors and generators to the global market. Many of its customers

A STRONG CENTRAL TEXAS PRESENCE SINCE 1971, TECO-WESTINGHOUSE MOTOR COMPANY'S FOCUS ON HEAVY MANUFACTURING TRULY STANDS OUT IN THE VAST ARRAY OF LOCAL HIGH-TECH COMPANIES (TOP).

THE LONGHORNS GRAZING IN FRONT OF THE COMPANY'S BUILDING JUST OFF INTERSTATE 35 REPRESENT TECO-WESTINGHOUSE'S SINGULAR CULTURE—AT ONCE STRONG, ADMIRABLE, DIFFERENT, AND DISTINCTIVELY TEXAS (BOTTOM).

in 19 states and offices in Canada, Chile, Mexico, and China.

TECO-Westinghouse's recent growth has led to the opening of a new division to service and remanufacture motors, both those made by the company and those made by its competitors. The company also recently began marketing products manufactured by other divisions of its parent company, including air conditioners and related products, motor controllers, and motor drivers.

The company attributes its success to its research and development efforts and its constant improvements to a product that has existed in one form or another for 150 years. "By adding new technology, increasing efficiency, and creating higher horsepower in our motors, we set ourselves apart in the industry and really create our own market niche," says Pipes.

An active sponsor of community activities, TECO-Westinghouse and its employees contribute to a number of events for the March of Dimes, United Way, YMCA, Project Graduation, the Round Rock Fireman's Fund, and local organizations from sports teams to high school bands. With a name as recognized on the Little League field as it is in the oil field, TECO-Westinghouse's local impact rivals its global reach.

name the company as their preferred supplier, thanks to a strong commitment to meeting customer needs with quality products and service.

"Through ongoing product innovation and the introduction of new products, we've been able to reinvent this company several times over to keep it vibrant and growing," says Pipes.

Heavy Duty

Because its product line is so specific, TECO-Westinghouse recruits nationwide for people with large-motor experience and expertise. The Round Rock site, now the company's worldwide headquarters, employs more than 600 people.

Every new employee receives in-depth training to learn the company's own manufacturing processes and product lines, a process that facilitates both on-the-job skill and safety. Thanks to this up-front commitment and ongoing safety awareness programs, TECO-Westinghouse maintains one of the lowest injury incidence rates in the industry. In fact, the company's safety manager has won the Safety Manager of the

Year Award from the Texas Safety Association.

On its 116-acre site, TECO-Westinghouse utilizes 430,000 square feet of building space to assemble the majority of its motors. The company also has sales and warehousing facilities

ON ITS 116-ACRE SITE, TECO-WESTINGHOUSE UTILIZES 430,000 SQUARE FEET OF BUILDING SPACE TO ASSEMBLE THE MAJORITY OF ITS MOTORS.

AUSTIN COMMUNITY COLLEGE

IN ONLY 25 YEARS, AUSTIN COMMUNITY COLLEGE (ACC) HAS BECOME an important educational resource for many local residents. ACC has helped many Austinites meet their goals. "We take people from where they are and move them to a level where they can be successful," says ACC President Dr. Richard Fonté.

IN ONLY 25 YEARS, AUSTIN COMMU-NITY COLLEGE (ACC) HAS BECOME AN IMPORTANT EDUCATIONAL RE-SOURCE FOR MANY LOCAL RESIDENTS. STRESSING IDEALS OF QUALITY, FLEXIBILITY, ACCESSIBILITY, AND DIVERSITY, THE COLLEGE MAINTAINS AN OPEN-ADMISSION POLICY AND OFFERS FRESHMAN AND SOPHOMORE ARTS AND SCIENCE COURSES, A VARIETY OF TECHNICAL/VOCATIONAL PROGRAMS, ADULT BASIC EDUCA-TION, AND CONTINUING EDUCATION CLASSES.

As a comprehensive community college, ACC is fully accredited by the Southern Association of Colleges and Schools. Stressing ideals of quality, flexibility, accessibility, and diversity, the college maintains an open-admission policy and offers freshman and sophomore arts and science courses, a variety of technical/vocational programs, adult basic education, and continuing education classes.

THE BIRTH OF A COLLEGE

 CC got its start in 1972, when voters in the Austin Independent School District passed a ballot proposition to authorize the creation of a community college. Under the leadership of its first president, Thomas Hatfield, ACC opened its doors in September 1973.

A succession of powerful and innovative leaders helped ACC grow and prosper: Dr. Cecil Groves made significant connections with the business community; Dr. Dan Angel successfully lobbied for the passage of an ad valorem tax to begin a new building campaign; and Dr. Bill Segura created ties with the Austin high-tech community. Now, Fonté is ably leading ACC into the next millennium.

EDUCATING CENTRAL TEXAS

 CC serves an area stretching from Smith-ville to Fredericksburg. In and around Austin, campuses include the Northridge Campus on Metric Boulevard near Braker Lane; Highland Business Center on Middle Fiskville Road; Riverside Campus, just off Riverside Drive; Pinnacle Campus at Highway 290 and Highway 71; Rio Grande Campus at the site of the original Austin High School downtown; the new Eastview Campus on Webberville Road and Govalle Avenue; and Cypress Creek Campus in Cedar Park.

ACC's current enrollment is more than 25,000 students, with an additional 18,000 enrolled annually in continuing education programs. The school addresses four major areas to serve its diverse student population and a wide range of individual and community needs. Through its university transfer education programs, students can earn associate of arts or associate of science degrees from one of 27 different academic disciplines. More than half of ACC's student base are enrolled in transfer education—popular due to its low tuition, flexible class schedules, and transferable credit hours.

A second focus area is workforce education, through which students can receive an associate of applied science degree or certificate in more than 40 work-related majors, such as high technology, hospitality, nursing/allied health programs, and other career areas. By providing higher education in these areas, ACC is addressing Austin's future workforce needs.

Through its continuing education programs, ACC offers a variety of alternative credit options. In courses ranging in length from one day to 16 weeks, students can study a variety of topics, from conducting business in Mexico to making jewelry. Many continuing education classes and seminars are taught at the college's new Highland Business Center, formerly the primary site of ACC's administrative offices. The school works directly with local corporations, either at an ACC campus or on-site, to teach business-related skills and topics, such as TQM and time management. Professional development and continuing education classes allow students to advance in their chosen careers and to maintain certifications.

A fourth educational concentration is adult basic education, through which ACC reaches largely underserved populations. From

literacy classes to GED prep courses, ACC helps those with basic education needs.

INITIATIVE IN EDUCATION

s both the workplace and people's lifestyles become technologically advanced, ACC is using innovative learning methodologies. Distance learning is a priority for the college, and all campuses now have interactive, two-way video for teaching and learning. Showcasing the possibilities of this two-way video technology is the vocational nursing program—nursing faculty at ACC's Riverside Campus in Austin provide instruction to students in Fredericksburg, 80 miles away, via a two-way video hookup. ACC students may also choose from several dozen classes offered via the Internet, and a number of courses are broadcast on ACC's local cable channel.

A new initiative for ACC is its participation in the Virtual College of Texas, a program that offers on-line classes from various community colleges statewide. Students at participating schools can take a class offered by another college in a different part of the state.

To meet the needs of a growing metropolitan area, ACC offers numerous programs in a variety of formats and at many sites throughout the Capital Area. Classes are offered from early morning to late evening, and a number of condensed courses help working or otherwise committed students complete classes in shorter semesters, at night, or on the weekends. ACC also participates in the Multi-Institution Teaching Center (MITC) in Williamson County, through which students can attain their associate, baccalaureate, or master's degrees by taking a flexible schedule of night classes at ACC's Cypress Creek Campus, or at Round Rock, Westwood, or Georgetown high schools. Workforce education programs are also offered at the MITC. And through ACC's Early College Start program, high school students can receive college credit for taking ACC courses.

Building on the success of its first quarter century, ACC will continue to link college and community, serving Austin's educational needs for many years to come.

AS A COMPANY DEVELOPING TOUCH SCREENS, RADIO frequency identification systems, satellite communications, scanners, point-of-sale systems, and digital communications, Wayne® doesn't appear at first glance to be in the service station business. After all,

what could digital communications have to do with filling the car up with gas at the local service station? But appearances can be deceiving, for Wayne is the name behind the industry's first fuel blending dispensers, the first gas pump touch screens, and the first pay-at-the-pump systems. Wayne develops and markets gasoline dispensers, point-of-sale systems, and peripherals for the retail fuel equipment market, bringing cutting-edge, innovative technology to an activity most people take for granted.

Wayne developed its technical expertise in the service station industry through more than 100 years of experience. Founded in Fort Wayne in 1891, Wayne was the first company to introduce self-service consoles to service stations in the late 1950s and the first to apply microcomputers to

fuel processing systems. In 1968, Wayne was acquired by Dresser Industries, now a $7.7 billion company with 3,600-plus employees worldwide. Dresser was acquired by the Halliburton Company in 1998. With this latest acquisition, Wayne is now part of a $16 billion energy services company.

AN INNOVATOR IN THE INDUSTRY

Today, Wayne takes the service station experience to a new level of speed and convenience, with innovations including pumps that accept cash, read bar coding, and use radio frequency identification for billing. The Wayne *TRAC*™ system is the first system enabling customers to pay for purchases using a transponder attached to their car or on their key chain, instead of paying with a credit card or cash. Sensors at the pump quickly recognize the transponder and automatically bill the charges to the customer's designated credit card. In the not-so-distant future, Wayne's combination of transponder technology and robotics will altogether eliminate the need for customers to even get out of their cars.

Wayne's Touch-N-Go™ system enables users to select fuel type and payment method by touching the screen, and offers added values including weather, news, and sports highlights; local public service information; or coupons. While fueling, customers can even order food from the connected convenience store or quick service restaurant.

Nucleus®, Wayne's state-of-the-art gas station controller, uses a PC-based, easy-to-use touch screen interface to control the station's entire operations, including in-store sales, connection to credit card networks, pumps,

car wash, underground monitoring equipment, and more. Using a Microsoft®-based software development environment, Wayne applies object-oriented programming techniques.

The benefits of these time-saving services are convenience for consumers and increased throughput for Wayne's customers, including the world's largest oil companies. Amoco, BP, Chevron, Mobil, Shell, Sun, Texaco, and Ultramar Diamond Shamrock rely on Wayne for these systems and for ongoing equipment and site services. With a 24-hour help desk answering service calls, Wayne provides both remote service and on-site repairs through its direct service network and authorized service organizations.

Wayne's emerging mass merchandiser and hypermarket business allows grocery stores and retail warehouse chains to offer customers added value with gas pumps in their store lots. Clients such as Albertson's, Randalls, Sam's Club, BJ's Wholesale, Kroger, HEB, and Wal-Mart are drawing more customers with the convenience of the on-site pumps. Wayne's bar code scanning product, Wayne *SCAN*, also allows members of retail warehouse chains to scan the code on their membership cards at the pump to receive reduced prices on gasoline. In the grocery segment, stores are extending their loyalty programs to offer rewards and discounts at the pump as well as in the store.

Wayne offers a unique three-pronged expertise to its clients, focusing its development on hardware, software, and total site services. To create the highest level of end user convenience, the company works to develop customer focused technologies and applies existing technologies from other industries to its own products.

IN ITS AUSTIN HEADQUARTERS, WAYNE EMPLOYS MORE THAN 500 PEOPLE IN MANUFACTURING, SOFTWARE DEVELOPMENT, ELECTRICAL ENGINEERING, ELECTRONIC MANUFACTURING, SERVICE, AND ADMINISTRATION.

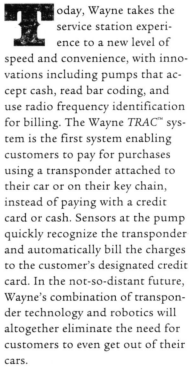

FROM AUSTIN TO THE WORLD

In its Austin headquarters, Wayne employs more than 500 people in manufacturing, software development, electrical engineering, electronic manufacturing, service, and administration. The company's largest manufacturing plant is located in Salisbury, Maryland, and international manufacturing sites include Canada, Sweden, the United Kingdom, Germany, Switzerland, South Africa, and Brazil. The company has been approved since 1994 to the ISO 9001 Quality Management System standard.

Says Wayne U.S. President John Ryan, "This is one of the only places where an employee can learn hardware engineering, electrical engineering, and mechanical engineering. We provide our employees a chance to hone their skills on many levels, giving them enormous opportunities for the future." To further extend employees' expertise and continuing education, the company offers a full college tuition reimbursement program.

A contributing member of the Austin community, Wayne extends opportunities for local high school and college students through a strong intern program. The company also works with the Austin State School through a program called Employment Plus, a support employment program for individuals with disabilities.

In addition to its local career initiatives in education, Wayne touches the community through a number of volunteer and charitable programs. Employees have participated in the March of Dimes Walk America, Angel Tree program, Salvation Army, and a school supply program. Wayne contributes to United Way and to several universities through a matching grants program. The company is also an active member of the Greater Austin Chamber of Commerce and the Round Rock Chamber of Commerce.

"Since moving our headquarters to Austin in 1996, we have become acquainted with many of the wonderful people and organizations in the area," says Ryan. "We look forward to becoming a true community partner in the years to come."

WAYNE OFFERS A UNIQUE THREE-PRONGED EXPERTISE TO ITS CLIENTS, FOCUSING ITS DEVELOPMENT ON HARDWARE, SOFTWARE, AND TOTAL SITE SERVICES (TOP).

WAYNE TAKES THE SERVICE STATION EXPERIENCE TO A NEW LEVEL OF SPEED AND CONVENIENCE, WITH INNOVATIONS INCLUDING PUMPS THAT ACCEPT CASH, READ BAR CODING, AND USE RADIO FREQUENCY IDENTIFICATION FOR BILLING (BOTTOM).

WILL IT BE THE CRISPY OYSTERS ON YUCCA-ROOT CHIPS with habanero-honey aioli? The almond-crusted sea bass with china princess mushrooms and black truffle corn cream? Or perhaps Jeffrey's cappuccino créme brûlée with chocolate-covered espresso beans

and mascarpone cookies? No matter what you order from Jeffrey's tantalizing menu, your choice is guaranteed to delight the taste buds. A friendly and sophisticated neighborhood bistro in eclectic Clarksville, Jeffrey's boasts a legacy of inventive and indulgent cuisine that is peerless according to many Austinites, whether they're celebrating a special occasion or just seeking an unforgettable meal.

Founded in 1975 by Jeff Weinberger and Ron and Peggy Weiss, Jeffrey's quickly became a local favorite. "We set out to create a comfortable, unpretentious atmosphere focusing on innovative food and informal, personalized service," says operating partner Ron Weiss.

Jeffrey's has grown from a 40-seat spot in a corner of the charming building that also housed a florist, a liquor store, and an ice-cream shop to occupying the entire

downstairs with seating for 80, plus an additional bar area. Over the years, the restaurant has successfully maintained its casually elegant atmosphere while enlightening and enlivening Austin's palates.

CHEF DAVID GARRIDO

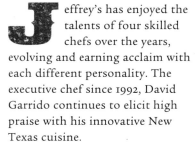

Jeffrey's has enjoyed the talents of four skilled chefs over the years, evolving and earning acclaim with each different personality. The executive chef since 1992, David Garrido continues to elicit high praise with his innovative New Texas cuisine.

Garrido's award-winning menus begin with only the freshest and highest-quality ingredients available. Using the best exotic ingredients from around the world—caviar from Russia, foie gras from New York, morels from Oregon, lamb from New Zealand—and using fresh local items such as baby

greens and goat cheese, Garrido energetically designs a creative menu each day. Prepared lovingly by hand, his breathtaking dishes satisfy Austinites' sophisticated tastes, yet Garrido will gladly accommodate any special request.

Customers appreciate Garrido's attention, as evidenced by Jeffrey's record volume of business over the past five consecutive years. Accolades continue to roll in: Jeffrey's is the only Austin restaurant to receive a two-star rating from *Texas Monthly* magazine; *Wine Spectator* magazine has bestowed its Award of Excellence on the restaurant every year since 1991; and in 1995, Garrido was invited to cook at the famed James Beard House in New York, and was one of three chefs chosen to cook at the 1997 Winter Escape in Hawaii. In addition, Garrido released his first cookbook in the summer of 1998, titled *Nuevo Tex-Mex* and published by Chronicle Books of San Francisco.

Over the years, Jeffrey's has remained a constant favorite in fine dining. Weiss attributes the restaurant's success to a team effort. "Everyone has value and input and truly enjoys their work. It's like hosting a party every night," he observes. "We enjoy treating people as if they were in our own homes. We are passionate about good food and good service, and we love to share that passion."

JEFFREY'S EXECUTIVE CHEF SINCE 1992, DAVID GARRIDO ELICITS HIGH PRAISE WITH HIS INNOVATIVE NEW TEXAS CUISINE (TOP).

A FRIENDLY AND SOPHISTICATED NEIGHBORHOOD BISTRO IN ECLECTIC CLARKSVILLE, JEFFREY'S BOASTS A LEGACY OF INVENTIVE AND INDULGENT CUISINE (BOTTOM).

THE PROGRESSIVE CORPORATION, ONE OF THE LARGEST AUTO insurers in Texas today, is a company that lives up to its name. From the way it sells its policies to the way it handles insurance claims, the company brings innovative, new ideas to the auto insurance industry. Founded in 1937, Progressive today provides a range of personal automobile and other specialty property-casualty insurance and related services throughout the United States and in Canada.

In 1988, the company underwent a complete transformation as a result of California state legislation. Consumers were unhappy with the auto insurance industry, and Progressive vowed to make a change. Since then, the company has literally redesigned every part of its business. Committed to providing innovative insurance products and top-notch service at the lowest possible cost, Progressive strives to make auto insurance easy to understand, buy, and use.

TOP-NOTCH SERVICE

Progressive lets customers choose when, where, and how to purchase a policy by selling through 30,000 independent agents, through a toll-free auto insurance rate comparison and shopping service (800-AUTOPRO®), and even over the Internet (www.progressive.com). Round-the-clock customer service lets policyholders call any time of day or night to get a question answered, make a payment, or immediately add or delete drivers or vehicles from their policy.

Assistance after an accident or other loss is Progressive's most important service, and Immediate Response® claims service is available at all times. Whether a claim representative comes directly to the scene of the accident or meets with the policyholder within a few hours, Progressive's goal is to turn an often harrowing ordeal into a hassle-free process that allows policyholders to get on with their lives as quickly as possible.

This combination of innovation and customer service has resulted in Progressive's strong growth, which consistently outpaces the industry average. In 1997, for example, Progressive's $4.6 billion net written premium represented a 36 percent increase over the previous year, while the industry as a whole grew approximately 5 percent. This growth has led to Progressive's standing as the fifth-largest auto insurance company in the nation and the fourth largest in Texas.

TAKING CARE OF ITS OWN

Progressive provides an atmosphere of open communication and innovation for its employees. Its 500 Austin staff members are encouraged to participate in creative problem solving, and are rewarded for the company's overall success with GainShare bonuses. In addition, the company's policy of promoting from within provides tremendous career opportunities.

Known for more than its services, Progressive has received recognition for its involvement in numerous area organizations and programs. With a strong interest in traffic safety, Progressive is a cosponsor of the Safe Ride Home program, which has provided thousands of free cab rides to drivers during holiday periods as an alternative to drinking and driving. Another regular Progressive program offers free vehicle identification etching to Austinites, whether or not they are Progressive policyholders.

These types of programs embody Progressive's core values, such as integrity and excellence, which help the company achieve its objectives of providing all consumers with competitively priced auto insurance and 24-hour, in-person services. Progressive's innovation and dedication to customer service are making a difference for consumers—a difference that is changing the insurance industry in Texas and across the nation.

THE PROGRESSIVE CORPORATION IS ONE OF THE LARGEST AUTO INSURERS IN TEXAS TODAY.

THE EXCITEMENT IS CATCHING ON THE CAMPUS OF NATIONAL Instruments, the Austin-based high-tech company that introduced hundreds of new products in 1998 with sales of $274 million. It's an excitement that originates in the corporate culture, and extends to engineers and scientists

CLOCKWISE FROM TOP:
SAYS NORMA DORST, SOFTWARE MARKETING MANAGER, "NATIONAL INSTRUMENTS IS A WELCOME AND RELAXED, YET EXCITING, ENVIRONMENT, FULL OF OPPORTUNITIES FOR INDIVIDUAL GROWTH AND ACHIEVEMENT."

NATIONAL INSTRUMENTS HARDWARE AND SOFTWARE PRODUCTS HELP COMPANIES COST-EFFECTIVELY MEET TODAY'S TOUGH PRODUCTION, TEST, AND MANUFACTURING CHALLENGES.

NATIONAL INSTRUMENTS PROVIDES SOLUTIONS FOR DIVERSE INDUSTRIES FROM AEROSPACE AND AUTOMOTIVE TO AGRICULTURE AND EDUCATION.

around the world using cutting-edge National Instruments hardware and software for their everyday applications and research.

"This company is built with the talents of innovative, entrepreneurial, energetic, persistent, and motivated people," says Dr. James Truchard, president and CEO of National Instruments. "We give them the opportunity to make a difference, and they choose National Instruments as a rewarding career, not just a job."

Truchard knows about being innovative and entrepreneurial. In 1976, he and two other researchers from the University of Texas founded National Instruments in a garage with $10,000 borrowed from a bank. The team realized their goal of creating products that allow engineers and scientists to generate accurate measurements and conduct reliable tests with personal computer technology.

Demand for National Instruments products has propelled the company to become the industry's leading supplier of computer-based instruments that help engineers and scientists do their jobs better, faster, and more efficiently while also saving money.

AN ENTREPRENEURIAL AND CREATIVE SPIRIT

Throughout its history, National Instruments has placed special emphasis on helping employees grow in their positions. When company leaders decided to go public in 1995, their motivation was to make stock available to all National Instruments employees—promoting employee involvement, energy, and ownership. Today, National Instruments employs approximately 1,500 people worldwide, with 1,250 in Austin.

Through forward thinking and employee encouragement, National

Instruments has achieved 22 consecutive years of double-digit growth. The company's growth promotes more opportunities for empowered employees. National Instruments hires the majority of its employees directly out of the country's top colleges and universities. The average age of employees is 31. An active internship program encourages students to experience the unique National Instruments culture while gaining job experience. Corporate leaders foster respect and responsibility for all employees from the outset of their jobs, resulting in rewarding long-term opportunities, involvement, and motivation.

To encourage future engineers and scientists with the best equip-

ment available, National Instruments actively cultivates relationships with educational institutions in Austin and around the world. In keeping with its own entrepreneurial and creative spirit, the company recently partnered with LEGO Dacta and Tufts University to develop a computer-programmed LEGO system for K-12 students using National Instruments signature LabVIEW™ software.

At home in Austin, National Instruments serves several community and arts organizations,

including the Austin Food Bank. Employees work with Junior Achievement and Austin Partners in Education, teaming with Cook Elementary School to provide mentoring and tutoring. The company is also part of a consortium funding updates to the Austin Independent School District's computer network. In addition, National Instruments donated $1.5 million worth of software to the Laptops for Learning program, a coordinated effort between several Austin companies and the University of Texas to provide discounted computers to engineering students.

Because of the company's continuous growth, National Instruments recently constructed a new corporate campus in Austin. The wooded campus on Little Walnut Creek reflects relaxed Austin ideals, in addition to the

company's own unique culture. Outside Austin, National Instruments maintains offices in 26 countries around the world.

REVOLUTIONARY SOFTWARE

National Instruments products serve two large markets—test and measurement, and industrial automation. The company's flagship product is LabVIEW, a revolutionary software product introduced in 1986 that was the first graphical program to use computer icons to emulate engineering instruments, such as oscilloscopes, waveform generators, and multimeters. The company has also had great success with its award-winning PCI eXtensions for Instrumentation (PXI™), a modular instrumentation system; LabWindows™/CVI; and other software products.

National Instruments develops products that help customers ranging from Fortune 500 companies to engineering start-ups in the telecommunications, semiconductor, and automotive industries. National Instruments products are used in such diverse applications as testing cars, blending coffee, and controlling experiments in outer space.

As National Instruments moves into the 21st century, the unique corporate culture continues to propel the company and its vision, ensuring lasting growth and success—not to mention excitement—for many years to come.

CLOCKWISE FROM TOP: RAY ALMGREN, DIRECTOR, TEST AND MEASUREMENT MARKETING AT NATIONAL INSTRUMENTS, EXPLAINS THE BENEFITS OF LABVIEW™, WHICH IS USED BY ORGANIZATIONS SUCH AS FORD, MOTOROLA, AND NASA.

NIWEEK™ IS THE ANNUAL NATIONAL INSTRUMENTS TECHNICAL CONFERENCE, WHERE HUNDREDS OF ENGINEERS, SCIENTISTS, AND BUSINESS PARTNERS FROM ALL OVER THE WORLD GATHER FOR IN-DEPTH TRAINING ON NATIONAL INSTRUMENTS HARDWARE AND SOFTWARE PRODUCTS AND APPLICATIONS.

NATIONAL INSTRUMENTS, LEGO DACTA, AND TUFTS UNIVERSITY INTRODUCED AN INNOVATIVE ROBOTICS PROGRAM FOR GRADES K-12, WHICH BRINGS ENGINEERING AND SCIENCE INTO THE CLASSROOM IN AN EXCITING WAY.

(FROM LEFT TO RIGHT) MARK FINGER, VICE PRESIDENT OF HUMAN RESOURCES; CARSTEN THOMSEN, ACTING VICE PRESIDENT, STRATEGIC PLANNING; PETE ZOGAS, VICE PRESIDENT OF SALES; TIM DEHNE, VICE PRESIDENT OF ENGINEERING; ALEX DAVERN, CHIEF FINANCIAL OFFICER; DR. JAMES TRUCHARD, PRESIDENT AND CEO; RUBEN MANGIN, VICE PRESIDENT OF MANUFACTURING; AND JEFFREY KODOSKY, VICE PRESIDENT OF R&D

SURREY, INC.

SURREY, INC. KNOWS THE SWEET SMELL OF SUCCESS. ONLY IN the case of this Central Texas company, it could be the distinctive aroma of English lavender, wild honeysuckle, fresh peach, or even honey apple. ★ Based just north of Austin in Leander, Surrey is a manufacturer of high-quality trans-

SURREY, INC. PRODUCES RETAIL LINES THAT INCLUDE BATH AND HOME FRAGRANCE PRODUCTS, AS WELL AS A VARIETY OF PRIVATE LABEL ITEMS (RIGHT).

UNDER THE LEADERSHIP OF (FROM LEFT) PRESIDENT MARTY VAN DER HAGEN AND CEO JOHN VAN DER HAGEN, SURREY HAS BUILT SEVERAL SUCCESSFUL RETAIL BRANDS, INCLUDING HILL COUNTRY SOAP COMPANY, THE PURE PLEASURE LINE, THE SIMMER SCENTS LINE, AND THE SURREY MEN'S LINE (LEFT).

parent glycerin and specialty soaps, as well as a line of potpourri, high-end scented candles, and other personal care and fragrance products.

The company's founder and CEO, John van der Hagen, began operations in Minneapolis in 1972, and moved his business and his family to the Austin area in 1976. Why Central Texas? "It was downhill from Minnesota, and we just coasted until it got warm," jokes van der Hagen. "We knew that Texas had a good business climate, that it was in a perfect spot for nationwide distribution, and that good employees were easy to come by."

DECADES OF GROWTH

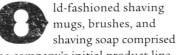ld-fashioned shaving mugs, brushes, and shaving soap comprised the company's initial product line, which was marketed with the nostalgic image of an English surrey.

Today, the familiar horse-drawn carriage remains the inspiration behind the company's name and logo. In 1980, when Surrey expanded its focus and began producing different types of soap, the business blossomed. The company completed an initial public offering in December 1997 and now trades on the Nasdaq system under the symbol SOAP.

"We use a proprietary process for manufacturing poured bar soaps," explains van der Hagen. "This allows us to produce unique and affordable soap products in large quantities with consistent quality." Over the years, Surrey has built several successful retail brands of its own, including Hill Country Soap Company, the Pure Pleasure line, the Simmer Scents line, and the Surrey men's line. The company recently launched two new product lines of soap and potpourri items in conjunction with General Nutrition Company.

Surrey also has a very successful private label and contract manufacturing business for such prestigious customers as Ann Taylor, Walt Disney, Neiman Marcus, Liz Claiborne, Revlon, Avon, Chanel, Tommy Hilfiger, and Elizabeth Arden. On the heels of a recent facility expansion, the company was able to land a major purchase order commitment for glycerin and specialty soap products from Bath & Body Works, a wholly owned subsidiary of The Limited, Inc. Van der Hagen estimates that Surrey will produce at least 1 million bars of soap a month for Bath & Body Works alone.

"Surrey is a one-of-a-kind company," says van der Hagen. "It's one-stop shopping for customers who want a variety of high-end products, and there's not another company like us in Texas."

While Surrey's specialty has long been focused on glycerin

soaps, it is quickly expanding into new product areas. The company, for example, has entered into the crafts market with its new soap-making kits, and has expanded its home fragrance offerings by introducing a full line of potpourri products and aromatherapy candles.

THE ELEMENTS OF SUCCESS

From glycerin soaps encasing colorful flowers to frog-shaped soaps on ceramic lily pads, many of the company's most unusual products are developed by van der Hagen himself, who spends a great deal of his time in Surrey's laboratory. "I didn't even have a chemistry class in high school," says van der Hagen. "But then again, nobody told Edison how to make a lightbulb—he figured it out himself."

In addition to his own sense of humor and penchant for creativity, van der Hagen credits the success of Surrey to good business acumen, perseverance, and the help of his family, all of whom work in the company.

Dedicated employees also keep the business running strong, according to van der Hagen. Surrey currently employs almost 200 people, many of whom have been with the company for more than

20 years. "We're a fun place to work, and we have a lot of laughs," says van der Hagen. "Our employees are proud of what they do and the quality of our products, and that pride is what drives the company."

Staff members find ample opportunities to excel on many levels, as Surrey often promotes from within and encourages involvement in community affairs. "We provide a lot of opportunity for a lot of people," says van der Hagen. "Additionally, we enjoy supporting the local community and being an integral part of it."

Going public has also propelled the company forward, allowing Surrey to expand its facility, and add new machines, tanks, and fillers in its approxi-

mately 100,000-square-foot office and manufacturing complex. The company now has the capacity to produce 30 million bars of soap each year and plans to keep on growing. "You can't stand still in business," explains van der Hagen. "We've worked hard to get here, and we know that Surrey will carry on for a long time."

Even with such forward-looking projections, it's likely that Surrey's neighbors will hardly notice the continued growth of this environmentally friendly company. "We're a clean business," adds van der Hagen. "We don't produce any pollution. In fact, you can hardly tell we're here, unless the winds are just right!" And then, it's just the sweet smell of success—or English lavender.

CLOCKWISE FROM TOP LEFT: SURREY'S ART DEPARTMENT CREATES PACKAGING AND SALES MATERIALS.

SURREY HAS AN EXTENSIVE RESEARCH AND DEVELOPMENT TEAM, AS WELL AS A FULL-TIME QUALITY CONTROL TEAM.

INGREDIENTS ARE MIXED TOGETHER IN THE COMPOUNDING AREA TO PRODUCE FINAL PRODUCTS.

THE COMPANY NOW HAS THE CAPACITY TO PRODUCE 30 MILLION BARS OF SOAP EACH YEAR AND PLANS TO KEEP ON GROWING.

I N THE EVER CHANGING AND INCREASINGLY COMPLEX WORLD OF health care, government officials and health professionals are challenged to simultaneously deliver high-quality services and serve as good stewards of funds provided by taxpayers. In Austin, EDS partners with the Texas Department of Health

(TDH), the Texas Health and Human Services Commission (THHSC), and other public and private entities to successfully accomplish this mission.

Many of the services EDS provides to the health and human services programs of the State of Texas are delivered by NHIC. Founded in 1977 as National Heritage Insurance Company, NHIC is a wholly owned subsidiary of EDS, a global leader in the information services industry based in Plano. Initially chartered to supply actuarial funds management and administrative services for the Texas Medicaid program, NHIC partners with the TDH to meet a wide range

of technology and administrative needs. Today, NHIC provides consulting and project management, technology, medical administration, and health claims processing to TDH. In 1998 alone, NHIC answered 2.9 million telephone inquiries, processed 32 million medical claims, and administered $4.2 billion in health benefit payments to Texans.

MEETING THE NEEDS

HIC has evolved to meet the changing needs of its customers and of Texans who depend on the state's public health care system. From 1980 to 1990, demands for

services provided through the Texas Medicaid program dramatically increased. As part of a plan to manage costs, the state decided to explore managed care as a health care delivery option. In 1993, NHIC assisted the TDH in developing a managed care program under the Star Health Plan, a highly successful pilot program that is continuing to be expanded into communities throughout Texas.

In 1995, as a further means of assisting the state in focusing resources on patient care rather than on program administration, NHIC developed TexMedNet. Used by medical providers to manage health insurance claims information, TexMedNet provides an electronic means to enable these providers to quickly and accurately file their claims, determine patient eligibility, retrieve payment information, and consult Medicaid policy and procedural information.

NHIC recently began a new contract with the TDH to perform Texas Medicaid Claims Administrator services. In this role, NHIC supplies health-insuring services, such as benefits funds management, provider relations, and claims and encounter processing. In addition, NHIC is responsible for the design, development, and implementation of a new Medicaid Management Information System (MMIS). This system, called Compass21, signals a new era in Medicaid administration technology.

"At NHIC, we capitalize on our understanding of the state's health care system, adding value for Texans who use the system and for the state agencies that facilitate the provision of care," says Drew Beckley, EDS state executive for health care. "To keep up with the constantly changing nature of health care delivery, we anticipate the changing needs of

NHIC's TexMedNet speeds submission and payment of Medicaid claims, and promotes provider participation in the delivery of health care services to Medicaid clients (top).

The new, centralized offices of NHIC, a wholly owned subsidiary of EDS, consolidate professionals from multiple locations throughout the Greater Austin area (bottom).

RIATA CROSSING
BUILDINGS I, II, & III

the system and how NHIC can most appropriately meet these needs by merging the best practices of the private and public health care sectors."

While the greatest portion of EDS' activities are focused on NHIC's services to the TDH, EDS also works with the THHSC. By providing consulting and strategic planning services to the Texas Integrated Eligibility System project, EDS has assisted the THHSC in developing the vision for streamlined and improved eligibility administration for a variety of health and human services programs.

Recently, Texas Medicaid officials called on EDS to create a system to safeguard the financial integrity of the Medicaid program. The company responded by developing the Medicaid Fraud and Abuse Detection System (MFADS). The most technologically advanced system of its kind, MFADS uses a highly advanced system of artificial intelligence to help uncover and prevent Medicaid fraud, abuse, and waste.

For the TDH, EDS designed and implemented ImmTrac, an immunization registry system. ImmTrac supports data collection and reporting of immunization activity, allowing medical providers, school districts, and parents secure access to a child's immunization record.

Making a Difference

With almost 1,000 employees in Austin in its new, three-building office complex at Riata Crossing, NHIC has a visible presence in the city. The company's new facility consolidates employees and operations formerly located in five different Austin locations. As an employer, NHIC focuses on teamwork and organizational learning concepts, providing personal development programs and ongoing training for employees. "The atmosphere at NHIC is cooperative and positive," says Sally Ward, the company's chief operating officer. "We have our own distinct culture, which has evolved to both fit and complement Austin's unique environment."

Various local organizations, particularly those that focus on promoting excellence in public education, are recipients of time and efforts donated by the people of NHIC. Through the EDS Education Outreach program, NHIC employees help improve the quality of the learning process through both the use of state-of-the-art technology and hands-on involvement. NHIC participates in the Austin-area Junior Achievement program, and also supports Barrington Elementary School through the Austin Partners in Education program.

Through parent company EDS, NHIC is part of a larger, worldwide community outreach effort. EDS is a founding sponsor and the technology provider to the JASON Project, a program designed to excite and engage students in science and technology, as well as to provide professional development opportunities for teachers. The EDS Technology Grant program provides financial awards to teachers of children ages six

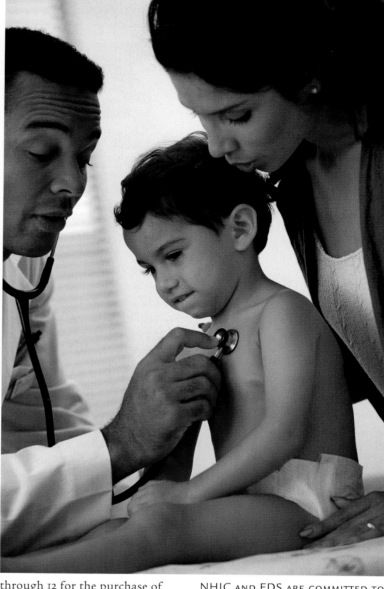

through 12 for the purchase of information technology products and services that will improve their pupils' abilities to learn. Additionally, EDS provided information technology support and results management for the Texas Special Olympics Summer Games in Austin, and continues this partnership now that the Summer Games event has been moved to Houston. In conjunction with EDS' annual Global Volunteer Day, NHIC and its employees participate in their own local outreach projects, including recent participation in the Habitat for Humanity Housing Blitz, as well as Caritas activities.

Part of a global company, but dedicated to the local Austin community, NHIC has become an important part of the city. With its tradition of growth and innovation, NHIC is certain to continue as a leader in its industry well into the new millennium.

NHIC and EDS are committed to the future through community involvement (left).

Behind-the-scenes work by NHIC ensures that physicians and their patients can focus on what really is important (right).

EEA (Energy Engineering Associates, Inc.)

USTIN'S HIGH-TECHNOLOGY FACILITIES ARE OFTEN noted for their style, their cost, or their size. However, it's what's behind the walls and above the ceiling that really makes them run. ★ "What makes a building more than shelter from the rain?

The invisible systems inside that provide comfort, safety, and added value," says Michael Hart, president of EEA (Energy Engineering Associates, Inc.). The company is a full-service engineering consulting firm specializing in the design of mechanical, electrical, telecommunications, security, fire protection, plumbing, and process systems for a wide variety of high-technology, industrial, institutional, and commercial clients.

LEADING EEA (ENERGY ENGINEERING ASSOCIATES, INC.) INTO THE NEW MILLENNIUM ARE (FROM LEFT) PRESIDENT MICHAEL HART, VICE PRESIDENT RICHARD CHILDRESS, VICE PRESIDENT RON JACKSON, AND VICE PRESIDENT FRITZ STINSON.

Combined Talents

 Going beyond the role of traditional engineering consultants, EEA offers services that other firms do not, including master planning, design standards, troubleshooting investigations, commissioning, and training. Strategic partnerships allow the firm to offer full-service capabilities. For example, EEA often serves as the prime design professional, hiring architects, structural engineers, and other professionals to get the job done. In other cases, EEA teams with leading contractors for design/build projects.

EEA's 50 employees include mechanical and electrical engineers, designers, CAD drafters, registered communications distribution designers, project managers, and administrative staff. The company is structured in client-based teams rather than discipline-based departments. "We create multidisciplinary teams made up of individuals with broad experience," says Vice President Fritz Stinson. "It gives us the flexibility to respond to clients quickly and knowledgeably with a few well-qualified engineers. With the same individuals working with a client year after year, we develop an in-depth understanding of our clients' needs and become part of their brain trust."

As a result, EEA has grown steadily into a full-service engi-

EEA's PROJECTS INCLUDE LARGE FACILITIES LIKE THIS 550,000-SQUARE-FOOT MANUFACTURING PLANT IN SINGAPORE.

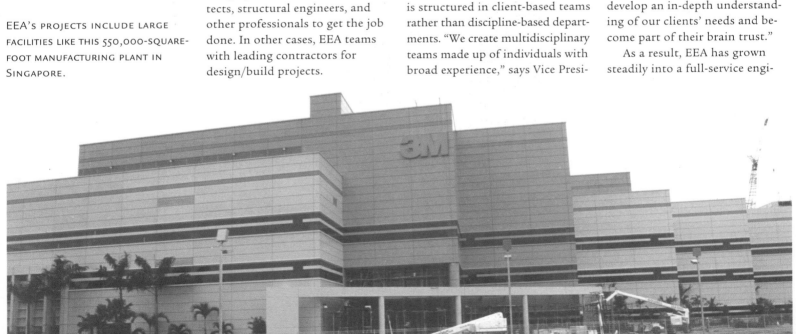

neering consulting firm. Through strategic partnering with large multinational manufacturers, EEA is now involved in the design of new facilities around the world. The firm's recent projects include a 550,000-square-foot manufacturing plant for 3M in Singapore (setting a new Singapore fast-track record), the new Motorola University campus in Austin, and the HVAC renovation of Exxon USA's headquarters building in Houston.

"We develop long-term relationships with clients," says Hart, who founded the company in 1977. "Our objective is to assist clients in constructing and maintaining profitable, comfortable, and energy-efficient facilities."

DIVERSE WORK FOR CLIENTS

The firm's prestigious and diverse list of clients includes 3M; Motorola; Exxon; Wilsonart International; Advanced Micro Devices; Dell Computer Corporation; USAA Insurance; University of Texas; Texas A&M University; Southwestern Bell; Graeber, Simmons & Cowan; Huntsman Chemical; Alcoa; Texaco; VTEL; and Marconi Aerospace (formerly Tracor, Inc).

Twenty years ago, EEA focused solely on energy efficiency projects, and received numerous energy-related awards at the state and national level. Today, much of EEA's work for long-term clients involves renovation, modernization, and ongoing services in industrial facilities. "Our experience solving problems inside existing buildings has helped us avoid problems with new facilities," says Vice President Ron Jackson. "We work hand in hand with the client defining goals, determining appropriate solutions, and often developing options they hadn't considered that save the client time, money, and aggravation."

EEA solves problems by developing solutions that range from commonsense quick fixes to innovative high-tech creations. The company has assisted large multinational corporations and small start-up companies develop first-class clean rooms, semiconductor

labs, and computer centers, while meeting budgets, time lines, and project goals.

OPEN COMMUNICATION

We listen to everyone from the top executives to the maintenance technicians to understand what they want and what they need," says Vice President Richard Childress. "We start with the big picture and work down to the details, helping them think through and plan for the future." Even when projects are complete, EEA remains available to clients as an information resource.

The open communication extends to interoffice relationships at EEA, which Hart describes as a culture of shared values and mutual respect. "We like to work with people we admire," he says. "It really changes the flavor of

an organization if you work with people you truly like." The company's bonus structure and profit-sharing pension plan provide motivation for teamwork. Because the firm hires for long-term stability and not to meet the needs of a specific project, EEA has a very low turnover rate.

"EEA is a can-do kind of place; we take personal pride in making a difference," says Stinson. "We give our engineers a lot of responsibility from the start. We hire people who bring talent and enthusiasm to the firm, and we get them together with clients and out in the field as soon as possible."

Many of the firm's employees volunteer their time to various professional, charitable, and service organizations. Says Hart, "It's a nice reflection of the kind of people we have at EEA."

THIS MASS FLOW CONTROLLER CALIBRATION FACILITY IS AN EXAMPLE OF EEA'S WORK IN AUSTIN.

REVOLUTIONARY IDEAS AND INNOVATIVE TECHNOLOGY HAVE helped Personique change the face of cosmetic surgery and become Austin's premier plastic surgery center. The Personique clinic is based on the principle of personal aesthetic plastic surgery with specific attention to the

care and happiness of patients. The unique qualities of Personique, however, lie within its comprehensive approach to enhancing appearance. Both the physicians and the entire Personique staff strive to ensure a unique and rejuvenating experience in cosmetic surgery.

According to Dr. Robert Ersek, Personique founder, "Patient education, specialized care, comfort, and a knowledgeable staff are factors that place Personique in the upper echelons of cosmetic surgery."

DISCOVERING THE BEAUTY WITHIN

The clinic maintains information on each cosmetic procedure it performs in an extensive library, and patients receive complete orientations in order to make educated choices. Personique also provides each patient with detailed information on the process of choosing a surgeon, which is one of the most important factors in

the success of aesthetic plastic surgery. The clinic advises prospective patients to conduct research into the surgeon's training and experience; check for certification

by the American Board of Plastic Surgeons or the American Society for Aesthetic Plastic Surgery; and check the surgeon's hospital affiliation. Prospective patients are advised to talk candidly with their surgeon, who should be happy to answer any questions and inform patients of the possible risk and side effects associated with surgery.

Computer imaging can be used to illustrate the appropriate changes one might expect of a particular procedure for the individual patient. The results of hair transplants, facelifts, eye and nose shaping, chemical peels, breast enlargement or reduction, tummy tucks, thigh lifts, and liposuction can all be depicted. Patients can also access Personique's Web site at www.personique.com for additional information on many procedures.

Laser surgery, Photoderm, and Endermologie are also available at Personique. Laser treatment of damaged skin reduces the appearance of wrinkles and sun damage,

PERSONIQUE'S STAFF OF BOARD-CERTIFIED PLASTIC SURGEONS INCLUDES (FROM LEFT) MARTIN SCHAEFERLE, M.D. AND ROBERT A. ERSEK, M.D.

PERSONIQUE PROVIDES A FULL RANGE OF SERVICES, INCLUDING HAIR TRANSPLANTS, FACE-LIFTS, EYE AND NOSE SHAPING, CHEMICAL PEELS, BREAST ENLARGEMENT OR REDUCTION, TUMMY TUCKS, LIPOSUCTION LASER SURGERY, PHOTODERM®, AND PERMANENT COSMETIC MAKEUP. ENDERMOLOGIE™, A NONINVASIVE FORM OF CELLULITE REDUCTION, IS ALSO AVAILABLE AT THE CENTER.

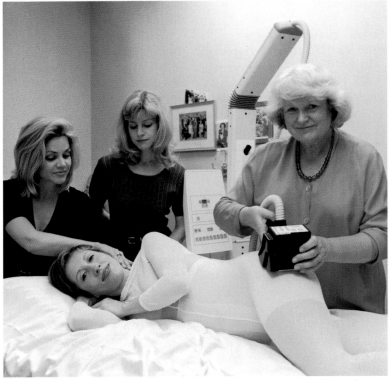

BARNES AND ELVINS PHOTOGRAPHY

while Photoderm® rids the legs of spider veins. Endermologie™ is a noninvasive, pressure-suction technique that reduces cellulite. These and other procedures are performed on-site in state-of-the-art surgical suites. Postoperative patients recover in comfortable, secluded rooms.

Personique uses "twilight anesthesia" for all surgical procedures. This type of outpatient anesthesia provides complete comfort and yet allows the individual to go home the same day surgery is performed. Outpatient surgeries reduce costs and are more discreet, and recovery at home is more pleasant than recovering in a hospital.

EXPANDING THE BOUNDARIES OF COSMETIC SURGERY

"Our clinic is dedicated only to elective cosmetic surgery and procedures," says Ersek. "By narrowing the scope of our patients and concentrating our energies on one specialty, we get the very best doctors and staff."

The skilled surgeons at Personique include Martin Schaeferle III, M.D. Schaeferle attended the University of Iowa, and his list of scholastic honors includes election to Phi Beta Kappa, a B.A. with honors as an undergraduate, and Phi Alpha Mu in medical school. He received his specialty training at the University of Utah and the University of Kansas.

Following his internship, Schaeferle served as an active-duty naval physician, where he earned the Naval Achievement Medal for his volunteer work with Korean civilians. In addition to doing cosmetic surgery, he served 18 years on the Washington State Maxillofacial Review Board and 10 years as part-time medical director of the Firefighters' Burn Center in Tacoma. Schaeferle continues to perform volunteer reconstructive surgery through the Heal the Children Foundation.

Ersek's interest in aesthetic plastic surgery came naturally, as he blended surgical prowess with his flair for artistic creativity and a genuine desire to help people feel better about themselves. He came to Austin from Pennsylvania

by way of Minnesota, attending Hahnemann Medical College in Philadelphia, the University of Minnesota Medical School, and Tulane University Medical School in New Orleans along the way. Upon arriving in Austin, he began performing cosmetic surgery, in addition to volunteering for Austin Smiles, an organization of charitable physicians who perform plastic surgery to correct the cleft palates of underprivileged youths throughout Latin America. Ersek is also the past president of the Lipoplasty Society of North America.

All the surgeons are certified by the American Board of Plastic Surgery and are members of the

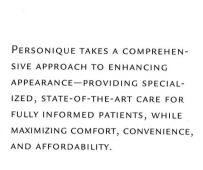

American Society of Plastic and Reconstructive Surgery, the American Society of Aesthetic Plastic Surgery, and the Lipoplasty Society of North America.

Personique's comprehensive approach to enhancing appearance—providing specialized, state-of-the-art care for fully informed patients, while maximizing comfort, convenience, and affordability—may be one of the most important advances in plastic surgery. Believing that having confidence in one's appearance runs more than skin deep, the staff and doctors at Personique are proud to practice their overall approach to cosmetic surgery.

PERSONIQUE TAKES A COMPREHENSIVE APPROACH TO ENHANCING APPEARANCE—PROVIDING SPECIALIZED, STATE-OF-THE-ART CARE FOR FULLY INFORMED PATIENTS, WHILE MAXIMIZING COMFORT, CONVENIENCE, AND AFFORDABILITY.

BARNES AND ELVINS PHOTOGRAPHY

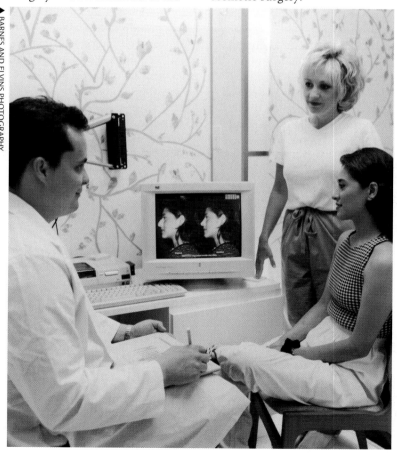

AT PERSONIQUE, COMPUTER IMAGING CAN BE USED TO ILLUSTRATE THE APPROPRIATE OUTCOME OF A PARTICULAR PROCEDURE FOR INDIVIDUAL PATIENTS.

WHEN AMD OPENED THE DOORS OF ITS FIRST WAFER manufacturing plant in southeast Austin in 1979, few locals knew much about high tech. But over the past 20 years, the high-tech industry and Austin have grown up together. ★ Founded in 1969 by Chairman and CEO W.J. Sanders III, AMD is a global supplier of integrated circuits for the personal and networked computer and communications markets. The company produces processors, flash memories, programmable logic devices, and products for communications and networking applications.

AMD's involvement in personal computers spans the entire history of the industry. The second-largest supplier of Microsoft® Windows®-compatible processors for PCs, the company has produced every generation of microprocessor for a wide range of applications. In addition to being a leading microprocessor supplier, AMD is a global communications company, producing integrated circuits for a wide range of telecommunications and local area network (LAN) applications.

Based in Sunnyvale, AMD has approximately 13,000 employees worldwide. While the company has manufacturing facilities in the United States, Asia, Japan, and Germany, more than 80 percent of its manufacturing occurs in Austin. Employing 4,400 people locally, AMD is one of the largest

▲ RICK WILLIAMS/AUSTIN

private employers in the city. With manufacturing and administrative support facilities located on a 138-acre campus on East Ben White Boulevard, the company currently occupies more than 2 million square feet in four AMD-owned buildings and several leased facilities. The company's wafer-fabrication facilities in Austin perform high-volume manufacturing.

BUILDING TOMORROW'S FUTURE TODAY

AMD's purpose, to "empower people everywhere to lead more productive lives," is fulfilled throughout the company by adherence to six core values: respect for people; integrity and responsibility; competition; knowledge; initiative and accountability; and customer success.

Through both corporate and individual employee actions, AMD strives to enhance the quality of life for its own employees and for the local community. Each year, AMD contributes financial resources and volunteer labor to more than 100 local nonprofit organizations in three targeted

areas: health and welfare, civic affairs, and education.

AMD focuses much of its energy on innovative education programs for the community. "We try to provide a link between the classroom and the clean room to enhance student and teacher achievement, through both targeted contributions and volunteer assignments," says Allyson Peerman, community affairs manager.

A unique partnership between AMD, other local high-tech companies, and Austin Community

CLOCKWISE FROM TOP: FAB 25, AMD'S STATE-OF-THE-ART MANUFACTURING FACILITY, IS ONE OF THE LARGEST AND MOST ADVANCED FABRICATION FACILITIES IN THE WORLD. IN 1996, FAB 25 WAS ONE OF TWO FACILITIES CHOSEN AS FAB OF THE YEAR BY *Semiconductor International* MAGAZINE.

A HIGH SCHOOL STUDENT SPENDING HER SUMMER AS AN INTERN AT AMD INSPECTS A WAFER FOR DEFECTS DURING THE MANUFACTURING PROCESS.

WORKFORCE DEVELOPMENT IS A PRIORITY FOR AMD AND FOR AUSTIN, AS THE SEMICONDUCTOR INDUSTRY'S GROWTH HAS FAR OUTPACED THE REGION'S AVAILABLE WORKFORCE. SUMMER INTERNS IN THE COMPANY'S ACCELERATED CAREERS IN ELECTRONICS (ACE) PROGRAM RECEIVE ONE-ON-ONE COACHING FROM THEIR SUPERVISORS.

◄ RICK WILLIAMS/AUSTIN

College helped create the Semiconductor Manufacturing Technology Program, which benefits the local community both by enhancing educational opportunities and by expanding the pool of highly skilled technical employees. AMD continues its involvement in the program by loaning instructors, providing curriculum guidance, and offering paid scholarships to deserving students.

Through partnerships with local schools, AMD employees routinely give students an extra dose of positive adult attention through mentoring, tutoring, reading, and other activities. The company works closely with both the Austin and the Del Valle Independent School Districts (ISDs). AMD's Accelerated Careers in Electronics (ACE) program allows high school students to take electronics courses for college credit and provides opportunities for students to apply for paid summer internships. For the past several years, AMD employees have taught the Junior Achievement curriculum to area elementary schools. The in-school program inspires young people to value free enterprise, to understand business and economics, and to be workforce ready.

This commitment to education has not gone unnoticed. Thanks in part to support from AMD, Smith Elementary in Del Valle won a national Blue Ribbon award from the U.S. Department of Education, the first ever awarded to a Del Valle school. For its ACE program, AMD won the Austin ISD Adopt-A-School's School-to-Work Award, and Exemplary Worksite

RICK WILLIAMS/AUSTIN

Awards from the National Tech Prep Network and the Governor's Office. Both the Del Valle and Austin school districts have named AMD the Adopter of the Year, and the City of Austin has honored AMD for its philanthropy.

AMD's popular holiday giving program allows employees to choose from several different events to share with Austin's less fortunate. From wrapping gifts for the Austin State Hospital to donating to Coats for Kids to providing food and gifts to needy families, AMD makes quite a difference in people's lives.

AMD employees have also built two homes for the Austin chapter of Habitat for Humanity; participated in a fund-raising walk for SafePlace; and helped with Special Olympics, United Way's Day of Caring, and Keep Austin Beautiful's Clean Sweep.

The company shares and encourages the spirit of volunteerism through its sponsorship of KVUE/Channel 24's Five Who Care and Five Kids Who Care programs

RICK WILLIAMS/AUSTIN

highlighting outstanding Central Texas volunteers.

AMD strives to support programs that focus on the future of Austin, whether through education or nonprofit organizations. Reflecting the company's values through its actions—especially those centering on people and knowledge—AMD not only helps to shape the future of Austin, but ensures its own continuing success as well.

CLOCKWISE FROM TOP:
IN A UNIQUE PARTNERSHIP, AMD DONATES ALL OF ITS USED COMPUTERS AND COMPUTER PARTS TO THE LOCAL GOODWILL'S COMPUTER WORKS PROGRAM. THE COMPUTERS ARE REPAIRED BY GOODWILL JOB-TRAINING CLIENTS AND THEN SOLD BY THE AGENCY AT REASONABLE PRICES. THE PROGRAM ALSO PROVIDES COMPUTERS TO LOW-INCOME CHILDREN AT DEEPLY DISCOUNTED PRICES.

HABITAT FOR HUMANITY IS A FAVORITE VOLUNTEER ACTIVITY FOR AMD EMPLOYEES. AN EMPLOYEE APPLIES GROUT TO THE UNDERPINNING OF A HABITAT HOME IN THE FINAL STAGES OF COMPLETION.

EACH YEAR, EMPLOYEES FROM AMD'S ENVIRONMENTAL HEALTH AND SAFETY DEPARTMENT PARTICIPATE IN AREA CLEANUPS TO PICK UP TRASH AROUND THE COMPANY'S SOUTHEAST AUSTIN FACILITY.

RICK WILLIAMS/AUSTIN

O N A SUNDAY IN 1979, 60 FAMILIES GATHERED TO WORSHIP in a rented schoolhouse in Austin. Their vision was to provide a safe haven where bruised, battered, broken, and bored people could find Christ. The day marked the beginning of Riverbend Church, a small congrega-

tion that has grown steadily over the years.

"From its inception," says Senior Pastor Dr. Gerald Mann, "Riverbend has sought to reach the cynical, the unchurched, and the skeptical with the good news of the healing, life-transforming power of God's amazing grace."

Although the church maintains its Baptist affiliation, it re-

flects the diversity of the Austin area, with members representing all ages, ethnicities, and religious backgrounds. Each Sunday, more than 5,000 people attend Riverbend's two worship services and three Sunday school sessions, traveling from all parts of Austin and its surrounding communities.

CONTINUOUS GROWTH

O n Easter 1998, Riverbend opened a classically designed worship center that seats approximately 3,000. With conscious decisions regarding the style of worship and building architecture, the church sought to create a user-friendly environment without the traditional trappings of most churches. Built of native limestone, the facility features a spectacular Hill Country view.

Bible study classes meet at least three nights a week, and numerous small learning groups gather throughout the month to discuss topics of interest to members. Classes for couples, singles, families, men, women, children, and dozens of other groups offer growth and support for members.

Riverbend's outreach programs are built on the strength of its volunteers, about 1,000 of whom help do everything from teaching Sunday school to greeting members to stuffing envelopes to caring for children during the service. The church itself supports a number of charitable causes, including local organizations such as the Ministry of Challenge, Angels Afoot, Caritas, Austin Area Candlelighters Childhood Cancer Foundation, Habitat for Humanity, Greater Calvary Baptist Church, and Austin Children's Shelter. "If you find a group that's doing something well," advises Mann, "don't copy it, support it. And if you find something that's not being done to meet a need, go out and do it."

Mann has received national recognition for his one-line, zinger prayers delivered to the Texas House of Representatives, as well as for his humorous comments and unique advertising techniques. He has been featured in numerous magazines, newspapers, and television shows. Each week, he broadcasts Riverbend's message into 70 million homes across the United States on *Real Life with Dr. Gerald Mann.*

According to Mann, Riverbend's growth has come from meeting a common need. "Hope is the greatest need felt by most people today," he says. "They want to know they are not alone in facing today's trials and tomorrow's troubles. In short, what we all want most is to know God is with us now and will be with us in the future."

"FROM ITS INCEPTION," SAYS SENIOR PASTOR DR. GERALD MANN, "RIVERBEND HAS SOUGHT TO REACH THE CYNICAL, THE UNCHURCHED, AND THE SKEPTICAL WITH THE GOOD NEWS OF THE HEALING, LIFE-TRANSFORMING POWER OF GOD'S AMAZING GRACE."

ON EASTER 1998, RIVERBEND OPENED A CLASSICALLY DESIGNED WORSHIP CENTER THAT SEATS APPROXIMATELY 3,000.

ROM POST-IT® NOTES TO THE VOLITION™ FIBER-TO-THE-DESK fiber-optic cabling system—and 50,000 products in between—3M creates products found in every corner of the world. Much of that innovation begins in Austin. ★ Austin is the headquarters of the 3M Electro and

Communications Markets Group, which includes Electrical Products, Electronic Handling and Protection, Corrosion Protection Products, Electronic Products, Telecom Systems, Visual Systems, and Corporate Services.

Based in Minnesota, 3M has had a presence in Austin through its distributors since the 1950s. Through the 1982 acquisition of a local company, APC Industries, Inc., 3M began a new legacy in Austin, and by 1984, established its research and development site. 3M Austin Center, a 1.2 million-square-foot facility with views of the Texas Hill Country, has received numerous awards for design and environmental excellence. 3M Austin also has a manufacturing facility on U.S. Highway 183, and approximately 1,800 people work at the two sites.

3M's corporate signature is innovation. Much more than a word or a mission, innovation is at the heart of all of 3M's philosophies, policies, and performance. Promoting entrepreneurship and freedom in the workplace to pursue innovative ideas, while committing to the highest standards of quality and ethics, characterizes 3M's principles of management.

Innovation at 3M leads to the development of unique and reliable products and services that

contribute to a better quality of life for its customers. "By applying core technologies to developing innovative solutions, we strive to invent new products, not just to improve existing ones," says Leo Dunn, vice president for Corporate Services at 3M.

With a vast range of products within each division, 3M Austin's client base also spans the globe. Dozens of industries—including major telecommunications service providers, major electronic manufacturers, power utilities, computer manufacturers, and electrical suppliers—look to 3M Austin for integrated solutions and ideas to help them grow.

EMPLOYEE AND COMMUNITY COMMITMENTS

Through its unique Lifestyle 2000 program, 3M Austin promotes the overall health and well-being of its employees. With on-site exercise and tai chi chuan classes, a noon lecture series with such topics as time management for working parents, and a toll-free hot line to answer employees' health-related questions, 3M Austin Center goes well beyond the typical office environment.

3M Austin is committed to helping improve and strengthen the local community. The company contributes to a number of education, health and human services, and arts and cultural programs through civic and service organizations, volunteerism, gifts in kind, and direct grants from the 3M Foundation.

The company sees a strong future in Austin and looks forward to being closely involved in the community for many years to come. "We have aggressive growth targets for the future and we strongly believe that Austin, through its resources and its atmosphere, is the right area to help foster that growth," says Dunn.

CLOCKWISE FROM TOP LEFT: 3M AUSTIN CENTER IS THE HEADQUARTERS OF THE 3M ELECTRO AND COMMUNICATIONS MARKETS GROUP, WHICH COMPRISES SIX BUSINESSES: ELECTRICAL PRODUCTS, ELECTRONIC PRODUCTS, ELECTRONIC HANDLING AND PROTECTION, TELECOM SYSTEMS, CORROSION PROTECTION, AND VISUAL SYSTEMS.

NATURAL LIGHTING, TREES, AND GREENERY ALL HELP TO CREATE A COMFORTABLE ENVIRONMENT INSIDE 3M AUSTIN CENTER, PUTTING EMPLOYEES AND VISITORS IN TOUCH WITH THE BEAUTY AND SERENITY OF THE TEXAS HILL COUNTRY.

THE 3M™ VOLITION™ FIBER-OPTIC CABLING SYSTEM BRINGS TO THE DESK THE POWER OF OPTICAL FIBER NETWORKING WITH THE EASE OF TRADITIONAL COPPER WIRE. THE SYSTEM WAS DEVELOPED AND IS MADE IN AUSTIN.

BASED ON LEADING-EDGE TECHNOLOGY, 3M MICROFLEX CIRCUITS ADDRESS THE NEED FOR ELECTRONIC PRODUCTS THAT ARE MORE POWERFUL, SMALLER, LIGHTER, AND ECONOMICAL. THE PRODUCT PLATFORM WAS DEVELOPED IN AUSTIN.

OW DO THE WORLD'S LARGEST PHARMACEUTICAL MANUFAC-
turers, chemical companies, oil producers, and other
firms control worldwide operations from the field to
the plant floor to the office? With help from Fisher-
Rosemount Systems. ★ Fisher-Rosemount Systems is

part of the Fisher-Rosemount group
of companies owned by Emerson
Electric Co. Fisher-Rosemount
is the largest of Emerson's business units and the world's largest
supplier of process automation
solutions. Products include process management systems, valves,
regulators, transmitters, analyzers,
services, and solutions. Founded
in 1890, Emerson is a worldwide
manufacturer of industrial products whose annual sales exceed
$11 billion.

As one of the world's largest
control system suppliers, Fisher-
Rosemount Systems boasts a
global workforce of 2,000 and
more than 8,000 installed systems.
While the company's worldwide
headquarters is located in Austin,
it maintains operations and technology centers in Minnesota,
California, Canada, England,
the Netherlands, and Singapore.

With 800 employees in Austin,
Fisher-Rosemount Systems makes
a significant contribution to local
community activities. In addition
to organizing and participating
in events such as blood drives and
school sponsorship programs, the
company supports numerous service and charitable organizations,
including United Way. Fisher-
Rosemount's employees are also
able to contribute to the educational
or cultural institutions of their
choice through a matching gift
program established by Emerson
Electric Co.

FIERY BEGINNINGS

The idea for the company
was born back in 1880,
when a fire raged through
the Iowa farm community of
Marshalltown. Exhausted fire-
fighter William Fisher decided
that there must be a better way to
maintain constant water pressure
than hand throttling the steam-
driven pumps. Several months
later, Fisher invented a constant-
pressure pump governor. The Fisher
Type I governor was patented in
1884, and by 1888, sales were so
strong that Fisher left his bicycle
and camera business to concentrate
solely on the new product.

Over the years, Fisher's company
developed numerous control valves
and became an industry leader.
In 1969, it became an independent
subsidiary of Monsanto and began
manufacturing a line of electronic
control instrumentation. The division responsible for the control systems moved to Austin in 1981.

Rosemount was founded in 1956
by Dr. Frank D. Werner, Robert
E. Keppel, and Vernon H. Heath.
The three met while working for
the University of Minnesota Aero-
nautical Research Laboratory in
Rosemount, Minnesota. Werner
developed a sensor for use on military jet aircraft, and the three
formed the Rosemount Engineering Company to mass-produce the
sensor for the U.S. Air Force. The
company, later known as Rosemount Inc., introduced its first
control system in 1973.

AS ONE OF THE WORLD'S LARG-
EST CONTROL SYSTEM SUPPLIERS,
FISHER-ROSEMOUNT SYSTEMS BOASTS
A GLOBAL WORKFORCE OF 2,000
AND MORE THAN 8,000 INSTALLED
SYSTEMS.

Emerson Electric Co., with the plan to build the world's largest instrumentation and control systems company, acquired Rosemount Inc. in 1976, and Fisher Controls in 1992, to form Fisher-Rosemount. Fisher-Rosemount Systems is an integral part of Fisher-Rosemount.

SERVICE THROUGH PROCESS CONTROL

Fisher-Rosemount Systems develops complete process automation solutions that help companies control programs across all levels of their operations. Solutions include software, hardware, expertise, services, and third-party alliances. Its product line includes RS3™, PROVOX®, and DeltaV™, award-winning platforms that help customers achieve higher value through full process automation systems. Its new PlantWeb™ field-based product combines intelligent field devices, scalable platforms, and modular software to provide not only process control, but also integrated asset management.

The company's customers are literally all over the map, with products and systems representing most major industries. Pharmaceutical manufacturers, oil and gas producers, chemical companies, pulp and paper process units, and food and beverage manufacturers all rely on Fisher-Rosemount

Systems to develop solutions that lead to powerful business results.

Through the firm's innovative Consult for a Day program, Fisher-Rosemount Systems experts meet with customers to investigate their toughest application problems. Working with the customer, they will identify and document possible opportunities for more efficient operation and additional cost savings.

Fisher-Rosemount Systems' primary focus is on customer satisfaction, through its employees, products, services, and support. Knowing that customer satisfaction begins with employee satisfaction, Fisher-Rosemount strives to treat all employees with dignity, respect, and fairness in an environment that facilitates individual growth and teamwork. Throughout the corporate culture, emphasis is placed on continuous improvement, innovation, ideas, and initiative.

Customers and industry analysts respond to Fisher-Rosemount Systems' companywide focus on service. *Control* magazine, one of the most widely read publications in the process control industry, has rated the company number one in customer service for three consecutive years. Fisher-Rosemount Systems has also been honored by the magazine as number one in large scale distributed control systems, batch software, and pro-

cess monitoring and control software. The company has received numerous other awards for its products, including the Leonardo Award for Technical Innovations in Manufacturing from Microsoft.

"Seventy percent of our business is repeat business," says Jim Hoffmaster, president of Fisher-Rosemount Systems. "Our customers understand that the value we bring through our products, combined with our excellent customer service and support, lets them leave the details to us so they can focus on their own success."

SULZER ORTHOPEDICS INC.

EVERY DAY, SULZER ORTHOPEDICS INC. IMPROVES LIVES around the world with its hip, knee, shoulder, and spinal implant systems. One of the top suppliers of musculoskeletal implants in the world, the company meets the ever changing challenges of orthopedic

medicine with products designed for everyone from the young and active patient to the more sedentary elderly population.

"Sulzer Orthopedics is a dynamic player in the musculoskeletal tissue repair industry," says Felix Scherrer, president of Sulzer Orthopedics and its affiliate, Sulzer Spine-Tech. "Our purpose is to improve the quality of patients' lives by improving musculoskeletal medicine."

GLOBAL REACH

Opened in 1981 as Intermedics Orthopedics, the company was acquired by Sulzer Medica, and changed its name in 1997 to reflect this affiliation. "As an integral part of Sulzer Medica," explains Scherrer, "we are part of a $1 billion global health care corporation that includes medical devices for orthopedic and spinal reconstruction and repair, cardiovascular, and dentistry, as well as leading research in biologic technology for tissue regeneration throughout the human body.

"Sulzer Medica is the medical technology arm of the Switzerland-based Sulzer Ltd., a 162-year-old, multitechnology corporation with more than $5 billion in sales. With

this financial stability," Scherrer continues, "Sulzer Orthopedics is in a good situation to improve our positioning in a marketplace where size, breadth, depth of product offerings, and financial stability of a supplier is increasingly important."

Thanks to its parent company, Sulzer Orthopedics also has access to a reliable, worldwide distribution network. Along with its customer-centered philosophy, this makes it a popular resource for health care delivery networks that must provide quality care as efficiently as possible.

In 1995, Sulzer Orthopedics built a state-of-the-art, 210,000-square-foot campus in northwest

Austin to house its research, development, and manufacturing facilities. On-site videoconferencing and satellite facilities enable communication with medical professionals worldwide, and a fully equipped training room provides opportunities for surgeons to acquire hands-on knowledge of Sulzer Orthopedics' products. The company is certified to the ISO 9001 international quality system standard as well as the European Medical Device Directive.

IMPLANT SOLUTIONS

Sulzer Orthopedics designs and manufactures a broad line of products to meet a vast range of patient

IN 1995, SULZER ORTHOPEDICS BUILT A STATE-OF-THE-ART, 210,000-SQUARE-FOOT CAMPUS IN NORTHWEST AUSTIN TO HOUSE ITS RESEARCH, DEVELOPMENT, AND MANUFACTURING FACILITIES.

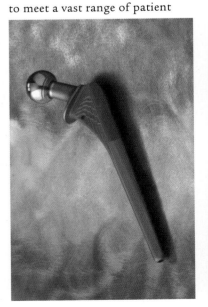

SULZER ORTHOPEDICS DESIGNS AND MANUFACTURES A BROAD LINE OF PRODUCTS TO MEET A VAST RANGE OF PATIENT NEEDS.

needs and surgeon philosophies. Its comprehensive knee systems, the Natural-Knee® and Apollo® Knee, have superior clinical results in endurance, comfort, and natural range of motion.

The firm's hip systems re-create the anatomic reality of the body in both design and leading-edge bone fixation technology. Sulzer Orthopedics offers a full range of design options to meet different surgeon preferences, including the Natural-Hip™, APR® Hip, Apollo® Hip, Precedent™ Revision Hip, and Inter-Op™ Acetabular System.

The Select® Shoulder System simplifies the management of complex shoulder fractures, and the MOST™ System meets the need for specialized implants in cases of severe bone loss and trauma.

Sulzer Orthopedics' affiliate, Sulzer Spine-Tech, has revolutionized spinal surgery with the BAK® Interbody Fusion System. The BAK System offers a less invasive approach to traditional spinal surgery, which results in minimal complications and quick back-to-work recovery time.

TECHNOLOGY LEADER

With more than 60 patent holdings, Sulzer Orthopedics has made major contributions to orthopedics technology, especially in the field of tribology—the study of wear, lubrication, and friction. The company is a leader in porous-coating technology, which promotes a long-lasting, biologic bond between the implant and natural tissues. Also, the firm's metal-on-metal hip implant technology has been shown to dramatically improve the longevity of implants.

In addition to technical innovations, Sulzer Orthopedics has focused on providing value-added services to meet the growing need for high-quality, cost-effective orthopedic solutions. The Joint Endeavor™ Program, for example, provides surgeons and hospitals with the means to achieve dramatic reductions in the length of hospital stays, complications, and their associated costs, while achieving significant improvements in quality, clinical outcomes, and patient satisfaction. Another unique service, the Practice Pro-Motion™

Kit, helps surgeons promote and grow their practices.

HELPING PEOPLE LIVE BETTER LIVES

Sulzer Orthopedics places a strong emphasis on preserving and protecting the environment, and is committed to reducing and minimizing waste. The company is a member of the Clean Texas Star program and has garnered awards from the Capital Area Corporate Recycling Council for its recycling program, and from the City of Austin for Excellence in Wastewater Pretreatment. In addition, Sulzer Orthopedics maintains a comprehensive water reduction program and recycles up to 70 percent of its waste. Through its Close the Loop program, Sulzer Orthopedics purchases office supplies with recycled content.

In 1997, Sulzer Orthopedics won the first BEST (Businesses for an Environmentally Sustainable Tomorrow) innovation award in energy efficiency. Other recent accomplishments include the

elimination of all VOC (volatile organic compound) cleaning solvents used in manufacturing processes.

In addition to proactive environmental management in the workplace, Sulzer Orthopedics' 500-plus Austin employees are involved in the community's environmental efforts by supporting an on-site recycling collection center and adopting a stretch of highway to maintain litter-free.

Sulzer Orthopedics and its employees also support community activities and charitable causes, including matching gifts programs benefiting the United Way and PBS/KLRU, Easter Seals campaign, Red Cross Blood Drive, the Salvation Army Angel Tree Christmas project, Austin Partners in Education, and St. Jude Children's Ranch Christmas Card Project.

With a staunch commitment to making the world a better place, coupled with its focus on developing better medical products, Sulzer Orthopedics is truly helping people live better lives.

SULZER ORTHOPEDICS IMPROVES LIVES AROUND THE WORLD WITH ITS HIP, KNEE, SHOULDER, AND SPINAL IMPLANT SYSTEMS.

CLEAR CHANNEL RADIO, INC.

USTIN'S HOMES, OFFICES, AND CARS WOULD BE AWFULLY quiet without Clear Channel Radio, Inc., a favorite source of entertainment for a wide variety of people. ★ Clear Channel Radio's bill of fare in Austin includes four stations: KPEZ FM (Z102), featuring

classic rock; KEYI FM (Oldies 103), with "the greatest oldies from the fifties and sixties"; KHFI FM, a contemporary hits format; and KFON AM (SportsFan), an all-sports station. KPEZ—on the air in Austin since 1982—is the oldest of the four. The others were acquired by Clear Channel in 1993.

While all four stations broadcast from the top of the company's office building on Barton Springs Road, the stations are unique in both their sounds and their styles. Some of the demographic profiles of listeners overlap, but the radio signals ultimately reach a diverse group of listeners. KHFI targets listeners aged 18 to 49, while Oldies 103 is most popular with listeners between ages 35 and 54. Z102 and SportsFan both target listeners in their 20s, 30s, and 40s.

GOOD MORNING

The radio stations love to interact with the community through their popular morning shows. *The Wake-Up Show* is personality oriented, focusing on lively conversation between cohosts and listeners. "We try to provide a fun, lighthearted escape for people gearing up for a long day at work," says cohost Karen Clauss, "It's

almost like Disneyland, but on the radio."

For the past several years, KHFI has been nominated as Radio Station of the Year by various broadcasting trade publications. These awards are based on programming and consistent ratings performance, when judged against the top contemporary hit music radio stations across the country.

The Official Morning Wake-Up Service on Oldies 103 entertains its listeners with news, trivia, contests, jokes, interviews, and phone conversations with an eclectic group of callers who often drive the theme of the show. "We put together the kind of fun and easy

show that people can listen to at home, at work, or even in the car with their kids," says host Connor Vernon.

Z-102 starts its listeners' days by featuring plenty of the classic rock they love, along with traffic information and the day's weather. Host Darren Todd adds to the presentation with his unique, irreverent spin on events in the news.

A CLEAR COMMITMENT

Founded by Lowry Mays, Clear Channel Communications, Inc. is a global diversified media company. The company operates, or is affiliated

◀ MARK COHEN

with, 441 radio stations, 18 television stations, and approximately 200,000 outdoor advertising displays in 25 countries worldwide.

"Our most important business assets are our FCC license and our people," says General Manager Judy Lakin. Clear Channel Radio has 80 full-time and 12 part-time employees. "We work hard and have lots of fun, and we try to provide a great environment for our employees."

While its parent company is a worldwide presence, Clear Channel Radio is greatly influenced by the uniqueness of the Austin area. "One of the greatest things about Clear Channel is the amount of empowerment given at the local level," says Lakin. "That flexibility

allows us to be involved in a wide variety of organizations in the Austin area, which not only helps our company grow and prosper, but ultimately has a great effect on the community."

Clear Channel Radio does indeed affect the community as a member of local organizations, including the Greater Austin Chamber of Commerce, Texas Association of Broadcasters, Ad Society, and American Women in Radio and Television.

All four stations host public affairs programming on Sunday mornings, presenting a wide range of community issues and serving as a forum for community leaders, educators, and government officials to discuss topics relevant to the

Austin community. Clear Channel Radio Austin has a strong, ongoing commitment to air announcements for various charitable causes throughout the year.

The company has a long-standing relationship with the Austin Parks and Recreation Department, with which it coordinates the annual Eggstravaganza, the city's largest Easter egg hunt, with proceeds benefiting the Recreation Center's various programs. Every Halloween, Clear Channel provides a safe environment and candy galore for hundreds of children in a Trick or Treat fair benefiting the Parks and Recreation Department. Each fall, thousands of people help beautify downtown Austin at the Clear Channel-sponsored Town Lake Cleanup, an event that won the Governor's Award for Excellence for Environmental Cleanup from the Texas Natural Resource Conservation Commission.

Each station frequently hosts individual community events, such as KHFI FM's annual Summer Jam, an all-day free concert held in Austin's South Park Meadows. More than 20,000 people come to hear entertainers such as Olivia Newton John and Kool & the Gang. Says Lakin, "We enjoy the opportunity to give something back to our listeners, and they have a great time."

With a formula that translates into popularity with listeners and success for the company, the Clear Channel family of radio stations plans to enliven and enlighten Austin for many broadcasts to come.

Z102'S DARREN TODD INTRODUCES THE MARSHALL TUCKER BAND TO THE CROWD AT DESSAU MUSIC HALL (LEFT).

Z102, THE CLASSIC ROCK STATION, ALWAYS HAS A LONG LINE OF LISTENERS WAITING TO JOIN IN THE EXCITEMENT (RIGHT).

CLEAR CHANNEL PROVIDES A SAFE ENVIRONMENT AND CANDY GALORE FOR HUNDREDS OF CHILDREN IN A TRICK OR TREAT FAIR BENEFITING THE AUSTIN PARKS AND RECREATION DEPARTMENT.

BUSINESS IS GLOBAL—PAPER IS OPTIONAL. TIME IS MONEY— Access Is Vital. ★ Less a slogan than a business philosophy, these words may explain why Austin-based PSI Technologies Corporation is a leading innovator in large-scale electronic storage, retrieval, and delivery

solutions using Internet/intranet and archival media. The company's cutting-edge technologies are revolutionizing the way businesses are linking their customers, employees, and shareholders to their information resources.

Every day, companies generate, send, and store printed documents by the millions, an immensely inefficient and costly practice for organizations that require frequent retrieval and timely delivery of information. PSI's innovative software products help companies wage the war on paper by processing high-volume, business-critical reports and statements into a user-friendly electronic format that offers immediate access and cost-effective distribution.

PSI supplies the permanent archiving of reports and state-

ments electronically—offering the same look and feel of a paper document—and delivers them on CD-ROM, on DVD, or over the Internet/intranet. Clients worldwide have improved productivity and achieved a competitive advantage in customer service, while saving millions of dollars by eliminating the cost of traditional paper methods.

SUPPLYING THE POWER OF INFORMATION

PSI's software and service solutions automate and simplify the storage, retrieval, distribution, and viewing of high-volume bills, statements, and reports—making businesses more efficient, more productive, and, ultimately, more profitable. The company develops

and markets a suite of products called Digital Xpress Reports (DXR).

DXR is a comprehensive client/server-based report and statement management solution that provides a reliable and efficient alternative to manual paper storage and delivery. RomComm, the service bureau division of PSI, uses DXR technology to electronically capture, store, and index data for storage on CD-ROM or DVD for viewing from a PC or through the Internet. Since its inception, RomComm has processed billions of pages of computer-generated statements and reports, including mutual fund and financial statements, 401(k) data, employee contribution reports, 1099 tax forms, bank reports, and retail bills. To continue meeting the needs of the information technology industry, PSI is employing its development expertise to pioneer products such as on-line intelligent and consolidated statements.

Companies in telecommunications, financial services, insurance, health care, transportation, retail, and many other industries rely on PSI to provide instant, easy access to their corporate information. PSI's customers—many of whom are required by law to maintain full-fidelity, "near replica" copies of all customer statements—save hundreds of millions of dollars by replacing paper and microfiche with CD-ROM and DVD storage and on-line delivery.

Not only does PSI's technology "freeze" information content in an unalterable form, but it also preserves the visual appearance of the original printed document, such as format, fonts, and graphics. Companies and their clients can quickly search, view, or data-mine any document, providing instant retrieval of results without the delays of standard searches through file or microfiche archives.

THE LEADERSHIP BEHIND PSI'S VISION: CEO AND FOUNDER PEDRO LANDA (RIGHT), AND PRESIDENT AND COFOUNDER PEDRO KAUFMANN

PRESERVING THE VISION

CEO Pedro Landa founded PSI Technologies Corporation, formerly known as Bacpac International, in Austin in 1982. The company's first products included the development of magnetic tape and optical media units to provide multi-PC users with a favorable alternative to backup and mass-storage devices. In 1985, the company became the first to offer a portable 25- and 60-megabyte tape backup device for microcomputer hard disks, as well as a portable laser optical disk system to permanently store digital information.

In 1987, the company changed its name to PSI Technologies Corporation and released its first source-document system, LaserSig, for bank-signature verification. Responding to the needs of its bank clients in managing computer data, PSI drew upon its optical-disk technology and developed Optical Fiche System (OFS) as a replacement for microfiche retrieval. It is from these core technologies that PSI has developed and expanded its product offering to what it is today.

A history of understanding and responding to its customers' needs enables PSI to provide both timely product solutions and quality service. PSI's engineering background drives its dedication to creating complete solutions for clients, focusing on each one individually. With ongoing customer education, on-site and on-line training, and around-the-clock technical support, PSI takes a very proactive role to ensure customer satisfaction.

Because technology in the information industry changes so rapidly, PSI serves as both the seller and the developer of its software products. In addition to its headquarters in Austin, the privately held company has affiliate offices in the United Kingdom, Canada, Argentina, Chile, Brazil, and Mexico.

The company's culture reflects both the innovation of its founders and the entrepreneurial spirit that is the essence of Austin. "Austin's vitality and energy help us foster and maintain our commitment to continually push the envelope of our technology," says PSI President and cofounder Pedro Kaufmann. "In a constantly changing market such as ours, it takes foresight and creativity to keep up. We were one of the first companies to perfect this technology, and we're confident PSI will remain on the frontier of the industry."

MERICUS DIAMOND, AUSTIN'S MOST SUCCESSFUL INDEPENdent jeweler, is a company based on brilliance—the brilliance not just of the diamonds it sells, but also of the concept that the store was founded upon. That concept is the store's promise to offer the largest selection of the finest quality jewelry at the lowest price and to back it up with a guarantee.

Although Americus Diamond carries a wide variety of jewelry, its specialty—as its name implies— is diamonds. "We buy diamonds directly from the cutters, who get them straight from the mines," says cofounder Richard Crawford. "Because we buy in volume and eliminate the reseller, we can offer the most beautiful diamonds at the best price."

This business philosophy has prevailed since 1983, when Crawford and his partner Kenny Hardin opened their business in North Austin with two showcases and $50,000 worth of jewelry they had made. Business boomed, and Americus Diamond now employs a staff of 10, with three on-site jewelers. Since 1994, the company has seen an average annual growth rate of 25 percent.

THE STAFF OF AMERICUS DIAMOND, WITH OWNERS AND COFOUNDERS KENNY HARDIN (FAR LEFT) AND RICHARD CRAWFORD (FAR RIGHT)

CRAWFORD AND HARDIN OPENED AMERICUS DIAMOND IN 1983, AND THE COMPANY HAS EXPERIENCED STEADY GROWTH SINCE ITS FOUNDING.

AUSTIN'S RING LEADER

Bridal jewelry comprises the majority of Americus Diamond's sales, and the store keeps more than 200 engagement rings in stock at all times. With diamonds of every shape and size—ranging from one-quarter carat to 10 carats—and a vast array of settings, customers have a slew of options from which to choose. Staff jewelers can also custom-make any piece of jewelry to the customer's precise specifications.

"We like to sell from a full wagon so that people can find exactly what they're looking for," says Hardin. "So many choices could be intimidating, but that's where our education process comes in."

Americus Diamond follows the Gemological Institute of America (GIA) grading scale for diamonds, a system that categorizes the gems into 230 different grades of color and clarity. Each stone has a different cut and a different price. Every salesperson at Americus Diamond completes a diamond-grading course through the GIA to better explain the various levels of quality.

"We educate our customers on the grading process, and how that affects both the look and the price of the diamond," says Crawford. "We let them look at the diamonds under a microscope, so they can get a better sense of the different levels of quality. It's a lot for people to

Americus Diamond's employees agree that it is an exciting place to work. The proof is in the store's low turnover rate, an anomaly in the retail business. The sales staff does not receive commissions; rather, all employees benefit from a profit-sharing plan. "Our employees are genuinely happy to work here, and because they present the facts about our merchandise, not a sales pitch, customers enjoy buying from them," says Crawford.

The partners of Americus Diamond credit the company's success not just to its impassioned, well-trained staff, but to the sophisticated Austin public. "Austinites are both highly educated and practical," says Hardin. "So they know that the jewelry they buy from us is the exact same as they could buy from the biggest names in New York or Dallas, but for literally half the cost. The intelligence of the Austin market has helped us tremendously."

Americus Diamond reciprocates the patronage of the Austin community by supporting a number of charitable groups and causes, from schools and hospitals to local sports teams and the Special Olympics. The company also belongs to the Greater Austin Chamber of Commerce and the Better Business Bureau.

"Austin has been great for us," says Crawford. "Like so many others here, we came for the quality of life, and found enormous opportunities."

CLOCKWISE FROM TOP: AMERICUS DIAMOND HAS ONE OF THE LARGEST SELECTIONS OF DIAMOND JEWELRY IN TEXAS.

THE CUT, COLOR, CLARITY, AND CARAT WEIGHT OF A DIAMOND DETERMINE ITS VALUE AND BRILLIANCE.

A ROUND DIAMOND WITH IDEAL PROPORTIONS IS THE MOST BRILLIANT OF ALL GEMSTONES.

learn, so the more we can help them make an educated purchase, the better they feel about it."

To further increase customers' knowledge and make them more comfortable, Americus labels every piece of jewelry in the store with the grade, the diamond weight, and the exact price.

ROCK-SOLID GUARANTEE

Once a purchase is made, Americus guarantees the quality of diamond as well as the workmanship. If a customer ever loses a diamond from its setting, the company will replace it for free. At any time, customers may trade in an Americus diamond for the full original purchase price toward any item in stock of equal or greater value. The firm also guarantees that its everyday marked prices are below its competitors' best prices, and if customers find a better deal, Americus will refund their money plus 25 percent of the difference. As confirmation of its quality and price guarantees, no one has ever taken advantage of the company's offer.

Customers have, however, come back to report on the success of their jewelry gifts or marriage proposals, some of which have taken place in the store and even the parking lot. "It truly is a fun business," says Crawford. "I don't know of any other place where you can meet so many people who are in love, excited about it, and celebrating it."

ORIGIN SYSTEMS, INC.

ERHAPS NOWHERE IS THE CREATIVITY OF THE SOFTWARE business more evident than at ORIGIN Systems, Inc. Known for setting new standards in interactive entertainment, this Austin company creates worlds of immersive simulation with unparalleled attention to

detail. But most of all, ORIGIN creates worlds of fun.

The company originated in 1979, when Richard Garriott began producing software on a shoestring budget with his brother, Robert, and pioneered computer gaming with the release of Akalabeth. In 1983, the Garriotts established ORIGIN with their father, astronaut Owen Garriott, and their friend Charles Bueche. Since then, the company has produced more than 50 highly acclaimed titles, including the award-winning Wing Commander™, Ultima™, Privateer™, and Crusader series of games. ORIGIN also

develops titles under the Jane's Combat Simulations brand.

In 1992, the company became a wholly owned subsidiary of Electronic Arts™ (EA) of San Mateo, California, a global leader in the entertainment software industry. The combined strengths of ORIGIN's unique product development expertise and EA's worldwide distribution power have expanded ORIGIN's influence around the world.

Despite the company's affiliation with EA, its Austin roots remain very important. ORIGIN's dedicated staff includes producers,

programmers, artists, designers, musicians, testers, marketers, and customer support teams. Many of its 220 employees are well-known local talents, including on-staff musicians who create award-winning interactive music. ORIGIN can also claim responsibility for helping several spin-off companies, ancillary businesses, and subindustries begin and succeed in Austin.

"We brought entertainment software to Austin, and we owe our success to this city," says Richard Garriott. "ORIGIN embodies all of Austin's best traits—creativity, music, brainpower—to form the perfect blend of high tech and art."

WIDESPREAD POPULARITY

In recent years, ORIGIN's cutting-edge products have skyrocketed in popularity. Since the launch of the first Wing Commander in 1990, the series has spawned four full sequels and numerous derivative products combining to generate sales of more than 5 million units worldwide. An animated television series based on the property, titled *Wing Commander Academy*, was broadcast on cable in 1996. Most recently, ORIGIN licensed the film rights for the Wing Commander property, which will serve as a basis for a major motion picture.

The company's medieval fantasy role-playing game, Ultima, remains one of the most successful series in the history of entertainment software. In 1997, the series broke new ground with the release of Ultima Online, the fastest-selling Internet-only game in history. Ultima Online brings to life the fantasy land of Britannia as a living, persistent, virtual world that exists only on the Internet and allows thousands of people to play simultaneously.

ROBERT PANDYA

ORIGIN SYSTEM'S DEDICATED STAFF INCLUDES PRODUCERS, PROGRAMMERS, ARTISTS, DESIGNERS, MUSICIANS, TESTERS, MARKETERS, AND CUSTOMER SUPPORT TEAMS.

"The depth and sophistication of our games has helped us to build an incredibly enthusiastic and hard-core fan base," says Garriott. That foundation of support, combined with the innovation of ORIGIN's Ultima Online product, helped sales quickly surpass the predicted volume more than tenfold. While ORIGIN credits much of its blazing success in the Internet market to the foresight of General Manager Neil Young and to the creativity of Vice President and Executive Producer Andy Hollis, it was a team effort that helped the company take the lead in on-line, multiplayer gaming.

ORIGIN's continued success is directly related to its reputation of producing high-quality, creative, and innovative games. Garnering numerous awards and accolades, ORIGIN titles are enjoyed by fans from around the world. In fact, ORIGIN often sells more units in Germany or Japan per capita than in the United States.

WORLDS OF FUN

lthough it takes a lot of hard work to succeed in the world of high-tech entertainment, ORIGIN and its staff haven't lost sight of what's important. "We're in the entertainment industry," says Garriott, "which means everyone is here to have a good time."

 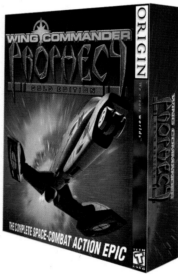

Thanks to ORIGIN's runaway success, the environment is a mixture of dedication and hard work with a good measure of fun.

In addition to developing award-winning entertainment software, employees might be found planning their design for a door decorating contest, racing toy cars in the hallways, creating a masterpiece for a Play-Doh® art contest, or stalking each other in a game of Laser Tag. Elaborate practical jokes are another favorite within the company. ORIGIN also welcomes pets and families at the office and hosts several events for employees and their children, such as an Easter egg hunt and a Christmas party.

Richard Garriott is also known throughout Austin for his legend-

ary haunted houses. Held in his home at his own expense, this Halloween tradition features elaborate sets and dozens of actors and technicians who help make the experience one of the most sought-after tickets in town.

During the years in which Garriott does not host a haunted house, he helps to sponsor Haunted Trails to benefit the Wild Basin Wilderness Preserve. The company also supports Handson Housing, Zachary Scott Theatre, and Paramount Theatre.

"Austin is such an amazing place because people and companies with the capacity to do so give so much back to the community," says Garriott. "The city has certainly given us so much, and we want to do our part."

NESTLED IN THE HILLS JUST WEST OF DOWNTOWN AUSTIN, ORIGIN HAS PRODUCED MORE THAN 50 HIGHLY ACCLAIMED ENTERTAINMENT SOFTWARE TITLES.

DELL COMPUTER CORPORATION

SAY "DELL COMPUTER CORPORATION" IN ANY CROWDED ROOM in Austin, and almost everyone will recognize the name—whether they know Dell employees, use Dell products, or benefit from Dell's extensive community outreach. The only Fortune 500 company headquartered in the region, the reach of Dell's impact stretches worldwide.

Founded in 1984 by Michael Dell, now the computer industry's longest-tenured chief executive officer, the company employs close to 26,000 people worldwide and approximately 18,000 in Central Texas. Austin is the company's birthplace and home to Dell Americas, the regional business unit for the United States, Canada, and Latin America. Headquartered just outside Austin on a 350-acre site in Round Rock, Dell also maintains manufacturing facilities in Austin; Limerick, Ireland; Penang, Malaysia; and Xiamen, China.

THE DIRECT APPROACH

The company began with a simple concept: By selling personal computer systems directly to customers, Dell could most efficiently and quickly understand and meet their needs. That formula has led to Dell's position as one of the world's leading computer systems companies, with 1999 fiscal year sales of $18.2 billion.

Dell's direct business model incorporates the concepts of selling directly to customers, building systems to order, and providing direct phone and on-line technical support as well as next-day, on-site service. This direct-to-customer approach saves customers both time and money, as they bypass computer resellers and avoid related price markups. Through its DellWare® program, the company designs and customizes products and services to the requirements of specific customers, sparing them additional time and cost.

Thanks to low inventory associated with the direct model, as well as relationships with key technology partners, Dell is able to incorporate the most relevant new technologies almost immediately. This gives the company a significant time-to-market advantage over competitors and gives customers higher-performance systems at a lower cost. Direct contact with thousands of customers every day enables Dell to constantly refine its products to meet customer demand.

High-performance desktop systems, notebook computers, servers, workstations, and storage products comprise Dell's extensive product offerings. The company's product lines include Dell Dimension® and OptiPlex® desktop computers, Latitude® and Inspiron® notebook computers, PowerEdge® network servers, Precision® workstations, and PowerVault® storage products. During 1998, Dell won more than 350 product and service awards worldwide for their quality, reliability, and performance.

MAINTAINING THE LEAD

Dell's ability to develop strategic solutions for emerging markets drives its success and positions it well for the future. One of Dell's strongest areas of recent growth is the Internet, as it further evolves its direct model through on-line

HEADQUARTERED JUST OUTSIDE AUSTIN ON A 350-ACRE SITE IN ROUND ROCK, DELL COMPUTER CORPORATION ALSO MAINTAINS MANUFACTURING FACILITIES IN AUSTIN; LIMERICK, IRELAND; PENANG, MALAYSIA; AND XIAMEN, CHINA.

▼ BOB DAEMMRICH

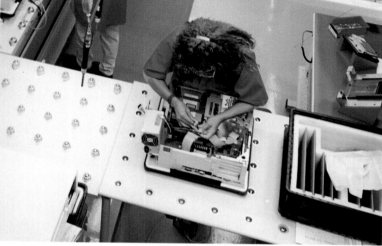

sales, service, technical support, and account management, resulting in on-line sales of more than $18 million per day. For corporate, government, and education accounts, Dell has developed a number of on-line programs such as a customized home page with critical information, including configuration, procurement, and technical data.

Another strong growth opportunity for Dell is in the consumer market, which is characterized by growing sophistication and change, encouraging new computer users and more rapid PC replacement. Already a leading supplier of PCs to corporate customers, government agencies, and medical and educational institutions, Dell products are also popular with medium and small businesses and home PC users. Today's savvy computer users search out the best system for the best price, and Dell is a consumer favorite, as evidenced by its consumer sales of approximately $3 billion a year.

COMMUNITY IMPACT

ell's direct and indirect economic impact on the Central Texas area is more than $5 billion and 50,000 jobs. These figures will continue to increase as the company's industry-leading growth rate stimulates significant reinvestment of jobs and facilities in the region. In addition to the major contributions Dell makes to the regional economy, the company strives to be a good neighbor through its community and environmental initiatives, for which it has received numerous awards.

Since 1995, the Dell Foundation has supported more than 100 programs and local services, particularly those serving community and children's issues in Central Texas. Recent grants funded programs for the Texas School for the Blind, Reading Is Fundamental, and the Austin Children's Museum.

Dell's community partnerships include work with the Children's Advocacy Center and CASA to help identify and serve young children at risk or in crisis. A partnership with the Austin Project provides technology access and training to East Austin families and children. In addition, a partnership with the Austin Museum of Art helps bring world-class exhibits, events, and educational opportunities to Central Texas. Dell-sponsored community programs include the annual Trail of Lights Festival, a favorite Austin holiday tradition featuring a mile-long stretch of lights and exhibits in Zilker Park.

Dell's employees make a significant impact on their own. An annual employee giving program benefits hundreds of environmental, health, and social services charities regionwide. The 1998 workplace fund-raising campaign raised more than $2.6 million in employee contributions. In addition, Dell volunteers give time and energy to projects, including Junior Achievement, fundraising marches, school mentor programs, school supply drives, and other volunteer efforts.

Michael Dell explains the symbiosis of Dell's relationship with the community: "Both Dell and Central Texas share a spirit of innovation and creativity. We strive to foster that spirit by giving back to the community, helping to maintain—and improve—the quality of life for our employees and for our neighbors."

CLOCKWISE FROM LEFT:
DELL'S DIRECT BUSINESS MODEL INCORPORATES THE CONCEPTS OF SELLING DIRECTLY TO CUSTOMERS, BUILDING SYSTEMS TO ORDER, AND PROVIDING DIRECT PHONE AND ON-LINE TECHNICAL SUPPORT AS WELL AS NEXT-DAY, ON-SITE SERVICE.

IN ADDITION TO THE MAJOR CONTRIBUTIONS DELL MAKES TO THE REGIONAL ECONOMY, THE COMPANY STRIVES TO BE A GOOD NEIGHBOR THROUGH ITS COMMUNITY AND ENVIRONMENTAL INITIATIVES, FOR WHICH IT HAS RECEIVED NUMEROUS AWARDS.

DIRECT CONTACT WITH THOUSANDS OF CUSTOMERS EVERY DAY ENABLES DELL TO CONSTANTLY REFINE ITS PRODUCTS TO MEET CUSTOMER DEMAND.

MC SOFTWARE CAN MAKE MILLIONS OF PHONE CALLS per second, process thousands of credit cards a minute, and route hundreds of airplanes an hour—at least, the software the company develops can help its customers do so. BMC Software develops software

products that improve the availability, performance, and recoverability of critical applications in complex computing environments. "We deliver solutions that help organizations reduce the complexity of managing the applications and data that are most important to their operations," says Max Watson, chairman, president, and chief executive officer.

As a worldwide developer and vendor of Application Service Assurance solutions, BMC Software's products focus on optimizing the service delivered to information technology (IT) professionals and their customers, maximizing return on investment in IT assets, and planning for and adapting to changing business requirements. The company is the world's 12th-largest independent software vendor, a Forbes 500 company, and a member of the S&P 500 with revenues exceeding $730 million in fiscal 1998.

A HISTORY OF LEADERSHIP

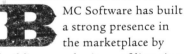ounded in 1980 with five employees and two products, BMC Software has a long history of industry-leading product development for large-scale computing environments. The company opened its research and development facility in Austin in 1985 and is now one of the largest software developers in town, employing more than 500 people.

BMC Software's corporate headquarters is in Houston, and the company maintains research and development offices in Houston, Austin, Sunnyvale, California; and Waltham, Massachusetts. BMC Software employs more than 3,400 people worldwide in the United States, Australia, Austria, Belgium, Brazil, Canada, Denmark, France, Germany, Hong Kong, Italy, Japan, Korea, the Netherlands, Singapore, Spain, Switzerland, and the United Kingdom.

BMC Software was ranked second in profits per employee (behind Microsoft), fifth in sales per employee, and fourth in assets per employee in a 1997 Forbes 500 survey. The company was ranked 12th among software-only vendors worldwide, and 20th in the world in *Software Magazine*'s 1998 Top 100 Software Companies. CEO Max Watson was named as one of the 1998 Top 100 CEOs by *Chief Executive* magazine. BMC Software was named as one of *Fortune* magazine's 1999 100 Best Companies to Work For.

LISTENING INTENTLY, RESPONDING INNOVATIVELY

MC Software has built a strong presence in the marketplace by building on a heritage of listening intently to customers and responding innovatively. PATROL™, BMC Software's flagship suite of distributed systems products, is widely recognized by customers and indus-

try analysts as the standard for managing applications, databases, and operating systems in the world's largest and most complex environments.

"We are known not only for the quality, reliability, and rapid deployment of our products, but also for our superior customer service and support," says Betty Otter-Nickerson, vice president of research and development and BMC Software's Austin site manager. "We focus on solving customers' specific problems while helping them plan for the long term."

BMC Software pioneered the concept of Application Service Assurance through application and data management across enterprises, and was the first software vendor to offer a complete solution for managing and monitoring the entire Internet enterprise. Leveraging this knowledge and strength in the management and movement of data, BMC Software is introducing new solutions for total enterprise-wide computing.

The firm's typical customer is a corporation or organization confronted with the task of managing billions of data entries essential to the daily activity of hundreds, thousands, and even millions of individuals. Credit card companies and banks who process millions of customer transactions a day, airlines who rely on the accuracy and timeliness of data to book

reservations and schedule flights, or governmental agencies and institutions responsible for maintaining the infrastructure upon which all businesses and every individual depends—all rely on BMC to help them manage their environments more effectively and efficiently.

RETURNING TO THE COMMUNITY

nown for its generosity to employees, BMC Software says a tangible thank-you to all those who make its success possible. The company is cubicle-free, says Otter-Nickerson, and almost every employee has a private office decorated to his or her individual taste or whimsy. BMC Software provides a home computer with a high-speed Integrated Services Digital Network (ISDN) line to any employee who requests one. It offers a generous salary package, bonuses, and stock options, and offers software developers an opportunity to own a piece of any sales their products generate. "Intellectual property is our company's greatest asset," says Otter-Nickerson. "We strive to keep our people happy, and we want them to be a productive part of our company for a long time to come."

BMC Software enjoys giving back to the community and sponsors a number of local charities and programs such as Habitat for

Humanity, the Austin State Hospital, KLRU's *Austin City Limits*, and the Austin Lyric Opera. The company also provides creative ways to contribute, such as the BMC Software Austin Olympics. Not only does the fund-raiser benefit BMC Software's Season of Giving charitable program, but it provides a fun atmosphere for employee interaction in events ranging from volleyball games to Scrabble tournaments to balloon-tying championships.

BMC Software attracts employees looking for a chance to shine while also maintaining a balance between life and career, says Otter-Nickerson. "We give people the opportunity to work in an environment as challenging and exciting as a small start-up, with the stability and financial strength of a large company," she says. "In turn, they give us the best effort they can. Everybody here is a hero."

IntelliQuest Information Group, Inc.

WHEN AUSTIN NEEDED TO ASSESS ITS OWN IMAGE AS an emerging city, it turned to IntelliQuest Information Group, Inc. to spearhead a community survey. To give back to the city where it was founded and is headquartered, IntelliQuest

donated its time and expertise to develop a pioneering study, the Austin Community Agenda '98. Presenting a nonpartisan look at quality of life and community involvement, the Community Agenda revealed the type of market-specific information gathering and analysis that has made IntelliQuest a success.

Founded in 1985 by Peter Zanden, IntelliQuest is a leading provider of information-based marketing services designed to help technology companies market smarter by supplying clients with timely, objective, and accurate information about technology markets, customers, and products. The company has incorporated sophisticated, cutting-edge technology to increase its product lines and expand its research coverage to include key international technology markets.

"Our singular mission is to help technology companies sell more products," says IntelliQuest president and CEO Brian Sharples. "Our products and services are designed to help our clients gain in-depth knowledge about their markets and fully understand their customers and prospects."

AN AUSTIN SUCCESS STORY

Today, IntelliQuest serves companies worldwide in technology-based markets such as personal and business computers, computer peripherals, software, Internet and on-line services, telecommunication, and technology publishing and advertising. The publicly traded firm has more than 400 employees located in Atlanta, London, New York, and Silicon Valley.

IntelliQuest uses its databases and software to help technology companies track product performance and customer satisfaction, measure advertising effectiveness,

assess brand strength and competitive position, determine price sensitivity, and evaluate new products, markets, or other business opportunities. The company designs comprehensive performance measurement systems and provides consulting services to help clients manage, retain, and extend customer relationships. IntelliQuest also licenses custom software applications for customer identification via electronic product registration, and offers associated database marketing products and services, including data enhancement, data cleansing, data mining, and professional services.

The company has developed many innovative products, such as the IntelliQuest Technology Panel, the technology industry's largest sample source of pre-profiled purchasers and users of technology products and services. Hailed as one of the most important media buying and marketing tools for the technology industry, the IntelliQuest Computer Industry Media Study (CIMS) provides a comprehensive view of readership, viewership, and product purchase behavior for technology influencers. The

Worldwide Internet/Online Tracking Service (WWITS) is the definitive source for size and growth on the Internet. Zona Research, Inc., a wholly owned subsidiary of IntelliQuest, focuses on Internet analysis. Zona's highly acclaimed industry analysts offer forward-looking perspectives on issues that are critical to success in the Internet market.

IntelliQuest and its employees are also recognized for their involvement in the community. The IntelliQuest Community Action team links the company and its employees with the community through programs such as Austin FreeNet, which provides access to the Internet through public libraries, schools, and community centers in the Austin area. IntelliQuest contributes employee time and expertise, equipment, and financial support to provide hands-on computer access and training.

Working in the Austin community, IntelliQuest and its dedicated employees enjoy a growing, fast-paced, and exhilarating environment. "We're a young company," says Sharples, "not only in years, but also in attitude and spirit."

INCORPORATED IN 1976, SAS INSTITUTE INC. IS THE WORLD'S largest privately held software company, with more than 5,000 employees worldwide. Some 3.5 million users at more than 30,000 customer sites in 12 countries use SAS software and solutions to achieve a competitive advantage through better

business decision making. The institute's customers cross the lines of industry, government, and education, and are among the most successful businesses in the world, including 97 Fortune 100 companies.

Headquartered in Cary, North Carolina, the institute opened the Austin regional office in 1985, where nearly 100 people are now employed. The only regional office with its own software development team, the Austin location also provides sales, marketing, consulting, and training for several states in the region.

SAS Institute marked its 21st year in business by continuing an unbroken record of double-digit revenue increases, earning 15 percent more in 1997 than in 1996. The company leads all major software vendors in percentage of revenue (32 percent) reinvested in research and development. This reinvestment helps the institute deliver continual improvements on products and services. The institute's annual SAS Users Group International (SUGI) meeting and SASware Ballot® survey enable customers to influence development priorities and technology directions.

SAS Institute's dedication to meeting customer needs through research and development, ongoing training, free software maintenance,

and free technical assistance is well recognized in the industry. In 1997 and 1998, the company received the Software Technical Assistance Recognition (STAR) award from the Software Support Professionals Association. *Database Programming & Design* magazine named the institute one of the 12 companies that "define the direction of the database industry," and *Software Magazine* selected the institute as Best Decision Support Tools Company.

SAS Institute employees work in an environment that integrates their personal needs with the company's business objectives. In addition to on-site facilities for health care, recreation, and fitness, the institute's work-life programs

address such topics as elder care, parent education, and adoption. With employee turnover at only 4 percent in an industry whose average is about 20 percent, SAS Institute reaps the rewards of unparalleled employee loyalty and talent.

SAS Institute's work-life initiatives and unique corporate culture continue to receive national praise. For nine consecutive years, *Working Mother* magazine has recognized the institute as one of the 100 Best Companies for Working Mothers. In 1998, the institute ranked number three on *Fortune* magazine's list of the 100 Best Companies to Work For and number four on *Business Week*'s list of family friendly U.S. companies.

An active corporate philanthropy program embodies the spirit of SAS Institute, donating to nonprofit organizations that enrich the community through education, the arts, environmental conservation, human services, and medical research. Austin employees support the Capital Area Food Bank, Recording for the Blind, Reading Is Fundamental, KLRU, Wild Basin, the American Red Cross, and Texas Association for Minorities in Engineering (TAME).

JIM GOODNIGHT, PRESIDENT AND CEO, DESCRIBES SAS INSTITUTE INC. AS "GREAT PEOPLE DELIVERING GREAT PRODUCTS AND SERVICES AROUND THE WORLD AND THE BEST STRATEGIC PARTNERS, ALL DEDICATED TO DOING OUR PART TO CREATE A WORLD WITHOUT BORDERS, WHERE INFORMATION FLOWS FREELY TO GIVE OUR CUSTOMERS A GLOBAL ADVANTAGE."

SAS INSTITUTE IS THE WORLD'S LARGEST PRIVATELY HELD SOFTWARE COMPANY, WITH SOME 3.5 MILLION USERS AT MORE THAN 30,000 CUSTOMER SITES IN 12 COUNTRIES USING ITS SOFTWARE.

SicolaMartin

I N FEWER THAN FIVE YEARS, SicolaMartin HAS EMERGED AS ONE OF the 10 largest, high-tech-focused marketing and advertising firms in the United States. How? By leveraging its foundation in consumer branding and promotions with its exceptional literacy in and insight into the technology industry. The

most common comment from prospective customers has been "They get it." Not just in terms of being experienced marketers, but in terms of truly knowing technology—from the silicon to the network and everything in between. As Tom Sicola, president and CEO, says, "When customers and prospects talk to us about their technology products, channels, targets, alliances, et cetera, we don't give them the RCA Victor dog look. We speak the same language because we have developed similar scar tissue, and we're ready to go."

SicolaMartin has developed a keen sense of the world in which technology companies must market their products and services—whether to businesses or consumers. It is a world like no other—fast, furious, and often unforgiving. Time in the technology world can be a strategic weapon or a most feared adversary. Helping companies succeed in an industry that moves faster than the speed of light requires a powerful combination of creative, big ideas and what SicolaMartin calls "intelligent innovations." These are innovations that offer the ability to dynamically integrate the very best in creativity, market-

WITH INNOVATIONS SUCH AS WEB-BASED "WORK SITES," SicolaMartin GIVES ITS CLIENTS THE ABILITY TO IN-STANTLY ACCESS INFORMATION AND WORK COLLABORATIVELY FROM ANY-WHERE IN THE WORLD, 24 HOURS A DAY, SEVEN DAYS A WEEK.

ing, and technology. Innovations that ensure that high-tech customers receive the "time-to-advantages" they need to stay competitive. That's time-to-market. Time-to-message. Time-to-change. Time-to-results.

Intelligent innovations leading to high-speed accuracy, creativity, and measurable results are part of the reason SicolaMartin now creates work around the world for international technology companies based in San Jose, Seattle, Boulder, Chicago, New York, Fort Lauderdale, and, of course, major cities in Texas. Another reason is a work style that is smart and

intense, yet fun, friendly, and service oriented.

SicolaMartin's intelligent innovations, such as Web-based creative focus groups, saved one client more than $40,000, cut four weeks out of the advertising testing process, and enabled copy revisions and best offer to be verified in fewer than 48 hours. And it simultaneously generated real-time leads for the customers. SicolaMartin's innovative use of the Web to present capabilities, creative concepts, and proposals to an IBM division in Raleigh led to a $500,000 contract without a single face-to-face meeting.

The company's recent deployment of Citrix® MetaFrame™, a leading technology solution from one of its major customers, has positioned it to be the first agency to successfully integrate Macs, PCs, and the new generation of low-cost thin-client devices and information appliances—a solution currently being used in 77 of the Fortune 100 companies to reduce the total cost of computing by as much as 57 percent. And it's a solution that is allowing SicolaMartin to break new ground in the use of its own

SicolaMartin HAS LEVERAGED ITS RETAIL AND CONSUMER MARKETING EXPERIENCE TO DELIVER HIGH-IMPACT, RESULTS-DRIVEN COMMUNICATIONS FOR ITS ROSTER OF LEADING TECH-NOLOGY COMPANIES.

First, we became the leader in memory.
Next came the widest range of MCUs.
Then, we had a flash.

HITACHI
Semiconductor

We'll send you the best thinking
on our embedded flash MCUs. Free.

HITACHI
Semiconductor

extranet, available to customers 24 hours a day, seven days a week, 365 days a year. Each customer has a password-protected Web site specifically designed for creative reviews, project management, and client communication. It's a paperless, fax-less, E-mail-less, FedEx-less way to conduct business across international time zones. And it lowers the cost of doing business, while improving the quality of work.

On the creative front, intelligent innovations in advertising and communications have earned the agency shelves of regional and national industry awards: for out-of-the-box television ads for Motorola semiconductors; eight-story-high, painted "billboard buildings" for 3M; and for naming and helping Citrix to

launch Thinergy, the technology industry's first ever worldwide conference on the new generation of thin-client computing devices and information appliances. And there are countless case studies to document the positive business results.

The company's innovative style is reflected in its culture, as well as in its work product. Employees find unique approaches within the corporate culture, such as FreshAire—a five-week sabbatical program that every employee receives after five years with the agency—and the SicolaMartin Three-Eyed Martian Award for innovation, initiative, and inspiration.

When Sicola is asked "What is SicolaMartin trying to accomplish in the world of marketing and advertising? What's your vi-

sion?" the answer is "To be one of the premier global agencies in an era of communication that we have branded as the PerfectCast™ era—a world where products and services will be perfectly targeted, easily understood, and instantly accessible. A world where advertising, promotion, and direct target-audience interaction will occur, not just on the Web or via your TV set, but also in your appliances—from toasters to refrigerators, from dishwashers to washing machines, from mirrors on your walls to the global positioning system in your car."

If it's true that the future belongs to those who see it most clearly, then SicolaMartin's vision and innovation certainly give it significant ownership in the years ahead.

CREATIVE USES OF ADVERTISING AND COMMUNICATIONS—FROM OUT-OF-THE-BOX TRADESHOW LAUNCHES TO STOP-YOU-IN-YOUR-TRACKS PRINT AD AND COLLATERAL CAMPAIGNS—HAVE EARNED SICOLAMARTIN NUMEROUS REGIONAL AND NATIONAL AWARDS.

CARDIOLOGIST IN LONDON TRANSMITS LIVE IMAGES OF a beating heart to colleagues around the world. Australian grade school students play Pictionary® with their peers—in California. A U.S. sales manager demonstrates a new product to his colleagues in

Europe. VTEL customers worldwide get the picture: better communication is visual communication.

What makes it possible? Video communications tools from Austin-based VTEL Corporation. VTEL develops and manufactures video communications technology, including videoconferencing systems, software, and services for commercial, education, health care, and government applications. Add multimedia streaming software expertise, and VTEL offers a complete line of communications solutions that combine the power of traditional videoconferencing with the global reach of the Internet.

VTEL knows that seeing is believing. "When our customers first see the quality and immediacy of VTEL videoconferencing, they are inspired by the possibilities," says Jerry Benson, VTEL president and chief executive officer. "They no longer are constrained by time, money, and other resources. Plus,

the growth and development of the Internet is opening doors for real-time video communications."

With installations in all 50 states and more than 30,000 systems deployed worldwide, VTEL enjoys a unique place in the telecommunications and networking marketplace. By building on nearly three decades of expertise in designing and managing private video networks, VTEL will soon introduce tools for the enterprise and virtual private networks and for the biggest public network of all: the Internet.

EXPANDING INTERNET VIDEO COMMUNICATIONS

In March 1999, VTEL acquired Vosaic LLC, an Internet software start-up founded at the University of Illinois by a core team of engineers who developed the legendary Web browser Mosaic. The little company—whose accomplishments include Webcast-

ing the first images from the Mars Pathfinder expedition in 1997—holds big promise for VTEL.

In summer 1999, VTEL is introducing new products that will change the oft-derided reputation of live audio and video over the Internet. VTEL streaming video and audio products are uniquely Java-based, which translates to increased accessibility and quality. Viewers can receive video over the Internet without having to download a plug-in, and Internet service providers can multicast live video and audio with unprecedented quality and clarity. VTEL demonstrated the power of this streaming technology in March 1999, when it helped deliver a live Webcast of the Grammy-winning band Smashing Pumpkins to more than 100,000 Web viewers simultaneously.

"VTEL wants to demystify live Internet video," says Benson. "We are demonstrating that it's possible to receive quality video on

THE SMARTSTATION IS VTEL CORPORATION'S AWARD-WINNING DESKTOP VIDEOCONFERENCING SYSTEM, BRINGING FULL-MOTION VIDEO TO THE DESKTOP.

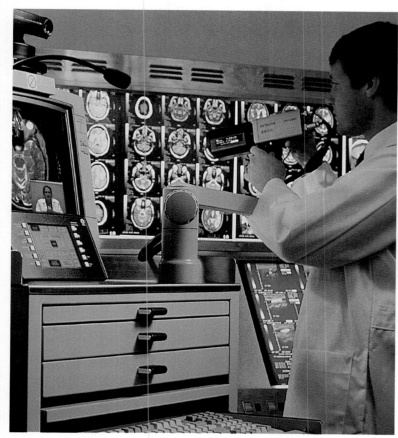

the Internet today, by using standards-based formats that do not require proprietary client players.

"The Java-based features of VTEL streaming technology will create incredible opportunities for both institutional and consumer applications," says Benson. "Now a videoconference can be streamed to anyone with Internet access and a Java-enabled browser."

The explosive growth of networked communications and the Internet is opening the door for VTEL products and services to help customers harness the potential of visual communications. In addition to the traditional real-time videoconferencing applications such as corporate training, distance education, and telemedicine, new products from VTEL eventually will enable countless applications of "time-shifted" video communications for corporate intranets and other private networks.

"The applications of streaming technology extend beyond the traditional domains of video-conferencing, such as distance education, corporate training, and telemedicine," adds Benson. "VTEL is bringing the power to distribute video communications to anyone with a computer."

While Benson is passionate about VTEL's new ventures into Internet software, he remains committed to the company's original mission: making videoconferencing as ubiquitous as a phone call. "In 1999, VTEL will release new products with a user interface that makes videoconferencing as easy as dialing a phone," says Benson. "Affordability, connectability, manageability, and usability will continue to be VTEL hallmarks."

ANOTHER GLOBAL COMPANY CALLS AUSTIN HOME

VTEL was founded in 1985 as SADL. It changed its name to VideoTelecom Corporation and then VTEL in 1993. The company is traded on the Nasdaq stock market (VTEL).

An Austin company since 1986, VTEL Corporation treasures its videoconferencing heritage, being one of the first telecommunications companies to design videoconferencing systems based on open PC architecture. Its history now propels the company into cyberspace and the Internet, with more than two decades of experience in creating and managing video networks.

With its corporate and manufacturing headquarters in Austin, VTEL also operates research and development activities in the Sili-con Valley and maintains a global services unit in King of Prussia, Pennsylvania. Outside the United States, VTEL operates offices in the United Kingdom, France, Germany, and China.

VTEL products and services are distributed through value-added resellers and partners in 61 countries. VTEL also provides installation, training, and support services in more than 130 countries worldwide. Its comprehensive after-market support programs include emergency on-site response across North America, and a 24-hour information line for domestic and international customers.

With nearly 250 employees in Austin, VTEL remains active in the Central Texas community, marked by its annual participation in the regional United Way campaign and its ongoing commitment to the Austin Children's Shelter. The company also is an active member in the Greater Austin Chamber of Commerce.

As one of Austin's original high-tech start-ups, VTEL continues to nurture new ideas in the ever changing business environment. And Benson's vision for video in every classroom and on every desktop is driving the company into the millennium. "The technological advances in computer networking and telecommunications that fueled the explosive growth of the Internet are now widening the path for video communications," he says. "The value of pervasive visual communications will be realized by all of us in the very near future."

1986 - 1998 ★

1986 Cypress Semiconductor (Texas), Inc.
1986 TechWorks, Inc.
1986 Wallingford Electronics, Inc.
1987 Brock Consulting Group, Inc.
1987 Higdon & Higdon, Inc.
1987 Shoreline Christian Center
1989 Analysts International Corporation
1989 Pinnacle Construction of Austin, Inc.
1989 r. j. kolar
1989 SI Diamond Technology, Inc.
1990 Trilogy Software, Inc.
1991 Delgado Design Group, Inc.
1992 Apple Americas Customer Support Center
1992 Ascension Orthopedics, Inc.
1992 Encore Orthopedics, Inc.
1992 IXC Communications, Inc.
1992 Randalls Food Markets, Inc.
1993 The Gottesman Company
1993 Micro-Media Solutions, Inc.
1994 Omnifax
1994 Pervasive Software Inc.
1994 Tokyo Electron America, Inc.
1995 Herman & Howry, L.L.P.
1995 Homestead Village
1995 Keane, Inc.
1996 CarrAmerica Realty Corporation
1996 DuPont Photomasks Inc.
1996 ICG Communications, Inc.
1996 Solectron
1996 The SMT Centre Inc.
1996 Wells Fargo
1997 Brigham Exploration Company
1997 Korn/Ferry International
1997 Renaissance Women's Center
1998 Watson Bishop London Galow, P.C.

YPRESS SEMICONDUCTOR (TEXAS), INC. IS IN ITS SECOND decade as an international, broad-line manufacturer and supplier of integrated circuits for a range of growth markets. The company supplies its products to leading providers of data communications, telecommunications,

personal computer, and military systems worldwide.

Cypress Semiconductor Corporation was founded in 1982 in San Jose, California, and has grown rapidly and profitably. Today, Cypress is an international company with about 2,500 employees and a worldwide sales network.

The company competes in high-volume, cost-sensitive markets, including those for SRAMs, FCT logic, and computer clock chips. Cypress has made rapid strides in other fast-growing markets, entering the high-density programmable logic arena and data communications with physical-layer products for emerging networking technologies, including ATM (asynchronous transfer mode) and fiber channel.

In addition to its Round Rock manufacturing site, Cypress operates other advanced wafer fabrication facilities in Bloomington, Minnesota. With assembly and test facilities in the Philippines, Cypress also has expanded its global design capacity with facilities in Mississippi, Colorado, Washington State, Oregon, Minnesota, Texas, England, India, and Ireland.

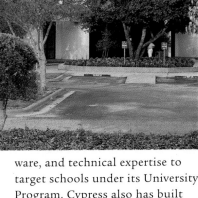

Cypress achieves strong results through technological innovation, solid management, and execution. From the start, Cypress' ground-breaking CMOS (complementary metal oxide semiconductor) technology outperformed competitive products that used far more power. Never satisfied, the company has become an industry leader through the introduction of newer and faster processing technologies.

Cypress has fostered a strong, loyal customer base, built through years of delivering high-quality products. The company maintains strong ties with the academic community, donating equipment, software, and technical expertise to target schools under its University Program. Cypress also has built one of the industry's strongest research and development organizations, positioning the company to maintain technology leadership and to respond quickly to changing market conditions.

CYPRESS PRODUCTS

Over the past decade, the semiconductor market has been marked by great change and volatility. Electronics are an integral part of almost every facet of the economy, and the proliferation of computer and communications equipment has prompted phenomenal industry growth, driving down prices and sharpening competition. As an acknowledged leader in an industry that has shown relentless growth, Cypress enjoys solid positioning in three of the largest semiconductor markets: personal computers, networking, and communications.

Cypress has built a reputation throughout the industry and with its customers for providing high-performance, high-quality products in every market it enters. The company is segmented into four divisions: memory products, programmable products, data communications, and computer products.

Across all its divisions, Cypress offers products that are mainstays in a broad range of industries and markets. They are used in personal computers, workstations, servers, and superminicomputers; telecommunications; data communications; networking products; military applications; and test and measurement equipment.

Cypress provides a wide range of RAM and RAM-based memory products, high-speed programmable read-only memories (PROMs), multichip modules, and non-volatile memory. Static RAMs (SRAMs) comprise the company's largest product segment. Cypress is also a leading provider of complex programmable logic devices (PLDs), small PLDs, and tools and software for PLD programming. The company supports high-speed data communications with a range of datacom products, from the physical-connection layer to system-level solutions. Its computer products offer timing technology products used widely in personal computers and disk drives, as well as universal serial bus (USB) microcontrollers and FCT logic.

Cypress recognizes the importance of bringing new, leading-edge products to market on a regular basis. The company's Top 10 Program tracks the most important new products through the production pipeline. The development of each product is supported by a cross-functional team of engineering, marketing, and production specialists, and the company's employee bonus plan is based on new product revenue.

The cornerstone of Cypress' success is the very high quality of

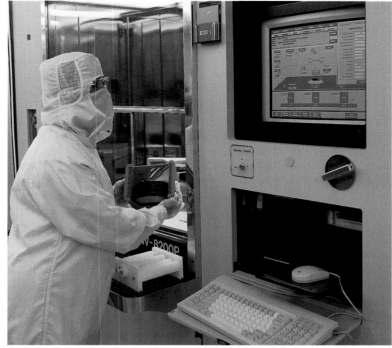

its products, services, and people. Cypress has been honored for product and service excellence by many of its customers, and has received the coveted STACK Level II certification, awarded to companies whose products meet tough standards for quality. The company also has received ISO 9000 registration, awarded to companies with exacting standards of quality management, production, and inspections. In 1996, the Defense Electronics Supply Center (DESC) awarded Qualified Manufacturer's List (QML) certification to Cypress' military offerings.

Corporate Culture

Cypress' culture is a product of the company's sophisticated technology and manufacturing. The firm goes to great lengths to hire and keep the best people

available. All employees are granted stock options and are eligible for quarterly profit-sharing bonuses, based on new product revenue. In this way, Cypress recognizes the contributions of all employees.

Cypress is a company that encourages individuals to do what it takes to get the job done, provides them with the proper tools to achieve these objectives, and rewards them for their efforts. The success of these individuals ensures that Cypress will be a leader in its industry well into the next century.

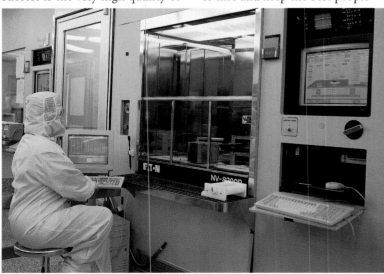

TechWorks, Inc.

USTIN-BASED TechWorks, Inc. is one of the world's leading computer upgrade companies, offering more than 200 personal computer and workstation upgrade products for more than 2,500 computer systems. Founded in 1986, TechWorks

has been recognized on three occasions by *Inc.* magazine's list of 500 Fastest-Growing Privately Held Companies in America. The first memory manufacturer to offer a lifetime warranty and an installation kit, the company has sold more than 5 million upgrades.

In 1998, TechWorks joined the family of companies operated by Melco, Inc. of Japan. Melco is the largest and one of the world's

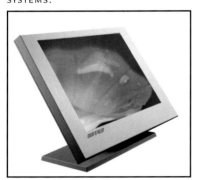

TechWorks, Inc. is one of the world's leading computer upgrade companies, offering more than 200 personal computer and workstation upgrade products for more than 2,500 computer systems.

leading suppliers of PC memory and computer enhancement products. The marriage of Melco and TechWorks created one of the largest third-party memory manufacturers in the world and positions the two companies to operate together as a major supplier of computer upgrade products worldwide.

Maximizing Customers' Investments

Because the best hardware and software in the world are only as good as how well and how fast they function, TechWorks delivers the ultimate upgrade products to maximize its customers' computer investment. TechWorks offers a variety of upgrade enhancement products for both PC-based and Macintosh computer systems, including graphics accelerators, processor accelerators, and flash card storage solutions for notebook computers, digital cameras, personal data assistants (PDAs), and

active matrix, thin film transistor (TFT) LCD monitors. The cornerstone of TechWorks' computer upgrades is the company's line of PowerRAM® memory upgrades for today's most popular computers and printers. Other products include TechWorks' Buffalo LCD displays, PowerCPU® processor upgrades, CDR, DVD, and wireless LAN network products.

TechWorks employs more than 100 people worldwide and almost 70 in Austin. The company also has a manufacturing and distribution operation in the United Kingdom. TechWorks products are distributed in more than 15 countries worldwide through distribution channels and are sold through the company's on-line store or toll-free direct sales line. Its customers include a vast range of corporations, government entities, and educational institutions, including almost every college, university, elementary school, and high school across the United States.

With its highest priority placed on achieving 100 percent customer satisfaction, TechWorks prides itself on its "outrageous customer service," including 24-hour delivery, a 30-day money-back guarantee, unlimited toll-free technical support, a lifetime warranty on PowerRAM memory modules, and quality control for its entire line of products. The company's speed in delivering products to customers allows even large clients such as the University of Texas to receive products the same day they are ordered. "Customer satisfaction is the basis of our entire business," says Yoshio Takahara, president and CEO of TechWorks. "As an international company, we are able to procure and provide the highest-quality product at the lowest price, which makes our customers very happy."

WHEN BROTHERS AND BUSINESS PARTNERS JOE AND Chuck Higdon founded Higdon & Higdon, Inc. in 1987, they recognized the need to help companies deal with an ever changing employee benefits environment. "We saw a problem and a solution,

and we started to develop a client-centered approach to employee benefits," says Joe.

"As the tag line on our logo says, we want clients to 'experience a new world of benefits,'" he explains. "First, we understand each client's unique situation, and second, we work to help each client understand the numerous plans and options available within the changing market conditions." Sometimes, this means bringing new ideas to the forefront. Early on, the company worked with the University Co-op to set up Prudential's first commercial preferred provider organization plan in the state of Texas.

Higdon & Higdon will celebrate the Lone Star millennium with clients of all sizes, all over the country. They have worked with small, emerging start-up companies to large, public companies, helping clients develop appropriate benefits plans every step of the way. According to Chuck, "Our growth has come because of our reputation for client service. This has allowed us to develop a loyal and diverse customer base." Approaching the $3 million annual revenue mark, Higdon & Higdon has enjoyed 20 to 30 percent annual growth and was named in 1997 as one of the city's Top 50 Fastest Growing Private Companies by the *Austin Business Journal*.

FINDING THE BEST SOLUTIONS

Many clients use Higdon & Higdon to help them manage the complicated benefits process throughout the year, and not just at renewal time. This means that Higdon & Higdon staff members serve as ongoing contacts for their clients' human resource departments, ready to fulfill the com-

▶ JAMES A. DUMAS, SPECTRUM PHOTOGRAPHY

pany's mission: "to be your creative support team on the cutting edge of benefit solutions." Staff members have extensive professional and academic expertise in the insurance, financial, and human resource fields. Partners Joe and Chuck have been designated as Certified Employee Benefit Specialists by the International Foundation of Employee Benefit Plans and the Wharton School of the University of Pennsylvania. To help clients keep abreast of the latest changes in benefits, Higdon & Higdon closely monitors federal and state legislation and holds

seminars for clients to explain major changes.

Chuck sums up the firm's success in three sentences: "We always give 110 percent. We do it right. We are loyal and honest to our clients."

"And for the next millennium," says Joe, "we hope to continue to grow not only in numbers, but also in knowledge and education. This allows us to work with clients who truly care about their employees, and we are rewarded by seeing real results that have the potential to not only enrich, but in some cases, save lives."

HIGDON & HIGDON STAFF MEMBERS SERVE AS AN ONGOING CONTACT FOR THEIR CLIENTS' HUMAN RESOURCE DEPARTMENTS, READY TO FULFILL THE COMPANY'S MISSION: "TO BE YOUR CREATIVE SUPPORT TEAM ON THE CUTTING EDGE OF BENEFIT SOLUTIONS" (TOP).

BROTHERS AND BUSINESS PARTNERS JOE (LEFT) AND CHUCK HIGDON FOUNDED HIGDON & HIGDON, INC. IN 1987 TO HELP COMPANIES DEAL WITH AN EVER CHANGING EMPLOYEE BENEFITS ENVIRONMENT (BOTTOM).

▶ JAMES A. DUMAS, SPECTRUM PHOTOGRAPHY

WALLINGFORD ELECTRONICS, INC.

WALLINGFORD ELECTRONICS, INC. EPITOMIZES AUSTIN'S entrepreneurial spirit. Founder Rick Wallingford originally created the business in 1986 as a sideline enterprise serving friends and family. Word spread, and within a few years Wallingford had a full-blown

success on his hands. In 1991, the company moved into its current facility, in which it expanded seven times before purchasing the building in 1997.

Today, Wallingford Electronics is one of Austin's largest computer builders and continues to rank as one of the city's fastest-growing privately held companies. Wallingford serves as president of the company, while his wife, Christienne, is chief financial officer and a majority stockholder, making it also one of the largest female-owned businesses in Austin.

BEST SOLUTIONS, BEST VALUE

Wallingford attributes the success of the company largely to the fact that it has not strayed from its original philosophy of providing the best value through quality products and innovative services. While the client base has expanded, the customer-centric emphasis is the same.

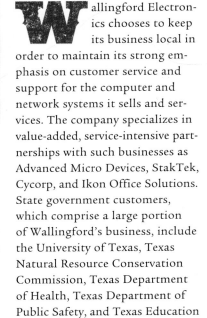

Wallingford Electronics assembles, configures, tests, integrates, and services computer systems and networks for some of Austin's largest companies and state agencies. Working closely with customers to determine their specific needs, the company designs solutions ranging from one to many thousands of computers. For large orders, the firm maintains a specifically configured software load unique to the client

and installs it on each machine before delivery, saving customers countless hours of internal support staff time.

LOCAL PRESENCE MAKES FOR FASTEST SERVICE

Wallingford Electronics chooses to keep its business local in order to maintain its strong emphasis on customer service and support for the computer and network systems it sells and services. The company specializes in value-added, service-intensive partnerships with such businesses as Advanced Micro Devices, StakTek, Cycorp, and Ikon Office Solutions. State government customers, which comprise a large portion of Wallingford's business, include the University of Texas, Texas Natural Resource Conservation Commission, Texas Department of Health, Texas Department of Public Safety, and Texas Education Agency.

With a service resolution time that is significantly faster than the industry average, Wallingford's first priority is making sure clients can get back to business as quickly as possible. "Because we build long-term relationships with our clients," says Wallingford, "we are extremely familiar with their systems and their technical needs, and we can quickly diagnose and solve problems. Our service is what makes a difference."

Knowing the ins and outs of its customers' operations, Wallingford Electronics brings increased efficiency to an area that needs it. "It's not uncommon in many organizations to hear stories about people who order computers and wait six months to get them, only to find out that they've been sitting in their own receiving department for three months," says Wallingford Vice

WALLINGFORD ELECTRONICS WAS FOUNDED IN 1986 BY RICK WALLINGFORD, WHO NOW SERVES AS PRESIDENT OF THE COMPANY; HIS WIFE, CHRISTIENNE, IS CHIEF FINANCIAL OFFICER AND A MAJORITY STOCKHOLDER (TOP).

TODAY, WALLINGFORD ELECTRONICS IS ONE OF AUSTIN'S LARGEST COMPUTER BUILDERS, AND CONTINUES TO RANK AS ONE OF THE CITY'S FASTEST-GROWING PRIVATELY HELD COMPANIES (BOTTOM).

President Ron Myers. Wallingford helps to streamline the process by working with the customer's procurement, purchasing, receiving, and information technology (IT) departments to reduce the delays and bottlenecks that impede the rapid deployment of computer systems to the end users. Wallingford precisely coordinates delivery quantities and times to match the customer's capacity, and even offers direct delivery to specified offices, applying the customer's own asset tags, filling in the inventory paperwork, and potentially bypassing the receiving dock altogether. Wallingford provides custom reporting on deliveries, configurations, and sales information. Clients can even track orders and past sales through Wallingford's Web site.

In addition to the individual computers it assembles, Wallingford offers a complete line of networking services from design, infrastructure installation, and maintenance, to workstation and server sales and deployment. In an industry where labor costs run higher than the parts when products need repair, Wallingford sets the standard for quality with a five-year labor warranty and a two-year parts warranty on all products. Extended parts and next-day, on-site service warranties are also available.

LONG-TERM SUCCESS, CLOSE-KNIT TIES

Wallingford's confidence in its product stems from the firm's reliance on only the finest components and its rigorous in-house testing process. All systems go through exhaustive tests before they are shipped to the client, a practice that results in long-term product success. The company's close-knit relationships with suppliers also account for Wallingford's quality products. "We look for the same qualities in vendors that clients look for in us," says Wallingford. "We work with those that provide the highest-quality product and back it up with consistently good service."

Approaching 100 employees, Wallingford Electronics is large enough to provide the resources customers need, yet nimble enough to respond quickly to those needs. The company's Microsoft-certified professionals are experts in problem diagnosis and resolution, and its service facility is A-plus certified by the Computing Technology Industry Association.

Wallingford Electronics has won numerous awards for quality and customer service, and is a State of Texas Qualified Information Systems Vendor, a registered historically underutilized business (HUB), and a General Services Commission catalog vendor. The company was cited in the *Austin Chronicle*'s Best of Austin issue for the best customer service, best computer repair, and best deals and bargains.

As much as they enjoy designing solutions for customers, the Wallingford staff delight in serving the community. The company supports numerous education and charitable organizations, such as public television station KLRU and Goodwill Industries. Wallingford Electronics is a Bedrock sponsor of SPLASH, and provides for closed captioning of local news broadcasts.

By building relationships throughout Austin, Wallingford Electronics is continuing its strong growth. "You can sense the energy and excitement here," says Myers. "It's the buzz of a company in the right position to do truly great things, and we're ready to take it to the next level."

THE COMPANY ASSEMBLES, CONFIGURES, TESTS, INTEGRATES, AND SERVICES COMPUTER SYSTEMS AND NETWORKS FOR SOME OF AUSTIN'S LARGER COMPANIES AND STATE AGENCIES. IN ADDITION, WALLINGFORD OFFERS A COMPLETE LINE OF NETWORKING SERVICES FROM DESIGN, INFRASTRUCTURE INSTALLATION, AND MAINTENANCE, TO WORKSTATION AND SERVER SALES AND DEPLOYMENT.

BROCK CONSULTING GROUP, INC.

ITH A SHARP EYE ON THE MARKET AND AN IN-DEPTH knowledge of transactions, Brock Consulting Group, Inc. takes the headaches out of finding, leasing, or developing real estate. Founded by President Vaughn Brock in 1987, the firm provides full-service real estate consulting, specializing in tenant representation and build-to-suit development.

With experience serving Austin's high-tech start-ups-turned-successes, Brock Consulting Group meets clients' current needs, while planning for long-term growth. "I learned long ago that entrepreneurs who build successful companies have done so by focusing on what they do best, while creating a superior team to whom they can delegate," says local venture capitalist Bob Fabbio. "I'm pleased to have Brock on my team when it comes to commercial real estate, because they make things happen and get things done."

As a tenant representative, Brock Consulting Group helps clients with every aspect of their real estate needs, saving them time and money by letting them concentrate on their own business responsibilities. To achieve this goal, Brock Consulting Group first analyzes a client's space require-ments, including location, image, size, and price. Using its own comprehensive computerized

(SEATED, FROM LEFT) ALEX CASTANO AND J. VAUGHN BROCK (STANDING, FROM LEFT) RAY ZVONEK AND DENNIS PETRAS

FOUNDED BY BROCK IN 1987, THE FIRM PROVIDES FULL-SERVICE REAL ESTATE CONSULTING, SPECIALIZING IN TENANT REPRESENTATION AND BUILD-TO-SUIT DEVELOPMENT.

database, the firm researches the market and prepares a report and physical analysis of all buildings meeting the client's requirements. Brock Consulting Group then analyzes each proposal received to determine how well it meets the client's requirements, and negotiates all aspects of the lease, including economic and legal points. Jon Sligh, of the Austin Diagnostic Clinic, says, "The professionals at Brock Consulting Group are relentless. They pursued every possible deal in the marketplace and expertly negoti-ated our final lease."

After the perfect location is found, the firm continues work-ing closely with its clients to handle all aspects of the transac-tion and development, including collaborating with the architect/ space planner, the tenant finish contractor, and the landlord to coordinate a smooth occupancy. As necessary, Brock Consulting Group works with lenders or eq-uity sources to secure financing or with the city or regulatory agencies on the permitting pro-cess. Once the transaction is com-plete, Brock maintains continual contacts with its clients to help them with key issues throughout the term of their lease and to stay abreast of their changing needs, including expansions and renewals.

"Meeting our clients' needs and ensuring their continued well-being is paramount to us," says Brock. "We build lasting relationships with them to help them plan for the future.

"We like to help companies grow," says Brock. "Part of the fun of this business is in really becoming part of their organiza-tion. They consider us as their

internal real estate department, because we work with them not only on facility needs, but also on other ongoing issues such as annually reviewing the landlord's operating expense calculations to ensure these conform to the lease provisions." Trilogy, Tivoli Systems, Dazel, Ventix, and TL Ventures are some of the high-tech firms whose real estate needs have been met in part by Brock Consulting Group.

DEVELOPMENT

In the commercial real estate development arena, Brock Consulting Group focuses on build-to-suit, joint venture, and fee-based development projects. In addition to handling the development and sale of corporate sites such as Dell Computer's 150-acre Round Rock headquarters and the 100-acre Round Rock site purchased by Scott & White Hospital, the company has developed several sites for state agencies, including the Texas Rehabilitation Commission, the Texas Natural Resources Conservation Commission, and the Office of the Attorney General.

Since its inception, the firm has developed 1.6 million square feet of commercial space, developed or remodeled more than 1,000 apartment units, and acquired almost 2,000 acres for development. Recent projects include the development of the 500,000-square-foot Boardwalk retail center in Round Rock, the development and sale of 100 acres of land for Scott & White Hospital's Round Rock clinic, the development of Semicon Business Park in southeast Austin, and the development of Hampton Cove Luxury Apartments in San Antonio.

Taking a turnkey management approach to development, Brock Consulting Group coordinates every aspect of a project. From negotiating with the land owner on the sale to working with the city on zoning, entitlement issues, and incentives, and from consulting with architects and engineers on building design to hiring surveyors to determine topsoil quality and topography, Brock Consulting Group understands every aspect of the development process. As a leasing and manag-

ing agent, Brock has leased millions of square feet of industrial and office space, achieving a strong record of success in a highly competitive market.

Staying involved in the community helps Brock Consulting Group keep abreast of the latest changes in both real estate and the Austin community. Employees participate both in volunteer and leadership roles in a number of community programs, and the company is an active member in professional organizations, includ-

ing the Commercial Brokers Leasing Association and the Industrial Facilities Management Association. "Vaughn Brock is a man of deep convictions and character. Thus, Brock Consulting Group works within a win-win framework, and for me this is an essential ingredient to any business relationship," says Gregory A. Soechting of Texas Copy.

"We are a very motivated team with a strong commitment to Austin," says Brock. "We know this city well, and we look forward to helping it continue to grow."

IN THE COMMERCIAL REAL ESTATE DEVELOPMENT ARENA, BROCK CONSULTING GROUP FOCUSES ON BUILD-TO-SUIT, JOINT VENTURE, AND FEE-BASED DEVELOPMENT PROJECTS. SINCE ITS INCEPTION, THE FIRM HAS DEVELOPED 1.6 MILLION SQUARE FEET OF COMMERCIAL SPACE, COMPLETED MORE THAN 1,000 APARTMENT UNITS, AND ACQUIRED ALMOST 2,000 ACRES FOR DEVELOPMENT.

OPEN HEARTS AND WELCOMING HANDS GREET MEMBERS and visitors at Shoreline Christian Center, one of Austin's fastest-growing churches. First established in 1987 as Austin Christian Faith Center, the church's rapid growth prompted its move from the pastor's house to

a doctor's office, to a hotel, to a small church building, then an old grocery store before settling into its new facility at Burnet Road and Shoreline Drive. Senior Pastor Robert Koke and his wife, Dr. Laura Koke, founded the church in their home after spending several years doing missionary work throughout Africa, Asia, Europe, and the former U.S.S.R. More than 12 years, five facilities, and thousands of members later, the name has changed, but the vision remains the same.

Today, the interdenominational Shoreline Christian Center can seat 5,000 people in its new facility. Members come from Austin and the surrounding cities and counties to take part in services, which feature a 25-piece worship team, a full choir, and state-of-the-art video and audio technology. "We combine inspiring messages, incredible music, and some of the friendliest people you could ever meet," says Pastor Koke. Shoreline places an emphasis on family and

youth ministry. Combining drama, illustrated sermons, and music, Shoreline creates a fast-paced, interactive learning experience for children, who attend their own service while their parents attend Shoreline's regular service. In addition to the main sanctuary (complete with a full-scale theatrical stage), Shoreline's facility features a 350-seat youth chapel, 28 classrooms, an indoor-playscape, and a preschool room that seats

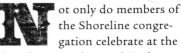

150. Decorated like a seaside village, the children's auditorium houses a stage and screens for various puppet shows, sermons, and ministry productions. The preschool has its own "western town," and classrooms each have a colorful, themed decor, such as Noah's ark or a family picnic.

To meet the needs of its ever expanding congregation, Shoreline's five-year ministry plan includes building a full gymnasium, a Bible school, on-site Christian education facilities, and an outdoor sports complex.

AN ARRAY OF CLASSES AND SERVICES

Not only do members of the Shoreline congregation celebrate at the church on Sundays and Wednesday nights, but they also meet in living rooms and office buildings all over Austin. More than 150 small groups come together regularly to discuss issues important to them. Whether in a singles or

PASTOR ROBERT KOKE AND DR. LAURA KOKE FOUNDED SHORELINE CHRISTIAN CENTER IN THEIR HOME IN 1987 (TOP).

TODAY, THE INTERDENOMINATIONAL SHORELINE CHRISTIAN CENTER CAN SEAT 5,000 PEOPLE IN ITS NEW FACILITY (BOTTOM).

SHORELINE CHRISTIAN CENTER
MOVED INTO ITS STATE-OF-THE-ART
FACILITY IN MAY 1998.

married group, workplace or home
group, or men's or women's group,
members find support among a
host of other congregation members. Specialty groups also meet
to discuss such topics as divorce
recovery, self esteem, and single
parenting. Shoreline's sports
teams—including softball, basketball, flag football, and volleyball—
provide yet another way for
members to reach out to others
within both the church and the
community. "Shoreline's small
groups are more than just one of
the ministries here," says Pastor
Koke. "They are the very lifeblood
of our church. We like to think of
ourselves not as a church that has
small groups, but as a church of
small groups."

In addition to adult Sunday
school classes, Shoreline's women's
and men's ministries both hold
weekly meetings and Bible studies
and host several events each year
featuring popular speakers. The
church's family focus underpins
many of its activities, most nota-
bly its parenting seminars. "We
want to provide as much support
as we can to families," says Pastor
Koke.

Shoreline also provides a strong
support network for its single
members and hosts popular activities, such as rafting trips and
meetings at local restaurants after

weekly services. The church regularly sponsors concerts featuring
nationally known Christian
artists.

Opportunities for involvement
also abound in Shoreline's dramatic, illustrated sermons, such
as last year's "Potter's Wheel," a
modern-day retelling of the bibli-
cal parable of the prodigal son.
More than 100 cast and crew members dedicate countless hours to
presenting different dramas three
times a year.

Shoreline's desire to reach out
to others transcends geographic
and cultural boundaries, and the
church organizes semiannual mis-
sions to Mexico, bringing clothes
and supplies to impoverished
communities. Shoreline members

are involved in prison outreach,
Special Olympics, and the Angel
Tree program.

"We get involved wherever our
sphere of influence takes us. Our
members truly enjoy making a
difference in others' lives," says
Pastor Koke. "It is truly exceptional
to see how friendly and enthusiastic the congregation is—the sincere
commitment they have to Jesus
Christ, and the way they get involved in ministry."

Shoreline's diversity also makes
it an exceptional place, adds Pastor
Koke: "Our members come from
every walk of life, every race, every
economic level, and every denomi-
nation. They come for the many
distinctions that make Shoreline
such a special place."

THE CHURCH PRODUCES SEVERAL
DRAMATIC OUTREACHES EVERY
YEAR, TOUCHING THE LIVES OF
THOUSANDS.

ANALYSTS INTERNATIONAL CORPORATION

IRTUAL ENGINEERING IS A DYNAMIC CONCEPT FOR MEETING technical-skill needs in the new millennium, and involves a team-oriented approach to information systems (IS) requirements. This next-millennium practice is a hallmark of Analysts International Corporation, whose

company motto is Excellence, Integrity, Innovation. In order to meet the needs of companies short on internal resources and long on projects, Analysts International created the RADD™ (Rapid Application Design and Development) team. The group helps clients tackle short-term projects that require special, fast-turnaround skills using prototyping and development tools, such as Microsoft Visual Basic®, Microsoft SQL Server®, and Microsoft Access®.

Analysts International provides a full range of information technology (IT) services, including the following: Year 2000 (Y2K); project management; Internet/ intranet, e-commerce development; on-site consulting; systems integration; software development & code maintenance; data and program conversions; documentation and testing; outsourcing services management (OSM)—such as help desk and legacy systems maintenance; mainframe-to-client/server migration; network design/install; systems support; and training.

CLIENT BENEFITS

Many clients view Analysts International as their virtual engineering department, as a hedge against the expansions and contractions of technical staffing that are typical during peak development periods.

"Our approach allows our customers to focus on results, rather than the means," says Analysts International Austin branch manager, Rick Young. "The client manages the delivery schedule and product design/definitions. We provide office space and tools, infrastructure, personnel management, and certified, 'road-tested' consultants with a fresh approach and proven, industry-standard project methodologies. Clients find that teaming with Analysts International lets them stay focused on their core business instead of fretting the details. As a result, they often find this creates a more positive and stable

atmosphere that helps them retain skilled internal staff because radical ramp-up and layoff cycles can be minimized or even eliminated."

ANALYSTS INTERNATIONAL CONSULTANTS

Analysts International consultants appreciate the professional and personal association provided by the company. A sense of camaraderie and community prevails through regular company activities, community service, and continuing education.

THREE DECADES OF GROWTH

Analysts International was founded in 1966 in Minneapolis, and the publicly held company now has more than 5,600 employees and 42 branch and field offices in the United States, Canada, and the United Kingdom. Analysts International serves more than 900 clients in nearly every sector of the business world. In the past 10 years, revenues have increased an average of 20 percent per year, passing $587 million in 1998. Much of this growth is due to its emphasis on building and maintaining long-term client relationships. This is evident in the fact that 90 percent of Analysts International's business is return business from existing clients.

IN TODAY'S TUMULTUOUS ADVERTISING ENVIRONMENT, STANDING out often means being loud and abrasive with an MTV style and a Dennis Rodman attitude. That's fine for some, but it misses the mark at Austin advertising and marketing agency r.j. kolar. Quietly and without much pretense, the 10-year-old

agency has grown to a staff of more than 40 people by focusing on the basics.

"The fundamental core of our success is our ability to listen to our clients and add value that builds a true partnership," says Rhonda Kolar, agency president. "Partnering has been our focus since we opened our doors."

ACT SMALL. THINK BIG.

The creative staff of r.j. kolar has won a number of awards with large, international accounts, as well as for smaller, regional companies. More important, the staff has won the respect of clients who appreciate strategic planning, hard work, and sense of ownership.

"Advertising and marketing are just a small part of what we do," Mike Kolar, agency vice president, says. "Regardless of the budget or deadline involved, we're committed to our partners."

For the agency's clients, the company's philosophy is to "Act small. Think big." "Act small" means keeping things in perspective and treating every client as the agency's most important account. It also means that there is little time for self-promotion or egos. Even r.j. kolar's logo is set in lowercase letters to stress that

emphasis is always placed on the clients first.

"Think big" spurs the staff to create big results through big ideas. Every job is an opportunity to communicate, inform, and persuade in a fresh, new, and creative way. A trip down the hallways of r.j. kolar is a testament to the type of people who have embraced this philosophy. The colorful walls are garnished with the agency's most recent work on retail and business-to-business accounts.

The company has been able to attract and retain quality employees to offer strategic, long-term value to its clients as well. Employees are viewed as partners, a benefit for clients that demand continuity from an agency.

The company also believes it has a responsibility to the community, and works with a number of pro bono partners, including the Leadership Enrichment Arts Program founded by Ada Anderson, the Chamber of Commerce, Austin Partners in Education, Austin Association for Retarded Citizens, and Coats for Kids. In partnership with the Austin Rodeo, the company offers $5,000 in scholarships to deserving college students each year.

"Anyone can make ads," Rhonda Kolar says. "We want to make a difference through our commitment, ideas, and strategies that shout as loud or whisper as quietly as necessary. That's the responsibility we feel as an advertising partner."

RHONDA KOLAR FOUNDED R.J. KOLAR IN 1989 TO PROVIDE QUALITY CREATIVE WORK WITH A TRUE COMMITMENT TO CLIENT SERVICES.

THE AGENCY'S PARTNERSHIP PHILOSOPHY PRODUCES MORE THAN JUST GOOD ADVERTISING—IT SERVES AS A PLATFORM TO BUILD STRATEGIC PARTNERSHIPS FOR BUSINESS-TO-BUSINESS AND CONSUMER ADVERTISING CLIENTS.

PINNACLE CONSTRUCTION OF AUSTIN, INC.

USTIN IS KNOWN FOR ITS FLAIR AND DISTINCTIVE style, which are amply evident in its favorite restaurants, stores, historic buildings, and offices. Contributing to the city's unique atmosphere is Pinnacle Construction of Austin, Inc., which is responsible for designing and building many of the city's most beloved hot spots and landmarks.

Pinnacle founder and CEO Beth Selbe Lasita entered the construction business in 1989, starting with small retail finish-out projects. "Our goal was to target the high-end restaurant and retail business, because it takes a special touch to work within that fast-paced, customized environment," says Lasita.

IN 1998, PINNACLE CONSTRUCTION OF AUSTIN, INC. REFURBISHED AN OLD DOWNTOWN BUS STATION, WHICH IS NOW THE OFFICE OF CITY NATIONAL BANK.

RESTAURANT EXPERTISE

Pinnacle's first big break in the restaurant business came in 1993 with the Bitter End Bistro & Brewery, a project of the San Gabriel Restaurant Group. The Bitter End was a keystone in Austin's warehouse district, and the company's largest and highest-profile project to that point. The full-renovation project earned Pinnacle not only recognition, but also numerous accolades and awards from *Texas Architecture* magazine, the Association of Builders and Contractors, and *Architectural Digest*. Pinnacle also won an excellence in construction award for the B-Side Tap Room, a 1995 addition to the Bitter End.

With the Bitter End as a feather in its cap, Pinnacle's client list quickly grew. The Arboretum Fresh Choice was the company's first from-the-ground-up restaurant project, and Pinnacle later built Chuy's first-ground-up restaurant on Highway 183. Other Austin favorites in Pinnacle's portfolio include the downtown Schlotzsky's restaurant in the Littlefield Building; Mezzaluna Gateway; Hangtown San Gabriel, Westlake, and Arboretum; Dick Clark's American Bandstand Grill; Cafe Josie; Pacifica; and Ruth's Chris Steak House in the Scarborough Building. To date, the company has worked on more than 50 restaurants in Austin, San Antonio, Arlington, Dallas, and Houston.

COMMERCIAL AND RENOVATION PROJECTS

While restaurant projects comprise almost 70 percent of Pinnacle's business, the company has also won awards for its numerous commercial projects and historical renovations. A former downtown bus station was rejuvenated by Pinnacle in 1998 and is now City National Bank. Pinnacle also won renovation awards for its work on Speakeasy at 412 Congress.

As a general contractor, Pinnacle provides construction management services, and works with all subcontractors and the design team. "We take a teamwork approach as most of our projects are fast track," says Lasita. "We join the team at the early stages of the project, working closely with the architects on scheduling and budgets." On average, it takes Pinnacle five months to complete a building from the ground up, and 90 days for smaller projects, such as interior finish-outs.

Pinnacle's success in meeting strict time lines and unique design specifications has helped the com-

PINNACLE BUILT CHUY'S FIRST GROUND-UP RESTAURANT ON HIGHWAY 183.

pany build a strong reputation for quality work. The majority of the company's new clients are referred directly by existing clients and even by the competition. "We understand and enjoy the challenges of the restaurant and renovation business," says Lasita. Strong relationships with others among Austin's restaurant, architecture, construction, and creative sectors help Pinnacle make each project a success, she adds. "Starting this business in any other city would have been much more difficult. Austin is so accepting—it embraces the local network and everything homegrown."

TEAMWORK

The concept of teamwork also prevails throughout Pinnacle's internal staff. "You never hear anyone say 'I' in this company—you always hear 'we,'" says Lasita. "We all help each other out whenever we can. We wouldn't have made it otherwise."

Pinnacle and its employees also enjoy helping others in the community. The company is an active participant in the Travis County Children's Advocacy Center; a member of the Greater Austin Chamber of Commerce and the Texas Restaurant Association; and an active member of the Central Texas chapter of the Associated Builders and Contractors, of which Lasita is past president. Pinnacle donated its time and services to help the group build a new facility and supports its education outreach programs through high school apprenticeship programs.

The company's impact on the community extends well beyond construction-related programs, as evidenced by its recent fundraiser to help fight the disease scleroderma.

Celebrating its 10-year anniversary in 1999, Pinnacle Construction of Austin, Inc. is constantly reaching new heights of success. The company was named by the *Austin Business Journal* in 1998 as number

14 on its list of Austin's Top 25 Woman-Owned Businesses. A number of high-profile projects are on the horizon. "It's exciting to see Pinnacle represented in some of the city's hot spots," says Lasita of the company's many projects dotting the Austin map. "It's nice to visit as a customer and hear other patrons complimenting our work. It's very rewarding to know that we were there from the very beginning."

PAUL BARDAGJY

PAUL BARDAGJY

PINNACLE HAS WON NUMEROUS HONORS IN ITS 10 YEARS IN AUSTIN, INCLUDING SEVERAL RENOVATION AWARDS FOR ITS WORK ON SPEAK-EASY AT 412 CONGRESS.

MANY OF AUSTIN'S FAVORITE HOT SPOTS ARE PINNACLE CLIENTS, INCLUDING THE DOWNTOWN SCHLOTZSKY'S RESTAURANT IN THE LITTLEFIELD BUILDING, MEZZALUNA GATEWAY, HANGTOWN WESTLAKES AND ARBORETUM, DICK CLARK'S AMERICAN BANDSTAND GRILL, CAFE JOSIE, NXNW RESTAURANT AND BREWERY, AND RUTH'S CHRIS STEAK HOUSE IN THE SCARBOROUGH BUILDING.

PAUL BARDAGJY

SI DIAMOND TECHNOLOGY, INC.

ICTURE A FULL-COLOR, ELECTRONIC BILLBOARD THAT CAN BE seen equally well in bright sunlight, at night, and from any angle. Or imagine an indoor video wall that has no seams between the images and is only a few inches thick. A futuristic dream? Actually, it is the current technology

being developed and marketed by Austin-based SI Diamond Technology, Inc. (SIDT).

SIDT has been working to revolutionize flat panel display technology since the company was incorporated in 1989. Using government contracts as its initial funding vehicle, SIDT quickly emerged as a leader in the new technology of diamond deposition for electronic and protective coating applications. In 1993, further commercial expansion was funded by a $5 million initial public offering.

"We are recognized as the world leader in diamond film technology," says SIDT President Dr. Zvi Yaniv. Within its industry, the company indeed maintains a very strong proprietary advantage and holds more than 50 patents on its products, as well as its innovative process for making screens by depositing a thin diamond film

on materials such as glass. In 1993, SIDT discovered that its thin diamond film technology provided an excellent cathode for field emission displays, and a series of acquisitions allowed the company to support development and fabrication for diamond field emission.

SIDT is today a publicly traded holding company consisting of two high-tech subsidiaries: Electronic Billboard Technology, Inc. (EBT) and Field Emission Picture Element Technology, Inc. (FEPET). Each subsidiary focuses on a specific technology, playing an integral part in SIDT's broader vision of providing cutting-edge solutions to the microelectronics and display industries. EBT, for example, commercializes its parent company's digitized sign technology by developing and providing products to the business and consumer markets using already-available

liquid crystal display (LCD) technology, along with SIDT's proprietary software and interfaces. Likewise, FEPET develops products for applications utilizing SIDT's proprietary field emission technology.

LARGER-THAN-LIFE TECHNOLOGY

In 1996, SIDT created the VERSAtile™ billboard, a new, VFD-based technology for large outdoor displays ranging in size from 12- by 23-foot poster video boards to 20- by 60-foot roadside billboards. Manufactured and marketed by EBT, the VERSAtile billboard offers a number of advantages to users, including low cost, high reliability, and excellent outdoor readability.

"This is the billboard of the future," says Marc Eller, chairman and CEO of SIDT. The cutting-edge technology allows advertisers

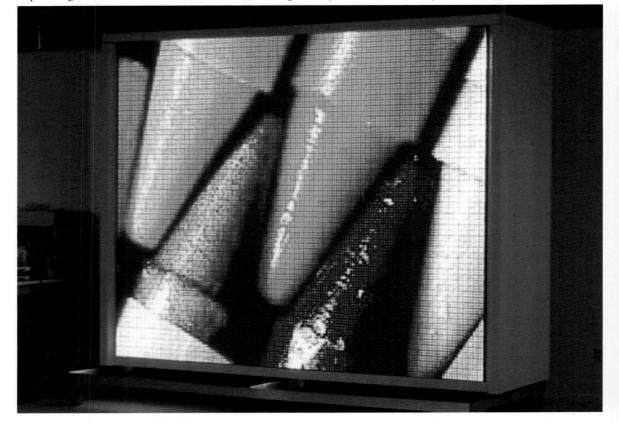

THE COLORFUL IMAGES ON EBT'S 10- BY 8-FOOT PROTOTYPE OF THE ELECTRONIC BILLBOARD ARE VISIBLE IN FULL SUNLIGHT.

to download programmed information electronically, eliminating the slow, dangerous, and expensive process of physically painting and pasting images on the billboard surface. Advertisers will be able to transmit content by modem, cable, or satellite, and will have an opportunity to control the placement and timing of advertisements from remote locations. Advertisers will also be able to target audiences by time of day and location (much like radio and television), use pictorial-quality images to produce visually exciting signs, instantaneously link billboards with promotional campaigns, and reduce costs by renting billboard space in relatively small increments instead of monthlong segments.

"These billboards offer such an increase in both information control and flexibility that we know they will soon be seen all over the world," says Yaniv. He envisions widespread use by advertisers and also hopes to offer the space free of charge to local governments to facilitate emergency communications.

Complementing its advances in state-of-the-art billboards, EBT manufactures and markets the VERSAtile electronic marquee, a thin, indoor messaging display panel that allows users to incorporate high-tech visuals to post messages, announce meetings, or highlight specials. Additionally, the company's Sun Visible High Resolution Color Display is used by fast-food restaurants and other drive-through businesses for order confirmation and advertising.

COMMERCIALIZING INNOVATIVE DISPLAY TECHNOLOGY

SIDT's second subsidiary develops, manufactures, and markets its proprietary thin diamond film technology for flat panel displays, such as flat screen televisions and other revolutionary products. In its simplest terms, this FEPET product is a unique, high-brightness, multicolor light source, intended for use initially in outdoor billboards,

indoor video walls, and alphanumeric displays such as those seen in airports. It provides key advantages over mainstream display technologies, such as higher brightness, low power consumption, and higher resolution for indoor billboards and signage. "This technology truly has an infinite market," says Yaniv, who predicts the product will eventually be used in countless locations, such as retail stores, office buildings, homes, sports arenas, cinemas, and more.

FEPET's latest development is HyFED™ display technology, a high-quality, thin display that combines the best properties of cathode-ray tubes and field emission displays using diamond/carbon films. "Besides being cost competitive in the market with the CRTs of today," says Yaniv, "the HyFED display can be made larger, brighter, and with higher resolution than conventional CRTs."

Over the years, the achievements of SIDT and its subsidiaries have not gone unnoticed. In fact, the company won the National Science Foundation's prestigious Tibbets Award for 1996 in recognition of its track record of excellence in commercializing technologies developed under federal sponsorship. With a decade of revolutionary technology under its belt and a current trend of growing revenues, SI Diamond Technology is well positioned to continue making the dreams of tomorrow the realities of today.

THE VERSAtile™ ELECTRONIC MARQUEE, A VIBRANT LIQUID CRYSTAL DISPLAY, IS A DYNAMIC, EYE-CATCHING ADVERTISING PLATFORM.

THE BancVIEW IS A FULL-COLOR, SUNLIGHT-VISIBLE, DRIVE-THROUGH DISPLAY CAPABLE OF RENDERING PHOTOGRAPHIC IMAGES.

IN 1990, JOSEPH A. LEIMANDT LEFT STANFORD UNIVERSITY JUST months before graduation to create a new kind of software company. The result: Trilogy Software, Inc., a company that would reengineer the way companies do business—the way they sell and market—by streamlining the sales and marketing process.

An entrepreneur with an eye for opportunity, Leimandt's experience as a consultant to computer companies had shown him that the system in which computers were ordered, shipped, and received was a mess. Shipments often arrived late, inventory and pricing information was often wrong, and parts were often missing or incompatible. His subsequent research into the sales and fulfillment process showed that many companies still used antiquated sales, configuration, and delivery procedures, such as giving salespeople bulky price books with incomplete or outdated information.

SEIZING AN OPPORTUNITY

Leimandt saw a tremendous market opportunity. He convinced several friends to join the venture, and together, the cofounders began to build the company. After financing the company's initial years on credit cards, their first big break came in 1992 when Hewlett-Packard bought and deployed Trilogy's software. Trilogy grew to more than 50 people, and signed on Silicon Graphics and AT&T as customers. In 1994, Trilogy signed its biggest account yet—a large deal with IBM.

Since its inception, Trilogy has grown to be the leader in enterprise sales and marketing solutions, and its innovative technology is helping to drive the way companies do business with their customers. Its Front Office suite of software solutions helps companies increase revenue and profit from their sales and marketing organizations by streamlining the customer fulfillment process from the point of sale through order entry.

For example, Trilogy's Selling Chain software integrates quotes, proposals, catalogs, pricing, financing, configuration, and ordering to provide an enterprise-wide solution for sales and order entry. Trilogy's suite of applications also helps customers derive increased revenues from direct sales to indirect channels over the Internet.

The innovation of Trilogy's software solutions has resulted in a vast increase in efficiency and millions of dollars worth of savings for customers in industries ranging from pharmaceuticals to financial services to consumer goods. Because every company and every industry maintains a unique selling process, Trilogy has developed a modular architecture that allows companies to map different components of Trilogy's technology to their reengineered business processes. In addition, Trilogy offers distinct value to every customer through industry-specific modules that solve some of the most challenging sales and marketing issues in that industry.

A WORLD OF ITS OWN

Trilogy's success stems largely from the enthusiasm and drive of its staff. The company is still growing exponentially, and today, has more than 800 employees.

FOUNDED IN 1990, TRILOGY SOFTWARE, INC. HAS GROWN TO BE THE LEADER IN ENTERPRISE SALES AND MARKETING SOLUTIONS, AND ITS INNOVATIVE TECHNOLOGY IS HELPING TO DRIVE THE WAY COMPANIES DO BUSINESS WITH THEIR CUSTOMERS.

Every new employee goes through an indoctrination dubbed Trilogy University, or TU, which graduates "classes" after a three-month training program. The new group of employees spends each day—from 8 a.m. to midnight during the first three weeks—learning and living together in preparation for their new roles as Trilogy employees. After a course on Trilogy's history, products, customers, and market, the employees dive directly into the action, with each student taking on mission-critical development, consulting, and marketing projects. Leimandt is the leading "professor," giving lectures, leading discussions, and tutoring students individually.

Many of the company's most successful initiatives have originated in TU. In past years, classes have designed and implemented base architecture that laid the foundation for nearly all its applications, and have represented Trilogy in deploying mission-critical software to Fortune 500 companies. They have also identified potential markets and developed a plan to dominate the space.

Trilogy's up-front investment in its employees reflects its belief in their talents and its conviction that the company is training the future leaders of the high-tech industry. Most new hires are recent college graduates, and the

average age of Trilogy employees is about 27. They are given great respect and responsibility, along with the latitude to define their roles and opportunities. And whether playing in a company softball game or volunteering for local charities, Trilogy employees have plenty of chances to carry their enthusiasm out of the office and into the community.

The combination of the best talent with an extremely entrepreneurial spirit creates an office that is both results-oriented and extremely flexible. An "anything goes" dress code means everything from suits and ties to shorts and sandals. Office hours depend on the personal preference of the employee. Perks, such as ski boats, fully stocked kitchens, weekly patio parties, and motivational trips to Hawaii and Las Vegas help employees perform and reward them for their successes.

The result is a palpable excitement and a companywide dedication to becoming a great organization—a sentiment evident at all levels of Trilogy. "If I don't wake up in the morning excited to come to work, happy to see the people I work with, it's just not worth it," says Leimandt. "You have to love what you're doing. You've got to have fun. It's an essential component of a successful company."

DELGADO DESIGN GROUP, INC.

ELGADO DESIGN GROUP, INC. (DDGI) SEES THE FUTURE in every one of its architectural blueprints. Founded in 1991 by the husband-and-wife team of Jesus and Patricia Delgado, DDGI provides architectural and interior design services that focus primarily on

FOUNDED IN 1991 BY THE HUSBAND-AND-WIFE TEAM OF JESUS AND PATRICIA DELGADO, DELGADO DESIGN GROUP, INC. (DDGI) PROVIDES ARCHITECTURAL AND INTERIOR DESIGN SERVICES THAT FOCUS PRIMARILY ON EDUCATIONAL, INSTITUTIONAL, AND COMMERCIAL PROJECTS. PICTURED IS BATY ELEMENTARY SCHOOL.

educational, institutional, and commercial projects. The firm also has a broad base of experience in governmental, recreational, commercial, retail, industrial, medical office-building projects, custom residential, and facilities management.

"We help our clients develop creative solutions to meet their needs today, as well as 10, 20, or 50 years down the road," says President Jesus Delgado.

TAKING DESIGN FURTHER

elgado Design Group offers facility planning and management to help its clients track their assets, including real estate, space, furniture, equipment, and occupancy. Through a business partnership with Aperture Technologies in New York, DDGI offers a unique software solution for facility management to help clients even after the project is over. "We use state-of-the-art technology to help clients determine the best design alternatives and to serve as a continual resource for them," says Delgado.

Taking design one step further than most architects, Delgado Design Group also offers interior office planning in conjunction with architectural design. "We deal intricately with the users of the space, looking closely at how they interact to plan the details of functionality and work flow," says Vice President Patricia Delgado.

The group's clients clearly recognize the value of such in-depth planning and responsiveness. "They're an outstanding firm with a can-do attitude," says client Tim Hess of Hensel Phelps Construction Company. "They take a proactive approach to find and resolve issues before they become problems."

Delgado Design Group has enjoyed steady growth since it set up shop in Austin, and estimates that 70 percent of its work comes from longtime clients. "We develop enduring relationships with clients," says Patricia Delgado, "so they feel confident in giving us any type or size of job."

One such long-term client is the South Austin Hospital Medical Center. Other repeat business comes from Texas Department of Transportation, Southwest Texas State University, Capital Metro Transit Authority, Austin Community College, and University of Texas Systems. Adding to its client list in Central Texas, Delgado Design Group has expanded to the southern region of Texas, establishing an office in Brownsville, where its projects range from new cultural centers to historic renovations.

In one year alone, DDGI completed designs for a new elementary school in Del Valle and a new middle school (Américo Paredes) in Austin, and also worked as part of a team to construct Austin Community College's new campus—Eastview Campus.

Delgado Design Group offers building assessment and code analysis services to help clients assess the ability of their property to meet state and federal regulations and standards, such as disability access. The firm also creates designs to retrofit facilities.

Active players in the Austin community, the principals of Delgado Design Group participate in many local organizations. "We love being involved in the community," says Patricia Delgado. "We feel that it is so important to understand the needs of the community, to get involved, and to give back."

DELGADO DESIGN GROUP COLLABORATED ON A NEW MIDDLE SCHOOL IN AUSTIN NAMED FOR THE AUTHOR AMÉRICO PAREDES (LEFT), SHOWN HERE WITH DDGI PRESIDENT JESUS DELGADO.

BUTTONING A SHIRT, PICKING UP A FORK, OR USING A PENCIL— everyday functions that many people take for granted— are made possible by one little joint in the hand," explains Jerome Klawitter, PhD. ★ Helping those unable to manage these simple functions is the reason

Klawitter founded Ascension Orthopedics, Inc., which develops orthopedic implants made of pyrolytic carbon for the small joints in the hand and foot. "Our intent is to make a replacement for these joints to provide a long-term, durable, and pain-free solution," he says.

RESTORING THE BODY

Joint replacements help relieve pain and restore mobility and function in patients suffering from rheumatoid and degenerative arthritis and post traumatic conditions. Rheumatoid arthritis, the most common disease, greatly affects the metacarpophalangeal (MP) joint in the hand. Ascension Orthopedics has developed an MP replacement joint in five different sizes, which fit approximately 95 percent of the population. The company will soon develop orthopedic replacements for other joints in the hands, toes, and the elbow.

While hip and knee replacements are quite common, they use a plastic and metal combination that does not work well in the small joints of the hand. "The only choice for the hand, until now, was a silicone rubber spacer, which helps to relieve some pain, but does not reestablish the function of a normal hand," says Klawitter. "Instead of using metal or rubber parts, we've designed parts made of carbon." The ball-and-socket design of Ascension Orthopedics' joint offers a similar range of motion to that of a natural finger joint.

While carbon occurs naturally in forms varying from coal to diamond, pyrolytic carbon is a manmade material formed by heating a hydrocarbon gas, such as propane or methane, to about 2,500 degrees Fahrenheit. The

heat breaks the chemical bonds to create a highly specialized carbon composition that doesn't occur in nature. The high strength and durability of the carbon are ideally suited for parts of the body subjected to constant repetitive movements, such as finger joints and heart valves. "It is biocompatible with the body, as well as biomechanically compatible," says Klawitter, who has studied this area since 1966.

Ascension Orthopedics was founded in 1992 by Klawitter and Stephen Cook, PhD. The founders met at Tulane University, where Klawitter was director of the Biomaterials Laboratory and where Cook still serves as Director of Orthopedic Research in the Department of Orthopedic Surgery. Klawitter left Tulane in 1980 to found a company to develop a mechanical heart valve replacement made of pyrolytic carbon based on his designs and patents. The company was sold in 1986, and soon after, he began to reexamine the possibility of pyrolytic carbon joint replacements. Klawitter came to Austin to work with existing medical products companies

JEROME KLAWITTER, PHD, FOUNDED ASCENSION ORTHOPEDICS, INC., WHICH DEVELOPS ORTHOPEDIC IMPLANTS MADE OF PYROLYTIC CARBON.

and to put together the highly qualified Ascension Orthopedics team.

Klawitter is as proud of this group as he is of the work they do. "It's amazing to see the impact one company can have on people and their families, both on the people we know here in Austin and the hundreds of thousands of people we can help around the world."

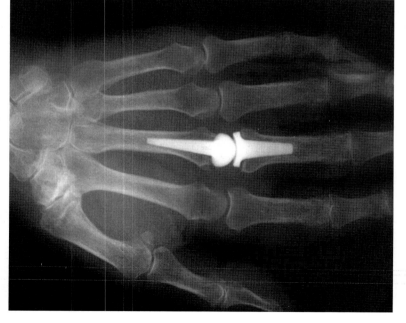

ASCENSION ORTHOPEDICS, INC. DEVELOPED THE PYROLYTIC CARBON METACARPOPHALANGEAL JOINT PROSTHESIS TO REPLACE THE SMALL JOINTS IN THE HAND AND FOOT, TO HELP RELIEVE PAIN AND RESTORE MOBILITY AND FUNCTION IN PATIENTS SUFFERING FROM RHEUMATOID AND DEGENERATIVE ARTHRITIS AND POST TRAUMATIC CONDITIONS.

APPLE COMPUTER, INC. HAS ALWAYS BEEN A GROUND-breaker, and its Americas Customer Support Center in Austin continues the trend of adapting to the dynamics of a constantly changing marketplace. ★ The site was opened in 1992 to consolidate two

geographically separate customer support centers located in Sunnyvale, California, and Charlotte, North Carolina. Choosing Austin for its quality of life and the availability of a highly qualified workforce, the company started with 350 employees and has since expanded to approximately 900.

. . . DOESN'T FALL FAR FROM THE TREE

Apple Computer, Inc. ignited the personal computer revolution in the 1970s, and is especially known for developing the Apple Macintosh® line of computers, introduced in 1984 and characterized by their intuitive ease of use. Apple is headquartered in Cupertino, California, and has manufacturing facilities in California, Ireland, and Singapore, with more than 9,000 employees worldwide. The company designs, manufactures, and markets personal computers and related peripherals and software to educational, home, business, and government customers through wholesale and retail channels, as well as directly to end users through its on-line store. In the United States, Apple is one of the major suppliers of personal computers for both elementary and secondary school customers, as well as for college and university customers.

More than 50 percent of the company's sales come through the Apple Americas Customer Support Center in Austin. The site encompasses the operations of sales support, logistics, finance, accounts receivable, information systems and technology, inside sales, field sales, Apple Assist end user support, and service provider support. "Our success in centralizing our customer service organization in an unbelievably competitive industry has led to our growth in new geographic and product markets," says Wayne Kozlow, site director.

Because the highest concentration of customer contact for the entire company occurs in Austin, the Apple Americas Customer Support Center is customer-centric in its organization, according to Kozlow. "We really are the crossroads of supply and demand, so we are committed to achieving a high level of customer satisfaction through our products, services, and people," he says. In 1995, the site achieved ISO 9002 certification for its presales support, order management, credit and collections, and revenue accounting processes.

Apple Americas Customer Support Center also reinforces employee development, measurement and accountability, encouragement of

diversity, and fun. Kozlow attributes the high morale of employees to the working environment, which fosters high productivity and recognizes performance, while encouraging a casual atmosphere with good opportunities for upward mobility.

APPLE TO THE CORE

In addition to ensuring customer satisfaction, the values of the Apple Americas Customer Support Center closely mirror those of the company. The Austin site encourages community involvement with a particular focus on education and children.

Employees participate in a wide range of activities, ranging from teaching Junior Achievement to sponsoring food drives, and the company enjoys a close relationship with Oak Springs Elementary School. Company employees participate in reading and mentoring programs, as well as hosting special activities such as a pen pal program, Halloween parties, and a yearbook project. Through such civic leadership within the Austin community and worldwide competitiveness within the personal computer industry, Apple Americas Customer Support Center will continue sharing the values and products of Apple Computer, Inc. with a new generation of computer users.

APPLE AMERICAS CUSTOMER SUPPORT CENTER OPENED IN AUSTIN IN 1992, AND NOW HAS SOME 900 EMPLOYEES IN SALES SUPPORT, LOGISTICS, FINANCE, ACCOUNTS RECEIVABLE, INFORMATION SYSTEMS AND TECHNOLOGY, INSIDE SALES, FIELD SALES, APPLE ASSIST END USER SUPPORT, AND SERVICE PROVIDER SUPPORT.

NCORE ORTHOPEDICS, INC. IS ONE OF THE FASTEST-GROWING orthopedic implant corporations in the world. Designing, manufacturing, and marketing products for the orthopedic device industry, Encore helps thousands of patients regain health, mobility, and independence. ★ The primary

operating subsidiary of Encore Medical Corporation, Encore Orthopedics is led by a management team with more than 120 years of combined experience in the orthopedic industry. The company began in 1992 as a member of the Austin Technology Incubator Program, and today employs more than 100 people. In 1997, it was ranked 145th on the *Inc.* 500 list of fastest-growing private companies in the United States, and the company went public in March of the same year.

"Our growth has continued to far outpace the industry's growth, and is the reward for our efforts to organize a quality sales force, with quality products, committed to serving the needs of orthopedic surgeons," says founder and CEO Nick Cindrich.

Encore's state-of-the-art, 70,000-square-foot facility houses all of the company's operations—sales, marketing, design, manufacturing, and administration. Encore holds ISO 9001 certification and European Certification (CE Mark), and maintains its own manufacturing facility, which helps the company not only expand its products line and sales, but also quickly respond to surgeons' requests and prototype new products. Encore's product-development personnel collaborate with a team of highly qualified design surgeons to constantly improve and update existing products and instruments while working on new offerings.

Encore prides itself on its excellent, user-friendly products and instrumentation, as well as its responsive, reliable service. The company maintains continuous contact with its surgeon and hospital customers, and hosts numerous programs, seminars, and site visits to facilitate a constant exchange of information on total joint replacements. This personal-

ized service helps surgeons best serve their patients while building thriving practices.

Encore distributes its products through a global network focusing on North America, Western Europe, and the Far East, which constitute 90 percent of the implant market. A strong network of exclusive sales agents are carefully selected, based on industry experience and technical knowledge.

LEADING-EDGE PRODUCTS

ncore has created a comprehensive line of total joint and trauma products, including the Foundation® Total Joint Replacement System for hips, knees, and shoulders; Vitality®, Revelation™, and Linear™ Total Hip Systems; True/Flex® Intramedullary Rod System; and True/Lok™ External Fixation System.

The company's recent innovations include its Revelation Hip Stem, which transfers physiological load to the bone and significantly improves the maintenance of bone stock. The company is also a leader in ceramic technology within the orthopedic device industry. A codevelopment effort is under way with the world-class French ceramics company Norton-Demarquest that should result in the introduction of the industry's

first successful ceramic knee femur. Additionally, a ceramic-on-ceramic total hip joint is currently being implanted in an FDA (Food and Drug Administration) clinical study, as is a similar metal-on-metal total hip clinical study. Both the ceramic and metal programs are intended to significantly reduce wear rates, thus reducing particulate debris and lengthening the life span of the total joint. With new spinal products and orthopedic-oriented biological products, Encore plans to extend its success by continuing its expansion into innovative new markets.

Encore maintains a strong commitment to customer service, and its responsive culture allows a quick and open exchange of information throughout all levels of the company. The combination of response and innovation is just one more reason Encore is a unique presence in the industry, challenging old rules and creating new paradigms to find success.

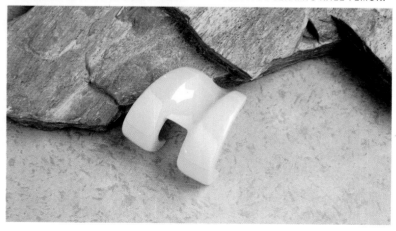

IXC COMMUNICATIONS, INC.

XC COMMUNICATIONS, INC. JOINED THE AUSTIN HIGH-TECH SCENE in 1992, and its tremendous growth since then shows no signs of slowing. One of the largest and fastest-growing communications companies in the world, IXC is helping to create the information infrastructure of the global communications market.

With more than 1,650 employees, IXC's rapid growth reflects both its external and internal successes in building a culture of open communication. The company empowers its employees to take ownership and initiative, welcoming ideas, innovations, and solutions at all levels.

INTEGRATED INFORMATION

One of the nation's leading suppliers of voice, video, and data transmission services, IXC offers innovative communications solutions to national and regional long-distance carriers and Internet service providers, local telephone companies, and cable and utility companies.

"As we approach the 21st century, satisfying the overwhelming demand for information has become increasingly dependent on a critical resource—communications network capacity," says Chairman and CEO Benjamin Scott. "What we are doing is providing integrated, network-based information delivery systems for businesses."

Recognizing the need for nationwide fiber-optic networks, IXC in 1994 began its trek to become the first-to-market provider of the nationwide network services required for advanced, high-bandwidth-intensive products and services. In 1998, IXC completed its state-of-the-art fiber route between Los Angeles and New York—the first time in more than a decade that a coast-to-coast fiber-optic network had been completed. The network incorporates the latest in fiber and optical transmission technologies to support all packetized applications, including the Internet, intranets, extranets, advanced data services, and multimedia communications.

The coast-to-coast portion of the network was completed as part of IXC's planned program to expand its network to more than 18,000 digital route miles and 400,000 total fiber miles. The ongoing expansion of IXC's network in the coming years will ensure that the company has the capacity and technology to meet the rapidly growing demand for high-speed data transmission, Internet connectivity, and other advanced communications applications.

STATE-OF-THE-ART SERVICE

IXC sells its services to wholesale or carrier services, retail, and emerging markets. Wholesale customers include carriers and resellers, cable companies, Internet service providers, utilities, competitive local exchange carriers, and others. Retail customers are primarily small- to medium-size businesses, who benefit in cost and quality by buying dedicated access to IXC's network. For emerging markets, the company's focus is on partnerships with international communications providers, cable companies, utilities, and other nontraditional outlets, as IXC continues to meet the growing demand for network capacity on a global level. International partnerships include joint ventures with MarcaTel in Mexico and Telenor AS in Norway to provide communications services in European countries.

Careful and continuing internal and external research helps IXC identify emerging trends, and the company has built a comprehensive portfolio of innovative products and services to meet the needs of its customers. IXC's

BENJAMIN L. SCOTT, IXC PRESIDENT, CHAIRMAN, AND CHIEF EXECUTIVE OFFICER

product line features private line, broadband, Internet, and long-distance switched and dedicated services. Private line services are the long-haul transmission of voice and data over dedicated circuits under long-term bulk contracts. With its long-distance switched services, IXC bills based on the actual minutes of use, including origination/termination fees. Broadband services offer frame relay, ATM (Asynchronous Transfer Mode), and IP (Internet protocol) transport.

The company's full line of long-distance products enables resellers to offer enhanced long-distance services, including outbound and inbound calling and card services. IXC's Private Line service is a point-to-point service designed for high-speed, full duplex transmission. The IXC Online software platform helps resellers with order processing in a real-time, user-friendly format. IXC Advanced Data Services use Frame Relay and ATM technologies to meet the growing demands

for increased bandwidth, higher access speeds, and effective congestion management.

Calling Austin Home

IXC makes its home in City View Centre, located on a seven-acre tract in the hills of southwest Austin. The spacious, modern facility features a mission control Network Operations Center, which keeps its finger on the pulse of IXC systems around the country. Equipped with the latest technology and systems for monitoring, managing, and maintaining fiber-optic networks, the Network Operations Center operates 24 hours a day to keep the network running smoothly across the nation. IXC's Customer Care Center also operates 24 hours a day, seven days a week to service IXC customers. Even the company's 16 conference rooms, each with a different Texas-specific name, offer state-of-the-art multimedia capabilities.

While embedded in the tradition of the communications industry, IXC's entrepreneurial spirit helps it focus on the future. As the information age continues to touch every corner of the world, IXC is there to provide the service and the solutions to make the transition into a new era as easy as possible.

RANDALLS FOOD MARKETS, INC. TRANSFORMS GROCERY shopping from a routine task into a pleasurable experience. Combining quality products, superb customer service, and unbeatable convenience, Randalls elevates the one-stop shopping experience to new heights.

Randalls designs its stores from the ground up to meet customers' needs and to appeal to their senses. Every store emphasizes the freshest foods available, from seafood to meat to produce, with a wide selection of organically grown fruits and vegetables. Certified Angus Beef, known as the best beef in the world, is available exclusively at Randalls. The Randalls bakeries are well known for their fresh breads and pastries, many made from scratch and baked on-site daily. Also famous throughout the state for its full catering services and wedding cakes, Randalls brings a unique touch to numerous special occasions. The store on Balcones Drive features the only kosher bakery in an Austin grocery store, and is overseen by a local rabbi.

Over the years, the company's stores have evolved to meet changing lifestyles and market demands. Randalls' newest stores reflect the spirit of Austin, providing such luxuries as full floral departments

with FTD-certified master floral designers, and, at one store, an outside deck where local musicians play and neighbors gather to listen while they enjoy a fresh bagel or a cup of coffee from the in-store Starbucks coffee shop.

Flagship Randalls on Bee Caves Road provides the premier shopping experience, with handsome aesthetic touches, a wide selection of freshly prepared meals to go, countless gourmet delicacies and specialty items, and a vast selection of everyday necessities. There is no other grocery store in Austin quite like it.

A TEXAS NATIVE

Founded in 1966, Randalls Food Markets debuted with two stores, adding a third two years later. During the 1980s, the chain expanded to 42 stores through acquisitions and construction. In 1992, Randalls entered the Austin market with the purchase of several existing grocery stores. Randalls built its first new store in Austin in 1995, and by remodeling current locations and building new stores, quickly established itself as an industry leader committed to growing with Austin.

Today, the business is run by Randall Onstead, chairman and CEO of Randalls and the son of cofounder and chairman emeritus Robert Onstead. Throughout its growth, Randalls' level of commitment to exceptional quality and customer service has remained steadfast. This commitment has guided Randalls as it has grown from a small operation into one of the largest privately held enterprises in Texas, with annual revenues of approximately $2.4 billion. With almost 18,000 employees statewide and 2,000 in the Austin area, Randalls attributes much of its success to a strong commitment to customer service.

EVERY RANDALLS FOOD MARKETS STORE EMPHASIZES THE FRESHEST FOODS AVAILABLE, FROM SEAFOOD TO MEAT TO PRODUCE, WITH A WIDE SELECTION OF ORGANICALLY GROWN FRUITS AND VEGETABLES.

"There's no doubt that we are growing bigger, better, and stronger every day, and none of this would be possible without our remarkable associates," says Randall Onstead. "Because of their dedication and commitment to serving our customers, we aren't just another ordinary grocery chain. We all strive to excel in every aspect of this business, especially where our customers are concerned. That is simply the Randalls way."

CONVENIENCE TO GO

Randalls knows that time is valuable to its customers, so it designs its stores to meet one-stop shopping needs. Many stores feature video rental, photo processing, a drive-through pharmacy, and dry-cleaning services. Wells Fargo electronic banking and ATM service are available in all stores. For added convenience, several Randalls locations offer on-site gas stations, in-store free child care while parents shop, and wellness centers offering a full line of health products.

To further expand efficiency and convenience, Randalls partnered with Peapod, an on-line grocery shopping and delivery service that allows customers to shop for their groceries at home with their personal computer. Customers can have their groceries delivered or they can pick them up in front of their local store.

The Randalls Remarkable Card program offers added value by rewarding loyal customers with electronic discounts and privileges, including video rentals, electronic/

paperless checking, check cashing, and more. The card is also tied to Randalls' Good Neighbor Program to support charitable organizations. Customers can designate the school, church, or charitable organization of their choice to receive 1 percent of their grocery purchases (excluding alcohol) as a quarterly donation from Randalls. This program has contributed $640,000 to more than 800 organizations in the Austin area.

In addition to its Good Neighbor Program, Randalls gives back to the community by supporting a variety of educational, environmental, and cultural philanthropic efforts. Randalls helps to raise funds for Any Baby Can, a local nonprofit agency that helps chronically ill children and their families in the Austin area. In 1998, Randalls introduced Randalls for Kids, an ongoing effort emphasizing children as the community's most valuable resource.

The company also sponsors Kindness for Kids, an annual,

monthlong campaign designed to raise public awareness about pediatric cancer while raising money for cancer research and treatment. This campaign has raised more than $50,000 for Children's Hospital of Austin. In 1998, the company introduced its Breast Cancer Awareness Month campaign, designed to promote breast cancer awareness by offering informational brochures and flyers, and offering mammography screenings at selected Randalls locations. Randalls is also an active member of the Capital Area Food Bank, and is involved with Tree Week on Shoal Creek, a partnership project to plant trees in Central Austin along Shoal Creek.

The diversity of Randalls' service programs reflects the company's commitment to its customers, both within the store and throughout the community. Realizing that the grocery industry is truly a service industry, Randalls has found a home in Austin, and developed a strong, loyal, and growing customer base.

RANDALLS DESIGNS ITS STORES TO MEET ONE-STOP SHOPPING NEEDS, WITH A WIDE SELECTION OF FRESHLY PREPARED MEALS TO GO, COUNTLESS GOURMET DELICACIES AND SPECIALTY ITEMS, AND A VAST SELECTION OF EVERYDAY NECESSITIES.

THE GOTTESMAN COMPANY

SANDY GOTTESMAN LIKES HIS WORK TO SPEAK FOR ITSELF. As president of The Gottesman Company and as the former regional partner and president of Trammell Crow Central Texas, Inc., Gottesman's premier commercial real estate developments speak volumes to help tell the story of Austin.

In 1973, Gottesman started his real estate career leasing commercial space for Trammell Crow Company. In 1977, he built his first warehouses for the company, subsequently overseeing the development of 1.5 million square feet of office space, 6 million square feet of warehouse space, and 1.9 million square feet of retail space. While at the helm of Trammell Crow Company, Gottesman oversaw the development of noted Austin office and retail complexes

THE GOTTESMAN COMPANY, FOUNDED IN 1993, IS A COMMERCIAL REAL ESTATE DEVELOPMENT COMPANY THAT SPECIALIZES IN OFFICE, RETAIL, INDUSTRIAL, AND LAND DEVELOPMENT.

such as the Arboretum, Braker Center, and Westbank Market.

In addition to the warehouse and office developments, Gottesman was involved in the restoration of the 300 block of Congress Avenue, including the historic Davis Hardware buildings; the design and construction of 327 and 301 Congress; and the restoration of 318 Congress. He has also been involved in a number of major public and private projects in partnership with the City of Austin and/or Travis County for major infrastructure improvements, including the Golden Triangle Road District and regional detention facilities along Walnut Creek. These facilities helped to alleviate downstream flooding and allowed for the development of many acres of greenbelt and trails in North Austin.

A NEW TRADITION

In 1993, Gottesman formed The Gottesman Company, a commercial real estate development company specializing in office, retail, industrial, and land development. The Gottesman Company's most recent projects

include Metric Center and Stone-Creek Park, an office development at Duval Road and Mopac Boulevard.

Gottesman is known for his ability to facilitate large and complex deals, handling the acquisition and assemblage of land for restaurants and major corporate users. As a private company, The Gottesman Company offers the resources and ability to structure transactions in the manner that is most advantageous to the client or venture partner.

As an owner and developer of projects, The Gottesman Company is not in the day-to-day property management business. Instead, the company relies on longtime business partner Trammell Crow Company to manage and lease a substantial allocation of its portfolio. Gottesman also enjoys long-term relationships with many local technical, design, and construction consultants, and chooses the best and most appropriate talent for each individual project.

Gottesman and other members of his company are active members of the Austin community, and contribute both time and expertise to a number of local charities and organizations. He has been honored with several local and state awards, including the Josiah Wheat Award of Merit for Historic Preservation from the Texas Historical Foundation, the Historic Preservation Award from the Heritage Society of Austin, and the Carl W. Burnette Award for Historic Preservation from the Austin Community Foundation. He was named Austin's Best Developer by *Austin Magazine* in 1986.

With more than 25 years of development experience in the Austin area, Gottesman creates projects of enduring value not only for investors and clients, but also for the community as a whole.

MICRO-MEDIA SOLUTIONS, INC. (MSI) MAY REACH MILLIONS of people across the nation each day, but some of its most important connections are made right in its own backyard. A publicly traded corporation, MSI is quickly earning a reputation for breaking bound-aries, through both its technology services and its impact on the community.

MSI provides advanced Internet broadcast delivery for a broad array of markets. The company's Internet Accelerator Portal™ division provides Internet integration services and high-speed Internet connectivity through its Internet-working facilities.

The Internet Accelerator Portal offers a unique suite of services designed to create private portals. A private portal is a turnkey service providing targeted Internet content to specific communities of interest. In other words, MSI creates and maintains virtual communities that appeal to a specific group of people.

The creation of private portals establishes secure virtual communities that can function totally independent of the World Wide Web. Accelerated communications delivered via Internet broadcasting and videoconferencing creates a renaissance for group buying and targeted advertising. These cutting-edge business arrangements will emerge as joint ventures between the community of interest and the Internet Accelerator Portal. Private portals produce a paradigm shift by transferring negotiating power from vendors to the consumer. This is accomplished with group buying and the ability to have one community voice that requests the same customer service previously only available to major corporations.

MSI offers clients broadband co-location/Webhosting services from the first BBN certified data center in their Austin facility. Through strategic alliances with GTE Internetworking and South-western Bell, MSI is positioned to become a market leader in facilitating broadband content via the Internet.

MAKING A DIFFERENCE

Deeply involved in the community, MSI's greatest outreach effort is to its own East Austin neighborhood. The company built its headquarters in the economically deprived area with the primary intent of helping the community. MSI hires and trains a nontraditional workforce, many from the neighborhood, in nontraditional, high-tech jobs. A huge investment in training, as well as great benefits and opportunities within the company, results in a loyal and enthusiastic staff numbering nearly 100.

MSI's involvement in the long-term renaissance of East Austin began with its renovation of a 39,000-square-foot, abandoned warehouse to house the company's corporate offices and its manufacturing, testing, programming, and distribution activities. Nearby buildings and houses soon followed suit with new signs or fresh coats of paint.

With its rapid rise to success and its powerful faith in its community, MSI is sure to lead its customers into the future, while continuing to make significant connections in its hometown.

Internet Accelerator Portal™

MICRO-MEDIA SOLUTIONS IS THE FIRST-EVER BBN CERTIFIED COMPANY.

HE FAX MACHINE HAS COME A LONG WAY SINCE ITS HUMBLE beginnings more than a century ago, and Omnifax continues to live up to its pioneering heritage in the industry, working to take fax technology and service to the next level. ★ The company traces its roots to the original

telautograph patented in 1888 by inventor and Omnifax founding father Elisha Gray. According to Gray's original patent, the telautograph "enabled one to transmit his own handwriting to a distant point over a two-wire circuit." The machines grew more and more sophisticated, and were soon found in virtually every form of private enterprise and public service.

The mid-1950s saw the development of facsimile technology, and in 1979, the Telautograph Corp. created the Omnifax brand name for its facsimiles. In 1993, Telautograph was acquired by Danka Industries, one of the largest independent distributors of photocopiers, fax machines, and associated supplies and services. The company changed its name to Omnifax and established its corporate headquarters in Austin in 1994.

Since arriving in Austin, Omnifax has become an integral part of the community. Besides creating 250 jobs in the Austin area, the company is involved in the Adopt-a-School program;

UNDER PRESIDENT RON PETRUCCI'S DIRECTION, OMNIFAX HAS ACHIEVED RECORD GROWTH.

supports the Capitol Area United Way, Habitat for Humanity, Austin's The Christmas Bureau, and America's Walk for Diabetes; and contributes to various community efforts through its employee program, Beans for Jeans.

FOCUSED ON COMMUNICATION

Omnifax is now, more than ever, a leader in the field of imaging communications, and maintains its own in-house engineering staff that actively develops new products, while also creating a new level of service and support for its customers. "Every aspect of our internal operations and our strategic direction is geared to deliver the best possible product and solutions to our customers," says President Ron Petrucci.

This goal begins with internal, two-way communication among the company's 700 employees, says Petrucci. "We have ongoing, open discussions to communicate our philosophy and goals, and at the same time, we listen to sugges-

tions and strategy coming from people throughout the company, whether in sales or service or shipping," he says. "The key to our success is the quality of our people, and some of the best ideas come from those doing their day-to-day job."

Petrucci also attributes the company's success to listening to its customers and perfecting exceptional service. "Our service is what truly distinguishes us," says Petrucci. "We have the most sophisticated product line in the industry, but the backup support behind our products really makes the difference."

As a result, Omnifax has developed innovative programs and services for its customers. The company's OMNISight is a unique program that helps customers control and manage their fax network and associated costs by providing specific facsimile network management data via a private and secure location on the Omnifax Web site. Utilized to analyze expenditures, equipment, and service trends, this real-time information helps customers make smarter purchasing and network management decisions. "This service allows us, as a partner, to maintain open communication with our customers to help them meet their needs and develop a

OMNIFAX HAS ALWAYS BEEN IN THE FOREFRONT OF TECHNOLOGY. THIS EARLY VERSION OF THE FIRST FACSIMILE WAS KNOWN AS THE TELAUTOGRAPH IN THE LATE 1800S AND EARLY 1900S.

more efficient network," says Petrucci.

Another Omnifax exclusive program, the company's OmniFlex is the first asset management system created to consolidate all fax-related costs—including equipment, supplies, and services—within one single payment. OmniSource, Omnifax's exclusive consumables division, provides customers with a single point of contact for all their supply needs. Customer profiles and master account records are automatically available to the Omnifax representative, ensuring price and product consistency no matter where a customer is located.

Omnifax manufactured its own products until the early 1970s, when it began cultivating steady relationships with several top manufacturers. Now the company uses its vast knowledge of the marketplace to choose the best products for the best prices, built to Omnifax specifications. "By incorporating requests from our customers, we take our research to each manufacturer partner to plan and develop specialty fax products that are unique to Omnifax," explains Petrucci.

"We can handle any need for any corporation," he adds. "By providing the most reliable, cost-effective, and fastest product line in the industry, we help our customers increase productivity

and save hundreds of thousands of dollars."

QUICK RESPONSE, QUALITY SERVICE

mnifax's knowledgeable customer support representatives provide initial and follow-up training to customers. More than 200 service technicians respond to service calls in all major cities within four business hours, outperforming the average industry response time by 50 percent. Every service technician carries a palmtop device with custom software that allows him or her to upload and download key account and support information from the site of the service call. For large installations, Omnifax's Pinnacle service package guarantees two-hour average response time in major markets for service calls, as well as no charge for packing and in-

stalling machines for relocation, replacement operator manuals, upgrading of firmware, and loaner machines.

The company was voted the number one service organization by users, not just for its quick response time, but also for its exceptional on-site repair capabilities. In fact, Omnifax technicians even service machines from other companies, as part of transition service to Omnifax products.

The Omnifax Process Implementation Team, the PIT Crew, was specifically designed for major account customers with large installed bases and new, large, multiple-site installations requiring nationwide coordination. The goal of the PIT Crew is to provide a smooth and quick transition to an Omnifax facsimile network with no disruption to the customers' employees and work flow.

Through a series of mergers and acquisitions, culminating in today's Omnifax corporation, Gray's original telautograph has been transformed into technologically advanced, must-have equipment for every business or organization in the world. Omnifax, the leading provider of fax equipment for Fortune 2000 companies, utilizes more than a century of experience to continually improve the future of communication.

OMNIFAX'S OMNISIGHT . . . TOTAL VISION FOR NETWORK SOLUTIONS IS AN INNOVATIVE, WEB-BASED SERVICE DESIGNED TO TAKE CUSTOMERS INTO THE NEXT MILLENNIUM AND BEYOND.

OMNIFAX OFFERS ONE OF THE MOST UNIQUE AND EXTENSIVE PRODUCT LINES IN THE FACSIMILE INDUSTRY.

MILLIONS OF PEOPLE USE PERVASIVE SOFTWARE'S DATA management and Web application software every day, but few have ever heard of the company. That's because Pervasive's products—built into some of the world's most popular software applications—

are designed to be invisible.

Pervasive Software is a leading provider of software for easily managing information—in Internet applications, in Web devices and appliances, and in packaged business solutions. Developers worldwide depend on Pervasive for powerful, easy-to-use Web development and deployment, high-performance embedded database, and reporting and data transformation solutions

Because many small and medium-sized businesses do not have a dedicated in-house database administrator, applications based on Pervasive products are a perfect fit. "We put a very sharp focus and a high premium on zero administration, developing information management systems that are virtually maintenance free," says Pervasive President and CEO Ron Harris.

The company was formed in 1994 as Btrieve Technologies, changing its name in 1996 to Pervasive Software Inc. Btrieve, the company's transactional database engine, was developed in 1982 and was among the earliest databases available for the PC platform.

Novell acquired the technology in 1987 and distributed literally millions of copies worldwide with its NetWare network operating system. The product's original architects, Doug and Nancy Woodward, teamed with Harris to buy the technology back from Novell in 1994 to found what would become Pervasive Software.

The company's flagship products—the Pervasive.SQL database engine with supporting tools and utilities, and the Tango Enterprise Web application and deployment environment—are designed specifically for use in applications for businesses without a dedicated database administrator. Pervasive.SQL is the first and only database that enables application developers to offer simultaneous transactional (lightning fast) and relational (sophisticated query) access to the same data.

Rich history and cutting-edge products breed success. In 1996, Pervasive was recognized as the Fastest Growing Private Company in Austin by the *Austin Business Journal*, and Harris was named Austin Entrepreneur of the Year for 1997. In 1998, Pervasive

earned a spot on the elite Texas Top 100.

WORLDWIDE DISTRIBUTION

Headquartered in Austin, Pervasive has offices in Toronto, Frankfurt, Paris, London, Brussels, Dublin, Tokyo, and Hong Kong. Pervasive's exclusively channel-driven product distribution model, the only one of its kind in the industry, relies on partners to embed and distribute Pervasive products to their end users. This network of original equipment manufacturers, distributors, manufacturing partners, independent software vendors, and value-added resellers offers a broad range of sales, consulting, application development, installation, service, training, and support to users of Pervasive-based applications.

As the company name implies, Pervasive database products are found worldwide in a broad range of applications. The Tango Enterprise product is behind such high-profile Web sites as BigE.com and theglobe.com, and organizations like Disney, Kodak, Intel, MGM Grand Casino, Taco Bell, Minolta, NASA, and other leading corporations depend on Pervasive's solutions to execute business-critical aspects of their operations.

Even as a worldwide success, Pervasive remains loyal to its Austin roots. The company and its almost 250 Austin employees actively contribute time and money to a number of community programs, including Blue Santa, Ronald McDonald House, Book Boosters, Child and Family Services, and the local humane society. As the company's employee base grows and as its markets boom, Pervasive is sure to remain an important part of the Austin economy for many years to come.

PERVASIVE SOFTWARE IS A LEADING PROVIDER OF SOFTWARE FOR EASILY MANAGING INFORMATION— IN INTERNET APPLICATIONS, IN WEB DEVICES AND APPLIANCES, AND IN PACKAGED BUSINESS SOLUTIONS.

WHEN TIM HERMAN AND RANDY HOWRY STARTED their own civil litigation firm in 1995, they knew they wanted to focus on the needs of local businesses. Today, Herman & Howry, L.L.P. helps the Austin business community resolve

disputes involving everything from contractual matters to patent infringement. The firm handles all types of business litigation, including partner/shareholder disputes; contractual disputes such as commercial or real estate contracts; fraud, deceptive trade, employment, and consumer law; oil and gas issues; securities; intellectual property disputes; insurance and employee benefits; professional and legal malpractice; defective products and catastrophic injuries; and regulatory and administrative licensing and enforcement issues.

"We are a trial firm that can handle any kind of business dispute," says Howry. "We help clients resolve their disputes by first finding the most appropriate process for the situation, whether it be mediation, arbitration, or litigation."

DRAWING ON EXPERIENCE

Herman & Howry's clients range from large corporations to small start-ups and individuals. With a broad base of experience in both administrative law and litigation, the firm's attorneys have handled and tried hundreds of cases, ranging from commercial, insurance, consumer, and intellectual property matters to cases involving torts, administrative law, and oil and gas issues.

While well equipped to represent clients in the courtroom, Herman & Howry appreciates the value of preserving business relationships while advancing clients' interests. The firm's experience in the courtroom provides a keen understanding of how both sides work to resolve disputes and translates into sage advice for clients.

When appropriate, firm members meet with clients early on to design a plan to find the best solution to their specific problems,

exploring dispute resolution options as an alternative to litigation in order to minimize clients' legal costs and lost time. If, however, litigation is necessary for the protection of clients' interests, it is undertaken with a commitment to success. Every matter is handled with an aggressive but ethical approach, developed through years of experience.

By using state-of-the-art computer technology and litigation support techniques, the firm helps clients achieve their objectives, often at a cost far lower than that of larger firms. Working in partnership with clients, the firm frequently provides representation through contingency fees or other nontraditional fee arrangements.

Concerned with giving back to the community in which they

work, the firm's partners participate in many community activities and serve on several charitable boards and charitable foundations, and all participate in the Travis County Bar Association's Volunteer Legal Services program.

Herman & Howry is focused on litigation. The firm's five lawyers often work together as a team, along with the firm's legal assistants and support staff, to deliver the best results for clients. "When our clients hire us, they know that we're the ones really doing the work," says Herman. "Because we hire the best people at all levels, we handle large and complex cases and still maintain the level of personal service that our clients expect and deserve."

HERMAN & HOWRY, L.L.P. WAS FOUNDED WITH A FOCUS ON THE NEEDS OF THE AUSTIN BUSINESS COMMUNITY. TO MAKE IT EASIER FOR CLIENTS TO COMMUNICATE WITH THE FIRM, HERMAN & HOWRY MAINTAINS A WEB SITE AT WWW.HERMANHOWRY.COM.

WITH A BROAD BASE OF EXPERIENCE IN BOTH ADMINISTRATIVE LAW AND LITIGATION, THE FIRM'S ATTORNEYS HAVE HANDLED AND TRIED HUNDREDS OF CASES, RANGING FROM COMMERCIAL, INSURANCE, CONSUMER, AND INTELLECTUAL PROPERTY MATTERS TO CASES INVOLVING TORTS, ADMINISTRATIVE LAW, AND OIL AND GAS ISSUES.

WHEN SEARCHING FOR THE PERFECT SPOT FOR ITS corporate headquarters, Tokyo Electron America, Inc. (TEA) knew it could call Austin home. Since moving to the city in 1994, the company has firmly planted itself in the local community, and its roots grow deeper and deeper.

Tokyo Electron Limited, TEA's parent company, began in 1963 as an import distributor of industrial electronic products in Japan. In the 1970s, the company expanded into manufacturing its own products through joint ventures with several of its principal suppliers. By the 1980s, the company had bought out its partners to become an independent manufacturer of equipment for the semiconductor industry.

When several of its principal customers expanded their operations to Europe and the United States, Tokyo Electron expanded, too, creating new, locally based organizations to serve them. In searching for a site for the headquarters of the newly created Tokyo Electron America, the company looked for a central location that could serve as a hub for its network of sales and service centers. Texas immediately topped the list because of its growing semiconductor industry.

After considering Dallas and other large Texas cities, Tokyo Electron selected Austin because

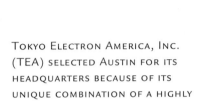

TOKYO ELECTRON AMERICA, INC. (TEA) SELECTED AUSTIN FOR ITS HEADQUARTERS BECAUSE OF ITS UNIQUE COMBINATION OF A HIGHLY EDUCATED WORKFORCE AND AN ATTRACTIVE LIFESTYLE.

THE TOKYO ELECTRON LIMITED (TEL) BOOTH AT SEMICON WEST SHOWCASES TEL'S COMMITMENT TO TECHNOLOGICAL EXCELLENCE AND CUSTOMER SATISFACTION.

of its unique combination of a highly educated workforce and an attractive lifestyle. "We felt that it would be easy to attract the very best people to Austin," says Louis Steen, vice president of marketing. "The countryside is beautiful, there is a world-class university here, and the recreational opportunities are outstanding. Also, the thriving high-tech industry in Austin provides a community that nurtures some of the most creative thinkers in the industry."

In October 1994, the 200 employees of Tokyo Electron America moved into temporary quarters near IH-35 and Ben White Boulevard. Just two years later, in August 1996, TEA moved its growing workforce of nearly 300 people into its permanent headquarters at 2400 Grove Boulevard. The Austin office acts as the central hub of TEA's sales and service network, with eight other major centers throughout the United States.

A LEGACY OF SERVICE

Like its parent company, TEA's mission is to provide high-productivity, state-of-the-art manufacturing equipment to the semiconductor industry. Total dedication to customer satisfaction is the parent corporation's driving philosophy, and was the impetus for the creation of the U.S. and European branches of the company.

"TEA started out as a distributor of equipment, not a manufacturer. For a distributor, service is the only value you can add to the product, and it became the core value of the company," says Steen. "That legacy lives on in the corporation today. Unlike many other manufacturers, we go wherever our customers go. That's why we felt it was important to create strategically located sales and

service operations throughout the United States. Our engineering service personnel are all TEA employees, not just subcontractors. This gives us greater control over the quality of not only our products, but also our customer service."

The majority of the company's promotional activities are face-to-face meetings with customers and potential customers designed to build rapport and trust. The goal is for the customers to feel as if they know each staff member, from field service engineer to CEO, and can count on them to be responsive.

In January 1998, the parent company opened Tokyo Electron Texas (TEX), a manufacturing and research site, next door to TEA. TEX produces the company's highly successful Clean Track line of microchip processing equipment. It is one of four manufacturing sites operated in the United States by Tokyo Electron Ltd. Other manufacturing sites, located in Massachusetts, Oregon, and Arizona, produce diffusion furnaces, plasma etchers, and thin film deposition tools for semiconductor production.

The company also has product and applications research and development at its Massachusetts and Arizona operations. Since the 1980s, when Tokyo Electron began developing its own proprietary designs for microchip manufacturing equipment, the company has focused on pushing forward the cutting edge of research and

development. In facilities in Japan and America, Tokyo Electron advances the state of the art in process technology and robust manufacturing solutions.

Equipment developed by Tokyo Electron researchers has helped fuel the drive toward packing increasing numbers of features onto ever smaller chips, bringing the cost of computer memory to phenomenally low levels. Recent advancements in photosensitive imaging materials and developing and etching equipment are being incorporated in a new generation of Clean Track equipment manufactured in Austin and Etch equipment manufactured in Massachusetts.

Just as the company seeks to build personal relationships with customers, it also seeks to build ongoing relationships with the communities in which it locates. Tokyo Electron actively supports Austin's environmental efforts by recycling many tons of paper,

aluminum cans, and other materials each year.

Though it develops its business strategies for the wider global marketplace, the company acts locally by recruiting employees from the Austin workforce, buying from local suppliers, and supporting local civic and charitable organizations.

Tokyo Electron is a major contributor to such activities as the Walk for Safe Families (operated by SafePlace, Austin's rape crisis center and battered women's shelter); KRLU Arts Auction; Meals on Wheels; United Way; Junior Achievement; the Motorola Marathon, benefiting Child and Family Services; Spirit of Christmas, in conjunction with Bank One; and Austin Partners in Education. In addition to its corporate funding of community activities, the company supports its employees' individual efforts to volunteer their time to make Austin a better community.

REQUENT BUSINESS TRAVELERS AND THEIR EMPLOYERS OFTEN have different priorities when it comes to choosing extended-stay lodging: one looks primarily for convenience and comfort, while the other seeks the best value. As more and more people are finding out, neither need look any farther than Homestead Village, which combines the best of both worlds.

Homestead Village is one of the leading developers, owners, and operators of moderately priced, extended-stay lodging facilities in the United States. Its parent company is Security Capital Group Inc., a Santa Fe-based management investment company. Recognizing the growing demand for extended-stay lodging, Security Capital created Homestead Village Hotels Incorporated, a company now publicly traded on the New York Stock Exchange.

SETTLING IN

According to recent industry trends, extended-stay travel is the fastest-growing segment of the hospitality market, and Homestead Village has been a pioneer in developing and serving this market. The company tested its first property in Dallas, and the initial reaction was so positive that it now operates more than 120 properties around the country, with antici-pated growth of 55 properties per year. Headquartered in Atlanta, the company employs 1,300 nation-wide and 40 in Austin.

Homestead Village established its first extended-stay hotel in Austin in 1995, and now has four properties: Arboretum, Austin Mid-town, Northwest, and Downtown/Town Lake, the newest location. Two additional sites—one at Interstate 35 and FM 1325 in Round Rock and one near the new Austin-Bergstrom International Airport—

will likely be developed in the future.

In its brief time in the Austin community, Homestead Village has already made its presence known. Staff members are involved in many organizations, including the Animal Trustees of Austin. The company is a member of the Greater Austin Chamber of Commerce, Better Business Bureau, Austin Business Travelers Association, and Austin Hotel/Motel Association. Whenever possible, Homestead Village supports local churches and women's shelters with the donation of linens and other necessities.

COMFORT AND VALUE

Homestead Village offers all the essentials for an extended stay at a surprisingly affordable cost. The typical stay at Homestead Village is five nights, and the average cost is $259 to $349 per week for a studio unit. A one-week stay at Homestead Village is comparable in cost to a three-night stay at a hotel.

BUSINESS TRAVELERS FIND ALL THE COMFORTS OF HOME AT A SURPRISINGLY AFFORDABLE PRICE AT HOMESTEAD VILLAGES' MANY CONVENIENT LOCATIONS.

EACH HOMESTEAD VILLAGE ROOM
HAS A SITTING AREA, A WELL-LIT
WORKSTATION WITH A DATAPORT,
AND A FULLY EQUIPPED KITCHEN.

For the most part, Homestead Village's customers are corporations seeking moderately priced, comfortable, and safe lodging for their employees. Frequent guests at Homestead Village are business travelers who are on extended-stay assignments, attending a training/ seminar function, or in the process of relocating to a new city. In Austin, Homestead Village's customers work in a variety of industries, including real estate, finance, and high technology, and the new downtown location is especially convenient for legislators during the legislative session.

The sites have 130 rooms, each with space to relax, work, and prepare meals. Beginning in size at approximately 400 square feet, each apartment has a bed, a sitting area with a comfortable easy chair or sofa, and a well-lit workstation with a dataport. A fully equipped kitchen allows guests to wake up to a fresh cup of coffee or fix themselves a quiet, relaxing dinner.

Most properties offer such personal services as dry cleaning, and all have on-site, 24-hour guest laundry, as well as an iron and ironing board in each room. Guests enjoy complimentary use of an off-site fitness club, as well as free cable and HBO.

Homestead Village creates a safe environment with lighted parking lots, uniformed security on-site after hours, and the industry's best electronic lock system on every door. Beautiful landscaping adds an aesthetic touch.

Generous business amenities also attract corporate clients.

Local phone service is free, as is personalized voice mail that's retrievable from outside the property. Photocopy and fax services are available during office hours, and incoming domestic faxes are complimentary. All messages, mail, overnight packages, and faxes are delivered to guests' rooms at the end of each business day.

CONVENIENCE AND SERVICE

In addition to providing excellent value for its customers, Homestead Village's main focal points are convenience and service. Each property is located near shopping, restaurants, and entertainment, with easy access to major thoroughfares. Homestead Village's staff is always happy to supply directions, maps, and information about local points of interest.

As a service-oriented company, Homestead Village is a strong believer in employee training and implements a curriculum-based training program for all employees. The seven different disciplines of

the training program focus on customer service and job skills. "Every employee—from the manager to the laundry room attendant—is trained to make the customer happy," says Jill Musca, general manager of Homestead Village. "Our service is what keeps guests content and what keeps them coming back."

Homestead Village is very proactive in its customer research and its properties are always evolving to meet changing customer demand. This attention to customer satisfaction pays off: Homestead Village's average occupancy rate is 90 percent and its recent national performance is double that of its competitors.

"The Austin economy remains one of the fastest growing in the country, and companies all over the country are doing business in Austin," says E.J. Schanfarber, company vice president. "They are discovering Homestead Village as an excellent and well-priced solution to their extended-stay needs."

KEANE, INC.

EANE, INC. IS READY FOR THE FUTURE, AND SO ARE ITS clients. The computer services company specializes in the development and maintenance of software for large corporations and government organizations, helping them meet their information technology

(IT) needs today while planning for tomorrow.

"In today's competitive environment, information technology is a critical business asset," says Austin Managing Director James Brewer. "IT, converted to business solutions, helps companies operate more efficiently, execute competitive strategies, and adjust to changes in rapidly evolving markets."

Keane, Inc. was founded in 1965 in Boston by John Keane. Despite its dramatic growth since then, its mission remains constant, says Brewer. "We're in business to help our customers plan, build, and manage software," he says.

AN INDUSTRY LEADER

he company's clients are typically state and local government agencies and Fortune 1,000 organizations in industries such as manufacturing, finance, banking, insurance, telecommunications, and health care. A public company, Keane reported 1998 revenues of $1 billion. Keane was listed in *Business Week's* 1998 Information Technology 100; *ComputerWorld* in 1998 listed it as one of the best places to work; and the *Wall Street Journal* in 1998 called its stock the best 10-year performer in total return to investors.

Keane's structure and business philosophy help to set it apart from the competition. While the company's headquarters is in Boston, 45 branch offices throughout North America and the United Kingdom allow Keane to hire locally and thus control costs for clients while positively impacting the local economy. A strong process approach to business also brings economies of scale. "We focus on productivity management," says Brewer. "By applying a commonsense methodology to every aspect of our work, we can ensure the most cost-efficient and effective solutions for our clients."

Keane's primary services include application development, E-commerce, Web-enabled technologies, application management, and year 2000 solutions. Other services offered by Keane include IT consulting, program management, technology migration services, help desk management, and enterprise health care solutions.

DEVELOPING CLIENT-SPECIFIC SOLUTIONS

e're solution oriented," says Brewer. "We work with clients to develop a complete understanding of their business issues, and then we find ways to help them drive down their costs, improve their time to market, and deliver increased value to their customers."

Keane's 70 full-time Austin consultants work closely with clients to develop solutions to their specific needs. For a local Central Texas hospital, Keane developed a client server software application to mine important information from its overwhelming amounts of data. Keane then helped the client put the mined data to use to improve the quality of patient care and to maintain costs.

In its few years in Austin, Keane and its employees have become active members of the community, participating individually and as a company in numerous local programs. At the corporate level, Keane, Inc. is a generous supporter of many charities through its corporate giving program. Locally, Keane's Austin employees organize and contribute to grassroots fund-raising efforts, such as a 1998 collection for Central American hurricane relief and Habitat for Humanity.

Keane foresees continued growth in the future, thanks in part to the company's focus on development of long-term client relationships. Says Brewer, "The greatest measure of our success is watching our clients succeed."

BASED IN BOSTON, KEANE, INC. HAS 45 BRANCHES ACROSS NORTH AMERICA AND THE UNITED KINGDOM THAT ALLOW THE COMPANY TO HIRE LOCALLY AND THUS CONTROL COSTS FOR CLIENTS WHILE POSITIVELY IMPACTING THE LOCAL ECONOMY. AUSTIN'S TEAM INCLUDES (TOP, FROM LEFT) BRIANT SIKORSKI, ADAM MARTINEZ, JAMES BREWER, BOB SINSKY, PETER MONTELEONE, (BOTTOM, FROM LEFT) NATALIE POTTER, MARIA TURNER, MYRA GONZALES, SUSAN HARBIN, MARTI MCCABE, AND ROSEMARY YOUNGBLOOD.

◄ PAUL TRAVES (F-16 PHOTOGRAPHY)

CarrAmerica knows that a corporate office is more than just work space—it is a revealing glimpse into the identity, purpose, and vision of a company. And finding the perfect space to convey the right image, while planning for future growth, is CarrAmerica's specialty.

CarrAmerica is a publicly traded national real estate investment trust with $4 billion market capitalization (NYSE:CRE). For more than 35 years, CarrAmerica and its predecessors have provided a full range of real estate services to customers, including property development, construction management, leasing, property management, and asset management. With a significant focus on development, the company can build facilities to suit corporations, associations, and institutional users. Through its executive suite affiliates, CarrAmerica also offers customers the flexibility of short-term executive suite leasing.

"We can accommodate the needs of customers looking for office space for one day or for 20 years," says Jeff Pace, vice president/market officer for CarrAmerica's Austin office. "We listen closely to understand what our customers really desire, and we provide a full and flexible menu of services."

The company owns, develops, and operates office properties in 15 markets throughout the United States, including Atlanta, Austin, Boca Raton, Chicago, Dallas, Denver, Los Angeles/Orange County, Phoenix, Portland, Sacramento, Salt Lake City, San Diego, San Francisco Bay Area, Seattle, and Metro Washington, D.C. Providing high-quality, well-managed, customized office space, CarrAmerica also possesses a long-term commitment to each market that enables customers to expand as their space requirements change.

"We have the professional, technical, and financial resources to provide responsive and flexible real estate services, allowing our customers to focus on their core business and future growth," says Pace. "Our goal is to provide pain-free and seamless avenues to meet

PAUL BARDAGJY PHOTOGRAPHY

our customers' general growth and real estate needs."

A National Company with a Local Commitment

CarrAmerica entered the Austin market in 1996 and quickly made its mark by focusing on Austin's fast-track companies looking for room to grow. Many of Austin's premier corporate developments proudly carry the CarrAmerica name, including Riata Corporate Park, a beautiful, campuslike setting on 50 wooded acres in the heart of Austin's northwest corridor. Riata's initial customers included DSC Communications, Pervasive Software, Janus, Allstate Insurance, Texas Instruments, and NetSolve, Inc. CarrAmerica's Riata Crossing will be home to EDS, and its City View Centre houses Holt, Rinehart & Winston and IXC Communications. The company also owns and operates Great Hills Plaza, Park North, and Braker Pointe. The firm's total Austin portfolio nears 1.5 million square feet and is still growing.

Concerned with more than turning a profit, the Austin office of CarrAmerica is very involved in local and national professional organizations, including BOMA,

IREM, and the Real Estate Council of Austin. As a company, and through the efforts of individual employees, CarrAmerica also contributes through financial support and volunteer time to the Make A Wish Foundation, the local chapter of the American Heart Association, and Austin Meals on Wheels.

Austin is an important component of CarrAmerica's growth. Says Pace, "We chose the city for its combination of strong fundamental job growth characteristics and its superior quality of life. We are thrilled to be a part of the Austin community, and will continue to facilitate its growth."

MANY OF AUSTIN'S PREMIER CORPORATE DEVELOPMENTS PROUDLY CARRY THE CARRAMERICA NAME, INCLUDING RIATA CORPORATE PARK, A BEAUTIFUL, CAMPUSLIKE SETTING ON 50 WOODED ACRES IN THE HEART OF AUSTIN'S NORTHWEST CORRIDOR (TOP).

CARRAMERICA'S CITY VIEW CENTRE HOUSES HOLT, RINEHART & WINSTON AND IXC COMMUNICATIONS (BOTTOM).

PAUL BARDAGJY PHOTOGRAPHY

uPont Photomasks, Inc. (DPI) is proud to call Round Rock home for its corporate headquarters. As the world's largest manufacturer of photomasks, DPI is widely recognized as the industry's technology leader, and serves many of the largest semiconductor producers in the world, including AMD, Hyundai, LSI Logic, Lucent Technologies, Micron Technology, Motorola, National Semiconductor, Philips, STMicroelectronics, and Texas Instruments.

Photomasks, a critical component in the production of microchips, are high-purity quartz plates containing precision images of integrated circuits. They are used by semiconductor manufacturers to optically transfer circuit images onto semiconductor wafers and other types of electronic components. Every semiconductor device, no matter how simple or complex, requires a unique set of up to 30 photomasks for efficient manufacture.

A Heritage of Excellence

In the mid-1980s, E.I. du Pont de Nemours & Co. (DuPont), a diversified, global company based in Wilmington, Delaware, entered the photomask business through the acquisition of Tau Laboratories, a small, independent supplier to the semiconductor industry. During the next 10 years, DuPont grew the business primarily through acquisitions of captive and independent photomask manufacturers. In 1996, DuPont elected to spin off the business through an initial public offering of stock, thus giving birth to DuPont Photomasks, Inc.

An Integrated Global Network

In order to deliver premier technology and service in the photomask industry, DPI has created a tightly woven, global network of production and service centers to meet the needs of its customers. A network of integrated production facilities allows photomasks to be delivered within 12 to 24 hours of DPI's receipt of design data. Locations include facilities in Rousset, France; Hamilton, Scotland; Hamburg, Germany; Ichon, Korea; Kokomo, Indiana; Santa Clara, California; and Round Rock. DPI also holds majority ownership positions in joint ventures in Taiwan and Shanghai, China, and has plans for new facilities in Gresham, Oregon, and Singapore.

In addition to the production of the photomasks themselves, DPI manufactures its own photoblanks and pellicles, two essential components in its product. The company's photoblank facility is located in Poughkeepsie, New York, and its pellicles facility in Danbury, Connecticut. DPI's ability to integrate its global facilities and share information worldwide results in high-quality products for its customers.

Strategic Partnering

s the industry leader, DPI is playing an increasingly influential

DuPont Photomasks, Inc. (DPI), the world's largest manufacturer of photomasks, is proud to call Round Rock home for its corporate headquarters.

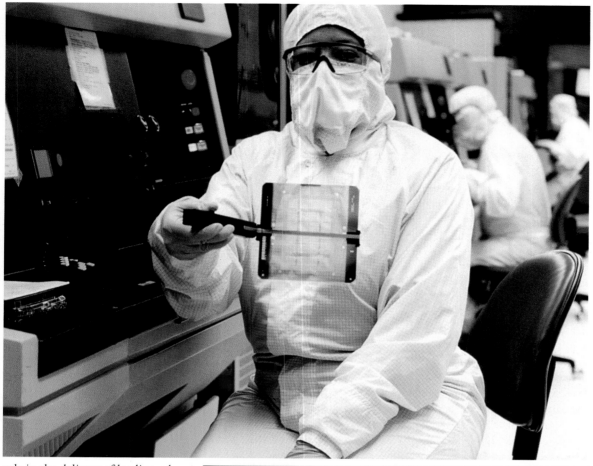

role in the delivery of leading-edge technologies that enable its customers to provide more advanced products around the globe. The company believes that the most expedient way to meet the increasing technology demands of advanced development in its industry is through collaboration. Partnering with its customers and suppliers, DPI is able to help define and accelerate future generations of technology.

An example of that industry-leading collaboration is the DPI Reticle Technology Center, LLC (RTC). Opened in 1997, the joint venture is a one-of-a-kind collaboration between DPI and three key semiconductor manufacturers: AMD, Micron Technology, and Motorola.

The RTC has engineers from DPI and its partners working side by side in a stand-alone facility, developing state-of-the-art photomask manufacturing processes. The venture allows these global leaders to share the education, experience, and excitement of working in tandem to develop new technology. A payoff of this focused effort is the manufacture of some of the world's most advanced photomask products.

RESPONSIBLE CITIZEN

 cornerstone of DPI's operating philosophy is its civic involvement. Every employee worldwide is encouraged to participate actively to help DPI earn its right to operate in the community. For example, at DPI's Round Rock site, the company is an active contributor to a variety of civic and service organizations, including the United Way and March of Dimes. Also, the company sponsors employees who volunteer their time during the workday to assist charities.

The contributions of DPI employees around the globe continue to make a difference in the many communities in which the company operates.

DPI is firmly entrenched in North America, Europe, and Asia, and is recognized by its customers as the technology leader among global photomask producers. As such, DPI is well positioned to continue its leadership role in the field, supplying the world with tomorrow's technology today from the company's headquarters in Round Rock.

ICG Communications Inc.

LTHOUGH A RELATIVELY NEW PLAYER IN THE COMpetitive field of telecommunications services in Texas, telecommunications veteran ICG Communications Inc. is making itself known. Offering local telephone, long-distance, and a variety of data communica-

ICG Communications Inc. uses the most up-to-date technology to provide consistently reliable service for its customers, including a fiber-based digital network and state-of-the-art Lucent 5ESS® switches in each of its five Texas markets (left).

ICG's business approach includes talking with customers about their business needs to help find a match with its products (right).

tions services, ICG—with more than 10 years of experience—has taken on the well-established local phone companies and plans to hit a home run.

In Texas, ICG was originally known as ChoiceCom, a venture between Central and South West Corporation (CSW), a utility holding company based in Dallas, and ICG Communications, a competitive local exchange carrier based in Englewood, Colorado. Established in December 1996, the original partnership, which combined the resources of both companies, was unique in that it marked the first time a major energy utility had teamed with a

telecommunications provider to create a local telephone company. In December 1998, ICG purchased CSW's interest in the ChoiceCom venture and is now its sole owner.

Even with the change in ownership, ICG continues to focus on Texas. Currently, the company serves five major Texas markets: Austin (the site of its regional headquarters), San Antonio, Houston, Corpus Christi, and Dallas.

ICG finds its market niche with Internet service providers and small- to mid-sized business customers utilizing 10 to 100 phone lines per location, including phone and fax lines, modems, and security systems. Prominent Austin customers include KJFK-FM radio, Apple Leasing, Travis County Medical Society, Capitol Chevrolet, and Onramp Access.

CHOICE IN SERVICE

ICG, as an alternative to the local Bell monopoly, offers its customers a choice in telecommunications. ICG's business approach includes talking with customers about their business needs to help find a match with its products. With dedicated door-to-door sales consultants who provide constant service and support to clients,

ICG is helping its customers grow their businesses.

"We differ from the incumbent local telephone companies by deploying local account sales and service teams to work face-to-face with customers who do not have the luxury of a telecommunications department," says Carey Balzer, ICG's senior vice president of marketing and the former president of ChoiceCom.

Because ICG knows many of its customers depend on phone service to conduct their day-to-day business, the company uses the most up-to-date technology to provide consistently reliable service, including a fiber-based digital network and state-of-the-art Lucent 5ESS® switches in each of its five Texas markets.

Bringing simplicity to the complex world of telecommunications also is a corporate mission. ICG offers one-stop shopping for local, long-distance, and enhanced telephony and data communication, so customers can make one call for answers to questions or solutions to problems. Customers are also able to keep their existing phone numbers, listings, and service options. "We want our customers to be able to concentrate on their own business, not ours," says Balzer.

Balzer's vision is to position ICG's Texas operations as the choice when customers are seeking an alternative to the Bell monopoly. "While many other companies are trying to compete with the incumbent telephone company, our plan is to be the dominant alternative telecommunications provider in our markets," explains Balzer.

CLOSE TO HOME

fter its purchase of ChoiceCom, ICG chose to keep Austin as its regional headquarters. The company was originally attracted to Austin by the city's growth and resulting opportunities, its highly qualified employee pool, and its central location. Since ICG's inception, the company has experienced rapid growth, and by the end of 1999, plans to employ more than 200 people, with approximately half of those in Austin.

ICG makes a strong commitment to Austin and all the Texas cities it serves. "While putting a digital switch in these cities is expensive, it was part of our ultimate commitment," Balzer says. But ICG's commitment goes far beyond the installation of a switch. The firm has donated much-needed equipment to libraries and schools, and employees have organized fund-raising drives to purchase clothing and school supplies for needy schoolchildren. ICG also contributes to several charitable organizations, and the Greater Austin United Way awarded frmer ChoiceCom and CSW Communications a 1997 Star Award for having the greatest percentage increase in employee contributions during the previous year.

"We hope to make a difference in Austin, both by being a good corporate citizen and by providing unmatched service and value for our customers," says Balzer. "We look forward to operating in Texas for many years to come."

CLOCKWISE FROM TOP: ICG HAS A STRONG COMMITMENT TO AUSTIN, AND SPONSORS BOTH CORPORATE INITIATIVES AND EMPLOYEE-ORGANIZED FUND-RAISERS TO BENEFIT CHARITABLE AND EDUCATIONAL ENDEAVORS IN THE COMMUNITY.

WITH DEDICATED DOOR-TO-DOOR SALES CONSULTANTS WHO PROVIDE CONSTANT SERVICE AND SUPPORT TO CLIENTS, ICG IS HELPING ITS CUSTOMERS GROW THEIR BUSINESSES.

"WE DIFFER FROM THE INCUMBENT LOCAL TELEPHONE COMPANIES BY DEPLOYING LOCAL ACCOUNT SALES AND SERVICE TEAMS TO WORK FACE-TO-FACE WITH CUSTOMERS WHO DO NOT HAVE THE LUXURY OF A TELE-COMMUNICATIONS DEPARTMENT," SAYS CAREY BALZER, ICG'S SENIOR VICE PRESIDENT OF MARKETING.

OLECTRON, A WORLDWIDE PROVIDER OF ENGINEERING AND custom manufacturing services to the electronics industry, is continuing a legacy begun by Texas Instruments in 1967. Solectron Texas began operation in 1996, when Solectron Corporation acquired Texas Instruments' custom

manufacturing services business. Building on the tradition, success, and vision established by Texas Instruments, the company's business has since doubled.

Solectron provides outsourcing solutions for both original equipment manufacturers (OEMs) and virtual companies. With approximately 700,000 square feet of manufacturing capacity at its Austin site, the company delivers a full range of design, manufacturing, and support services to the leading OEMs in the network equipment, telecommunications, workstation, mainframe/midrange computer, personal computer, computer peripheral, avionics, test/control, medical, and semiconductor equipment industries.

Solectron offers its customers competitive outsourcing advantages such as access to advanced manufacturing technologies, shortened product cycles, reduced cost of production, and more effective asset utilization.

"With Solectron as their partner, OEMs can focus on their core competencies—research and development, sales, and marketing—and be assured that Solectron will deliver the highest-quality product with

the fastest time to market at the lowest total cost," says Ron Shelly, president of Solectron Texas.

Solectron's primary goal to provide total customer satisfaction leads to an ongoing and intense measure of customer satisfaction. A comprehensive feedback process keeps the company tuned to customers' changing requirements.

A CULTURAL CONVERGENCE

he cultural transition between Texas Instruments and Solectron was quite easy. Maintaining the same location, the same services, and the same customers, Solectron also mirrors its predecessor's core values. Emphasis on worldwide responsiveness to customers, innovation and excellence, respect for employees, integrity, shareholder value, and social responsibility reflects the convergence in beliefs and practices.

Solectron's continued commitment to excellence has resulted in more than 150 quality and service awards, including the 1991 and 1997 Malcolm Baldrige National Quality Award for Manufacturing. Solectron was the first company to win the award twice. Other

quality awards include the 1995 City of Austin Quality Award, the 1996 State of Texas Quality Award, and ISO 9001 and 9002 certification. Solectron was also named by *Industry Week* as one of the world's 100 Best Managed Companies and by *Computerworld* as number three in its 100 Best Places to Work in Information Systems ranking.

With a long history in Austin, Solectron Texas plays a large role in the community. From board memberships to communitywide efforts, the company is very involved with community and education organizations, including United Way, Junior Achievement, Austin Partners in Education, Science Academy, Inroads Central Texas, and Capital Area Training Foundation. The company (as Texas Instruments) was also a charter founder of Neighborhood Longhorns and TFAME (Task Force of Austin Major Employers).

Solectron's strong commitment to the community is equaled by its commitment to the environment. The company has won numerous awards for its environmental sensitivity and its cutting-edge recycling and waste reduction programs. Such innovative approaches have helped Solectron Texas become one of the fastest-growing companies in its industry, with revenues nearing $5 billion. The company employs approximately 2,250 people in Austin and more than 21,000 worldwide.

"Our rapid expansion in Texas is a response to the growing trend for OEMs to outsource more of their electronics manufacturing functions to partners like Solectron," says Shelly. "We are firmly committed to the Central Texas area, and we are excited to continue growing our presence in one of the high-technology centers of the world."

WITH APPROXIMATELY 700,000 SQUARE FEET OF MANUFACTURING CAPACITY AT ITS AUSTIN SITE, SOLECTRON DELIVERS A FULL RANGE OF DESIGN, MANUFACTURING, AND SUPPORT SERVICES TO THE LEADING OEMs IN THE NETWORK EQUIPMENT, TELECOMMUNICATIONS, WORKSTATION, MAINFRAME/MIDRANGE COMPUTER, PERSONAL COMPUTER, COMPUTER PERIPHERAL, AVIONICS, TEST/CONTROL, MEDICAL, AND SEMICONDUCTOR EQUIPMENT INDUSTRIES.

 RIGHAM EXPLORATION COMPANY MOVED TO AUSTIN and struck oil—literally. ★ Founded in Dallas in 1990, Brigham Exploration Company relocated its corporate headquarters to Austin in 1997. "We came for the quality of life and the synergy with the entre-

preneurial high-tech community," says Ben M. "Bud" Brigham, the company's CEO, president, and chairman of the board. "We're more similar to a high-tech company than a traditional oil and gas exploration company because cutting-edge technology is the basis of our business."

Brigham Exploration is an independent exploration and production company that applies 3-D seismic imaging and other advanced technologies to systematically explore and develop onshore oil and natural gas provinces. The company pioneered the acquisition of large-scale, onshore 3-D seismic surveys for exploration, obtaining extensive 3-D seismic data and expertise to capture undiscovered oil and natural gas reserves.

While 3-D imaging was previously used in the industry as an offshore developmental tool, Brigham Exploration recognized the opportunity to leverage advanced computer technology and 3-D seismic imaging to create a cost-effective and highly accurate exploration tool. The company's strategy, to utilize large-scale 3-D seismic surveys to systematically explore proved oil and gas producing provinces in the onshore United States, proved very successful, with a cumulative 64 percent success rate for more than 400 drilled wells.

The successful and rapidly growing company quickly caught the interest of outside investors. Brigham received its first equity funding in 1992, when it raised $10 million from General Atlantic Partners, a Connecticut-based venture capital firm. The company went public in May 1997, raising $24 million in its initial public offering to further fuel the company's growth strategy. "We've

experienced continual growth since we started," says Brigham, explaining that the best measure of growth for independent exploration companies is proved oil and gas reserves. Brigham Exploration's proved reserves have grown from 14 billion cubic feet equivalent (bcfe) with a value of $18 million in 1995 to 98 bcfe with a value of $82 million by the end of 1998.

The company's current exploration activities are primarily focused on natural gas prospects in three core areas: the Anadarko Basin of western Oklahoma and the Texas Panhandle; the onshore Gulf Coast of Texas and Louisiana; and West Texas. Brigham's 3-D seismic imaging technique is environmentally friendly, because not only does the process use non-intrusive sound waves to survey the land, but the efficiency and accuracy of the method mean fewer wells are drilled.

Brigham Exploration's staff of 65 includes geophysicists, geologists, petroleum engineers, computer application specialists, and others focused on the niche of advanced 3-D exploration technology. "By combining years of ex-

ploration experience with cutting-edge technology, we've created a new breed of independent oil and gas exploration companies," says Brigham.

Brigham Exploration leverages its high volume of operational activity and experience to enhance its 3-D seismic data processing. The company partners with Veritas Geoservices Ltd., using its seismic data processing workstations in-house to process almost 100 square miles of 3-D seismic data every month. In addition, Brigham utilizes its own in-house processing workstation for special testing and research.

The application of advanced 3-D seismic exploration technology by Brigham Exploration has helped to set the standard for the rest of the oil and gas exploration industry, and Brigham hopes to create an Austin-based alliance of industry partners to further advance the field. Says Brigham, "We look forward to building a strong network within the oil and gas industry in Austin, to become more familiar not only with our industry peers, but with the community as a whole."

THE APPLICATION OF ADVANCED 3-D SEISMIC EXPLORATION TECHNOLOGY DEVELOPED BY BRIGHAM EXPLORATION COMPANY HAS HELPED TO SET THE STANDARD FOR THE REST OF THE OIL AND GAS EXPLORATION INDUSTRY (TOP).

BRIGHAM EXPLORATION IS AN INDEPENDENT EXPLORATION AND PRODUCTION COMPANY THAT APPLIES 3-D SEISMIC IMAGING AND OTHER ADVANCED TECHNOLOGIES TO SYSTEMATICALLY EXPLORE AND DEVELOP ONSHORE OIL AND NATURAL GAS PROVINCES (BOTTOM).

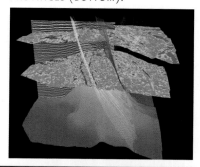

▲ GARY RUSS

HE CONTRACT ELECTRONIC MANUFACTURING BUSINESS IS THE fastest-growing segment in electronic manufacturing today, and Austin's SMT Centre Inc. is taking a leading role in this dynamic industry. ★ As technology continues to evolve at a record pace, companies are under

THE SMT CENTRE INC. (SMTC) IS AN ELECTRONIC CONTRACT MANUFACTURING PARTNER AND A GLOBAL FULL-SERVICE PROVIDER FOR THE ELECTRONIC MANUFACTURING SERVICES INDUSTRY (LEFT).

SMTC OFFERS DESIGN SERVICES, PCB ASSEMBLY AND TEST, SYSTEM INTEGRATION, SOFTWARE LOADING, CONFIGURATION AND TESTING, SYSTEM-LEVEL FUNCTIONAL TESTING, END PRODUCT PACKING, DISTRIBUTION, AND WARRANTY/REPAIR (RIGHT).

intense pressure to reduce cycle times to market while leading in technology advancement. This evolution provides the opportunity for corporations to rethink strategies and reshape operations to focus on core competencies such as product direction, design, marketing, and sales. The SMT Centre Inc. (SMTC) helps them to do so as an electronic contract manufacturing partner and a global full-service provider for the electronic manufacturing services industry. "Our ability to be a true manufacturing extension of our customers is the cornerstone of our success," says Vice President/General Manager Rick Winter.

The SMT Centre was founded in Toronto in 1985 by three pioneers in the application of surface mount techniques in circuit board manufacturing. SMTC's second U.S. expansion in as many years brought the company to the Austin market in 1996, when it acquired the electronics assembly division of Radian International.

WORLD-CLASS MANUFACTURING EXCELLENCE

The evolving technology of electronic manufacturing has enabled SMTC to fine-tune the extremely techni-

cal and complex process of building and testing circuit boards through to full configuration of box or system level products, thus bringing a high level of added value to its customers in the computer, networking, datacom, telecom, RF/wireless, PCMCIA, and instrumentation markets.

Strategically partnering with its customers, SMTC takes ownership of its complete manufacturing operations and provides services that encompass all aspects of the customers' production, test, packaging, and end product distribution. The company offers design services, PCB assembly and test, system integration, software loading, configuration and testing, system-level functional testing, end product packing, distribution, and warranty/repair.

Most of SMTC's local customers are Austin-based companies with worldwide operations. "This is an increasingly global business," says Winter. "The majority of our customers could have their products built anywhere in the world, but they choose SMTC because we're local to them, and provide a world-class product and service to meet their manufacturing and logistic demands on a global basis."

Headquartered in Toronto, SMTC has additional manufacturing sites in Austin, San Jose, Charlotte, and Cork, Ireland, and will open in Mexico and China in 1999. As the company expands its manufacturing presence, SMTC plans to follow its proven franchise approach in which the same highly successful business model, focused business systems, and established processes are adopted. "At each site, we have the same business systems, the same equipment, the same training techniques, and the same quality standards," says Winter. "Employees can literally go from one plant to another and find everything familiar."

A TEAM APPROACH

Since its founding nearly 15 years ago, SMTC's strategy has been to provide an exemplary standard of service by dedicating people, resources, and assets to each customer. "Keeping manufacturing partnerships simple and straightforward is the advantage customers desire," says Winter.

To that end, the company's TOPS model—Team Oriented Production System—defines customers as individual business units and assigns them to a dedicated busi-

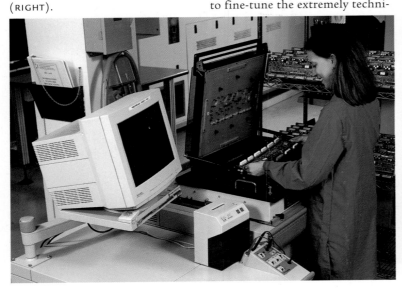

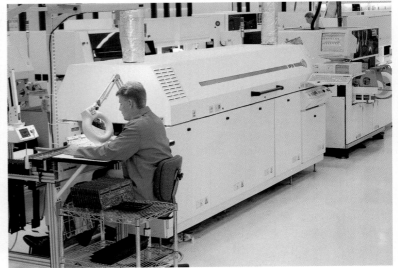

At SMTC, MANUFACTURING EXCELLENCE CONTINUES TO EVOLVE, FOCUSING ON TECHNOLOGY ADVANCEMENT, QUALITY PROCESSES, AND CONTINUOUS IMPROVEMENT TO MEET CUSTOMERS' CHANGING NEEDS.

ness and manufacturing unit. Each team is tailored to meet the individual needs of its customers, and is supported by manufacturing assets, business systems, and team personnel who have the experience and the authority to make important and timely decisions. Each program manager has complete ownership of his or her unit, and oversees all aspects of the business, including equipment and assets, inventory, manufacturing personnel, and the dedicated manufacturing processes. The team is comprised of individuals that represent all disciplines of a manufacturing environment, including customer service, master production scheduling, material management, manufacturing and test engineering, supplier quality, and documentation control.

"The paramount advantage of TOPS is that customers gain the benefit of having their own manufacturing unit without the associated cost or effort," says Winter. SMTC's incentive-based team approach helps provide continuous improvement in quality, manufacturing processes, cycle time, delivery methods, and cost, as every team member receives bonuses based on the quality level of the products,

on-time delivery, and revenue generated.

MATERIAL AND MANUFACTURING EXPERTISE

SMTC has defined the art of supply management by creating what it calls a single enterprise environment that mutually benefits customers, suppliers, and the company. Corporate commodity managers are experts on market conditions and industry trends, and they negotiate individualized supply agreements for each customer. The customer teams then execute the material flow with key suppliers on a local basis. "Centralizing this aspect of the business affords us excellent visibility at the supply base and strength in numbers," says Winter.

At SMTC, manufacturing excellence continues to evolve, focusing on technology advancement, quality processes, and continuous improvement to meet customers' changing needs. The company's expertise and experience involve advanced manufacturing in micro BGAs, BGAs, 15 mil PQFPs, MCM technologies, and complex circuitry layouts. The company also boasts proven experience in the manufacture and testing of RF/wireless,

and PCMCIA technology, as well as in full system level/box builds, product configuration, packaging, and distribution. SMTC is ISO 9002 certified, and its internal quality data collection system allows for weekly product quality reports to customers.

With a growing base of blue-chip customers and some 2,000 employees worldwide, the company continues to experience exceptional growth. Having more than 400 employees at its Austin site, SMTC has quickly earned a strong reputation as a great employer, a key player in the local community, and an invaluable part of its customers' manufacturing strategy.

WELLS FARGO BANK, WHICH WAS FOUNDED IN 1852, has served Texans for more than 115 years. Since opening its first office in the state in 1881, the bank has established a long tradition of growth and success. In 1996, Wells Fargo moved into the

Austin area, and two years later, merged with Norwest Bank. Norwest will change its name to Wells Fargo midyear 2000. With more than $2 billion in total assets, the new Wells Fargo has become one of the largest financial services companies in Greater Austin.

Prior to the merger, Wells Fargo and Norwest already had a substantial presence throughout the United States. Based in Minneapolis, Norwest had banking "stores," or branches, in 16 states, and San Francisco-based Wells Fargo had banks in 10 states. Today, the new Wells Fargo serves approximately 20 million customers and operates nearly 6,000 banking locations in all 50 states and on the international front. With more than 100,000 employees, Wells Fargo is the nation's largest originator of mortgages, the largest commercial real estate lender, the largest bank-owned insurance agency, and the number one Internet bank. Wells Fargo also offers the largest network of supermarket locations and is the nation's largest lender to small businesses.

Both Wells Fargo and Norwest had established a major presence in Austin through a series of acquisitions in 1996. Wells Fargo bought

First Interstate Bank, and Norwest purchased Liberty Bank, Victoria Bancshares, Cattlemen's State Bank, Texas Bank, Fidelity Bancshares, Franklin Federal, First State Bank of Austin, and Founders Trust Company. As a result of the Wells Fargo and Norwest merger in 1998, a strong local presence was immediately established—42 banking stores serving approximately 150,000 households in Austin and the nearby communities of Bastrop, Dripping Springs, Round Rock, Burnet, Marble Falls, and Kingsland.

COMBINING STRENGTH AND VISION

At the time of the Wells Fargo and Norwest merger, the combined company had assets of $191 billion, and the new Wells Fargo became the nation's seventh-largest bank. This merger of equals combined Norwest's community banking approach with Wells Fargo's technological innovation. The new company chose the 147-year-old Wells Fargo name and its stagecoach logo. Richard Kovacevich, formerly chairman and CEO of Norwest Corporation, now serves as president and CEO of Wells Fargo & Co.

The merger combined remarkable financial strengths and business philosophies, as evidenced by Wells Fargo's adoption of Norwest's vision statement. "We want to satisfy all the financial needs of our customers and help them to succeed financially," says Gary Valdez, president of the Austin market. "That's our vision. We also want to be recognized as the premier financial services company in our markets and be regarded as one of America's great companies."

Becoming one of America's great companies is a goal that the

IN 1998, WELLS FARGO AND NORWEST BANK MERGED, BECOMING THE SEVENTH-LARGEST BANK IN THE NATION. BOTH BANKS HAD ALREADY ESTABLISHED A MAJOR PRESENCE IN AUSTIN THROUGH A SERIES OF ACQUISITIONS IN 1996.

new Wells Fargo is quickly reaching. It was named by *Fortune* magazine as the most admired U.S. super-regional bank and among the top 10 percent of the nation's most admired companies in all industries. The bank was also ranked first by *Fortune* for customer satisfaction among commercial banks. Additionally, Norwest was ranked by *George* magazine in 1998 as one of the country's 10 most generous companies. This recognition was due to its community investment programs, corporate giving, employee volunteerism, and the PartnerShares stock option plan Wells Fargo offers to all team members. The company also was cited by *George* for its retain and retrain program, which locates new positions for employees whose positions have changed as a result of the merger. Wells Fargo's goal is to retain its valuable employees throughout the merger process.

"We've created a work environment where all team members care, and are committed individually and as a team to do their best. We value diversity, recognize contributions, and provide opportunity for personal growth, challenge, reward, and fun," says Thomas Honig, chairman and CEO of the Greater Austin Region.

A Lively History

In adopting the Wells Fargo name in midyear 2000, Austin's new bank also will inherit a colorful history of realized opportunities and great successes. In 1852, Henry Wells and William G. Fargo, eastern express businessmen, founded Wells, Fargo & Co., in San Francisco and Sacramento to do express and banking business

for the gold rush. In 1858, Wells Fargo helped finance the nation's first cross-country stage line. Coaches of John Butterfield's Overland Mail Company crossed 900 miles of Texas territory on their 21-day journey between Missouri and California.

Wells Fargo agencies and express routes spread across the western plains and mountains, and by 1888, the company had established direct ocean-to-ocean service, with large transportation networks and offices in the Northeast and the Midwest.

Wells Fargo returned to the Lone Star State aboard the iron horse—the steam train of the Southern Pacific Railroad—in 1881. The rails reached El Paso on May 10, and soon after, M.B. Davis, El Paso's first Wells Fargo agent, opened for business. By 1883, Wells Fargo had 44 offices along the tracks in Texas.

Despite stagecoach bandits and train robbers, Wells Fargo continued to grow. By the early 20th century, Wells Fargo had more than 10,000 offices nationwide, plus an extensive network in Mexico and overseas agencies from Shanghai to Berlin.

In 1918, the federal government assumed operations of the nation's railroads and express as a wartime measure. Wells Fargo, American Express, Adams, and other express companies' offices, equipment, and employees were merged into one vast American Railway Express, but Wells Fargo continued its banking operations in San Francisco.

Convenient Business

Today, Wells Fargo is a full-service banking and financial institution. The

bank offers consumers checking and savings accounts, insurance products, annuities, credit cards, mortgages, home equity loans, all types of personal loans, residential construction loans, and safety deposit box services. Wells Fargo's Private Client Services, which is touted as being "better than a bank and better than a brokerage," manages investments, trusts, and other financial needs for individuals.

For business customers, Wells Fargo provides depository services, lines of credit, equipment financing, construction loans, international banking services, foreign exchange, treasury management, investments, Small Business Administration loans, small-business loans, brokerage, and trust management services. Wells Fargo's 25 Austin business bankers work on behalf of small- and medium-sized businesses, and long-standing customers include many of Austin's most prominent businesses and organizations.

Wells Fargo offers convenience at all levels by providing 42 full-service banking locations in the Greater Austin area, ATMs throughout the city, 24-hour customer service, and telephone and Internet

IN ADOPTING THE WELLS FARGO NAME, AUSTIN'S NEW BANK INHERITS A COLORFUL HISTORY DATING BACK NEARLY 150 YEARS. NORWEST CAN ALSO TRACE DEEP HISTORICAL ROOTS IN AUSTIN THROUGH ITS MANY ACQUISITIONS IN THE CITY.

WELLS FARGO OFFERS CONVENIENCE AT ALL LEVELS BY PROVIDING 42 FULL-SERVICE BANKING LOCATIONS IN THE GREATER AUSTIN AREA, ATMS THROUGHOUT THE CITY, 24-HOUR CUSTOMER SERVICE, AND TELEPHONE AND INTERNET BANKING 24 HOURS A DAY. EVERY BANKING LOCATION THROUGHOUT THE CITY HAS ON-SITE TEAM MEMBERS WHO WORK DIRECTLY WITH CUSTOMERS.

banking 24 hours a day. Customers can even bank while they shop by taking advantage of Wells Fargo's eight full-service branches in Albertson's, Randalls, and Wal-Mart.

Every banking location throughout the city has on-site team members who work directly with customers. "We are a customer-centric organization," says Rick Burciaga, executive vice president. "We try to meet our customers' needs in terms of both services and convenience."

"It is very important to us to serve our local customers and to have the ability to meet with them face-to-face at any one of our locations, as well as offering the many options of advancing technologies such as the Internet," adds Valdez. "In the future, we want to continue to broaden our branch network in those areas of Austin that are growing, and where we feel we can provide convenience."

A TRUE COMMUNITY BANK

Supporting local communities and promoting their long-term success are integral elements of Wells Fargo's community vision. Through contributions of volunteerism, financial support, and leadership experience, Wells Fargo supports numerous charities and nonprofit organizations in the Austin area, including Children's Hospital of Austin, Arts Center Stage, Austin Community Development Corporation, and Junior Achievement. The bank gives back to the community as much as 2 percent of its net income each year. Additionally, Wells Fargo is solidly committed to the Community Reinvestment Act, and provides loans and services to low- to moderate-income families through a variety of agencies and its own community development programs. Wells Fargo also was a major sponsor for the opening of the Austin-Bergstrom International Airport.

What differentiates Wells Fargo from its competition, says Honig, is that Wells Fargo operates at the local level. "We have local managers who have been in the area for years, we make decisions at the local level, and we have a local board of directors. We're also very active in the community and encourage our team members to participate in programs special to them. We are truly a community bank."

SUCCESSFULLY MOVING A COMPANY INTO THE NEW MILLENNIUM is a challenge, no matter where the company is located or what the company does. It poses an even greater challenge in a city that is itself evolving into one of the country's leading technology centers. In Austin, the need for leaders

with the right mix of skills, experience, and cultural compatibility is critical—leaders who can successfully guide businesses in a developing, rapidly changing economy.

That's why many Austin companies turn to Korn/Ferry International, an executive search firm that specializes in helping companies find the senior-level management they need to grow and prosper. "The growth of Austin businesses has outpaced local growth of senior management talent, so the demand to recruit people into Austin has dramatically grown," explains Rob Golding, managing director of Korn/Ferry's Austin office.

Executive search brings value to clients because the search consultant provides a client with domestic and worldwide knowledge of the managerial market within its industry, as well as a sophisticated network of relevant industry contacts to identify suitable candidates for each assignment. The search process involves working with clients to understand their businesses or organizations, as well as their inner culture and thinking. This means that a top search consultant not only can advise on a strategic hire, such as that of a chief executive officer, but also can offer insight into the development and implementation of major strategic human resource programs.

Korn/Ferry works on behalf of its clients to find the highest-caliber applicants possible to fill a special position. The search process begins by working to understand clients' businesses and corporate culture and then defining their objectives and specifications for the particular position. Korn/Perry initiates an exhaustive research process, including the use of its extensive proprietary database, to identify and assess potential candidates.

After engaging in a thorough screening process to develop a long list of candidates, followed by an in-depth interview process, Korn/Ferry identifies candidates for the client to interview, eventually narrowing down the field to a lead and a back-up candidate. With objectivity and confidentiality, Korn/Ferry works closely with the client throughout the entire process, and conducts ongoing follow-up as well.

FutureStep

Korn/Ferry doesn't limit the search to traditional methods, however. In a joint venture with the *Wall Street Journal*, Korn/Ferry launched an Internet-based executive search tool called FutureStep. Through FutureStep, Korn/Ferry can communicate with, interview, and qualify a vast pool of candidates via the World Wide Web. With this and another service called K/F Selection, an advertising-based search, Korn/Ferry is, says Golding, "the first firm to offer these vertically

integrated searches, providing a cost-effective and dynamic solution for clients' employee needs."

The Austin office of Korn/Ferry International specializes in executive searches for a variety of industries, including advanced technology, financial services, biotechnology, pharmaceutical, and others. Clients range from Fortune 500 companies to small start-up firms. With the goal of becoming the benchmark search provider in Austin, the firm has quickly developed a reputation for quality and integrity.

Korn/Ferry's Austin office is committed to dedicating a portion of its time to pro bono causes, such as a recent search for the executive director of the Texas Fine Arts Association. In addition, the company is very active in the United Way and other service organizations. "We are committed to building enduring relationships in Austin, both in the business world and in our community, and we look forward to growing with our clients and our city," says Golding.

THE AUSTIN OFFICE OF KORN/FERRY INTERNATIONAL SPECIALIZES IN EXECUTIVE SEARCHES FOR A VARIETY OF INDUSTRIES, INCLUDING ADVANCED TECHNOLOGY, FINANCIAL SERVICES, BIOTECHNOLOGY, AND PHARMACEUTICAL, WITH CLIENTS RANGING FROM FORTUNE 500 COMPANIES TO SMALL START-UP FIRMS. (FROM LEFT, STANDING) MELE JUILLERAT, DEBBIE DE HAAS, DICK BEAL, AND DAVID HARAP; (FROM LEFT, SEATED) KRISTINE NGUYEN, GINA BABER, AND ROB GOLDING

▶ ROBERT GODWIN

RENAISSANCE WOMEN'S CENTER

THE RENAISSANCE WOMEN'S CENTER OPENED ITS DOORS to Austin women on Labor Day, 1997. Since then, the center, Austin's first women's hospital, has worked hard to bring a new dimension in women's health care to Austin. Nestled on a wooded hillside 10 minutes southwest

of downtown Austin, the 75,000-square-foot hospital is designed to treat women in all stages of their lives.

AN IDEA IS BORN

The Renaissance Women's Center was created when a group of obstetric physicians in Oklahoma City conceptualized a facility containing both a hospital and their offices. Such a center would allow the physicians to provide efficient care for patients in the hospital and in their offices without losing time traveling between the two. At the Renaissance Women's Center, patients would be no more than one floor away. Both the physicians and the patients loved the results.

The center's parent company, Universal Health Services, Inc., built additional facilities in Oklahoma City before moving to Austin. Attracted by the region's growth, health-conscious population, and quality of life, Universal met with a group of Austin doctors and found enthusiasm and support.

Today in Austin, the Renaissance Women's Center is a fully licensed hospital with a difference. The center offers general surgical services, bone density screening, mammograms, maternity care, and gynecologic services. The hospital houses medical and surgical facilities, a radiology department, LDRP (labor/delivery/recovery/postpartum) suites, a nursery, an in-house pharmacy, and a laboratory. These services are combined with the physicians' offices and exam rooms upstairs to make the Renaissance Women's Center a convenient way for women to meet their health care needs.

The Renaissance Women's Center delivers nearly 150 babies a month. While the majority of births are uncomplicated, the center is designed and equipped to handle emergencies. Four operating rooms are staffed 24 hours a day, and in-house anesthesiologists and OB/GYNs provide analgesic and surgical support.

In addition to emergency surgical services, the Renaissance Women's Center has expanded its scope to provide a wide range of inpatient/outpatient surgeries, including general, urologic, orthopedic, podiatric, cosmetic and reconstructive, gynecologic, and infertility procedures. The center offers advanced surgical technology and skilled, compassionate nurses who have chosen to specialize in women's surgical care.

◄ GREG HURSLEY

THE RENAISSANCE WOMEN'S CENTER, A 75,000-SQUARE-FOOT HOSPITAL, IS DESIGNED TO TREAT WOMEN IN ALL STAGES OF THEIR LIVES.

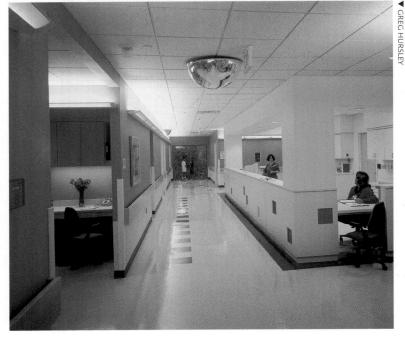

◄ GREG HURSLEY

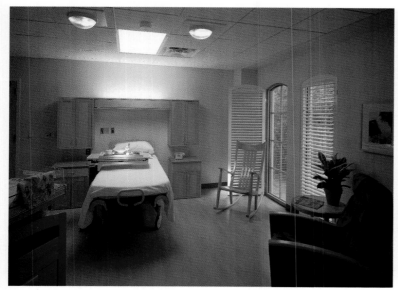

GREG HURSLEY

The Renaissance Breast Center provides state-of-the-art breast services, including screening and diagnostic mammography, early diagnosis of breast cancer through stereotaxtic biopsy, bone density screening, and consultation regarding the management of all types of breast disease.

Through its wellness education program, the Renaissance Women's Center provides a series of health-related classes and seminars that address the needs of women through all stages of their lives. Facilitators hold classes and support groups on everything from adolescent and parenting concerns to postmenopausal issues. With many free classes and scholarships available, the Renaissance Wellness Center is accessible to women from all economic backgrounds.

Patients appreciate the special attention, as well as the convenience and familiarity of coming to one place for all their health care needs. "We offer all of the services women need throughout their lifetime," says Center Chief Nurse Executive Hilda Guevara.

A BRIGHT FUTURE

The Renaissance Women's Center was designed for women, and it strays far from the typical look of traditional health care facilities. Works by local women artists grace the walls, and the center's vibrantly colored open spaces take advantage of abundant natural light.

Patient rooms set a new standard in luxury. Each professionally designed private room is beautifully decorated to provide a com-

fortable and spacious homelike setting. Every room has a balcony overlooking the adjacent canyon, and a television and VCR. New mothers can rock their babies in rockers handmade by a local Austin artisan. The center has an open visitation policy, and families are welcome to stay.

The center is active in many local events and organizations that benefit various health-related causes. The center's employees participate in the March of Dimes Walk America, the Susan G. Komen Foundation's Race for the Cure, and the Danskin Triathlon. The hospital also supports local organizations through donations and by volunteering.

All of the center's 100 full-time employees embrace the facility's mission and commitment to women's health, and their enthusiasm is evident. "The vast majority of our employees come here because they truly believe in the concept of focusing wholly on women's health," says Guevara. "We're the only hospital in Austin with a waiting list of people who want to come work here."

Although the Renaissance Women's Center receives glowing feedback from its patients, it constantly strives to improve and expand its services. "We survey each patient to learn how we can better meet her needs," says Guevara. "It's just good medicine."

GREG HURSLEY

WATSON BISHOP LONDON GALOW, P.C., ONE OF Austin's newest law firms, combines extensive courtroom experience with a fresh outlook. Founded by Austin Mayor Kirk Watson, Dan Bishop, Alice London, and Jerry Galow—four of

Austin's top trial attorneys— in 1998, the firm specializes in business litigation and plaintiff's personal injury litigation, and capitalizes on a past track record of litigation success.

"Our focus on litigation and advocacy allows us to bring a high caliber of quality to our representation of clients," says Watson, the firm's managing shareholder. "Among the different lawyers in this firm, we have tried a remarkable variety of civil cases. Because of our diverse experience, we are able to approach every litigation dispute with a fresh approach—an effort to think outside the box— regardless of whether we are negotiating around a table or trying our case at the courthouse."

The firm brings deep Texas roots and a fresh outlook to trying complex cases focusing on personal injury, business disputes,

class actions, and mediation services. "Our goal was to form a law firm that could represent both people and businesses who had litigation disputes," says Bishop. "Toward that goal, we brought lawyers together from a top-notch personal injury law firm and a

well-known commercial litigation firm. The result has been a legal team that is capable of handling virtually every kind of litigation situation." The law firm includes four associates—Chris Dodds, Phillip Schmandt, Joe Brophy, and Cory Smith—in addition to the shareholders.

The partners' vast business litigation experience includes complex business disputes, oil and gas litigation, technology litigation, trade secret litigation, and insurance coverage issues. Personal injury cases handled include class action lawsuits, professional malpractice, defective product lawsuits, and vehicular accidents, particularly automobile/truck collisions and victims of accidents caused by drunk drivers. The firm handles product liability litigation and general negligence litigation, and has headed more recently in the direction of environmental class action.

Self-described hard-hitting, aggressive litigators, Watson Bishop London Galow represents businesses of all sizes, as well as individuals. "When clients find themselves in need of trial lawyers, we add the firepower they need to win," says Galow. "It's like the difference between seeing a family doctor or a brain surgeon. You don't always need a brain surgeon, but when you do, you need the best."

Watson Bishop London Galow's office is located in the historic Littlefield Building, Austin's first true skyscraper, built in 1910 by Texas cattleman George Littlefield. "We each have Texas roots and a long history in Austin," says Bishop. "We share a sense that we can make history and that we're a real part of the community, which is why the building appealed to us."

WATSON BISHOP LONDON GALOW PARTNER MAYOR KIRK WATSON (ON LEFT) WELCOMES PRESIDENT BILL CLINTON, WHO ATTENDED THE OPENING OF AUSTIN'S NEW AIRPORT. CONGRESSMAN LLOYD DOGGETT ALSO PARTICIPATED IN THE CEREMONY (TOP).

WATSON BISHOP LONDON GALOW, P.C. WAS FOUNDED IN 1998 BY (FROM LEFT) DAN BISHOP, ALICE LONDON, WATSON, AND JERRY GALOW (BOTTOM).

DENSITY OF QUALITY

What truly distinguishes us is our density of quality," says London. "Lots of firms litigate, but they don't have the stellar record of accomplishment that we do." Each partner is board certified in personal injury trial law by the Texas Board of Legal Specialization, and Bishop and Watson are also board certified in civil trial law.

Each partner brings to the firm unique accomplishments and distinguished honors. Watson graduated as the highest-ranking student from the Baylor University School of Law, where he served as editor in chief of the *Baylor Law Review*. In 1996, he was honored as Baylor's Outstanding Young Alumnus and the Young Baylor Lawyer of the Year. He was also named the Outstanding Young Lawyer of Texas in 1994 by the Texas Young Lawyers Association.

Bishop received his law degree from the Baylor University School of Law, where he also was editor in chief of the *Baylor Law Review*. Bishop served as a briefing attorney for the Texas Supreme Court and on the Supreme Court Advisory Committee on Evidence, and he is a member of the American Board of Trial Advocates. He was president of the Austin Young Lawyers Association in 1989 and has served on the board of the Texas Young Lawyers Association.

London was named the 1993 Outstanding Woman Lawyer in Litigation by the Travis County Women Lawyers Association and the 1990 Outstanding Young Lawyer by the Austin Young Lawyers Association. London is a graduate of the University of Texas School of Law, and has served as an adjunct professor, teaching the trial tactics course at the law school.

Galow, also a graduate of the University of Texas School of Law, is active in the trial law community and has received recognition as one of the nation's top litigators for representing the University of Texas' National Mock Trial Team in 1985. Galow's team took national honors, and he was named the outstanding speaker in the competition.

INVOLVED IN THE COMMUNITY

Watson Bishop London Galow combines an impressive track record and solid legal counsel with a commitment to involvement in the local community. Watson was elected mayor of Austin in 1997. He was appointed in 1991 by Governor Ann Richards as chair of the Texas Air Control Board, the state environmental agency responsible for air quality. Bishop served as chair of the Homeless Committee for the Texas Young Lawyers Association, and has spoken to local schools about the role of the jury in the

civil justice system. London serves on the board of SafePlace and does additional volunteer work for Mothers Against Drunk Driving. Galow has coached youth basketball and soccer teams, and has served as the president of the Lost Creek Neighborhood Association. In addition to the many professional and civic leadership roles the partners hold, the firm conducts an annual clothes drive benefiting the Clothes Closet at the Central East Austin Community Organization.

"We are all committed to Austin in many different ways," says Bishop. "It's a cornerstone of our partnership and an ideal for our future."

FROM TOP:
WATSON BISHOP LONDON GALOW'S OFFICES ARE LOCATED IN ONE OF AUSTIN'S HISTORIC DOWNTOWN BUILDINGS.

THE FIRM'S LAWYERS HAVE LITIGATION EXPERIENCE IN SUCH DIVERSE AREAS AS COMMERCIAL DISPUTES, PERSONAL INJURY, OIL AND GAS, AND SECURITIES FRAUD.

THE FIRM'S STRENGTH IS A TEAM APPROACH AT THE COURTHOUSE. (FROM LEFT) CHRIS DODDS, BISHOP, PHILLIP SCHMANDT, CORY SMITH, LONDON, AND GALOW

TOWERY PUBLISHING, INC.

EGINNING AS A SMALL PUBLISHER OF LOCAL NEWSPAPERS in the 1930s, Towery Publishing, Inc. today produces a wide range of community-oriented materials, including books (Urban Tapestry Series), business directories, magazines, and Internet sites. Building on its long heritage of excellence, the company has become global in scope, with cities from San Diego to Sydney represented by Towery products. In all its endeavors, this Memphis-based company strives to be synonymous with service, utility, and quality.

A DIVERSITY OF COMMUNITY-BASED PRODUCTS

Over the years, Towery has become the largest producer of published materials for North American chambers of commerce. From membership directories that enhance business-to-business communication to visitor and relocation guides tailored to reflect the unique qualities of the communities they cover, the company's chamber-oriented materials offer comprehensive information on dozens of topics, including housing, education, leisure activities, health care, and local government.

In 1998, the company acquired Cincinnati-based Target Marketing, an established provider of detailed city street maps to more than 300 chambers of commerce throughout the United States and Canada. Now a division of Towery, Target offers full-color maps that include local landmarks and points of interest, such as parks, shopping centers, golf courses, schools, industrial parks, city and county limits, subdivision names, public buildings, and even block numbers on most streets.

In 1990, Towery launched the Urban Tapestry Series, an award-winning collection of oversized, hardbound photojournals detailing the people, history, culture, environment, and commerce of various metropolitan areas. These coffee-table books highlight a community through three basic elements: an introductory essay by a noted local individual; an exquisite collection of four-color photographs; and profiles of the companies and organizations that animate the area's business life.

To date, more than 80 Urban Tapestry Series editions have been published in cities around the world, from New York to Vancouver to Sydney. Authors of the books' introductory essays include former President Gerald Ford (Grand Rapids), former Alberta Premier Peter Lougheed (Calgary), CBS anchor Dan Rather (Austin), ABC anchor Hugh Downs (Phoenix), best-selling mystery author Robert B. Parker (Boston), American Movie Classics host Nick Clooney (Cincinnati), Senator Richard Lugar (Indianapolis), and Challenger Center founder June Scobee Rodgers (Chattanooga).

To maintain hands-on quality in all of its periodicals and books, Towery has long used the latest production methods available. The company was the first in the country to combine a desktop workstation environment with advanced graphic systems to provide color separations, image scanning, and finished film delivery under one roof. Today, Towery relies on state-of-the-art digital prepress services to produce more than 8,000 pages each year, containing well over 30,000 high-quality color images.

AN INTERNET PIONEER

By combining its long-standing expertise in community-oriented published materials with advanced production capabilities, a global sales force, and extensive data management expertise, Towery has emerged as a significant Internet provider. In keeping with its overall focus on community-based

TOWERY PUBLISHING PRESIDENT AND CEO J. ROBERT TOWERY HAS EXPANDED THE BUSINESS HIS PARENTS STARTED IN THE 1930S TO INCLUDE A GROWING ARRAY OF TRADITIONAL AND ELECTRONIC PUBLISHED MATERIALS, AS WELL AS INTERNET AND MULTIMEDIA SERVICES, THAT ARE MARKETED LOCALLY, NATIONALLY, AND INTERNATIONALLY.

STEVE DAVIS

resources, the company's Internet sites represent a natural step in the evolution of the business. There are two main product lines within the Internet division: introCity® and the American Community Network (ACN).

Towery's introCity sites introduce newcomers, visitors, and long-time residents to every facet of a particular community, while also placing the local chamber of commerce at the forefront of the city's Internet activity. The sites include newcomer information, calendars, photos, citywide business listings with everything from nightlife to shopping to family fun, and on-line maps pinpointing the exact location of businesses, schools, attractions, and much more.

ACN, Towery's other Internet product, is the only searchable on-line database of statistical information for all of the country's 3,141 counties and 315 metropolitan statistical areas. Each community's statistical profile includes vital information on such topics as population, workforce, transportation, education, taxes, and incentives. ACN serves as a national gateway to chambers of commerce, private companies, and other organizations and communities on the Web, making it an ideal resource for finding and comparing data on communities suitable for a plant or office location.

DECADES OF PUBLISHING EXPERTISE

In 1972, current President and CEO J. Robert Towery succeeded his parents in managing the printing and publishing business they had founded nearly four decades earlier. Soon thereafter, he expanded the scope of the company's published materials to include *Memphis* magazine and other successful regional and national publications. In 1985, after selling its locally focused assets, Towery began the trajectory on which it continues today, creating community-oriented materials that are often produced in conjunction with chambers of commerce and other business organizations.

Despite the decades of change, Towery himself follows a long-standing family philosophy of unmatched service and unflinch-ing quality. That approach extends throughout the entire organization to include more than 130 employees at the Memphis headquarters, another 60 located in Northern Kentucky outside Cincinnati, and more than 50 sales, marketing, and editorial staff traveling to and working in a growing list of client cities. All of its products, and more information about the company, are featured on the Internet at www.towery.com.

In summing up his company's steady growth, Towery restates the essential formula that has driven the business since its first pages were published: "The creative energies of our staff drive us toward innovation and invention. Our people make the highest possible demands on themselves, so I know that our future is secure if the ingredients for success remain a focus on service and quality."

▶ JONATHAN POSTAL

TOWERY PUBLISHING WAS THE FIRST IN THE COUNTRY TO COMBINE A DIGITAL DESKTOP ENVIRONMENT WITH ADVANCED GRAPHIC SYSTEMS TO PROVIDE COLOR SEPARATIONS, IMAGE SCANNING, AND FINISHED FILM DELIVERY UNDER ONE ROOF. TODAY, THE COMPANY'S STATE-OF-THE-ART NETWORK OF MACINTOSH AND WINDOWS WORKSTATIONS ALLOWS IT TO PRODUCE MORE THAN 8,000 PAGES EACH YEAR, CONTAINING WELL OVER 30,000 HIGH-QUALITY COLOR IMAGES (TOP).

THE TOWERY FAMILY'S PUBLISHING ROOTS CAN BE TRACED TO 1935, WHEN R.W. TOWERY BEGAN PRODUCING A SERIES OF COMMUNITY HISTORIES IN TENNESSEE, MISSISSIPPI, AND TEXAS. THROUGHOUT THE COMPANY'S HISTORY, THE FOUNDING FAMILY HAS CONSISTENTLY EXHIBITED A COMMITMENT TO CLARITY, PRECISION, INNOVATION, AND VISION (BOTTOM).

John Anderson, originally from Washington, D.C., moved to the Austin area in 1990. A graduate of the University of Texas, he specializes in photographing people and food.

Gary Dillard studied photography at Austin Community College. A registered nurse for more than 12 years, he purchased his first 35mm camera 10 years ago. Dillard now specializes in scenic, fine art, and infrared photography.

Ron Dorsey received a bachelor of fine arts degree from the University of Texas. As the owner of Ron Dorsey Photography, he has amassed a clientele that includes Balfour, Motorola, Dell Computer Corporation, and *Playboy*. A Vietnam combat veteran, Dorsey enjoys backpacking and fishing in his spare time.

Mary Lee Edwards, a native of Corpus Christi, graduated from the University of Texas with a bachelor of fine arts degree. Her photographs have appeared in numerous publications and exhibitions, and are part of the permanent collections of the Mexic-Arte Museum, Center for American History, Texas Humanities Resource Center, and Harry Ransom Center.

Coles Hairston, an award-winning Austin-based location photographer, graduated from the University of Texas and studied at the Brooks Institute of Photography. His clients include AT&T, Austin Convention and Visitors Bureau, Bluewater Industries, Embassy Suites, Texas Library Association, and Trinity University. Hairston's photographs have appeared in *Austin Magazine*, *Builder/Architect*, and *Pinnacle*.

Jim Hargan practices freelance photography and writing full-time from his home in the mountains of North Carolina. His work has appeared in numerous magazines, calendars, postcards, and books, including *Compass American Guides: North Carolina*, the *New York Times*, the *Atlanta Constitution*, and *Farm & Ranch Living*, as well as Towery Publishing's *Charlotte: Nothing Could Be Finer*; *Celebrating a Triangle Millennium*; and *Huntsville/Madison County: To the Edge of the Universe*. Hargan and his wife live in the Smoky Mountains community of Possum Trot.

James Innes is a professional photographer specializing in architectural, aerial, and travel images. He has photographed more than 1,000 commercial projects for some 200 clients, including Motorola, *Texas Monthly*, SynerMark,

Drenner & Stuart, the *Flick Report*, DuPont, and Riata. Innes has traveled extensively in Europe, Israel, Mexico, America, and the Virgin Islands.

Pamela Johnson moved to the Austin area 15 years ago. She attended Ontario College of Art & Design and is currently the owner of Westbank Gallery in Austin. Johnson specializes in custom corporate artwork.

Cindy Light was born in Austin and raised in Chicago. She has specialized in performance photography since 1973 and has covered the Texas music scene extensively. Light's images have appeared on several CD covers, including Paul McCartney's *Paul Is Live* and Stevie Ray Vaughan and Double Trouble's *Live Alive*. Her work has also appeared in the *New Yorker*, *Bass Player*, *Austin Chronicle*, *Stereo Review*, and *Guitar World*.

Gary Lockhart is an ultra-close-range aerial photographer employed by www.blimpphoto.com. He has provided photographs for the Texas Department of Transportation, City of Austin, Motorola, 3M, Lyndon Baines Johnson Library, *Texas Highways* magazine, and Towery Publishing's *Austin: Lone Star Rising*. Lockhart has also flown his company's blimp inside the capitol rotunda for an aerial photograph of the state seal embedded in the floor, and inside the Alamodome for aerial video of a 1993 George Strait concert.

Karen Maier is a freelance photographer and owner of Time Stop Photography. A native Texan, she grew up in a military family and traveled all over the world. As an adult, Maier continues to travel, capturing images of people, places, and landscapes. At home, she does commercial photography, portraits, and the occasional wedding.

Karen Marks is a native Austinite currently pursuing a degree in biology. She is the visual resource collection coordinator for Bat Conservation International, and her photographs have appeared in *Reader's Digest*, *Ranger Rick*, and a Girl Scout calendar. In her spare time, Marks enjoys exploring the outdoors with her husband and two children.

Dennis Oliver is a photographer, poet, songwriter, and engineer. His work in process control and electrical engineering taps the logical and satisfies the scientific elements of his curiosity. Writing sonnets and country

APHERS

songs is Oliver's expression of intellect and emotion. Photography has allowed him to share with others his view of the infinite beauty in the world.

Laurence Parent received a bachelor of science degree in petroleum engineering from the University of Texas. Owner of Laurence Parent Photography, he has contributed photographs to *Texas Monthly*, *National Geographic*, *Newsweek*, the *New York Times*, *Outside*, and *Texas Highways*. Parent has published 21 books and his images have appeared in numerous calendars.

Van Redin received a bachelor's degree in photojournalism from Stephen F. Austin State University and specializes in publicity stills for major motion pictures. His clients include Faulkner Construction, Sony Pictures Entertainment, Warner Bros., and 20th Century Fox. Redin, a native Texan, moved to the Austin area in 1976.

Donovan Reese is a Dallas-based photographer who journeys worldwide to capture travel-related scenic images. Shooting a wide variety of formats from 35mm to panoramic, he specializes in photographs of business, industry, and urban abstract architecture. Reese is represented by Tony Stone Images, Panoramic Images, and PhotoDisc, and has published works for various giants of business and industry.

Doug Richardson moved to Austin in 1977, and attended Baylor University, St. Edwards University, Stephen F. Austin University, and Austin Community College. The owner of Richardson Photography, he specializes in images of action sports.

Lance Schriner, originally from Chicago, received a bachelor of fine arts degree from the University of Texas. As owner of Lance Schriner Photography, he concentrates on commercial, studio, and illustrative images.

Lisa Adriene Smith is currently studying at Austin Community College and is employed by Images. She specializes in animal photography.

Walt Stoneham Jr. spent nine years in California after earning his bachelor of journalism degree from the University of Texas. Now a commercial photographer, he owns Austin-based Walt Stoneham Jr. Photography.

Park Street has amassed a clientele that includes Dell Computers Corporation, Health South, Steck-Vaughn, Capitol Records, and Whole Foods. Specializing in corporate, editorial, and advertising photography, he has traveled to 52 countries.

Peter Tata has worked in the architectural photography industry for 20 years. His photographs have appeared in *Builder Magazine*, *Interiors*, *Professional Builder*, and *Woman's Day Kitchens & Baths*. Originally from Detroit, Tata moved to Austin in 1986.

Lela Jane Tinstman has pursued careers in medicine, homemaking, teaching science, and business, only to return to her first love—photography. Her work has appeared in books, encyclopedias, magazines, calendars, and travel and environmental brochures, and her photographs have been exhibited in one-man and juried shows. She shares her love of photography with her husband, Bob.

Janice R. Tyson received her bachelor of business administration degree in accounting and is currently pursuing an associate of applied science degree in photography from Austin Community College. She has been a resident of Austin since 1986.

William Wasp, a New York City native, moved to Austin in 1997. Currently working for a major financial institution based in New York, he balances the daily demands of his securities and information services corporate career with the creative and artistic energies of his image work. Wasp's photography work has appeared in Austin's Pasillo de Artes and Laughing at the Sun galleries, and has taken him throughout the Southwest and the eastern seaboard.

Tina Weitz is a nine-year veteran architectural photographer. She enjoys creating hand-manipulated Polaroids and photographing small Texas towns. A board member of the Austin Visual Arts Association and a member of the Texas Photographic Society, Weitz focuses her attention on the Central Texas area.

Additional photographers and organizations that contributed to *Austin: Lone Star Millennium* include Allsport, Austin Children's Museum, GeoIMAGERY, Rick Hastie, International Stock, and the University of Texas at Austin's College of Fine Art.

INDEX OF PROFILES ★